Praise for *Remaking the World*

"This remarkable book offers a lively historical reconstruction of decolonization and superpower competition, but also explains how these fundamental dynamics of the twentieth century shaped one another. In clear and captivating prose and with an admirable balance between global view and textured case study, *Remaking the World* is destined to feature on syllabi, exam reading lists, and many a bookshelf. Jessica Chapman has given us a compelling account of the world we have all inherited."—John Munro, author of *The Anticolonial Front: The African American Freedom Struggle and Global Decolonisation, 1945–1960*

"In this significant contribution to Cold War history, Chapman deftly explores decolonization as a coherent global phenomenon, while capturing the complexity and specificity of individual national movements. With clear, persuasive writing and nuanced analysis, *Remaking the World* charts the collision between decolonization movements and the Cold War that shaped the twentieth century, making it an essential text for scholars and students alike."—Vanessa Walker, author of *Principles in Power: Latin America and the Politics of U.S. Human Rights Diplomacy*

"*Remaking the World* is a perfect classroom book. Incisive, broad in coverage, and written in clear and accessible prose, it expertly captures the explosive intersection of the global and the local, as the geopolitical forces of the Cold War ran up against the complex dynamics of decolonization. Chapman's astute analysis is certain to benefit students and more established scholars alike." —Scott Laderman, author of *Empire in Waves: A Political History of Surfing*

"Jessica Chapman has written a sweeping history of the Cold War's fateful collision with the global process of decolonization in India, Egypt, the Congo, Vietnam, Angola, and Iran. Put together, these cases reveal a tangled web of misunderstandings, miscalculations, and misplaced priorities on the part of both Washington and Moscow that often carried tragic consequences for postcolonial societies as well as the superpowers themselves." —Paul Thomas Chamberlin, author of *The Cold War's Killing Fields: Rethinking the Long Peace*

"In this masterful new synthesis, Jessica Chapman demonstrates that the true costs of the Cold War were paid by the inhabitants of the Global South. Chapman's penetrating analysis and crisp narrative beckons us to abandon once and for all the 'triumphalist' account of that epic conflict. Comprehensive and accessible, this thought-provoking study is required reading for anyone who seeks a full understanding of how the Cold War shaped the modern world."—John Sbardellati, author of *J. Edgar Hoover Goes to the Movies: The FBI and the Origins of Hollywood's Cold War*

"*Remaking the World* is an astonishingly well-written, lucid, and engaging synthesis of the intersection of the Cold War and decolonization and its impact in the so-called Third World. Chapman masterfully relates the agency of Asian, sub-Saharan African, and Middle Eastern actors in shaping their postcolonial national destinies without disregarding the meaningful roles assumed by the United States, the Soviet Union, and China in conditioning the history of the Global South after 1945. This is a remarkable scholarly balancing act accessible to everyone."—Pierre Asselin, Dwight E. Stanford Chair in US Foreign Relations at San Diego State University

"*Remaking the World: Decolonization and the Cold War* artfully and accessibly distills a rich scholarly literature on the double-helix of decolonization and the Cold War. In the wake of the international, transnational, and cultural turns, scholars have rethought the notion of a Europe-centered Cold War globe backlit by a few tropical hot spots scattered here and there. Chapman helps us to see instead the holistic and lateral connections between the superpower conflict, anticolonial nationalism, and the retreat of the Columbian empires."—Jason Parker, Texas A&M University

Remaking the World

REMAKING THE WORLD

DECOLONIZATION AND THE COLD WAR

JESSICA M. CHAPMAN

UNIVERSITY PRESS OF KENTUCKY

Editorial and Sales Offices: The University Press of Kentucky
663 South Limestone Street, Lexington, Kentucky 40508-4008
www.kentuckypress.com

Cataloging-in-Publication data is available from the Library of Congress.

ISBN 978-0-8131-9748-7 (hardcover : alk. paper)
ISBN 978-0-8131-9762-3 (paperback)
ISBN 978-0-8131-9750-0 (epub)

This book is printed on acid-free paper meeting
the requirements of the American National Standard
for Permanence in Paper for Printed Library Materials.

Manufactured in the United States of America.

 Member of the Association of
University Presses

For Bill and Mia

Contents

Introduction

If the first half of the twentieth century was defined by warring empires, the second half became a battle over what would emerge in the wake of their collapse. The post–World War II era was dominated by two deeply interconnected global phenomena: decolonization and the Cold War. Decolonization was both a legal process of transferring sovereignty from colonial powers to indigenous leaders and, as the postcolonial theorist Prasenjit Duara writes, "a movement for moral justice and political solidarity against imperialism."[1] It was both global and highly specific, as each decolonizing country grappled with a unique colonial past and navigated distinct challenges en route to independence. This liberatory project unfolded in the shadow of the Cold War, a superpower competition that emerged in the wake of World War II as the disintegration of Europe's great empires coincided with the ascendance of the United States and the Soviet Union as global hegemons, guided by warring ideological systems. Washington and Moscow would insert themselves into power vacuums generated by imperial collapse. Existential crises gripped both powers as they aimed to construct novel—and oppositional—world orders from the rubble of empires. As Leslie James and Elizabeth Leake argue, the Cold War and decolonization were "not isolated, parallel, phenomena" but "a broader movement of intertwined, if sometimes paradoxical, local and global change."[2] Both were imaginative projects, fueled by differing ideas about how to replace the collapsing European imperial order with new political, economic, and social structures.

The first chink in the armor of Europe's empire came with World War I, which witnessed not only the Bolshevik Revolution but also the birth of a generation of anticolonial leaders bent on achieving national self-determination. Following on these major disruptions, the interwar years ushered in a new era of globalization, marked by integrated financial markets, new modes of mass communication, increased human migration, and population growth that combined to erode the existing geopolitical system. The Great Depression and World War II fundamentally altered the balance of global power, inexorably weakening Europe's imperial giants, emboldening anticolonial nationalists the world over, and ushering in two rival superpowers, the United States and the Soviet Union. The ensuing Cold War—fueled, expanded, and prolonged by the rapid process of decolonization that gripped the world in the decades after World War II—continued for four and a half decades, spanning every corner of the globe. By the mid-1950s the superpower competition that had initially focused on Europe shifted its main theater to the Third World. Soviet and American efforts to harness the decolonization process for their own ideological and geopolitical ends served as a critical backdrop for independence struggles the world over.

Between 1945 and 1965, more than fifty nations proclaimed their independence from a system of European empires that had taken more than four centuries to consolidate. Independence sometimes resulted from peaceful negotiations, but the attainment of full sovereignty all too often required violent struggles. This process reached its peak in the early 1960s, followed by a second wave of decolonization in the Portuguese colonies in the mid-1970s. Following the Vietnamese communist victory over the United States, the Cold War was transformed by a series of strategic realignments and the radicalization of Third World revolutionary nationalism, both occasioned by the Sino-Soviet split. The dismantling of Europe's formal imperial system was not complete until the end of apartheid in South Africa in the early 1990s.[3] Even then, hegemonic power structures remained in place across the Third World, ensuring ongoing indebtedness to and dependence on Western states, corporations, and institutions. Throughout this process, Cold War dynamics would frequently restrict the parameters of political, economic, and cultural transformation, dramatically increase the violence associated with decolonization, and forestall the complete undoing of colonial-era power structures.

With Europe's great empires in retreat, newly ascendant superpower rivals, the Soviet Union and the United States, launched a fierce competition to fill the gaping global power vacuums left in their wake. The decolonizing Third World—or what is now often referred to as the Global South—included key strategic sites and contained vast natural resources and mineral wealth that both superpowers deemed vital to their economic and military strength. Moreover, the political orientation of newly independent states seemed critical in the ideological battle between communism and liberal democratic capitalism, two totalizing and totally irreconcilable political and economic systems. In the zero-sum game of the Cold War, strategists in Washington and Moscow deemed any small victories for their adversaries to be significant threats to their own survival. Both superpowers therefore posited alternatives to the old imperial system—rooted in their overarching ideologies—aimed at winning allies in the Third World. Just as critically, they sought to keep newly liberated countries from falling into the enemy camp. Moscow called for a radical anticapitalist, anticolonial revolution. Washington, calling for democracy while too often aligning with authoritarian guardians of the status quo, pleaded for a more gradual, orderly transition to independence.

Modernization and development programs constituted one of the key mechanisms by which the superpowers sought to make inroads into the Third World. Indeed, the question of modernization rested at the heart of post–World War II international history. As historian Todd Shepard has argued, in the early years of the Cold War the Western powers came to see decolonization as an inevitable stage in a narrative of progress; it was no longer something to be resisted but something to be controlled. Imperialists therefore replaced the old language of "civilizing mission," long used to justify their empires, with talk of a "modernizing mission."[4] This modernizing mission, though rooted in long-standing civilizational precepts, emerged largely in reaction to a mid-1950s Soviet thrust to win over allies in the Third World by exporting its planned industrialization model, backed with Soviet aid and technical assistance.[5] In turn, the Western powers cited the need for protracted tutelage in political, technological, economic, and even cultural modernization to carve out ongoing metropolitan influence in their former colonies. Asserting their unique abilities to provide such tutelage, the Cold War superpowers swept into the Third World with competing models of modernization and development, rooted in their diametrically opposed views of the history of the world and its proper trajectory. Their development aid programs were designed to fast-track "backward" societies from their purportedly primitive states to the supposed pinnacles of modernity that they each claimed to embody. Developments in the Third World would become no less than "a litmus test of their core ideas about the nature and direction of historical change."[6]

To their great frustration, however, the superpowers regularly encountered resistance from their interlocutors in the decolonizing and postcolonial world.

Although Third World elites often framed their political agendas in terms designed to win support from the two Cold War behemoths, they walked a fine line between seeking crucial international support for their own modernization and development projects and maintaining independence of action and fidelity to their own nationalist visions.[7] In the early Cold War, anticolonial figures and postcolonial leaders of various political stripes came together to form movements for Afro-Asian solidarity, aimed at securing independence, and nonalignment, focused on steering postcolonial countries clear of the two Cold War blocs. The Afro-Asian movement, inspired by Nehru at the dawn of Indian independence, was most closely associated with a 1955 meeting in Bandung, Indonesia. The Bandung generation sought to construct a sense of Third World solidarity on the grounds of shared colonial experiences. By uniting, its participants hoped to steer a "third way" in the Cold War by beckoning the United Nations to uphold human rights, promote self-determination, and settle interstate conflicts. This was part of what Matthew Connelly has termed a "diplomatic revolution" in international affairs, by which Third World actors angled for support from world public opinion and international organizations like the United Nations (UN) as they challenged the dominant global order imposed by Cold War superpowers.[8]

The Afro-Asian bloc faced numerous obstacles, including a lack of internal cohesion and frustration with the UN's limited ability to influence events in the Third World. It never became the formidable presence in global politics that its founders imagined, and far too many postcolonial elites got sucked into the ideological rigidity of the Cold War as they pursued the backing of powerful international allies. But in the early stages of the Cold War, especially, leading Afro-Asian figures like Egypt's Gamal Abdel Nasser, India's Jawaharlal Nehru, and Ghana's Kwame Nkrumah became some of the most influential players in the Third World. In the early 1960s, Nasser and Yugoslavia's Joseph Broz Tito seized on Nehru's philosophy to establish a movement for Cold War nonalignment that would inspire a generation of Pan-Africanists while provoking the ire of the Afro-Asian bloc.[9] Despite a host of internal schisms and a limited record of success, movements for Afro-Asian solidarity and nonalignment speak to the determination held by many members of the Third World to remain independent of powerful Cold War forces.

These Third World solidarity movements stood alongside other developments that also belied the bipolarity of the Cold War. While the Western and communist blocs squared off into rival alliance systems, both were dogged by persistent internecine quarrels. Washington's North Atlantic Treaty Organization (NATO) allies often balked at its overtly anticolonial positions and its penchant for military intervention, while the Soviet Union's putative Chinese allies issued withering public criticisms of Moscow's insufficient support for radical nationalist movements, challenging its position as the world's revolutionary lodestar. China's rhetorical attacks on Soviet "revisionism" often dragged the latter into staking more radical positions in favor of national liberation movements in places like the Congo and Vietnam than it would have otherwise. Washington, too, found itself stumbling recklessly into Third World conflicts in reaction to real or imagined Soviet aggression out of a perceived need to protect its international credibility and prestige, considerations that factored heavily into the Cold War competition that focused so intensely on perception.

As the contest wore on, both superpowers lost control of their images, as well as their fragile alliance systems. By the mid-1960s, both camps were fracturing along additional fault lines. Stalwart US allies like Britain and France, by then resigned to the end of their empires and fully persuaded of the futility of trying to contain the forces of nationalism, grew outspokenly opposed to American policies as the war in Vietnam went awry. In the Soviet bloc, the simmering Sino-Soviet split reached a full boil. Meanwhile, Cuba and Vietnam positioned themselves as prototypes for liberation movements around the world, threatening to displace both Moscow and Beijing as the vanguard of socialist revolution.

The appeal of the Cuban and Vietnamese revolutionary examples stemmed from their ability to stave off what many in the Third World had come to see as a heavily militarized American project of neoimperialism without succumbing to Soviet or Chinese control. From the anticolonial perspective, the global revolution at hand entailed much more than simple transfers of power from imperialist masters to local leaders. Decolonization posed a fundamental challenge to the Southern Hemisphere's absolute subordination to the North, and to the global power structures that grew out of colonial-era epistemologies of race, civilization, and culture. Postcolonial leaders contended with remnants of colonialism ranging from inherited governing institutions, educational systems, and national boundaries to foreign control of natural resources and ongoing economic dependence. They challenged a global system of racial oppression that united people of color around the world, including African Americans who saw their quest for civil rights and equality as part of the global process of decolonization. That process would require unraveling the deep-seated and complex legacies of colonial rule, legacies that interventions by Cold War superpowers only seemed to reinforce.

Odd Arne Westad, a preeminent scholar of the Cold War in the Third World, has gone so far as to argue that "the Cold War was a continuation of colonialism through slightly different means."[10] Although both powers were avowedly anticolonial, the Soviet and American programs bore the unmistakable imprints of imperial thinking about colonized people's political immaturity and need for foreign tutelage, which resulted in chauvinistic attitudes toward their counterparts in the decolonizing world. Their condescending approach to postcolonial elites, combined with the intensity of the Cold War conflict and the catastrophic results each side feared would result from a loss, led both Soviets and Americans into the trap of replicating older patterns of domination.

Yet their ability to dominate was more limited than they anticipated. The Cold War rivals squared off in a world transformed by the slackening of rigid imperial controls, which unleashed an array of movements and conflicts that controverted Soviet and American designs on the decolonizing world. As the superpowers sought to win and control allies in the Middle East, Asia, Africa, and the Caribbean, they had to contend with a range of local and regional considerations that were often much more important to their Third World counterparts than were Cold War imperatives. Blinded by their ideological visions and chauvinistic approaches to postcolonial elites, Soviet and American policymakers made too little effort to understand, much less adapt to, these contexts. When indigenous allies, responding to local customs, needs, and conditions, diverged sharply from their superpower patrons, Soviet and American policymakers tended to respond with frustration, condemnation, and retribution rather than undertaking wholesale reconsiderations of their policies.

All too often, as relationships with indigenous nationalists grew sour, and modernization and development efforts failed to produce the desired political results, the Cold War superpowers contributed to the militarization of Third World conflicts. Stunningly, every one of the Cold War's hot eruptions took place in the decolonizing and postcolonial world. Those conflicts were not initiated by the superpowers but grew out of caustic combinations of the challenges of decolonization, feuds over foreign-owned corporations and lingering metropolitan control over resources, preexisting local and regional rivalries, internecine struggles for power and resources, border disputes, ethnic and religious tensions, and more.[11] Cold War interventions poured fuel on these fires, often making them much longer and deadlier and frequently perverting or foreclosing the messy but necessary civil conflicts by which postcolonial peoples struggled to chart their new, independent paths. Superpower involvement in the decolonizing process came at great human cost and altered fundamentally what the Third World and its constituents would become, contributing to the emergence of several important states, movements, ideologies, and conflicts that shape our world today.[12]

Several key questions rest at the heart of this volume: What were the primary concerns, conflicts, and objectives among decolonizing and postcolonial elites in the countries under study? On what grounds did the United States, the Soviet Union, and, in many cases, China come to regard certain countries or regions as important Cold War battlegrounds in political, military, economic, or ideological terms? What were Soviet and American visions of modernization and development in the Third World and how did these interact with postcolonial leaders' plans to modernize and develop their own countries? How and why did some nationalist figures in the decolonizing and postcolonial world attempt to remain neutral parties in the Cold War, and with what levels of success? How did anticolonial and postcolonial political elites conceive of US, Soviet, and Chinese involvement in their affairs? How did they view the relevance of the Cold War to their movements, especially relative to other local, national, and regional considerations? In what ways did the Cold War alter the process of decolonization both as a global phenomenon and at the local level? In what ways did decolonization alter the dynamics of the Cold War and affect the politics and diplomacy of the superpowers? How did the Sino-Soviet split and the subsequent fragmentation of the communist world alter the trajectory of the Cold War and decolonization and change the nature of their intersection? And, finally, what were the key turning points in the relationship between these two global processes?

The first chapter addresses many of these questions through a chronological overview from World War I to the Soviet collapse, highlighting key developments in the international system as decolonization unfolded in tandem with the Cold War. Readers may refer to that timeline for overarching context as they make their way through six case studies on India, Egypt, the Congo, Vietnam, Angola, and Iran. By following each of these countries' trajectories from early anticolonial movements through the end of the Cold War, readers will be able to track connections between the processes of decolonization and the Cold War across time and space. These cases—spanning Asia, Africa, and the

Middle East—were selected for their overall geopolitical significance and for their representativeness of a range of key characteristics of the Cold War in the Third World. The six countries discussed in this volume broke free from Britain, France, Belgium, and Portugal, each of which adopted distinct approaches to both colonial rule and decolonization. Taken together, these case studies speak to shifting Soviet, American, Chinese, and Cuban policies; the centrality of modernization; movements for Third World solidarity and nonalignment; the role of the United Nations; the often-outsized influence of regional actors like Israel and South Africa; the significance of the Sino-Soviet split; and seminal post–Vietnam War shifts in the international system. Each case in this volume can be credited with at least one geopolitical "turning point," demonstrating that the Cold War and decolonization were mutually constitutive processes in which local, national, and regional developments altered the superpower competition as much as it transformed them.

India, gaining independence from Britain in 1947, set the stage for the global cascade of decolonization that was to come. In pursuit of true independence—rather than the neocolonial subjugation he feared—Nehru engendered movements for Afro-Asian solidarity and nonalignment and hailed the promise of state-directed modernization and development. Yet, economically underdeveloped and plagued by regional conflicts with Pakistan, India found itself repeatedly ensnared in the superpower rivalry. Cold War–era India presaged the difficulties many decolonizing and postcolonial countries would face as they sought to avoid falling into either superpower bloc while pursuing the monumental task of unifying disparate populations within the arbitrary national borders inherited from imperial oppressors.

Egypt rested at the heart of the Middle East region that both Washington and Moscow deemed critical for its oil reserves and its strategic location. The 1956 Suez Crisis provided the Cold War one of its tensest moments, elevating Nasser to the fore of Arab nationalism, revealing cracks in the Western alliance, occasioning a rare moment of Soviet-American cooperation, and presaging the Arab-Israeli conflict that would consume the region for decades to come. When the United States stepped in to replace Britain as the dominant Western power in the Middle East just as the Soviets sought to make inroads, the superpowers' Cold War calculations butted up against their regional clients' concerns that centered to a far greater extent on the Arab-Israeli conflict and the competition between politically conservative and Nasserite regimes. The Egyptian case illustrates how both superpowers attempted to adapt their policies to fit a region that largely belied Cold War frameworks, while revealing a stubborn tendency to revert to those frameworks when faced with a potential loss of influence.

Following its independence from Belgium in 1961, the Congo emerged as the first Cold War hot spot in sub-Saharan Africa. The ensuing Congo Crisis featured an emerging Afro-Asian bloc in the United Nations, highlighting the geopolitical reconfigurations wrought by decolonization while simultaneously pointing to the limits of UN influence over Africa's decolonization process. Washington's involvement in the assassination of the Congo's first prime minister, Patrice Lumumba, spurred charges of neocolonialism and criticism of American racism but also led to the installation of a pro-US dictator. Meanwhile, Beijing and Moscow's rivalry for influence in the Congo contributed to the Sino-Soviet split, while Cuban intervention cemented for the Caribbean nation a revolutionary role in the continent. All of this would converge to fuel Angola's bloody civil war a decade hence.

Vietnam's protracted wars for independence constituted the marquee event of the Cold War in the decolonizing world. Driven first by the logic of the domino theory and then by the theory of credibility, the United States assumed from France the burden of fighting Vietnamese communists, only deepening its commitment in the face of mounting evidence of the war's futility. Chinese support for North Vietnam, meanwhile, compelled the Soviet Union to step up its own involvement in the conflict for fear of ceding the revolutionary vanguard. By the war's end, the United States was humiliated and the long-simmering Sino-Soviet rivalry became an open split. Washington, seeking to capitalize, pursued rapprochement with Beijing and détente with Moscow. Even as the supposedly monolithic socialist bloc fractured, the Soviet Union—buoyed by its victory in Southeast Asia—adopted a more aggressive approach to the Third World as the United States pulled inward to lick its wounds. Hanoi's victory, meanwhile, signaled to Third World nationalists across the globe that it was, indeed, possible to defeat one Cold War superpower without succumbing to the control of another. The geopolitical reconfigurations wrought by the Vietnam War conditioned the final chapter of the Cold War in the decolonizing world.

Angola, upon gaining independence from Portugal rather suddenly in the mid-1970s, featured heavily in that final chapter. Soviet and American involvement in Angola's bloody civil war was determined largely by the actions taken by their Cuban and South African allies, and to a lesser extent by Chinese and

Zairian machinations. Both superpowers initially sought to avoid the fray but, for reasons that centered largely on image and prestige, increased their involvement not only in Angola but in a chain of crises that beset southern Africa. Washington's initial involvement was cut short by congressional interference that Ronald Reagan would later attribute to the "Vietnam Syndrome"; Reagan in the 1980s would revive American intervention in Angola as part of his campaign to support "freedom fighters" in their efforts to roll back communism. Perhaps most notably, it was in Angola that Soviet-backed Cuban revolutionary forces played by far their biggest role on the continent and boasted the greatest impact. Signifying the demise of the Cold War geopolitical system, Moscow and Washington would collaborate to negotiate an end to the conflict in Angola just months before the fall of the Berlin Wall.

Iran, the final case study in this volume, featured turning points that bookended the Cold War. The 1946 Azerbaijan Crisis informed American perceptions of Soviet behavior and shaped the emerging US containment strategy. It contributed to Washington's determination to stave off Soviet inroads into the oil-rich Persian Gulf, which led it to authorize the first CIA-backed coup against a foreign government in 1953 and, thereafter, to support the US-friendly shah despite his clear dictatorial tendencies. Blinded by their commitment to the anticommunist shah, successive American presidents overlooked signs of popular discontent that erupted in 1978–1979 in the Iranian revolution. That revolution resulted in the creation of an Islamic republic, which signaled the emergence of a third way in the international system that elided both Soviet and American ideological structures. Nonetheless, officials in both Washington and Moscow read developments in Iran through familiar Cold War lenses, leading them to table détente and reinvigorate the Cold War in the Third World.

Each of these cases illustrates in a different way that breaking free from imperial control, either formal or informal, was no cure all. On the contrary, each country examined here faced an onslaught of postcolonial problems that played out under the long shadow of the Cold War. Yet each of these cases transformed the Cold War in the process, often prolonging, deepening, and expanding the geographic reach of a superpower rivalry that was once limited to Europe and a handful of other strategic sites. One can hardly overstate the extent to which this collision between the Cold War and decolonization shaped the world that emerged at the end of the twentieth century.

1

Decolonization and the Cold War

Contesting the Global Order

World War I (1914–1918) augured the beginning of the end of the European colonial system by which a handful of relatively small powers imposed their dominion across all corners of the globe. That process of colonization unfolded in waves over a period of more than four centuries, but it was the final phase, from the 1870s to the outbreak of war in 1914, that was marked especially by heightened competition and tension among empires. Just after the turn of the twentieth century, Europe squared off into two rival alliance systems that would turn a minor diplomatic incident—the assassination of Austrian archduke Ferdinand by a Serbian nationalist—into a global conflict, as one nation after another declared war in keeping with its alliance pledges. European armies paraded off to fight, almost gleefully expecting to return home quickly from a short and glorious war. Instead, the fighting would last for four years, and approximately 8.5 million soldiers lost to combat wounds or disease would never return home. An even greater number of civilians—estimated as high as 13 million—died of starvation, disease, exposure, military encounters, and massacres amid a new kind of total war aimed at destroying an entire population's will to resist.

Several empires disintegrated completely while others were left limping. The Austro-Hungarian and Ottoman Empires collapsed, czarist Russia was overthrown by the Bolsheviks, and Germany was roundly defeated, fatefully left to chart its political future through hostile and punitive international waters. Meanwhile, the victors, namely Britain and France, had suffered nearly the same devastating losses as the vanquished. They sacrificed a generation to the trenches and squandered their wealth and power in pursuit of a pyrrhic military victory. Both powers had gone deeply in debt to the United

States and lost important footholds in the colonies upon which their standards of living depended. Weary and demoralized in the war's wake, they struggled not only with material weakness but with a wavering faith in European cultural superiority that underpinned the entire imperial project.

Colonized peoples also suffered and sacrificed greatly during the war in ways that undermined the very premise of European colonization as a "civilizing mission." Contrary to popular conceptions that World War I was narrowly confined to the Western front, fighting took place in Europe, Africa, and the Middle East, with forays into Central Asia and the Far East.[1] Perhaps even more significantly, the European powers drew extensively on their colonies for manpower and raw materials as the war dragged on. Critical resources were extracted, and millions of colonized peoples were conscripted to serve as soldiers or laborers ("beasts of burden") in service of a cause that benefited them not at all. This only laid bare the exploitative nature of the colonial relationship. The barbaric and irrational character of the war only further belied European claims of cultural and moral superiority that colonizers had long relied on to justify their imperial projects. Furthermore, the devastating outcome of the war made clear that colonizers were not invincible, reinvigorating dormant resistance movements and spawning new ones. Thus, as World War I drew to a close, Europe's empires faced internal weakness and an impaired ability to project power abroad just as many of their colonial subjects awakened to their desire to struggle for independence.

While the United States and revolutionary Russia certainly cannot be credited with creating anticolonial nationalism, they did much to focus and inspire early twentieth-century movements for independence. The havoc wrought by World War I posed a crisis to the existing international order that demanded a solution. US president Woodrow Wilson and Vladimir Lenin, the leader of Russia's Bolshevik Party, responded with competing visions for the future of humanity, competing visions that, in due time, would set the United States and the Soviet Union on a collision course over nothing less than "the soul of mankind."[2] While they both spoke of self-determination, Wilson and Lenin had almost oppositional understandings of the term. Foreshadowing Washington's approach to the Cold War, Wilson saw it as a means of alleviating colonial oppression through long-range, systematic reforms that could reduce pressure on empires, thereby serving as a bulwark against radical revolution.[3] He expected colonial peoples to achieve independence eventually, but only after years of tutelage from "civilized" patrons who would enable them to mature politically and embrace the democratic and capitalist traditions that he saw as markers of social progress.[4] Lenin, on the other hand, preached the concept of self-determination as a revolutionary tool to be wielded in the wholesale destruction of the European imperial system. The term implied the radical overthrow of colonial empires as an important aspect of the world anticapitalist revolution that Marxist-Leninist doctrine predicted.[5]

A generation of anticolonial leaders first latched onto Wilson's wartime promises of liberty and self-governance, but, disillusioned by his failure to address the colonial world—much less to acknowledge its representatives—at the 1919 Versailles peace conference, many soon gravitated instead toward Lenin's more radical, revolutionary vision.[6] For most anticolonial nationalists, independence would have to wait until after World War II, but, during the interwar years, vibrant movements to that end percolated throughout the colonized world. Chief among them was a movement for Indian independence from British rule, led by Mohandas K. Gandhi, that would launch the era of decolonization with its eventual success in 1947. Iraq and Egypt also gained nominal independence during these years but under conditions that largely retained for Britain the benefits of colonial control. Both countries would undergo more comprehensive revolutions after World War II, bringing them squarely into the crosshairs of the Cold War. Meanwhile, anticolonial leaders from French Indochina and Algeria to Dutch Indonesia bided their time, organizing to the extent they were able under the watch of oppressive colonial regimes. In many cases, future revolutionary leading lights spent significant chunks of the interwar years outside of their home countries—in Europe, the Soviet Union, and China—where they could develop their movements, build international support networks, and consort with like-minded comrades.

In March 1919, against the backdrop of the Russian civil war, the Bolsheviks created the Comintern to promote global revolution.[7] But the Soviet Union in the interwar years was consumed, above all, with consolidating its own hold on power and laying down socialist roots at home. Joseph Stalin, who emerged from a power struggle following Lenin's death to assume leadership of the Soviet Union in the late 1920s, was far less interested than his predecessor in promoting world revolution, especially in the colonies whose socioeconomic conditions failed to conform to the Marxist-Leninist model.[8] The development of a comprehensive Soviet commitment to promoting revolution in the developing world would not materialize until Nikita Khrushchev took power three decades later. Meanwhile, however, the interwar period sharpened the divide between the capitalist United States and the communist Soviet Union.

As the Kremlin spent the interwar years struggling to ensure its survival, build a socialist state, and establish itself as the vanguard of anticapitalist and anticolonial revolution, the United States emerged as the dominant economic power in the world. In the 1920s, the United States rejected global leadership in the form of Wilson's League of Nations but extended its cultural, political, and economic reach around the world.[9] After World War I, from Washington's vantage point, the weak and chaotic Bolshevik regime posed no direct security threat to the United States.[10] But Americans feared that, should the contagion of Bolshevik ideas infect the rest of Europe, the future of liberal democratic capitalism would be in peril. And the suspicion was mutual. Following the 1918 allied military intervention into the Russian civil war on behalf of the anti-Bolshevik forces, Lenin concluded that all the belligerents in the conflict—including the United States—were imperialist aggressors bent on snuffing out the socialist ember before it could catch flame.[11]

Fundamentally, the American model of liberal internationalism and the Bolshevik aspiration for world communist revolution could not coexist in the long term, as each predicted—alas, hinged on—the other's demise. The ideological clash discussed here simmered throughout the 1920s and saw a brief cooling during the Popular Front period in the second half of the next decade. Yet, to the Americans, the global Great Depression of the 1930s imperiled US dominance and called into question the entire capitalist system, opening the door for communist appeals in Europe and the colonies. Communist and fascist advances in those years threatened to undermine both European security and the open market system that underpinned US-led global capitalism. The Soviets and the Americans were on a collision course for the Cold War that would commence after World War II, when the Soviet Union, though still much weaker than the United States, emerged as a stronger, more legitimate rival. But first, they would team up to defeat the Axis powers.

From Grand Alliance to Cold War on the Periphery

The Grand Alliance that brought the United States, the Soviet Union, and Great Britain together to defeat Hitler and the Axis powers was a strained marriage of convenience at best. Mutual suspicion and fundamentally opposed interests, both in terms of how to fight the war and how to structure the postwar world, marked the relationship from the outset. FDR sought a postwar order framed along the lines of the 1941 Atlantic Charter that called for self-determination, no territorial aggrandizement, a reduction of trade restrictions, and global economic cooperation. Stalin, on the other hand, was determined to secure a territorial buffer zone of "friendly" states to protect the Soviet Union against the type of catastrophic military invasions it had suffered twice in the first half of the twentieth century. It is easy to see why the Allies made common cause against the Nazis, but it is equally unsurprising that the alliance disintegrated at the war's end.

Although FDR may have been able to soften the emerging Soviet-American conflict with his realpolitik approach and the strength of his personal relationships with Churchill and Stalin, it is difficult to see how he could have avoided the Cold War altogether.[12] His death in April 1945 meant that Harry Truman, a far less experienced and much less nuanced statesman, would preside over the chaotic developments in the postwar world. By the time of the Potsdam Conference in July 1945, the United States was armed with a monopoly on nuclear weapons that only reinforced Truman's natural tendency to take a hard line against Soviet adventurism. Two months after the United States dropped nuclear weapons on Hiroshima and Nagasaki to end the war in the Pacific, dystopian British novelist George Orwell—predicting a world divided and enslaved by nuclear armed superpowers—was first to apply the term "Cold War" to the clash between the United States and the Soviet Union.[13]

The ideological conflict that had been brewing between the United States and the Soviet Union since 1917 had, by the end of World War II, morphed into an unprecedented geostrategic standoff that, as Orwell observed, was inseparable from the concurrent process of decolonization. As Europe's two leading colonial powers, France and Britain, faced precipitous decline, the United States emerged from World War II as by far the most powerful nation in the world. Leaders of the United States recognized their country's preponderant power on the world stage but worried about a date not far in the future when it could be overwhelmed by Soviet might, should they fail to act preemptively to shore up US strategic interests.[14] The world appeared perilously unstable, and rampant poverty and political turmoil seemed to offer the perfect breeding ground for communist movements in both Europe and the periphery. Communism, they believed, was a pathology destined to infect those not immunized against it with doses of economic vitality and democracy.

As the Cold War emerged from the ashes of World War II, American officials developed an understanding of the Soviet Union as a wily and rapacious power, poised to capitalize on global instability and human suffering, albeit more often through intimidation and subversion than via overt military aggression. In early 1946 George Kennan, an American diplomat stationed in Russia, penned a sobering assessment of a paranoid, irrational, and predatory Soviet Union that would respond only to the logic of force.[15] This missive was, in part, a response to Stalin's vitriolic anticapitalist speech just days before, which Justice William O. Douglas described as "the Declaration of World War III."[16] Kennan's insights, elaborated the next year in the supposedly anonymous "X Memorandum" published in *Foreign Affairs,* formed the basis of a containment policy that would be applied initially to a series of strategic points including Europe, the Turkish Straits, and the oil-rich regions of the Middle East. Far from revelatory, Kennan's telegram simply put elegant and actionable words to perceptions of the postwar Soviet threat that were already rapidly gaining currency in US foreign policymaking circles. Those perceptions were informed by the Kremlin's domineering approach to Eastern Europe, which, by March 1946, former British prime minister Winston Churchill deemed lost behind an "Iron Curtain."[17] Anglo-American officials also fretted over the strength of communist movements in war-ravaged western Europe— especially in Italy and France—where they saw the real possibility of ceding critical ground to the Soviet bloc. The urgent need to jump-start European economic recovery to avert such losses underpinned the 1948 Marshall Plan.

Outside of Europe, Moscow's backing for separatist movements in Azerbaijan, and its refusal to withdraw troops from Iran according to wartime agreements, sent worrying signals that the Kremlin's word could not be trusted. The 1946 Iran Crisis seemed to indicate aggressive Soviet designs on strategically vital, resource-rich parts of the world that had previously been under Western dominion. Its resolution confirmed suspicions that Moscow would, whenever possible, pursue those designs through intimidation and subversion, relying heavily on local proxies, and that it would back down in the face of stalwart resistance from the United States. The Iran Crisis laid the foundation for Washington's emerging strategy of containment, with profound ramifications for the future of Iran, specifically, and the Third World more broadly.

The containment policy resulted as much from pressure on the United States to fill power vacuums in the decolonizing world, left by retreating European powers, as it did from Soviet aggression. Before the war's end, nationalists in Iran and Egypt were protesting vigorously against British control, and London began the process of relinquishing India, its prized colony. India's independence in 1947 inaugurated the era of decolonization and, with the emergence of Jawaharlal Nehru, introduced movements for Third World solidarity and nonalignment. At the same time, Indonesia struggled for independence from the Netherlands, the United States promised independence to the Philippines, and Ho Chi Minh and the Viet Minh proclaimed an independent Vietnam.[18] In the months and years following World War II, Britain and France implored the United States to support efforts to restore colonial control in colonies like Algeria, Malaya, and Indochina, while Britain withdrew from the Mediterranean, calling for Washington to step into the breach. In his 1947 Truman Doctrine speech, formulated in a desperate attempt to salvage the Western position in Greece and Turkey following Britain's precipitous retreat, the president issued an unbounded pledge of US support for "free peoples" in their struggles against "totalitarian regimes."[19] Ironically, this speech, combined with the announcement of plans for Marshall Plan aid later that year, "hardened attitudes in Moscow," leading to a fundamental reassessment of Soviet foreign policy in preparation to wage a more vigorous Cold War against the United States.[20]

By the late 1940s, the decolonizing world remained on the periphery for both Washington and Moscow, but a series of events would soon shift it to the strategic center of the Cold War contest. In 1949, American officials greeted the "twin shocks" of the Soviet Union's first successful nuclear detonation and Mao Zedong and the Chinese Communist Party's (CCP) victory in the Chinese Civil War as evidence of the rapid acceleration of communist aggression in Asia, and a concomitant reduction in US power. In the summer of 1950, the outbreak of war in Korea only seemed to confirm Sino-Soviet designs on the continent. American officials, who were previously as concerned about their European allies' desperate and outmoded policies in the decolonizing world as they were about threat of communist revolution, began to view the entire world as divided between two hostile camps.[21] The Cold War was moving beyond the borders of Europe to become a global chess match in which Third World countries would become essential pawns.

In 1950, the Truman administration's resulting adoption of a new national security strategy, NSC-68, globalized and militarized the containment strategy.

"The whole success of the proposed program," claimed the authors of the new policy, "hangs ultimately on recognition by this Government, the American people, and all free peoples, that the cold war is in fact a real war in which the survival of the free world is at stake."[22] Under the new regime, no expense was too great, no response too severe, and no outpost too remote in the global fight against communism. For a time, the United States would continue to draw distinctions between strategically significant and insignificant sites on the periphery, but the die was cast for a total collapse of such distinctions by the mid-1950s in response to the Soviets' more activist turn to the Third World.[23]

Americans were suddenly seeing red all over the global map. Truman articulated fears of a renewed Soviet assault on Iran, and the communist orientation of Ho Chi Minh's Vietnamese government took on a newly sinister cast. Armed with a dramatically increased defense budget, the United States made a fateful commitment to support the French War effort in Indochina, and to recognize the alternative noncommunist government installed by the French in southern Vietnam. The Cold War and decolonization had begun to intersect in ways that would only deepen and determine each other's courses in the decades that ensued. By and large, though, the Truman administration continued to have little interest in the Third World beyond its direct implications for the superpower conflict and the disposition of European allies. The globalization and militarization of the American strategy of containment paved the way for a reorientation of the Cold War toward the decolonizing world, but it was not until President Dwight D. Eisenhower took office in January 1953—and especially after Stalin's successors launched a game-changing "economic offensive"— that the United States began to confront the Third World in a concerted way.[24]

The Cold War Meets the Third World

In the mid-1950s, the pace of decolonization picked up rapidly. The number of nation-states doubled between 1955 and 1965 as former colonies claimed their independence. As the focus of the Cold War shifted to the Third World, the conflict assumed a more multipolar character. While the Soviet Union and the United States ramped up their competition for influence in the developing world, the People's Republic of China (PRC) started to challenge Soviet primacy in ways that would heighten superpower intervention in the global process of decolonization and impede efforts to establish peaceful coexistence between Moscow and Washington. At the same time, the Soviet Union and the United States had to contend with nascent Third World solidarity movements, which China manipulated as part of its earliest effort to displace the Soviet Union as the leader of world revolution. As they competed for allies in the decolonizing world, Washington, Moscow, and Beijing all had to navigate a range of complicated national and regional politics that did not conform neatly to either their ideological assumptions or their strategic objectives.

President Dwight D. Eisenhower and his secretary of state, John Foster Dulles, took office in early 1953, against the domestic political backdrop of McCarthyism. The shock of the CCP victory and the subsequent outbreak of war in Korea, coupled with high-profile espionage cases including those of Alger Hiss and Julius and Ethel Rosenberg, fueled a scourge of anticommunist hysteria in the United States. The American people were beset by fears that communist agents had infiltrated their own government en masse to facilitate a Soviet plot to take over the world and to bring down the United States by brainwashing their friends and neighbors.[25] Although Eisenhower and Dulles harbored serious qualms about the excesses of Senator Joseph McCarthy's anticommunist witch hunts, they shared popular concerns about recent communist gains in Asia and faced significant political pressure to mount a vigorous foreign policy response to communist threats worldwide.

In Eisenhower and Dulles's "zero-sum" outlook, a gain for communism in any nation, regardless how small, remote, or strategically insignificant, reduced American security.[26] This assumption was predicated on their understanding of communism as a movement directed by Moscow and imposed upon vulnerable populations. As Dulles put it in April 1954, international communism was "a vast monolithic system which, despite its power, believes that it cannot survive except as it succeeds in progressively destroying human freedom."[27] The challenge for Eisenhower was to deter Soviet aggression and meet the challenge of communism in every jungle, city, and desert while reining in US defense spending, which he believed was spiraling out of control under the regime of NSC-68. His solution took the form of a new national security strategy known as the "New Look."

The New Look strategy, approved by Eisenhower in October 1953, is best known for its emphasis on nuclear deterrence, or "mutually assured destruction," as a mechanism for discouraging Soviet adventurism while reducing expenditures on conventional weapons. Its second prong was an increased reliance on bilateral and multilateral alliances, such as the Southeast Asia Treaty Organization (SEATO), formed in 1954 in an effort to cordon off the communist PRC and North Vietnam, and the 1955 Baghdad Pact (later the Central Treaty Organization, or CENTO), the primary instrument by which the United States sought to curb Soviet advances and temper the forces of neutralism in the Middle East. The third prong was psychological warfare (or propaganda), designed not only to counter Soviet appeals but also to promote the benefits of America's democratic way of life. The fourth prong was covert operations. Under the cloak of plausible deniability, the Central Intelligence Agency (CIA) worked surreptitiously to influence political developments in decolonizing and postcolonial countries, even going so far as to orchestrate coups in Iran (1953) and Guatemala (1954) and to conspire in the 1961 assassination of Patrice Lumumba, the first democratically elected prime minister of the Democratic Republic of the Congo. While each of the four prongs of this strategy was designed in large part to deter Soviet advances in the Third World, the Eisenhower administration possessed no clear vision for how to respond to the wave of anticolonial revolutions that was sweeping across Asia, Africa, and the Middle East, or to the rash of socialist movements in Latin America, where nationalist figures increasingly rejected what they saw as American neoimperialism. Caught between the forces of McCarthyism at home, the threat of communist expansion abroad, the waning fortunes of European empires, and the emerging forces of anticolonial nationalism, Eisenhower's approach to the Cold War in the Third World was often reactive.

Just as the new American president was grappling with his new Cold War strategy, the game changed with Stalin's death in March 1953. The menacing figure so closely associated with Soviet aggression and ideological rigidity in the early postwar period was suddenly gone, leaving the future of Moscow's policy and leadership in flux. If Stalin was to blame for the Cold War, as many held, it stood to reason that his death might open the door to an early thaw. At first, his successors did seem to display a greater willingness to resolve international disputes peacefully, but dreams of an early end to the superpower clash soon scattered to the wind as the main battleground shifted to the developing world.[28]

By 1955, the flamboyant, hot-tempered Nikita Khrushchev emerged from a bitter succession struggle within the Kremlin to become the clear Soviet leader. Condemning Stalin as unnecessarily provocative toward the

West and insufficiently supportive of communist revolutionaries abroad, he would enact a wholesale transformation of Soviet foreign policy centered on what would turn out to be contradictory objectives of "peaceful coexistence" with the West and increased support for revolutionary nationalists in the decolonizing world.[29] Eager to redress Stalin's neglect of potential allies outside of Europe and to reassert the Soviet Union's lapsed position as the leader of global revolution, he set out to build alliances with revolutionary-nationalist figures in the Middle East, Africa, South and Southeast Asia, and Latin America.[30] In 1955, Khrushchev initiated direct Soviet engagement with Asia and Africa by brokering an arms deal with Egypt via Czechoslovakia, personally visiting India, Burma, and Afghanistan, and inviting a number of Third World leaders to the Kremlin.

The shifting focus of Cold War competition from Europe to the decolonizing world, and Moscow's renewed commitment to leading the revolutionary process outside of Europe, exacerbated Sino-Soviet tensions. Contrary to American perceptions of communism as a monolithic movement, the alliance between Moscow and Beijing was strained from the outset. China had always bristled at its subordinate position in the relationship, and the cracks became deeper after Stalin's death. Competition for leadership of the world communist revolution, to which the Soviet Union and China both hitched their political stars, was at the heart of the conflict. This was a geopolitical power struggle but also an ideological one. The Soviet Union's overriding goal was always to replace capitalism with socialism; it only supported anti-imperialism as a means to that end. China, on the other hand, pursued a revolutionary agenda with anti-imperialism at the core.

The PRC made its debut in global politics in the mid-1950s, at the 1954 Geneva Conference and the 1955 Bandung Conference. China was, at that point, hardly a diplomatic powerhouse. It was still excluded from the United Nations, not formally recognized by many countries, and itself still in the very early stages of economic development. Until the end of the decade, Beijing would swallow its objections to what it saw as Moscow's insufficiently revolutionary policy of peaceful coexistence and defer to the Soviet Union in most international arenas.[31] Within a few short years, however, events in the decolonizing world would unleash a significant competition between Moscow and Beijing's respective revolutionary agendas of anticapitalism and anti-imperialism.[32] As historian Jeremy Friedman writes, "For the leaders of the Soviet Union and the People's Republic of China, formally committed to an ideology that predicted world revolution, establishing their leadership of the world revolutionary process was both an ideological necessity and a grand strategic imperative."[33] As China attempted to leverage the appeal of its militant revolutionary ideology among Third World leaders to seize the vanguard, the Soviet Union was forced to accommodate Beijing's agenda or risk ceding primacy among revolutionary nationalists in the developing world.[34] This would draw Moscow more deeply into Third World conflicts than it intended, which placed it increasingly in conflict with Washington, thereby undermining efforts at peaceful coexistence with the West.

As part of their effort to assert Beijing as the hub of anticolonial revolution, Chinese diplomats made sure they were front and center as Third World leaders came together in solidarity to oppose what Ghanaian leader Kwame Nkrumah called "neo-colonialism."[35] The term "Third World," a concept itself borne out of the bipolar superpower conflict, first appeared in a 1952 article by French demographer Alfred Sauvy. Sauvy identified a three-tiered stratification of international society: the First World comprised the capitalist West united in the NATO alliance; the Second World included the Soviet Union and its socialist satellites bound together in the Warsaw Pact; and the Third World was made up of the darker peoples of the Southern Hemisphere who had long labored under colonial oppression and now yearned for independence, equality, dignity, and opportunity on the world stage. According to Sauvy, "What interests each of the two [developed] worlds is to conquer the third, or at least to have it on its side."[36] Leaders of the Afro-Asian bloc and the subsequent nonaligned movement thus aimed to create a united front to prevent newly liberated nations from falling under the thumbs of either Cold War behemoth.

In April 1955, a diverse group of anticolonial nationalists convened the first Afro-Asian conference in Bandung, Indonesia, to explore prospects for Third World solidarity and neutralism in the Cold War. The meeting was dominated by what one historian has referred to as the "three titans" of neutralism: India's Jawaharlal Nehru, Egypt's Gamal Abdel Nasser, and Indonesia's Ahmed Sukarno.[37] There was little to unite the disparate group of twenty-nine nations represented at the conference aside from their shared history of oppression at the hands of European imperial powers and their attendant experiences of cultural and racial discrimination. Six of the delegates had recently concluded military-economic agreements with the United States and Britain, whereas the majority of the countries represented were sympathetic toward, if not formally aligned with, the communist powers. The leaders of the conference derided these sorts of attachments that, they claimed, perpetuated the toxic division of the world, instead urging a strategy of Third World solidarity and Cold War neutrality. In a rousing speech, Sukarno suggested that a common set of desires among Bandung participants would trump their cultural, religious, political, economic, and racial differences. "We are united," he announced, "by a common detestation of colonialism in whatever form it appears. We are united by a common detestation of racialism. And we are united by a common determination to preserve and stabilize peace in the world."[38]

The Final Bandung Communiqué declared that "colonialism in all of its manifestations is an evil which should speedily be brought to an end" and warned against "the dangerous situation of international tension existing and the risks confronting the whole human race from the outbreak of global war." The latter was an especially threatening prospect in the age of a thermonuclear arms race that posed a unique peril to the Global South, where much of the superpowers' destructive testing was already taking place, and where neither ruled out the prospect of a nuclear attack. The attendees voiced their commitment to human rights and self-determination, pledged economic and cultural cooperation, and identified the United Nations as the primary vehicle for pursuing their shared goals. Perhaps the most significant product of the conference was the emergence of a what Third World intellectuals and politicians referred to as the "Bandung Spirit," the feeling of hope and promise that percolated as the colonized world stepped up to assert itself as a legitimate global player, independent of First and Second World powers.

Washington and Moscow reacted very differently to the Bandung Conference and the subsequent creation of a more explicit movement for nonalignment. The Eisenhower administration was highly suspicious of Cold War neutralism, fearing that it could ultimately result in the Soviet takeover of key points in the Middle East, Africa, and Southeast Asia, or at least cut off the United Sates from strategic positions and critical natural resources.[39] Khrushchev's Kremlin actually shared many of the same expectations. Moscow, though skeptical of the neutralists' reliability as allies for local communists, saw an opportunity to block the formation of new US-backed alliance systems and to deny the Western powers access to military and economic assets in Third World regions. And since the Soviet ideological system cast anti-imperial revolutions as steps along the path to socialism, Soviet officials viewed neutralism as a temporary condition that would eventually yield to closer relations with the Soviet bloc.[40]

Early Cold War Hot Spots: Southeast Asia and the Middle East

In the 1950s, Southeast Asia and the Middle East were the geographic hubs of the Cold War in the Third World. Events in Indonesia and Indochina in the former region, and Iran and Egypt in the latter exemplify the complexities that emerged as the exigencies of decolonization and the Cold War became more deeply intertwined. In each of these cases, the United States felt compelled to fill political, economic, and military voids left by retreating European colonial powers that were among its closest allies. The Soviet Union, cautiously but with increasing boldness, made overtures to postcolonial leaders in the hope of capitalizing on the shifting political winds at the end of empire. Where China became involved, it urged greater revolutionary militancy and, over time, dragged Soviet officials grudgingly to support more radical forms of revolution than it preferred. Whether they dealt with neutralist or overtly aligned leaders, all three of these Cold War giants met with determined nationalist resistance to their efforts to control allies' political behaviors.

In the years after World War II, Southeast Asia witnessed the triumph of nationalist movements against British, French, and Dutch colonial forces. Following the PRC's triumph in 1949 and the outbreak of war in Korea in 1950, the region that was once of tertiary concern to Soviet and American leaders took center stage. The PRC exercised its earliest support for revolutionary communist forces in Korea and Vietnam, asserting its claim to communist world leadership and prompting Washington to convulse over fears that Southeast Asia would soon be swallowed up by communism. To American officials, the stakes of such an outcome were diffuse. A communist takeover of the region would deprive the United States and its allies of access to vital resources while making them available to foes in Beijing and Moscow, isolate Japan in a sea of red, cut off important shipping and communications routes, imperil US offshore military bases, and enhance China and the Soviet Union's power and prestige at the expense of American credibility. The psychological significance of Southeast Asia—especially Indochina, where the conflict was seen as a symbolic battle between East and West—was at least as important to US policymakers as its geostrategic significance. Washington spoke in metaphors of "dominos" and "bandwagons" to explain the fear that a communist takeover in Indochina could undermine the credibility of US commitments and weaken its ideological appeal, leading to successive losses in neighboring and distant countries. To forestall such an outcome, Eisenhower was determined to hold the line in response to crises in Indochina and Indonesia, just as Khrushchev and Mao were determined to exploit them, however cautiously.[41]

During Eisenhower's second term, a CIA intervention in Indonesia backfired, pushing the neutralist Sukarno closer to China and the Soviet Union. The United States responded by ramping up support for opposition forces in a vicious spiral of superpower intervention that fueled the slaughter unleashed later in the decade by the US-backed rebel coup that toppled Sukarno's regime. Likewise in Indochina, Washington's commitment to preventing the spread of communism inspired policies at odds with its stated mission of spreading democracy. After the 1954 Geneva Accords that divided the country in two, Eisenhower committed full US support to South Vietnam's Ngo Dinh Diem, who resembled more of a strongman dictator than the exemplar of democracy his American backers hoped he would become. China and the Soviet Union, meanwhile, offered diverging advice to Ho Chi Minh's revolutionary government in the North, with Beijing calling for a violent, confrontational approach and Moscow urging a patient, political process. In the coming years, the Soviet Union would grudgingly follow China ever deeper into the Vietnam conflict, and the war would exacerbate Sino-Soviet tensions to the point of an open split. Meanwhile, Hanoi proved frustratingly difficult for either side to control as it persistently prioritized its own nationalist considerations even as it pursued socialist revolution and war. As in Indonesia, superpower intervention into a postcolonial civil conflict deepened internecine rivalries and heightened the violence that would be unleashed during the American war in Vietnam, the marquee event of the Cold War in the Third World.

Meanwhile in the Middle East, with Britain in retreat, both Cold War superpowers understood well the strategic importance of the region containing some 60 percent of the world's oil reserves. Both sides viewed capturing the allegiance of Middle East governments as an absolute imperative to secure access to oil while depriving the enemy, to obtain rights to strategic bases and transit routes, and to prove to postcolonial nationalists the ideological appeal of their respective political and economic models. Going into the 1950s, the United States held the clear upper hand in the region in political and military terms, but its close alignment with British imperialists and its increasing association with Zionist Israel allowed the Soviet Union to make inroads into the Arab world.

In 1953, the Eisenhower administration's first Cold War crisis in the Middle East struck in Iran, where the CIA first ventured to unseat a legitimate postcolonial government. The putsch started off rocky but ultimately succeeded in replacing Prime Minister Mohammad Mosaddeq with the pro-US shah. The takeaway for Washington was that this sort of covert meddling in the internal affairs of postcolonial states would serve US interests well. Iran under the shah would prove a reliable ally for the United States for some time to come, but the events of 1953 planted the seeds of a more virulent form of nationalism and anti-Americanism that would erupt in the 1970s.[42]

The 1956 Suez Crisis, one of the tensest episodes of the Cold War, pitted Egyptian president Gamal Abdel Nasser—the undisputed leader of Arab nationalism—against Britain, France, and Israel in a standoff that resulted briefly in Soviet-American cooperation. Although Eisenhower was suspicious of the Egyptian leader's neutralism, disturbed by his recent arms deal with the Soviet bloc, and outraged by his decision to nationalize the Suez Canal, the United States was unwilling to give up entirely on Nasser and drive him even further into the Soviet camp. Nothing could be more harmful to the US reputation in the Middle East than an association with unvarnished European imperial action against the forces of nationalism, and Eisenhower therefore rejected a hasty intervention against the popular and determined Egyptian regime. When Washington's closest European allies disregarded American pressure to stand down, instead invading Egypt in October 1956, Eisenhower and Khrushchev grudgingly joined ranks, for very different reasons, to compel them to withdraw.[43]

This was a turning point for American involvement in the Middle East, and the Third World more broadly, as the United States realized it could no longer straddle the line between bolstering European imperialism and supporting a host of nationalist ambitions. Washington recognized that waning European power and influence in the former colonies created a diplomatic, military, and political vacuum that it would have to compete with the Soviet Union to fill. The Eisenhower Doctrine, which indicated US willingness to intervene unilaterally in the Middle East to defend its friends and allies against communism, constituted the first stab at a policy to avert Soviet advances in the Arab world.[44] Meanwhile, although the Soviet Union was heartened by recent shifts in the Middle East, Khrushchev approached Arab nationalism with an abundance of caution, warning that nationalist leaders could turn on local communists at any time.

By 1958, events in the countries discussed here combined with a number of other developments in the Third World to make decolonization a top priority for the socialist powers. In 1957, Ghana became the first majority-ruled sub-Saharan African country to claim independence in the modern era. Its leader, Kwame Nkrumah, saw Ghana's liberation as a harbinger of things to come in an independent, and perhaps even united, Africa. The Afro-Asian People's Solidarity Organization (AAPSO) conference in Cairo later that year, and the overthrow of Iraq's Hashemite monarchy and Guinean independence in 1958, also helped spur a dramatic increase in Soviet economic and technical aid for developing countries. As George Mirsky, a Soviet expert on the Third World, recalls, Khrushchev increasingly threw his hat in the ring of national-liberation movements, especially in Africa, "to use post-colonialist momentum, break into the 'soft underbelly of imperialism' and win sympathies of the millions of people who woke up to the new life."[45] Moscow not only stepped up the magnitude of its aid, it shifted the objectives of its aid policy from simply strengthening relationships with friendly governments to guiding recipient countries along a socialist path of development.[46]

As the Soviet Union ramped up its support for national-liberation movements and postcolonial governments, US officials began to realize that it was not just the philosophy of communism but the model of planned industrialization that appealed to the developing world. Already by 1956, Dulles conceded that the United States had "very largely failed to appreciate the impact on the underdeveloped areas of the world of the phenomenon of Russia's rapid industrialization. Its transformation from an agrarian to a modern industrial state was an historical event of absolutely first class importance." He went on to observe that developing countries saw "the results of Russia's industrialization and all they want is for the Russians to show them how they too can achieve it."[47] Eisenhower condemned Soviet efforts to exploit the economic and political vulnerability of emerging nations but acknowledged that the United States must design a policy to counter Moscow's appeal. He proposed a robust program of economic aid and trade agreements that would prevent "the entire house of freedom" from collapsing under the pressure of "communist imperialism."[48] But Eisenhower's somewhat haphazard economic aid program stalled in Congress. And in the words of historian Odd Arne Westad, "To the Eisenhower administration it was more important to spoil the chances for a successful left-wing development strategy than it was to impose its own version of development on newly independent countries."[49] It was not until John F. Kennedy took office in January 1961 that the United States began to develop a coherent strategy to counter the appeal of Moscow's economic model.

The "Year of Africa" and the "Decade of Development"

Kennedy's 1960 presidential campaign took place during what the United Nations dubbed the "Year of Africa," in recognition of the tide of anticolonial revolutions sweeping through the continent. That February, in a speech before South Africa's parliament capping a monthlong tour of Britain's former and current colonies on the continent, British prime minister Harold Macmillan conceded the inevitability of decolonization and highlighted its significance to the Manichean Cold War struggle:

> The wind of change is blowing through this continent. . . . As I see it, the great issue in this second half of the twentieth century is whether the uncommitted peoples of Africa will swing to the East or the West. Will they be drawn into the Communist camp? Or will the great experiments in self-government that are being made in Asia and Africa, especially within the Commonwealth, prove so successful, and by their example so compelling, that the balance will come down in favour of freedom and order and justice?[50]

This speech reflected a reality that the aforementioned events in Asia and the Middle East had already laid bare: the British imperial system was coming apart at the seams, not unlike that of the French, the Dutch, and others. In Britain's and France's African colonies, then, independence often resulted as much from crises in the metropole as from organized anticolonial movements. Some colonies like Ghana and Guinea achieved independence quickly and bloodlessly, whereas others like Kenya and Algeria endured long, violent conflicts.[51]

The Algerian war for independence, from 1954 to 1962, brought to prominence Pan-African philosopher Frantz Fanon and became an early rallying point of African decolonization. Algeria's highly visible struggle against France highlighted layers of racial and civilizational oppression that transcended colonialism and seemed to define the relationship between North and South, a perspective that contributed greatly to the radicalization of Third World anticolonial movements in the early 1960s.[52] Furthermore, as historian Matthew Connelly has noted, the Algerian War demonstrated the ability of nationalist revolutionaries to challenge the bipolar power structure of the Cold War by driving wedges between Paris and Washington on one hand and Moscow and Beijing on the other.[53] Washington's overriding desire to avoid the odious taint of colonialism set it at odds with Paris, while Sino-Soviet competition over claims to ideological rectitude and revolutionary primacy in the Third World fractured the unity of the socialist bloc. By the end of 1960, the Algerian War alongside a crisis unfolding in the Congo seemed to indicate that Africa was leaning toward China's preferred course of armed struggle for national liberation over Moscow's program of peace and disarmament.[54]

That year, following Belgium's sudden and unexpected grant of independence to the Congo, Moscow and Washington intervened to turn the ensuing struggle into a proxy conflict. Superpower intervention in the Congo Crisis, marked most famously in 1961 by the US-backed assassination of independent Congo's first prime minister, Patrice Lumumba, contributed to the balkanization and failure of the Congolese state. The drama unfolding in Congo seemed to unleash the floodgates of African independence and helped ignite a subsequent wave of violent and messy wars for national liberation in Portuguese Africa, especially in neighboring Angola.

In 1961, faced with such rapid changes to the map of Africa, as well as ongoing challenges to colonialism and its legacies in Asia, Africa, and Latin America, JFK took office convinced that the Cold War would be won or lost in the Third World, where he deemed his predecessor's efforts insufficient.[55] To Kennedy, the fate of the decolonizing world would depend on its path to economic development. He enlisted in his administration the leading lights of a new social-scientific concept known as modernization theory. The most notable of these was Walt W. Rostow, author of the 1960 book *The Stages of Economic Growth: A Non-Communist Manifesto,* which outlined a series of stages of economic growth through which every society progresses naturally before reaching the pinnacle of US-style capitalism.[56] This served as a direct rebuttal to Marxist predictions that societies were destined to pass through a series of economic stages leading ultimately to communist utopia. By the time Kennedy took office, modernization theorists believed the United States faced a foreign policy emergency, as Soviet economic intervention threatened to derail the natural economic evolution of an ever-growing number of independent, underdeveloped countries in the Third World. Only an active US development policy could thwart the communists' nefarious plot.[57]

In a 1961 speech to Congress in which he made his case for the most robust and sustained foreign aid policy in US history, Kennedy proclaimed the 1960s the "Decade of Development." He warned, "The ability to make long range commitments has enabled the Soviet Union to use its aid program to make developing nations economically dependent on Russian support—thus advancing the aims of world communism." The new president argued that the United States possessed moral and economic obligations to help poorer countries resist communism and develop their economies in a manner consistent with freedom and democracy. "To fail to meet those obligations now would be disastrous," he claimed, and in the long run more expensive and more threatening to American security and prosperity, as "widespread poverty and chaos lead to a collapse of existing political and social structures which would inevitably invite the advance of totalitarianism into every weak and unstable area."[58] Kennedy created a number of initiatives to prevent such a catastrophic outcome, including the Peace Corps, counterinsurgency programs and—for Latin America—the Alliance for Progress, an ambitious but ultimately unsuccessful effort to promote prosperity and stability south of the border.[59] He pursued a similar program in Iran to shore up the embattled US-backed shah, with equally disappointing results.

Missiles in Cuba, War in Vietnam, and the Sino-Soviet Split

Latin America, long considered to be within the US sphere of influence and critical to national security as per the Monroe Doctrine, was integral to American strategic thinking about the Third World throughout the Cold War. It took on a new prominence after the 1959 Cuban Revolution brought Fidel Castro to power, enabling the Soviet Union to establish a foothold in Latin America.[60] Initially, it was not clear that Castro was entirely anti-US or pro-Soviet. But by the time Kennedy took office, he had cast his lot with the Kremlin. Cuba stood as a communist bridgehead to Latin America, with Castro's regime threatening to foment revolution throughout the hemisphere.[61]

New to the presidency, Kennedy made the naïve and rash decision to enact a CIA plan inherited from Eisenhower's administration to enlist Cuban refugees in a plot to oust Castro. This plan followed the same logic as the 1954 CIA-backed ouster of pro-communist Guatemalan President Jacobo Árbenz, which Eisenhower carried out as part of a larger effort to quash communist activity in Latin America. The April 1961 Bay of Pigs debacle made a fool of Kennedy at home and abroad. Everything that could go wrong, did. The refugees involved with the amphibious landing were captured immediately by Castro's forces, the anticipated uprisings never occurred, and Kennedy refused to send US forces to support the refugees even after the operation was unveiled as a CIA plot. This unmitigated foreign policy failure gave his Republican foes fodder to question his vigor in the fight against communism, emboldened Castro to ask for stronger measures of support from his communist allies, encouraged Moscow to test the strength of Kennedy's Cold War commitments, and contributed to Khrushchev's decision to ship Soviet missiles to Cuba the following fall.

The October 1962 Cuban Missile Crisis, the closest the world has ever come to nuclear war, illuminates several key developments at the heart of the Cold War in the Third World. Khrushchev's decision to send missiles to Cuba seems reckless—almost incomprehensible—until you consider it in the context of the deteriorating Sino-Soviet relationship. As Castro operated under the constant threat of Yankee aggression, Khrushchev's personal authority, and with it the credibility of the Soviet Union as an ally of revolutionary communists across the Third World, suffered at home and abroad. Domestically, expectations that the Soviet Union would come to the aid of its revolutionary brethren in general, and especially in Cuba, were on the rise. And Khrushchev's sense of personal responsibility to guarantee the success of Third World revolutions grew stronger as Beijing stridently accused him of betraying the revolution with his revisionism and appeasing imperialists at the expense of world communism.[62] From the outset, Khrushchev's support for Castro, whose aspirations to stir up revolution across the Caribbean and Latin America were aggressive enough to make Moscow uncomfortable, was largely aimed at excluding Chinese revolutionary influence in the region. On paper, installing Soviet missiles in Cuba made a certain sense in terms of balancing the missile gap and responding to the American placement of missiles in Turkey, the Soviet Union's own backyard. More importantly, however, it was Khrushchev's determination to prove his revolutionary mettle in the face of Chinese challenges that enabled Castro to persuade his Soviet patron to make such a risky gambit.

Khrushchev's gamble backfired. Upon discovering the missiles in Cuba, Kennedy's administration outmaneuvered him diplomatically, drawing him so close to the brink of nuclear conflict that he had no choice but to back down. Castro was furious with what he perceived to be a Soviet betrayal, notwithstanding the pledge Khrushchev obtained from the United States renouncing future plans to invade Cuba. China immediately seized the opportunity to exploit Khrushchev's humiliation, launching a media campaign to denounce the Soviet withdrawal as a "Munich" and to condemn Khrushchev's revisionism for "show[ing] vacillation in a struggle and dar[ing] not to win a victory that can be won." Chinese leaders charged the Soviet Union with "adventurism" for sending the missiles in the first place and "capitulationism" for withdrawing them.[63]

China's anger over Khrushchev's handing of missiles in Cuba, combined with Moscow's lack of support for Beijing in a second Sino-Indian border war that took place simultaneously, brought the ideological conflict between Mao and Khrushchev to a head.[64] Over the coming months, Moscow and Beijing made some grudging efforts to repair the relationship, but, as historian Lorenz Lüthi writes, by July 1963 "it was clear that only a complete ideological surrender of one side could save Sino-Soviet relations."[65] The period between the summer of 1963 and late 1965 constituted the most intense period of direct competition between China and the Soviet Union for allies and influence in the developing world. Mao launched an all-out ideological assault against Soviet revisionism, implying that the center of world revolution had shifted from Moscow to Beijing.[66] While China stepped up its efforts to promote an alternative development model in the Third World and made a bold attempt to cut the Soviets out of the Afro-Asia bloc altogether, the Soviets tried to paint the Chinese as irresponsible and unreliable allies.[67] In an effort to undercut Chinese appeal, Moscow emphasized a new willingness to accept armed struggle in the developing world, even as it continued to pursue peaceful coexistence. Beijing, for its part, made an ill-fated diplomatic bid to hold a second Bandung conference excluding the Soviet Union and launched a marginally more successful foreign aid program aimed at demonstrating that its revolutionary commitment extended beyond the realm of armed struggle to include the critical work of postcolonial political and economic development. This Sino-Soviet competition for leadership of world revolution converged on Vietnam, which, by 1965, took center stage as the primary Cold War battleground not only between capitalism and communism but also between the competing revolutionary alternatives proffered by Moscow and Beijing.

By the mid-1960s, against the backdrop of a stalemated war in Vietnam, both Moscow and Beijing made dismal assessments of their progress in the conflict against imperialism, and their interest in Third World intervention ebbed considerably. Following grave setbacks in Algeria and Indonesia, China's revolutionary foreign policy was in tatters. As the PRC focused its attention inward on the Cultural Revolution, it backed away from its confrontational stance and sought to avoid open conflict with the United States. China continued to proclaim its revolutionary rhetoric but did very little to back it up. For Moscow, recent events in Congo, Cuba, and elsewhere drove home sharp limits on the Soviet Union's ability to direct movements in the decolonizing world from afar. Coups against Algeria's Ben Bella and Indonesia's Suharto in 1965, and Ghana's Kwame Nkrumah in 1966, made clear the precarious nature of the postcolonial regimes Moscow depended on for the success of its revolutionary policies. Furthermore, the Six-Day War in the Middle East undermined the Soviet alliance with radical Arab regimes, which had, in many ways, been the crowning achievement of Moscow's foreign policy in the Third World.[68] Moscow's influence faded across the Global South, seeming to prove the massive Soviet aid program in the developing world a colossal waste of money and energy.[69] The 1970s, however, would witness a bloody encore of Soviet interventionism in the Third World, to which the United States ultimately responded in kind.

American Defeat, Socialist Fragmentation, and Cold War Realignments

The end of America's War in Vietnam augured a series of major global transformations that defined the final phase of the Cold War. As Lien-Hang Nguyen writes, "The crisis in American Power, the breakdown of unity within the Marxist-Leninist order, and the apogee of revolutionary Third

World Movements in 1970s can all be traced to the Vietnam War and its aftermath."[70] A turning point came in January 1968 with the North Vietnamese Tet Offensive, which exposed the brutality of America's war in Vietnam, adding fuel to a global antiwar movement that challenged the basic claims of "development," "progress," and "human rights" that undergirded the West's Cold War project.[71] Americans were scarred by their nation's failures—both military and moral—in Vietnam. Throughout the Cold War, the American public had exuded confidence in both the righteousness of US foreign policy and their country's ability to effect global change. The Vietnam War, costly in human, economic, and political terms, pointed to sharp limits on American power and led many to decry it as immoral; some would even go so far as to deem the violence unleashed on Vietnam criminal. Amid a public outcry to restore morality to America's global leadership and ensure that the country would never stumble into another such misadventure, President Richard Nixon and his national security advisor, Henry Kissinger, initiated a wholesale transformation of American foreign policy focused on the latter with a veneer of lip service to the former.

In 1969, Nixon rode to the White House on campaign promises of a secret plan to end the war in Vietnam. His plan consisted of investing South Vietnamese forces with greater fighting responsibility, which, combined with stepped-up bombing attacks on North Vietnam and a secret expansion of the war into Laos and Cambodia, would enable the United States to draw down its troop levels without letting up pressure on the enemy. In a July 1969 stopover in Guam, Nixon announced that, henceforth, America's Asian allies would be expected to shoulder the burden of their own defense with only economic and materiel support from the United States. Although Nixon's goal was to explain his administration's Vietnamization strategy, the Nixon Doctrine would become the basis of his approach to the Third World writ large. Nixon and Kissinger viewed the developing world as a geopolitical sideshow into which their predecessors had foolishly allowed themselves to be dragged, at great expense to American power, credibility, and prestige. In the Third World, then, they aimed to shore up friendly, stable regimes that would prevent Soviet encroachment, avoid drawing the United States into unnecessary conflict, and enable them to focus on the great power game. Their primary diplomatic objective was to exploit hostilities within the communist camp to improve diplomatic relations with both China and the Soviet Union.

As catastrophic as the Vietnam War was for the United States, Nixon and Kissinger recognized that it had also wrought great damage on communist bloc cohesion. Kissinger believed that the United States could leverage the Sino-Soviet split to weaken its adversaries' global positions, advance American diplomatic objectives, and pressure both the Soviet Union and China to compel their North Vietnamese allies to negotiate a face-saving settlement. This wedge strategy threatened Moscow with the prospect of a US-China alliance should the Soviet Union fail to cooperate with Washington on ending the Vietnam War and resolving other pressing international problems.[72] Nixon and Kissinger's pursuit of détente also promised desired progress on a number of key issues, from trade to arms control, and flattered the Kremlin by seeming to confer US recognition of the Soviet Union's great power status. Beijing also welcomed American overtures for rapprochement. Gripped by what Westad calls "one of the great geopolitical misunderstandings of the twentieth century: that the Soviet Union was the ascending power and that the United States was a power in decline," Chinese officials regarded an alliance with Washington as a welcome source of protection against future Soviet aggression.[73]

In the mid-1970s, the Cold War's novel reconfigurations converged on southern Africa, where a coup in Portugal suddenly unleashed a brutally violent final wave of decolonization. Renewed Soviet adventurism, America's "Vietnam Syndrome," South Africa's security woes, the Sino-Soviet rivalry, and Cuba's global revolutionary ambitions all combined to fuel massive foreign interventions in the civil war that resulted in Angola. Cuba, sensing an opportunity to realize its long-sought revolutionary dreams in Africa, courted Soviet support for direct military intervention to combat a US-backed South African invasion. Moscow, awash with a spirit of "Third World optimism" following its recent success in Southeast Asia, overcame its initial reluctance to back the large-scale introduction of Cuban troops.[74] Not only was Moscow motivated to support its Cuban ally's bid to bolster Angola's Marxist forces, it was also determined to hold the line against Chinese and US challenges to its position in Africa. Following a congressional vote to cut off US funds for covert operations in Angola, the Cuban- and Soviet-backed faction prevailed. But southern Africa's chain of crises was hardly resolved, and Angola's civil war raged for another quarter century, fueled until 1988 by foreign interventions inspired by Cold War rivalries.

The United States, China, the Soviet Union, and Cuba all drew lessons from the Angolan War that would shape the final phase of the Cold War in the Third World. With the Angolan debacle following closely on the heels of Saigon's fall, the United States appeared weaker than ever in the Third World. Americans on the left only grew more anti-interventionist, while neoconservatives began plotting to restore American vigor. In 1980, following a one-term interlude with Jimmy Carter in the Oval Office, neoconservatives would prevail with the election of arch–Cold Warrior Ronald Reagan. Officials in Beijing, finding that the grass was hardly greener on the other side of the Iron Curtain, aired their disdain for American weakness and fatalism in the face of Soviet power. The Soviet Union, on the other hand, was intoxicated by its victory in Angola. "The world," Soviet strategists believed, "was turning in our direction."[75] Officials in Moscow mistakenly gleaned from their intervention in southern Africa that they could provide bold support for revolutionary movements in the Third World without damaging the process of détente with the United States.[76] The Soviets continued to gloss over troubling signs of weakness in their own economy to focus on promoting the forward march of socialism in the Third World. Between 1978 and 1982, Soviet military aid to almost thirty countries amounted to $35.4 billion.[77] Moscow dove headlong into its largest military interventions of the Cold War in Ethiopia and the Horn of Africa, again in concert with Cuban allies, who took from their Angolan adventure that they could turn the tide of history. Far from adding to Moscow's success, however, these interventions sparked profound crises, including a crippling famine in Ethiopia and the long-term failure of state-building in Somalia. Moreover, they poisoned the well of détente with the United States that Jimmy Carter attempted to revive when he took over as president in January 1977.

Human Rights, Revolutionary Transformations, and the End of the Cold War

Carter came to office intent on restoring morality to American foreign relations. In the wake of the Vietnam War, the Watergate scandal, and revelations by the Senate Select Committee on Intelligence (Church Committee) of covert activities abroad, he argued that the future of US global leadership depended on reorienting US foreign policy away from Cold War rivalries—and the attendant habit of supporting Third World authoritarian leaders—toward human rights and nonintervention. "His policy of human rights," argue David Schmitz and Vanessa Walker, "sought to create a post–Cold War foreign policy that changed the fundamental nature of American relations with the Third World while still protecting essential American interests."[78] By focusing on human rights as a metric for gauging the rectitude of American policies and for evaluating the foreign governments with which it engaged, Carter was picking up on a major thrust in domestic and global politics that predated his election.[79] Although driven by idealism, Carter was enough of a realist to recognize that national security interests would sometimes trump human rights considerations, as would be the case in Cambodia, Iran, and Nicaragua. By the end of his first and only presidential term, in the face of a series of events in the Third World that once again stoked the flames of Soviet-American rivalry, Carter would largely scrap his commitment to human rights and nuclear arms control.

The Islamic Revolution in Iran was chief among the crises that reinvigorated the Cold War for its final decade. Carter's continuation of his predecessors' support for the authoritarian shah of Iran was a prime example of his pragmatic—and selective—approach to integrating human rights into American foreign policy. Iran had been a key pillar of US national security policy in the Persian Gulf since the overthrow of Mosaddeq in 1953. The shah helped shore up American access to Gulf oil and, under the Nixon Doctrine, had increasingly assumed responsibility for defending Western interests against Soviet-backed threats in the region. Washington failed to realize the extent to which its support for this brutal, repressive regime had fueled not only resistance to the shah but also virulent anti-American sentiment, both of which would be unleashed with a vengeance in a 1978 popular uprising. By early 1979, Ayatollah Khomeini and his cohort of radical Islamists seized control of that movement, establishing an Islamic republic bent on restoring the religious foundations of Iranian society.

The new Iranian regime, suspicious of both superpowers, rejected both the Soviet and American models in favor of an ideology born and bred in the Third World, a momentous event that would both transform and transcend the Cold War. Yet both Washington and Moscow were slow to grasp that the Islamic Revolution in Iran introduced into the international system an ideological force that elided the East-West rivalry. Instead, they fell back on assessing its strategic implications largely in Cold War terms. American officials initially sought to make connections with revolutionary moderates who could ensure the continuity of US interests in Iran, only to conclude amid the catastrophic 444-day hostage crisis that the unstable Iranian regime was dangerously vulnerable to Soviet machinations by which the Kremlin could usurp America's dominant position in the Gulf. Soviet officials, meanwhile, initially believed Iran would end up back in the US camp, due to a shared antipathy to communism. When the hostage crisis rendered that impossible, Moscow began to fear a US military intervention to overthrow the Islamic Republic and restore a friendly regime.

It was in this context that Soviet officials decided to invade neighboring Afghanistan in a desperate attempt to prop up its embattled communist government. Should Afghanistan fall to rebel forces, Moscow would lose its critical wedge between Islamic Iran and Pakistan, a staunch US ally. The Soviet Union's regional security seemed equally threatened by the prospect of US military intervention in the Gulf, hints that its Afghan allies might be shifting toward the United States, and the growing influence of Islamic revolutionaries in Afghanistan. On December 25, 1979, Soviet tanks rolled into Afghanistan, sparking American fears of a Soviet plot to seize control of the Persian Gulf and driving a stake through the heart of détente.

The collapse of détente resulted, in part, from the Soviet Union's vigorous support for revolutionaries in in Afghanistan, southern Africa, and Nicaragua, where the Cuban and Soviet-backed Sandinistas had just overthrown the pro-US Somoza dictatorship. But Carter's reinvigoration of the Cold War in response was also heavily determined by the vicissitudes of US domestic politics. In a presidential election year, he found himself humiliated by the drawn-out, heavily televised Iran hostage crisis, caught on his heels by the Soviet invasion of Afghanistan that seemed to show a Kremlin eager to exploit the weakness of his foreign policy retrenchment, and doddering through an economic recession. Desperate to prove his mettle on the world stage, Carter elevated the voice of his national security advisor, Zbigniew Brzezinski, a dyed-in-the-wool Cold Warrior, over the more tempered advice of his dovish secretary of state, Cyrus Vance. Nevertheless, eleventh-hour shows of strength against the Soviet Union in Afghanistan, a botched effort to rescue the hostages in Tehran, and renewed investments in nuclear technology were not enough to spare him from a trouncing at the ballot box. Reagan, an old Cold Warrior from Hollywood, would replace Carter in the White House on January 20, 1981, just minutes before the hostages were finally released.

Reagan decried the "Vietnam Syndrome," which he believed was preventing the United States from pursuing its anointed role as the leader of the free world. He campaigned on promises that he would beef up national defense, fight communism abroad with renewed vigor, and restore a sense of American pride and patriotism. Far from rejecting a role for morality in American foreign policy, he insisted the United States had a moral duty to support "freedom fighters" in their anticommunist struggles. Denouncing détente as "a one-way street that the Soviet Union has used to pursue its own aims," Reagan brought to the White House a plan not just to contain communism but to roll back Soviet expansionism.[80] He sought to accomplish this by tying up Soviet troops and resources in the Third World, most notably in Afghanistan, which he sought to turn into a "Soviet Vietnam," and in Latin America, where he proved willing to skirt legal frameworks to support right-wing forces against Cuban and Soviet-backed communists. He paired this Third World strategy with a costly missile defense program known as "Star Wars" that was designed not only to bolster US defenses but to turbocharge the arms race, forcing the Kremlin to spend itself into the ground. By January 1983, Brezhnev's successor, Yuri Andropov, proclaimed to a group of Warsaw Pact leaders that it was "no exaggeration to say that we are faced with the greatest attempt by imperialism to put a brake on the process of social change in the world, to bring to a halt the progress of socialism and, at least in certain areas, press it into reverse."[81]

Reagan's second term coincided with the ascendance of Mikhail Gorbachev, who would lead the Soviet Union through a series of domestic and foreign policy reforms designed to stave off collapse. In the final years of his presidency, Reagan joined his Soviet counterpart in working to resolve crises on the periphery that seemed only to perpetuate superpower conflict. In 1991, Americans greeted the collapse of the Soviet Union with a triumphalism that largely ignored the newly decolonized world, which had moved past the Cold War into new phases of conflict and development. Caught up in the superpower rivalry in ways that had warped decolonization processes and layered untold violence atop existing regional, ideological, religious, ethnic, and class rivalries, nation-states across the Global South found that they were neither colonized nor decolonized. An incomplete process would continue to play out long after the fall of the Berlin Wall, irrevocably marked by Cold War distortions.

2

India

The Promises and Perils of Nonalignment

"At the stroke of the midnight hour, when the world sleeps," proclaimed India's first prime minister, Jawaharlal Nehru, on August 14, 1947, "India will awake to life and freedom. A moment comes, which comes but rarely in history, when we step out from the old to the new, when an age ends, and when the soul of a nation, long suppressed, finds utterance."[1] Despite these lofty sentiments, independent India was born in crisis. The Indian Congress Party was forced to accept the subcontinent's partition into two states, a solution that almost immediately led to a scourge of bloodletting among Hindu, Muslims, and Sikhs. The subcontinent was afflicted by the all-too-common challenge of establishing postcolonial political borders that reflected the complex social, cultural, ethnic, and religious realities on the ground. Partition spurred a massive wave of human migration, as some 11.5 million people desperately crossed borders in search of safety while between 225,000 and 500,000 people lost their lives. So began a bitter and ongoing rivalry between predominantly Hindu India and the majority Muslim state of Pakistan, a regional rivalry that would soon become ensnared in the global Cold War, leading to an arms race, a series of wars, and incalculable human suffering.

Indian independence was a harbinger of things to come, the first domino in the post–World War II collapse of the colonial system. As historian Robert J. McMahon writes: "Britain's withdrawal from what had stood for centuries as the most glittering jewel in its vast colonial domain formed the opening act in one of the great historical dramas of the modern era. The curtain was beginning to close on the era of Western colonialism; before long, dozens of other new nations would follow the path to freedom blazed by India and Pakistan."[2] Nehru believed India had a unique role to play in guiding the newly liberated countries of Africa and Asia through the choppy international waters of the Cold War.

India's first prime minister was born in Allahabad on November 14, 1889. His father, Motilal Nehru, was an agnostic lawyer, a modern secularist who effectively resisted caste restrictions and religious divides. Jawaharlal, who was educated at home by an English governess and tutors, grew up with British, Muslim, and Hindu friends. The Muslim-Hindu divide that wracked South Asia was never significant in his early life. At fifteen, his father sent him to study in Britain, where he would remain for seven years before returning home to practice law with his father—to him a great drudgery—while dreaming of liberating India from British rule. In 1919, with the emergence of Mohandas Gandhi's nonviolent independence movement, he discovered a vehicle for pursuing that dream. Led by Gandhi, the Indian Congress Party, founded in 1885, was devoted to Swaraj, meaning "self-government." In the 1920s and 1930s, under Gandhi's tutelage, Nehru alternated between several stints as Congress Party president and no fewer than nine separate jail sentences imposed by British colonial officials, as they worked to thwart the party's agitation for independence.

In the late 1930s, Gandhi began to groom Nehru as his successor and formally named him as such in January 1942. The two paragons of Indian nationalism disagreed on several key principles. Nehru accepted Gandhian nonviolence as a tactic but insisted there remained a place for violence that was justified and aboveboard. And Nehru, a self-proclaimed socialist, embraced industrialization as a means of national advancement, whereas Gandhi condemned it as the root of capitalist abuses. Yet the two agreed on a uniquely Indian path to independence, and Gandhi's faith in Nehru's character overrode his concern about policy differences. In 1945, Nehru emerged from his last—and longest—stint in colonial prison at the age of fifty-five. As India's anointed nationalist leader, he took a leading role in negotiating independence.[3]

From the earliest days of his political career, Nehru preached what would become known as nonalignment, a policy of steering a diplomatic course independent of former colonial masters, regional hegemons, and the Cold War's two major power blocs. Insisting that peace and freedom were indivisible, he warned postcolonial leaders against falling into the trap of ongoing dependence on foreign powers.[4] As early as 1923, he expressed concern that independent India, if not truly autonomous, might become "a cheap and

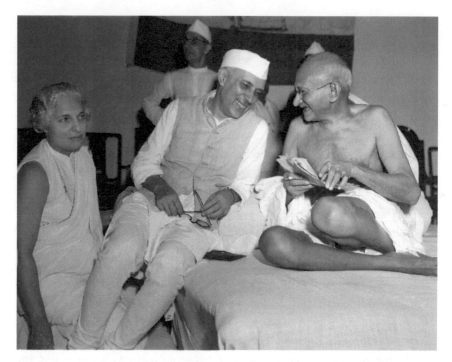

A bespectacled Mohandas Gandhi, the Mahatma, who eventually led India to its independence, laughs with the man who was to be the nation's first prime minister, Jawaharlal Nehru, at the All-India Congress committee meeting in Bombay, India, on July 6, 1946. Pictured to Nehru's left is Madam Vijaya Lakshmi Pandit. Nehru took office as president of the Congress during the session. Gandhi's philosophy of nonviolent resistance, including civil disobedience and fasts, drove India to independence in 1947 after nearly two hundred years of British rule. The father of modern India, the Mahatma, which means great soul, was assassinated in 1948 for his tolerance of other religions. (AP Photo/Max Desfor)

insufficient replica of the countries of the West" rather than "a shining example to the rest of the world."[5] In 1946, responding to the news of Philippine independence from the United States, he remarked cautiously: "We hope this really signifies independence, for this word has become rather hackneyed and outworn and has been made to mean many things. Some countries that are called independent are far from free and are under the economic or military domination of some great power."[6]

To Nehru, who famously proclaimed, "dams are the temples of modern India," the key to true independence lay in development. Like Ghana's Kwame

Nkrumah and Egypt's Gamal Abdel Nasser, he "wanted to achieve economic independence, promote industry, stimulate agricultural productivity, fight poverty, deliver health care, and improve education."[7] He viewed this as critical not only to securing the dignity and prosperity of his people but also to ensure the legitimacy and survival of India's postcolonial state. Nehru's embrace of centrally planned development—aimed at establishing "national self-sufficiency" and avoiding "the whirlpool of economic imperialism"—traced back to the 1930s, when the Congress Party charged him with drafting a development policy in anticipation of winning independence. Looking to the Soviet Union as an exemplar of planned economies, he considered state-directed development of heavy industry to be the path to ensure India's independent future. While India's first Five-Year Plan, launched in 1951, largely responded to crisis conditions, the second Five-Year Plan in 1956 constituted a bold project in line with Nehru's developmentalist vision.[8]

Nonalignment was conceived as a means of providing India and other postcolonial states the space necessary to develop independently while also enabling them to court critical foreign aid. Drawing on the Gandhian tradition of nonviolence, Nehru asserted India as a peacemaker in a conflict-ridden world, a broker between East and West, and "the third pole of attraction for those unwilling to be thrown about like pieces on the chessboard of superpower confrontation."[9] Nehru's promise to take an ethical stand on global issues while avoiding being reduced to a "pawn" or "plaything" of other powers appealed to national pride and a sense of morality rooted in ancient Hindu ethical precepts. Moreover, with much of the population mired in abject poverty after independence, Nehru was convinced that remaining unattached from both the Soviet and American spheres of influence would be the best way to attract desperately needed economic development aid from both camps.[10]

Initially, Nehru was frustrated in his efforts to gain the attention of either Cold War superpower. So long as Stalin occupied the Kremlin, Soviet relations with India were hampered by his view of postcolonial governments as tools of Western imperialism.[11] Stalin deemed moderate India hopelessly reactionary and bourgeois. Suspicious of Nehru, whom he viewed as "little more than an Anglo-American stooge," the Soviet leader expected India to tilt toward the West.[12] As long as Stalin was alive, then, both India and the Soviet Union remained closer to the People's Republic of China (PRC) than they were to each other. It was not until after Stalin's death in 1953 that his successor, Nikita Khrushchev, began to court India and other nonaligned countries as part of an overhauled diplomatic strategy toward the Third World.

In the immediate aftermath of independence, many of Nehru's policies did indeed lean toward the West. New Delhi, in dire need of economic assistance, appealed to the United States, which seemed the most likely source of development aid given recent precedents set by the Truman Doctrine and the Marshall Plan. Nehru, however, quickly grew frustrated with the Truman administration, which continually rebuffed his aid requests on the grounds that South Asia was peripheral to Washington's pressing security concerns amid the rapidly intensifying Cold War. Although the vast subcontinent was home to approximately one-fifth of the world's population, American officials had yet to see it as an area of critical strategic importance. Given India's size, population, and dominance in South Asia, Truman's foreign policy advisors gave it more attention than Pakistan, but their enthusiasm was tempered by trepidation over Nehru's leadership.

American officials considered Nehru's independent diplomatic path perilous. The paragon of nonalignment, who commanded the attention and allegiance of nationalists throughout the Third World, seemed to hold the power to advance—or thwart—American global interests. Officials in Washington were frustrated by Nehru's implication of moral equivalence between the US and Soviet sides, and distressed by waves of anti-American sentiment in India. "Indians," writes historian H. W. Brands, "found American culture insipid, and American preachments of equality, coming from a country with a long and continuing history of oppression of the nonwhite races, seemed the height of hypocrisy."[13] As charges of "new imperialism" mixed with condemnations of America's lowbrow culture and backward race relations flowed from a region of dubious strategic import, US officials opted to watch South Asia from the sidelines through the 1940s.[14]

Several factors, aside from an inherent distrust of Nehru and frustration with anti-Americanism, dictated this hands-off approach. To avoid stepping on British toes and overextending America's national security apparatus, the Truman administration preferred to leave South Asian security to the United Kingdom, which possessed vastly greater knowledge and experience of the region. Moreover, Pakistan's geographic location made it a potentially valuable strategic ally that the United States could not afford to alienate. Situated near the Soviet Union's southern border, South Asia's Muslim state could be used to gather intelligence, establish American airbases, and defend or recapture oil fields in the Persian Gulf. In a concerted bid to distinguish itself from India and win Washington's support, Pakistan openly rejected non-alignment and issued targeted appeals to the United States using virulently anticommunist rhetoric.[15] Yet the Truman administration embraced its own version of nonalignment toward conflicts on the subcontinent that would prove just as frustrating to India and Pakistan as India's policy of Cold War neutralism was to the United States. Washington refused to pick sides.

The first real challenge to Washington's policy of South Asian fence sitting came in early 1949, as an Indo-Pakistani dispute over the princely state of Kashmir drew the United States reluctantly into the affairs of the subcontinent. The conflict traced back to the moment of independence, when Kashmir was presented the option of joining either of the partitioned states. A clash between Indian and Pakistani troops erupted after Kashmir's Hindu maharaja ceded control of the state to India over the objections of its nearly 80 percent Muslim population, which favored attachment to Pakistan. This was just the beginning of an ongoing struggle over the fate of Kashmir, which represented far more than just a plot of land. As Brands notes, the Kashmir dispute highlighted India and Pakistan's "differing conceptions of nationhood."[16] Pakistan defined itself as a Muslim religious state, whereas India asserted itself as a secular one, the survival of which depended on the separation of religion from politics, and the coexistence of a variety of religious communities. New Delhi's governing legitimacy—and the integrity of the Indian state—thus depended on rejecting Pakistan's premise that religious disposition should dictate national affiliation.

When fighting initially broke out, the Truman administration made every effort to avoid getting involved in what it saw as a no-win situation, even going so far as to embargo shipments of military supplies to both sides. American officials were afraid of committing to one side over the other but also worried that the dispute, if left unsettled, could jeopardize US interests in the region. By 1949, UN mediation efforts stalled, pulling Washington into the diplomatic breach. As the United States pushed for a compromise solution, it increasingly blamed India for the impasse.[17] Nehru, for his part, resented American intervention and came to believe that the United States was openly siding with Pakistan in the dispute.

With the crisis in Kashmir ongoing, the late-1949 Chinese communist victory fundamentally altered Washington's assessment of South Asia, elevating its strategic significance. The first Soviet nuclear test within days of Mao

Zedong's triumph, on top of increasingly divisive conflicts in Indochina and Indonesia, seemed to signal the deterioration of Western power—and US preponderance—in Asia. The subcontinent was now home to the greatest number of Asian peoples outside of communist control, with India left standing as the largest noncommunist country in the world. Truman's National Security Council warned, "Should India and Pakistan fall to communism, the United States might find themselves denied any foothold on the Asian continent."[18] US officials were convinced the line must be held against this unthinkable outcome.

American audiences thus bristled with anticipation when Nehru's first state visit to the United States was announced for October 1949. In the wake of China's collapse, India seemed to hold great promise as a "new anchor" for democracy—and bulwark against communism—in Asia. However, the visit turned out to be spectacularly unsuccessful. Nehru found his hosts to be brash, condescending, and materialistic, while the Americans deemed him uncooperative, self-righteous, and dangerously rigid and dogmatic.[19] These perceptions built on a long-standing set of stereotypes that colored how Americans viewed Indians, and vice versa, rendering them, in the words of historian Andrew Rotter, "comrades at odds."[20] Nehru and Truman often talked past each other, uncovering fundamental differences that could not be papered over. While US officials were interested in India only insofar as it could be won over to the Western bloc, Nehru refused to budge on his policy of nonalignment. Even more troubling to his American hosts, he insisted that colonialism, not communism, posed the greatest threat to world peace. He declared his intention to recognize the new communist government in Beijing, upsetting American hopes that India could be deployed to contain Chinese power in the region. Meanwhile, "Kashmir remained a running sore infecting all aspects of bilateral relations," which stalled on the heels of Nehru's tour.[21] Ongoing tensions over economic aid also strained relations, as officials in New Delhi believed that Washington, generally unresponsive to its urgent requests, was manipulating aid as nothing more than a cynical tool to lure India into its camp.

In the summer of 1950, the outbreak of war in Korea precipitated a series of events that further strained relations between Washington and New Delhi, diminished India's relative significance to the United States, and ultimately drew Washington and Karachi closer together.[22] While both India and Pakistan initially condemned North Korean aggression, Nehru refuted Washington's claims that the conflict was a product of Chinese and Soviet aggression. To him it was fundamentally an indigenous dispute among Koreans that attracted outside intervention. Furthermore, Nehru resisted the Truman administration's efforts to link the Korean conflict with matters in Taiwan and Indochina. Not only was he personally contemptuous of American actions in those arenas, he faced domestic critics who lambasted him and his ministers as "tools of the Anglo-American imperialists."[23] He refused to support UN Security Council resolutions to repel the North Korean invasion by force—and then to reunify Korea—fearing that doing so could tarnish the reputation of the nonaligned movement and poison relations with China and the Soviet Union.

Long before war erupted, India had a stake in peacekeeping in Korea. In 1948 the country's most experienced diplomat, K. P. S. Menon, had been elected chairman of the UN Temporary Commission on Korea, a body charged with overseeing elections and monitoring the withdrawal of US and Soviet troops to their respective positions relative to the thirty-eighth parallel. When war commenced, rather than entering the fray—which would have required that India make a choice between the United States and the UN on one side and China and the Soviet Union on the other—Indian officials dug in to search for compromise solutions. Washington's rash decision to cross the thirty-eighth parallel, its rejection of various peace initiatives, and a scourge of vehement public attacks on Nehru's diplomatic activities led to a blossoming of anti-American agitation across India.[24] US officials, although increasingly frustrated with this anti-Americanism, not to mention Nehru's obstinacy, eventually gave in and made a private request that India take the lead in formulating a peace deal. New Delhi's proposed settlement served as the basis for the armistice, signed on July 27, 1953, that provided the blueprint for India's robust participation in future UN peacekeeping efforts.[25]

For the remainder of Truman's administration, Indo-American relations remained hampered by Washington's ambivalence toward South Asia, India's open hostility toward the United States, and Nehru's dogged refusal to pick sides in the Cold War. But Indian officials faced a deepening economic crisis and widespread famine that compelled them to court American support. In late 1950, they came hat in hand to request 2 million tons of food grains, indicating that the request represented a "formal turning point," as India had reached the conclusion that US support was vital to its national stability.

Truman's White House, viewing India's predicament in Cold War terms, was inclined to step in. According to a National Intelligence Estimate sent to

Secretary of State Dean Acheson on January 30, 1951, "The present threat of famine in India promises to create conditions ideally suited to the subversive activities of the Communist Party of India." Days later, Truman delivered to Congress a strong message—later titled "India Food Crisis—Opportunity to Combat Communist Imperialism"—requesting that it send the 2 million tons of grain to India in emergency food relief. Reflecting its distrust of and even distain for Nehru, though, Congress stalled, eventually passing a compromise bill that only further aggravated anti-American sentiment in India, where the public saw Washington's manipulation of desperately needed food aid as an effort to undermine neutralism and compromise India's diplomatic autonomy.[26]

But the funds were enough to seed a community development program in India, which would become a model for similar pursuits in other decolonizing countries. As historian Daniel Immerwahr explains, apostles of community development believed it would help foster solidarity, establish democratic deliberation, and encourage civic action on the local level to help communities absorb "the economic and political shocks of modernization."[27] Only by strengthening communities from within, the logic went, could they be adequately armed to resist the lure of communism. As Congress provided little guidance on how the allocated $54 million in aid to India should be spent, Nehru and US ambassador to India Chester Bowles hatched a plan to invest the funds in community development. Building on a rural development project in Etawah that had been spearheaded privately in 1946 by New York architect and urban planner Albert Mayer, with Nehru's backing, the Indo-US technical agreement of 1952 launched grassroots community development programs in 16,500 villages. By the mid-1960s the movement expanded to cover almost the entire country, but it ultimately failed to spur grassroots democracy and collapsed in the 1970s under Indira Gandhi's administration.[28] Meanwhile, the issue of food aid persisted as a thorn in the side of US-Indian relations into 1953, when both the United States and the Soviet Union transitioned to new leadership, auguring a new phase in India's Cold War.

President Dwight D. Eisenhower replaced Truman in January 1953, just two months before Stalin's death. Eisenhower brought to the White House a new national security strategy known as the New Look, a key pillar of which was the establishment of bilateral and multilateral pacts aimed at enlisting a broader swath of allies in regional defense. The Korean War led the Truman administration to evaluate the Soviet Union as a much more dangerous, aggressive, and unpredictable power than previously thought. Eisenhower agreed with his predecessor on that assessment but believed the irresponsible and unsustainable explosion of military spending resulting from NSC-68 could be partially mitigated through mutual defense agreements. As the United States looked to bolster its capacity to defend Western interests in the oil-rich Middle East, Pakistan emerged as a promising potential ally in a strategically significant location.[29]

Between 1953 and 1955, the Middle East emerged as a primary concern for American strategists. Worried about vulnerabilities opened by Britain's dwindling influence in the oil-rich Persian Gulf region, Eisenhower and his secretary of state, John Foster Dulles, aimed to shore up the region's defenses against Soviet encroachment. That led to the CIA-sponsored coup against Iranian prime minister Mohammad Mosaddeq and the installation of the pro-US shah, Mohammad Reza Pahlavi, and prompted American officials to intensify their search for other allies to share the burden of regional defense. Of the options available, Secretary of State John Foster Dulles was most impressed by Pakistan, which he declared after a May 1953 visit was the one country in the Gulf region "that has the moral courage to do its part in resisting communism."[30] Eisenhower and Dulles juxtaposed Pakistan favorably with India, which continued to criticize the United States and eschew any kind of military alliance. Nehru, who maintained his refusal to accept aid with political strings attached, butted up against a US defense establishment that was interested in Third World states only insofar as they could be wooed away from the Soviet orbit and into the Western camp. A frustrated Eisenhower concluded, "India would rather see Pakistan weak and helpless in front of a Russian threat than to see that country grow strong enough to give substance to its hope of annexing Kashmir."[31]

Washington announced its military commitment to Pakistan in February 1954, followed in May by the formal conclusion of the Mutual Defense Assistance Agreement. This Pakistani-American strategic partnership cemented Karachi's alignment with the West and drove a deeper wedge between Washington and New Delhi, plunging bilateral relations to their lowest point since independence. Anticipating Indian outrage, US officials promised New Delhi that the pact was directed solely against communism, and the weapons sent to Pakistan were for defensive purposes only, not directed against India. Furthermore, they hoped to mollify India with promises of massive economic aid on which Nehru's development strategy depended. From Washington's perspective, the commitment to Karachi by no means signaled a move away from the approach established under Truman of attempting to balance diplomacy toward both South Asian powers. But Dulles and his team were unwilling to sacrifice a bird in the hand—Pakistan—for the sake of appeasing the inscrutable Indian bird in the bush.[32]

Nehru, however, could not help but see Washington's military commitment to Pakistan as a direct threat to his country's dominant position on the subcontinent. Arguing that the pact was tantamount to taking Pakistan's side in the dispute over Kashmir, he claimed that the United States had not only completely altered the "roots and foundations" of any future settlement of the issue but that it was assisting Karachi in the "encirclement" of India.[33] While Nehru may have misapprehended Washington's intentions, he was not far off the mark when it came to Pakistan's understanding of the alliance. The United States saw it as a tool to secure a Western defense perimeter around the Middle East, but Karachi's aim was to bolster its regional position against India. In the coming years, the Pakistani-American military pact would exacerbate regional conflict, impede US-Indian relations, lead Pakistan to become an increasingly out-of-touch military dictatorship with ever-growing dependence on the United States, and ultimately fall short of both Pakistani and American expectations.

Nehru was critical not only of the US-Pakistan alliance but of Eisenhower's larger national security strategy. He pounced on the United States as a warmongering state following a January 1954 speech in which Dulles announced "massive retaliation," a strategy by which the United States would simultaneously save money on conventional arms and deter communist aggression by the threat of nuclear annihilation. Nehru was equally contemptuous of Washington's overall expansion of military pacts into the Middle East and Southeast Asia. He would be particularly concerned about the Southeast Asian Treaty Organization (SEATO) concluded in 1954 and the Baghdad Pact (CENTO) formed in 1955, both of which included Pakistan. Friction between Washington and New Delhi flared at the Geneva Conference held to negotiate peace in Indochina, where the flamboyant leftist K. P. S. Menon led the Indian delegation charged with chairing the International Control Commission. "Widely despised in the US," writes Roby Barrett, "Menon became a symbol of India and Nehru's leftist tendencies, and of the danger posed by the nonaligned movement."[34] Frustrated by Washington's posture in Geneva, Nehru referred to Eisenhower's signature pattern of defense pacts as "a wrong approach, a dangerous approach, and a harmful approach, jeopardizing both India and the general peace of the world."[35] Nehru insisted that the United States, through these pacts, had delivered the Cold War directly to South Asia, an outcome he had dedicated his life and career to avoiding. As historian Robert McMahon writes, "Nehru's dream of a region holding itself aloof from superpower rivalries lay shattered."[36]

American officials, blinded by the Cold War belief that nonalignment was little more than a pit stop along the way to communism, fundamentally underestimated Nehru's determination to retain an independent role for India in foreign affairs. His commitment to nonalignment only grew in response to US policies, especially the regional alliance systems that he regarded as a form of colonialism. In hopes of spearheading an Afro-Asian bloc of nonaligned states, the Indian prime minister took a leading role in the limited Colombo Conference in May 1954 and the much larger Bandung Conference in April 1955. He sought to attract international support for—and Afro-Asian commitment to—what he termed the principles of *panchsheel:* nonintervention and peaceful coexistence. He was also motivated by a desire to offset American alliance systems by consolidating India's connection with China. Wary of the potential influence of American allies at Bandung, Nehru extended an invitation to Beijing. Determined to undermine China and derail nonalignment, the United States coached representatives from SEATO countries to make sure American principles of anticommunism and collective security got equal hearing alongside his preachments of neutralism.[37]

The final conference declaration, which emphasized the brotherhood and common struggles of Afro-Asian peoples, did not include an endorsement of *panchsheel* but instead noted a right to collective defense that directly contradicted Nehru's nonaligned diplomacy.[38] "Bandung," writes Brands, "demonstrated the diversity of views among Asian and African states, effectively killing Indian hopes for leadership of a coherent movement between the superpower blocs."[39] Celebrated in the United States, the outcome of Bandung was a setback but not a disaster for Nehru, who remained a major figure on the world scene, as committed as ever to a nonaligned India.

Nonalignment, however, never signaled a lack of engagement. To the contrary, Nehru regularly swallowed his frustrations to make explicit, simultaneous efforts to court both of the dueling communist powers as well as the United States. Given recent strains to its relationship with the United States, New Delhi was especially heartened by new overtures from Moscow following Stalin's death. While Nehru promoted nonalignment at Bandung, the Soviet Union was developing a new foreign policy strategy designed to attract Third World countries into its orbit. Nikita Khrushchev emerged from a bitter power struggle to promote peaceful coexistence and competition with the West while simultaneously opening a second front of the Cold War in Asia, Africa, and the Middle East, where he sought to win new allies with generous economic assistance packages.[40] The new Soviet leader flatly rejected Stalin's "two camps" theory, introducing instead a new flexible approach to the Third World based on the calculation that closer relations with nonaligned countries would undermine Western power and influence throughout the Afro-Asian world, reduce the effectiveness of anticommunist alliance systems, and assert the Soviet Union as a formidable global power.[41] He lashed Stalin for neglecting India's vast potential, and rejected his predecessor's dismissal of the South Asian giant as a Western puppet.[42] India was among the first and most important targets of the Kremlin's new strategy. Menon, who was now New Delhi's ambassador to Moscow, deemed the situation "extremely favorable to us" and angled to take advantage of opportunities stemming from the Soviet volte-face.[43]

In pursuit of rapprochement with India, Khrushchev played on widespread anti-American sentiment and appealed to shared Soviet-Indian interest in planned economies. In February 1955, Moscow and New Delhi concluded a deal for Soviet technical and financial assistance to build a large steel plant at Bhilai, a development project long sought by India. Khrushchev then invited Nehru to visit the Soviet Union in July, followed later that year by Khrushchev and Soviet premier Nikolai Bulganin's visit to India, which Nehru called a "feast of friendliness."[44] Though the Nehru-Khrushchev talks were short on details, Czech historian Vojtech Mastny claims that the results "were sufficient to encourage Khrushchev's hopes that he could use India to move the 'correlation of forces' in the struggle with the United States decisively in Soviet favor."[45]

These events deepened American officials' concerns about what they read as a Soviet "economic offensive" in the Third World. They worried that India, in the wake of the US-Pakistani military alliance, was slipping out the Western grasp toward alignment with the communist bloc. Meanwhile, Eisenhower realized that Nehru, however distasteful, represented Washington's only hope of keeping India out of more radical hands. Afraid that Soviet domination of India "would be certain to cost us the entire Middle East," the president took the lead on promoting an expanded aid program for India.[46] Yet he faced an inhospitable domestic political environment. American fears and suspicions of Nehru only intensified in the wake of his visit to the Soviet Union. Newspapers across the United States abounded with condemnations like a *Detroit Free Press* editorial entitled, "Nehru Likes Any Color Just So Long as It's Red," and a *Washington Star* column proclaiming, "He has sided officially with the enemies of this country."[47] Eisenhower's administration faced stiff resistance from Congress, which reduced aid to India by $20 million in 1956. For the time being, widespread public and congressional disillusionment made the prospect of significant aid to India, even as a means of countering Soviet maneuvers, unrealistic.[48]

In short order, though, a series of domestic and international developments slowed Nehru's gravitation toward the Soviet Union and began to stem the tide of anti-American sentiment in India. Nehru found himself pleasantly surprised by Washington's firm response to the Anglo-French misadventure in the Suez Canal. At the same time, brutal Soviet moves in Hungary, coupled with China's heavy-handed actions in Tibet and aggressive claims in the Himalayas, undermined his trust in international communism. None of these events eliminated distrust between Washington and New Delhi, nor did they quash the burgeoning Soviet-Indian friendship. But they opened space for Nehru to approach the White House for assistance as Indian officials grew increasingly concerned that rapidly evaporating foreign-currency reserves could subvert India's Second Five-Year Plan (1956–1961). In August 1956, following Nehru's visit to the United States in which he and Eisenhower established a surprising rapport, the United States agreed to provide New Delhi with $360.1 million in surplus agricultural commodities over the next three years.

On January 3, 1957, Eisenhower's National Security Council (NSC) produced a new policy statement on South Asia. The NSC noted ongoing contradictions between US strategic goals and India's adherence to nonalignment. "Nevertheless," the statement concluded, "over the longer run, the risks to U.S. security from a weak and vulnerable India would be greater than the risks of a stable and influential India. A weak India might well lead to the loss of South and Southeast Asia to Communism. A strong India would be a successful example of an alternative to Communism in an Asian context."[49] Within a few months, Eisenhower established an interagency task force charged with developing a robust aid program for India, warning that the

Soviet Union would step in to aid countries like it if the United States stayed aloof. That same month, with India teetering on the edge of economic disaster, the Indian Communist Party achieved a few unexpected victories in national elections, lending urgency to NSC recommendations that the United States help India close its foreign exchange gap.

As David Engerman writes, India "became a new sort of Cold War hotspot, defined not by the fact or even the threat of armed conflict, but by superpower economic competition."[50] Soviet and American development aid policies toward the subcontinent would set a pattern for Cold War economic competition in the Third World.[51] Eisenhower's aid policies toward India presaged the John F. Kennedy administration's obsession with modernization as a tool to gain leverage and influence development in Third World nations, while Soviet aid to India served as the model for Khrushchev's "non-capitalist path" by which noncommunist states could be developed—and groomed for communist conversion—following centralized state plans.[52] According to CIA estimates, Soviet credits to India between 1954 and 1983, largely earmarked for industrial construction like steel mills and oil refineries, exceeded $3.2 billion. This was in addition to a steady stream of military aid that helped India maintain a substantial military advantage over Pakistan.[53] Over the course of India's Second Five Year Plan, the country witnessed an influx of foreign planners and economists.[54] Nehru, for his part, courted military and economic assistance from both Cold War superpowers while making commitments to neither. He continued to pursue the fragile dream of nonalignment, himself setting a pattern for how many Third World leaders would interact with their superpower patrons.

For Washington, the project of stepping up aid to India posed major challenges to its ongoing—and fundamentally contradictory—effort to maintain friendly relations with both India and Pakistan. Eisenhower, in his second term, faced the increasingly complex challenge of "saving" India from the type of economic dislocation that American strategists feared would usher it into the Soviet camp, without delivering a death blow to the Pakistani-American alliance. By early 1957, many in Washington were already starting to view that alliance as more of a liability than an asset. Eisenhower vented behind closed doors that the US military commitment to Pakistan had been a "terrible mistake," and several other American officials began questioning whether the pact with Pakistan was worth the costs.[55] Leaders in Karachi had become increasingly dependent on American aid, which they used to bolster the military at the expense of what Americans considered to be more pressing development

projects. This, in turn, led to simmering domestic opposition, political instability, and cycles of repression that worried American officials. Moreover, Pakistan's demands for economic and military aid seemed more focused on
strengthening its position against India than on the US priorities of defending
the Middle East and blocking Chinese advances in the region.

If the Eisenhower administration was not yet ready to give up on Paki-
stan, it certainly was unwilling to save the alliance at the expense of watching
India go red. "No American wants to see Communists take over in India,"
asserted State Department officials, framing the country's problems in starkly
Cold War terms. To highlight the urgency of the situation, they warned,
"Once a country, like China, comes under Communist control it is lost to
the free world; no amount of dollars can buy it back." On March 4, 1958,
John Foster Dulles publicly unveiled an emergency aid package for India
aimed at averting such an outcome. The package included a $225 million
loan in addition to promises of wheat and other food grains.[56] Although this
was only half the amount Nehru requested, it was but the first installment in
an American aid program that would continue to grow during Eisenhower's
second term.[57]

Predictably, this hefty aid package infuriated Karachi and strained relations on the subcontinent, fueling the arms race already underway between
India and Pakistan. Pakistani officials, who viewed this aid announcement as
an unmistakable sign that American foreign policy was leaning toward India,
put out feelers to the Soviet Union and China. Especially after it was discovered that an American U-2 spy plane shot down over Soviet airspace in May
1960 had departed from a US airbase in Pakistan, leaders in Karachi began
to wonder if the wavering alliance with Washington was worth risking Soviet
hostility. Meanwhile, American strategists deemed US aid to India essential,
regardless of its deleterious effects on relations with Pakistan, leading to a
marked improvement in US-Indian relations.

Yet American officials remained troubled by signs that aid had done little
to halt India's gravitation toward the Soviet Union. The friendship between
Moscow and New Delhi deepened as both powers found themselves increasingly at odds with China. A Sino-Indian border dispute in 1959 exacerbated
the deterioration of relations between China and the Soviet Union that was
already well underway. A violent conflict erupted between China and India
over their contested border when India offered asylum to the Dalai Lama—
the Tibetan religious leader—and thousands of his followers following

Tibet's rebellion against Chinese rule in March 1959.[58] Mao expected that China's military alliance with the Soviet Union, not to mention socialist solidarity, would guarantee Moscow's support in this conflict with a nonsocialist foe. The Kremlin, however, blamed China for the aggression, and accused it of violating the alliance treaty by failing to consult the Soviet Union.[59]

Pinned uncomfortably between Mao and Nehru, Khrushchev declared neutrality, a move that only deepened the wedge between Moscow and Beijing. China read the Kremlin's lack of support as a prime example of Soviet bourgeois revisionism and a victory for Washington's wedge strategy designed to break up the Sino-Soviet alliance. While suspicion brewed between China and the Soviet Union, Moscow and New Delhi drew closer. In September 1959 they concluded a Soviet industrial development credit agreement worth $375 million, at that point the largest outside the socialist camp.[60] It was becoming increasingly clear that the Kremlin's strategy of peaceful coexistence, in which India was viewed as an essential ally in the competition with the West, was fundamentally incompatible with Mao's strategy of international class struggle, in which India was classified as an enemy.[61]

Just as Moscow had come to view India as an indispensable ally, a new administration in Washington also seized on the South Asian giant as a critical player in the international system. John F. Kennedy, inaugurated in January 1961 on the heels of Khrushchev's "wars of national liberation speech," was convinced that the Cold War would be won or lost in the Third World. He and his cabinet, comprising the best and brightest stars of American finance, industry, and higher education, lambasted Eisenhower's administration for reacting slowly and responding insufficiently to key changes in the character and geography of the Cold War. Kennedy's secretary of state, Dean Rusk, warned, "The battles for Africa, Latin America, the Middle East, [and] Asia are now joined, not on a military plane, but for influence, prestige, loyalty and so forth, and the stakes there are very high."[62] Washington's flat-footedness in the Third World had, in Kennedy's estimation, enabled the Soviet Union to shift the global balance of forces to its advantage. As the new administration rolled out a suite of programs aimed at reclaiming that edge, Nehru's India and the neutralist bloc— proverbial Cold War chess pieces still up for grabs—assumed a position of special significance.[63]

Kennedy's team charged their predecessors with overemphasizing formal alliances and military pacts, like the one with Pakistan, at the expense of friendly relations with nonaligned countries. By showing greater tolerance toward neutralism and mobilizing development aid as a diplomatic tool, the new administration hoped to lure nonaligned states into the Western camp, thereby thwarting Soviet and Chinese designs.[64] Their eyes were trained especially on India, a bellwether for the nonaligned world, where they believed a major increase in development aid was necessary to halt Soviet influence and establish the South Asian giant as a regional counterweight to China. To that end, Kennedy's spring 1961 foreign aid request to Congress earmarked $500 million in development support for India alone, compared with only $400 million for the rest of the world.

The administration's new approach seemed to yield benefits almost immediately. In May 1961, Vice President Lyndon Baines Johnson reported after a trip to New Delhi that "Nehru, during our visit, was clearly 'neutral' in favor of the West." In coming months, that optimism would be tempered by ongoing tensions in the US-Indian relationship—Nehru still objected to US actions in Vietnam, Berlin, and on the issue of disarmament—but the foundation seemed to be on solid ground.[65] Pakistani leaders, however read the stepped-up program of US aid to India as a sign that their nominal ally was now siding openly with the enemy. That belief was cemented by Washington's refusal to intervene on Pakistan's behalf to resolve the ongoing dispute over Kashmir, though the United States did continue to send regular arms shipments. Pakistani leaders, feeling betrayed, began to inch away from what they saw as a dangerous overreliance on the United States. Moscow and Beijing were waiting in the wings, eager to make inroads in South Asia. In early 1961, the Soviets extended a $30 million loan to Pakistan, while Karachi made overtures to its Chinese neighbors. Pakistan's President Muhammad Ayub Khan announced that he saw no reason why Karachi could not "do business" with Moscow.[66]

Even as Kennedy sat back and allowed the US-Pakistani relationship to deteriorate, new conflicts cropped up to stymie a full Indo-American embrace. In December 1961, the Indian army invaded three Portuguese colonies along the Arabian sea, reclaiming in just thirty-six hours the long-contested territory of Goa. Washington, sympathetic to India's objection to ongoing Portuguese colonial rule on the subcontinent, had put pressure on its NATO ally to relinquish its claims on Goa. But US officials also warned Nehru against taking violent action. Following the invasion, then, the United States felt obliged to condemn Indian aggression before the UN Security Council. Both Kennedy and Nehru, though frustrated by this episode, remained intent on improving relations. But Goa damaged India's image within the United States, making it more difficult for the White House to promote its generous aid policy.[67] In the spring of 1962, the Senate Foreign Relations Committee cited India's assault on a NATO ally as justification for a vote to reduce aid to India by a quarter. Senator Stuart Symington called Nehru "probably one of the most aggressive persons in the world" and questioned the policy of aiding a country that espoused "pro-Soviet neutralism."[68]

Indian officials, for their part, remained deeply concerned over continued US arms shipments to Pakistan, particularly the recent sale of American F-104 fighter jets. Insecure about their own arsenal, they appealed to Moscow, which proved eager to supply India with MiG fighters to counter Pakistan's American-made jets. Kennedy tried, unsuccessfully, to block the sale. As historian Robert Rakove writes, "Washington stood by in a partial state of paralysis: wary of being a bystander to an influx of Soviet technical advisors in India but also chary of either sharing advanced weaponry with a nonaligned state or of contributing to a dangerous military escalation in South Asia."[69] NSC official Robert Komer warned, "Sooner or later, of course, we are going to have to become arms purveyors to India or it will inevitably turn more to Moscow."[70] Yet the United States, still refusing to pick sides in the Indo-Pakistani conflict, made yet another ill-fated effort to resolve the main point of dispute on the subcontinent: Kashmir. In spring 1962 the United States voted for a UN Security Council resolution calling for negotiation on the issue. The move backfired, infuriating Nehru. Washington's UN votes on Goa and Kashmir, combined with its sale of fighter jets to Pakistan, aroused the Indian leader's suspicion about American intentions and impeded Kennedy's dreams of luring India into the Western camp.

Such was the state of relations between Washington and New Delhi on October 20, 1962, when China launched an attack across the disputed border into India amid one of the gravest standoffs of the Cold War: the Cuban Missile Crisis. The resulting Sino-Indian War would contribute to fundamental shifts in the international system and a reconfiguration of power in South Asia. Nehru, whom a frustrated Mao had recently characterized as a "half-man, half-devil," overestimated the support he could expect from Moscow.[71] In a brief respite from the deepening Sino-Soviet feud, Beijing provided Moscow with the courtesy of almost two weeks' notice of the impending attack. With the Soviet Union facing the threat of total war with the United States, Khrushchev sidelined his misgivings about Mao and assured Beijing that the Kremlin would not take India's side.[72] Furthermore, he promised to delay the pledged shipment of MiGs to New Delhi, even after having completed a delivery of the very same jets to China. Following the invasion Moscow kept its promise, ignoring New Delhi's pleas for "moral support," instead encouraging India to negotiate on Chinese terms. An October 25 article in *Pravda* went so far as to endorse Beijing's line that India's policy was led by Western imperialists.[73]

India's poorly equipped and ill-prepared forces were overrun almost immediately, but its leaders dug in their heels and refused to give in to Chinese demands to negotiate. On November 14, the Indian army went for broke, launching an ill-conceived offensive that led quickly to disaster. Days later, with his army in a state of near-total collapse, Nehru saw no choice but to plead with the United States for direct military intervention. Not only did he ask for dozens of squadrons of fighter jets; he also requested American crews to operate them. To Kennedy, India's predicament was boon, a watershed event that Washington could leverage to secure New Delhi's alignment with the West. He agreed to many of Nehru's requests but warned that such a significant military buildup would take time. Before the United States had a chance to begin that process, China declared a unilateral cease-fire and began pulling back troops. On November 20, Beijing announced that it had secured a satisfactory border settlement and demolished its South Asian neighbor's "arrogance" and "illusions of grandeur."[74] The defeat was nothing short of humiliating for Nehru, who emerged from the crisis a broken man.

Meanwhile, the fragile Sino-Soviet solidarity on display at the beginning of the border war collapsed in the face of the Cuban Missile Crisis. Khrushchev's October 28 decision to withdraw missiles from Cuba prompted Chinese recriminations. In Mao's view, the Kremlin had sacrificed the socialist cause on the altar of peaceful coexistence, betraying its revolutionary ally Fidel Castro in the process. The Soviet Union was, in Chinese eyes, a revisionist power that could no longer be trusted to spearhead global revolution. Khrushchev lashed back, arguing that the Soviet Union had withdrawn missiles from Cuba in service of peace, whereas China's decision to start a war with India was just the type of rash and reckless behavior that would fuel violent conflict and undermine revolutionary progress.

It was only after China announced a cease-fire that Khrushchev, swayed by Mao's vitriol and threatened by Nehru's overture to the United States, rallied to India's side. A chastened Nehru praised Khrushchev for his "exemplary" handling of the Cuban Missile Crisis and blamed reactionaries in his own government for the foolhardy decision to push for a military solution on the border. While Indian-Soviet relations had reached a low point from which they would only climb, Khrushchev's reversal in the Sino-Indian war presaged his final break with China the following year. Thenceforth, China's emergence as the common enemy of both India and the Soviet Union would increasingly define the interdependent relationship between the two powers.[75]

The Sino-Indian border war also proved a turning point in Washington's relationship with India. Kennedy believed the Chinese offensive had transformed South Asia into a hot new theater of the Cold War. Washington must step into the breach or accept Chinese regional hegemony. Although the cease-fire eliminated the need for the American air cover Nehru had requested amid the fighting, Kennedy pressed on with supplying India with arms and equipment to fend off future Chinese aggression. In principle, he supported an American commitment to provide India with air defense and resumed efforts to resolve the perennial Kashmir problem. The president announced plans to increase military, financial, and diplomatic involvement on the subcontinent and approved an emergency military aid program for India up to $60 million. "Emergency military assistance," writes Rakove, "was granted to India with the express purpose of aiding in its hour of need *and* establishing a long-term foundation for closer ties."[76] Kennedy, working closely with British prime minister Harold Macmillan, also unveiled a joint Anglo-American military aid package to India worth $120 million.

Predictably, Pakistan objected to the US decision to supply India with military equipment. Frustrated by what they perceived as Washington's repeated refusal to respond to Pakistan's security concerns while moving ever closer to its chief regional enemy, its leaders inched closer to China. In February 1963, drawn together by their common enmity toward the United States, China and Pakistan reached a border agreement that served as the basis for future cooperation. In the months leading up to his death, Kennedy tried to salvage Washington's relationship with Pakistan, as difficult a partner as it may have been. In the hope of creating a regional anti-Chinese alliance, he continued efforts to bridge the divide between India and Pakistan, perhaps by finding a solution to the conflict in Kashmir. He was disappointed, however, to find that American military assistance in no way persuaded Nehru to make concessions on Kashmir, much less to throw India's support behind the deepening US involvement in Vietnam. By the end of his life, Kennedy found his diplomatic goals in India largely unrealized, while a clash between the United States and Pakistan seemed all but inevitable.

With the balance of power in South Asia in flux, the United States, India, and the Soviet Union all underwent leadership changes that were as turbulent as they were transformative. On November 22, 1963, Kennedy was struck down by an assassin's bullet as his motorcade rolled through the streets of Dallas. His successor, Lyndon B. Johnson, came to office with little foreign policy experience and none of Kennedy's passion for South Asia or the Third World. Nehru's death was less sudden, but no less dramatic. Independent India's first prime minister—the global figurehead of nonalignment—suffered a minor stroke in January 1964, setting off a divisive secession struggle that raged until he died of a ruptured aorta that May. The death of independent India's first and only prime minister unleashed a torrent of mourning in the capital so overwhelming that the military was called in to maintain order. That, combined with uncertainty over who would succeed Nehru, fueled rumors of a military coup. His ultimate replacement, Lal Bahadur Shastri, a relative unknown, was viewed by many as little more than an interim prime minister. Although he possessed little experience with foreign policy, he would preside over a war with Pakistan before his own death in 1966 led to the election of Nehru's daughter, Indira Gandhi. In the Soviet Union, meanwhile, Khrushchev was ousted in October 1964—the same month China exploded its first nuclear weapon—to be replaced by Leonid Brezhnev.

Kennedy's approach to South Asia had been riddled with flawed assumptions; namely that Washington would be able to paper over the rivalry between India and Pakistan to create a regional alliance against China. His administration had managed only to drive Pakistan deeper into Chinese arms, while ramping up US aid commitments to India just as New Delhi was enjoying a renaissance in its relationship with Moscow. Johnson's approach to South Asia made matters worse, undoing much of the progress his predecessor had made in courting India. "Indian hopes," writes Rakove, "once inflated by Kennedy, came crashing down as the contours of Johnson's policy toward New Delhi emerged."[77] In the spring of 1965, consumed with the escalating war in Vietnam, LBJ postponed scheduled visits to Washington by both the Indian and Pakistani prime ministers. This came at a critical time, as tensions were once again brewing on the subcontinent, this time over the Rann of Kutch, where India and Pakistan maintained overlapping border claims.

When fighting erupted there in April, India sounded alarm bells over the fact that Pakistan appeared to be using US-supplied weapons. This was in direct contravention of provisions stating that weapons supplied to both countries through the Military Assistance Program (MAP) could only be used for legitimate self-defense, internal security, or regional collective security.[78] Indian officials were quick to remind Washington of its repeated guarantees that Pakistan would not be allowed to use US military equipment against India. Johnson responded by forbidding the use of American arms by either country. While seemingly neutral, this move severely disadvantaged Pakistan, which procured its weapons almost exclusively from the United States, whereas India sourced military equipment from a range of countries, including substantial troves from the Soviet Union.[79] Pakistani leaders, who had recently returned from a weeklong tour of China, had ample reason to suspect a pro-Indian bias in Washington.

Ultimately, the skirmishes in the Rann were less notable for their militarily outcome than for the scars they left on US diplomacy with both India and Pakistan. The United States had, since the early 1950s, been committed by alliance to Pakistan, while flirting increasingly with India. "Had the South Asian powers settled their long-standing differences amicably," writes historian H. W. Brands, "American leaders might have continued their double game. But with the outbreak of war, neither would brook Washington's two timing."[80] Both counties lost confidence in the United States, preventing it from playing even a minor mediatory role on the subcontinent. Rather than working to mend fences, Johnson chose to step up pressure on India and Pakistan, calling for a comprehensive review of US aid programs to both countries. Meanwhile, he insisted on personally reviewing all future loans and grants to the subcontinent prior to Congress passing the next year's aid bill. The result was a restriction on aid to India, including that which had already been committed, leaving New Delhi profoundly disappointed by Washington's refusal to deliver on the promises Kennedy made following the border war with China.

Just as US relations with both Pakistan and India reached their nadir, a crisis erupted over Kashmir that posed what McMahon calls "the greatest threat to the peace of the subcontinent since 1948."[81] In early August 1965, Pakistani irregular forces infiltrated an Indian-occupied section of Kashmir. Within a month, a series of escalatory military moves by both sides led Pakistan to invade the extreme southern portion of Kashmir using US-supplied tanks. UN Secretary U Thant pleaded for an immediate cease-fire, asking both sides to withdraw to the demarcation line previously established by the UN. While the United States supported the UN appeal, India further escalated the conflict, invading Punjab in violation of Pakistan's territorial integrity. The United States responded by halting arms shipments to both counties.

On September 22, Pakistan reluctantly acceded the UN cease-fire proposal, pausing the war after seventeen days of fighting. To stave off Western mediation of the conflict, Soviet premier Aleksei Kosygin stepped in to broker the Treaty of Tashkent. The treaty, signed on January 10, 1966, restored the status quo under international supervision. "Though motivated by the narrow goal of preempting Western mediation," writes Mastny, "[the treaty] stands out as the most constructive accomplishment in the history of Soviet-Indian relations."[82]

India's prime minister Shastri died in Tashkent, Uzbekistan, the day after the treaty was signed. His cause of death was listed as a heart attack, though his family refused to accept that explanation, and conspiracy theories abound. Shastri's demise paved the way for a new era of leadership under Nehru's daughter, Indira Gandhi, who was sworn in as prime minister on January 24, 1966. Like her father, she was a true patriot, having grown up among leaders of the Congress Party fighting for freedom. Frustrated as a child by the repeated rejection of her appeals to join the party's membership, she took matters into her own hands to organize a children's brigade, the Vanar Sena (army of monkeys) aimed at ending dependence on Britain.[83] Unlike her British-educated father, she received most of her schooling in India and reputedly felt a much deeper connection than he to her Hindi heritage. When the widowed Nehru was elected prime minister in 1947, she was the closest thing the country had to a first lady. Before her father died, he started pushing her to assume a leading political role. During Shastri's short rule, she distinguished herself as a formidable figure, the obvious one to take over the helm when he died.[84]

Unlike her idealistic father, Gandhi was a realist. Faced with a severe drought, food shortages, and famine at home, she valued pragmatism above theory. In foreign affairs, she sought to win much-needed international support for India from a position of strength. In March 1966, en route to the United States for a presidential summit, she mused: "The weaker your position, the stronger must be your stand. To appear to bend and accept is a sign of immense strength."[85] Johnson went into his meetings with Gandhi determined

US president Lyndon B. Johnson and his wife, Lady Bird Johnson, present a bouquet of roses to India's prime minister, Indira Gandhi, at the White House Lawn in Washington, DC, on March 28, 1966. Man at right is unidentified. (AP Photo)

to pull back on commitments to both India and Pakistan in the wake of their most recent war. Fed up with difficult allies and intractable problems in the Third World, and increasingly consumed with the deepening morass in Vietnam, he concluded that the United States could disengage from South Asia without threatening the country's greater Cold War security interests. LBJ made clear to Gandhi that the United States would seek to lower its profile and limit its policy objectives in South Asia.[86] Yet, Johnson was persuaded by a combination of Gandhi's charms and his advisors' counsel that it would be wise to continue sending desperately needed food aid to India. While the United States fought in Vietnam to spare Asia from communist takeover, it could not stand by and let the continent collapse due to India's starvation. Johnson's hope was to strengthen India so that it could join Japan in defense against Chinese communist aggression in Asia. He called for India to rein in its population growth, "revamp its outmoded agricultural methods," and make peace with Pakistan.[87] Moreover, he believed he had secured from Gandhi a much-needed guarantee that India would at least tacitly support US policy in Vietnam in exchange for a steady supply of food aid.

On her way home from Washington, Gandhi visited the Soviet Union, where she struck out in her bid to win support for several heavy-industry projects. This failure only redoubled her determination to rectify the imbalance in New Delhi's relationship with Moscow, a relationship in which India was far too dependent upon Soviet whims. Recognizing that the Soviet Union could only be persuaded to act according to its own interests, she presented India as the lone country capable of preventing further Chinese expansion. She urged Moscow to approach the subcontinent with aid policies to diminish ongoing conflicts with Pakistan that, she argued, prevented India from standing up forcefully against China. She also made clear to the Kremlin that generous development and military aid policies would be necessary to prevent New Delhi from turning toward the Western camp. Like her father, though, she remained committed to preventing any power from "taking over management of the subcontinent."[88]

India moved markedly closer to the Soviet Union after the 1965 war, as Soviet military aid to India outpaced Washington's for the first time. Between 1965 and 1970, the Soviet bloc shipped India some $730 million worth of weapons in an effort to woo Gandhi into a formal alliance. Brezhnev also aimed to bolster New Delhi's conventional strength sufficiently to sideline Indian hard-liners who were pressing to develop a nuclear arsenal.[89] Geopolitical disputes, coupled with Gandhi's determination to preserve her father's policy on nonalignment, stood in the way of a full embrace. In the summer of 1968, India refused to vote for a UN resolution condemning the Soviet invasion of Czechoslovakia, simultaneously signaling its willingness to open border talks with China without preconditions. Yet, for Indian officials, Moscow could be counted on in ways that the United States could not.

Pressure from the Soviet Union and the nonaligned bloc alike forced Gandhi to break her vague promise to Johnson that India would support—or at least not actively oppose—US actions in Vietnam. Although Gandhi's pledge may have been well intentioned, she almost immediately found it impossible to keep. In a meeting with fellow neutralist leaders, Nasser of Egypt and Tito of Yugoslavia, her refusal to denounce US aggression in Southeast Asia seemed insufficiently neutral. She later recalled, "I was accused of having turned too pro-American." Moreover, giving comfort to the United States as it pummeled the Soviet Union's North Vietnamese ally threatened India's more reliable relationship with Moscow. Thus, during a July 1966 visit to Moscow, she added her signature to a communiqué denouncing the "imperialists in Southeast Asia."[90] Johnson, prone to taking diplomatic slights personally and intolerant of any country that presumed to criticize American actions in Vietnam, responded by tightening the noose on aid shipments to India. He ordered them to be released month-to-month in a way that thwarted any type of long-term planning by the Indian food ministry, and even halted them completely for several months at the end of the year. For the remainder of his administration, the Vietnam War stood in the way of improving relations with India, as with much of the world. Ultimately it brought down his presidency, ushering the Machiavellian rule of Richard Nixon and his national security advisor, Henry Kissinger.

America's long and disastrous sojourn in Vietnam did much to transform the contours of international relations, intensifying the Sino-Soviet split and dealing crippling blows to American credibility. In pursuit of what he considered to be an honorable exit from Vietnam, Richard Nixon took office in January 1969 with a plan to improve relations with both China and the Soviet Union. He aimed to play the two communist giants off one another to enlist them both in forcing Hanoi to negotiate on American terms. Triangular diplomacy, which involved improving relations with both pillars of international communism, would have been unthinkable in previous administrations. Yet Nixon, who built his political career on staunch—even virulent—anticommunism, had the unique credentials to change course without attracting charges of appeasement. Still, after two decades of rabid US hostility toward China, Nixon and his national security advisor, Henry Kissinger, realized they had to tread carefully. They would need a go-between with connections to both Washington and Beijing. In a move that would prove catastrophic for South Asia, Nixon turned to Pakistan's new prime minister, Agha Yahya Khan, to carry his messages to Beijing. Yahya rose to the occasion, playing a critical role in setting up Kissinger's surprise trip to China in July 1971, which paved the way for Nixon's historic visit to Beijing announced later that month. But the bill would soon come due for that diplomatic favor, and the price Washington ended up paying was immense.

Even as Yahya did Nixon's bidding in China, he faced the virtual unraveling of the Pakistani state. A separatist movement in the East—the territory now known as Bangladesh—had been building steam since before he took over for Ayub in 1969 amid great domestic turmoil. In March 1971, Pakistani troops rolled into Dacca, killing as many as 100,000 in short order. But the rebels refused to cave, continuing to fight for independence as a horrified world watched the Pakistani army commit genocide against its own people. By some estimates, more than a million people died at the hands of the army and from communal fighting between Muslims and Hindus. The fighting prompted a massive wave of refugees to flee across the border into India, where they put a heavy strain on Calcutta and its environs. Just six weeks after the fighting commenced, 3.1 million refugees spilled into India, and that number nearly tripled by the end of the summer. New Delhi faced a staggering $200,000 million-per-month price tag to feed and house the displaced. With India aiding and abetting the rebels, Pakistan was treading water on the battlefield, prompting it to make the fateful decision in early December to strike across the border at Indian installations in West Bengal. "This foolish move," writes Brands, "provided all the excuse New Delhi needed and it sealed Pakistan's fate." New Delhi immediately extended diplomatic recognition to Bangladesh and ordered Indian forces to march on Dacca. Within ten days, Indian forces captured the city. On December 16, Pakistan's army surrendered, bringing the fighting to an end.[91]

Shifting alliance politics transformed this regional conflict into a Cold War hot spot, with devastating effects. Despite the almost total lack of ideological affinity between China, a secular socialist state, and Pakistan, a Muslim nationalist project, China sided with Pakistan in a bid to challenge the Soviet position in South Asia. Motivated as always to check Beijing's designs on the subcontinent, especially given the recent Sino-American rapprochement, the Soviet Union predictably sided with its old friend, India. By late summer, the conflict provided the impetus for New Delhi to sign a formal pact with Moscow, which Gandhi had long resisted in service of nonalignment. Nixon had nothing but disdain for Gandhi, whom he referred to as a "bitch" following the so-called "dialogue of the deaf" between the two leaders that took place in Washington in November 1971. Beholden to Pakistan, and invested in seeing its new friends in Beijing succeed at Moscow's expense, Washington adopted a decidedly pro-Pakistani stance. Nixon and Kissinger's rapprochement with China had forced India to rely more heavily on the Soviet Union, and dictated Washington's increasingly indefensible support for Pakistan.

The staggering violence unleashed by Pakistan's army quickly spurred cries for Nixon and Kissinger to distance the United States from its old, troublesome ally. The American consul in Dacca cabled Washington to condemn the "mass killing of unarmed civilians, the systematic elimination of the intelligentsia, and the annihilation of the Hindu population." The ambassador in

New Delhi was "deeply shocked at the massacre" and feared that US credibility would be harmed by association with "a reign of military terror."[92] Without consulting the White House, the State Department took steps to limit arms shipments and economic aid to Pakistan, while the Senate worked to ban military aid to what many were coming to view as a genocidal regime.

Nixon and Kissinger, loath to reveal Pakistan's secret role in the China gambit, brushed off criticisms of their failure to intervene in South Asia's humanitarian crisis by saying that it was a regional—not an international—problem. Yet, Nixon did not remain neutral. When India finally invaded Pakistan in response to a slew of provocations, the White House responded by canceling orders for the small amount of arms India was purchasing from the United States, cutting off economic aid to India, and introducing a resolution in the UN Security Council demanding that Indian forces withdraw from East Pakistan. Moscow's veto, however, held up the Security Council until India's victory was complete. In a futile last-ditch effort to block Indian advances, the United States dispatched a nuclear aircraft carrier to the region, only cementing in Indian minds "the image of the United States as a treacherous bully and the Soviet Union as a friend in times of need."[93]

Nixon and Kissinger had shamelessly elevated power politics above humanitarian considerations for the world to see. Nixon recalls Kissinger saying to him at the time, "We can't allow a friend of ours and China's to get screwed in a conflict with a friend of Russia's."[94] Yet that is exactly what happened, deepening the Indian-Soviet bond in the process. Moscow rejoiced at the first trouncing of a mutual Chinese-American ally in conflict with a friend of the Soviet Union. India, however, faced diplomatic fallout, especially within the neutralist sphere. All but a handful of states had voted for the UN cease-fire resolution, and all nonaligned countries cast their vote for a statement that blamed India, albeit not exclusively, for the war. The nonaligned bloc, consisting largely of Muslim states that believed Hindu India was bent on humiliating their religious brethren, abhorred New Delhi's decision to continue fighting in defiance of the General Assembly resolution. India emerged from the war with the Soviet Union as its only remaining ally. "Yet, paradoxically," writes historian Lorenz Lüthi, "the decisive military victory on the battlefield and the destruction of the Muslim rival as a potential threat seemed to open the way for India 'towards playing a great-power role.'"[95]

After the 1971 India-Pakistan war, Gandhi took a critical step away from nonalignment by signing a Treaty of Friendship and Cooperation with the

Soviet Union. Since 1969 the Soviet Union had been pushing for such a treaty, which it hoped would serve as the foundation of an anti-Chinese collective security arrangement for Asia.[96] Brezhnev envisioned building on the Soviet-Indian entente to establish India as a Soviet bridgehead in Asia, through which he could launch a major expansion of Soviet influence in the Third World. Gandhi, however, proved much more willing to accept the Kremlin's largesse than to submit to its direction.[97] As Mastny writes, "Gandhi wanted India to be seen as indispensable for the global balance but not used as anybody's balancer."[98]

One major point of contention between the partners was nuclear proliferation. Moscow, which shared Washington's chagrin when India refused to sign the Non-Proliferation Treaty (NPT) in 1968, made a futile effort to persuade India to halt its nuclear program. India's nuclear ambitions also placed the country at even greater odds with the rest of the nonaligned movement. Gandhi, however, had come to connect the possession of nuclear weapons with the type of great-power status to which India aspired. After 1971, following China's accession to the UN, all the world's nuclear powers were permanent members of the Security Council, and all members of the Security Council were nuclear powers. There seemed only one route to membership in that exclusive club.[99]

Following India's first "peaceful" nuclear test—disarmingly nicknamed "Smiling Buddha"—in 1974, Moscow reluctantly accepted the fait accompli, convinced that continuing support for Gandhi was the only way to prevent a right-wing turn in Indian politics. Soviet diplomats hoped the test would, at least, diminish China's stature in the region. New Delhi insisted that its weapons program was peaceful—not intended to start an arms race in the region but to display India's technological capacity on par with that of the great powers. However, in 1976, once India rejected Pakistan's proposal to make the area a "nuclear free zone," the latter secured from China a promise to help launch its own nuclear weapons program, further destabilizing the South Asian powder keg.[100] "Unlike the U.S.-Soviet process of arms control," writes Mastny, "developments in South Asia had the effect of multiplying military conflicts, raising the prospect that the region would become the world's first nuclear battlefield."[101]

In 1977, Gandhi was voted out of office, to be replaced for a three-year interregnum by a new coalition government headed by Morarji Desai. India's new leader, prone to condescension toward the Soviet Union, broadcast a desire to improve relations with both Washington and Moscow. Despite the

Kremlin's frustration with this new tack, Cold War developments ensured an increase in Soviet arms shipments to India under Desai's brief term. Tensions between China and the Soviet Union went from bad to worse, elevating India's role as a regional counterweight to Beijing. Then, in December 1979, the Soviet invasion of Afghanistan disrupted the balance of power on the subcontinent, making Moscow even more reliant on India.

Though privately critical of Soviet aggression, Indian officials publicly parroted Moscow's line that Soviet troops had invaded Afghanistan at the invitation of its government. Gandhi, the eternal realist who returned to office in 1980, lent public support to the Soviet war, acknowledging that Moscow could only be expected to pursue its own national interests. Later that year, the Soviets granted India a $1.5 billion credit to purchase military equipment over the next fifteen years. With this, India became one of the world's largest arms importers, the great majority of which were Soviet.[102]

When Ronald Reagan took office in early 1981, he furnished Pakistan with a massive military aid program—amounting to $2.5 billion—to bolster regional defenses against Soviet aggression in Afghanistan. Protests erupted immediately in New Delhi, where officials were less concerned about the threat from Pakistan than they were over the signals this sent about American priorities in South Asia. Amid this turmoil, however, Gandhi, made a concerted effort to chart a more balanced relationship with Washington and Moscow. She established a personal rapport with Reagan that would have been unthinkable under Nixon.[103] Yet, as Radchenko writes, "In the early 1980s India's relations with both superpowers effectively stagnated."[104] India had become less, not more, secure, thanks to its Soviet-backed militarization. Regional conflicts abounded, as India's former satellite Bangladesh turned against it, raising fears of Chinese intervention, and a new conflict between India and Pakistan over Kashmir erupted in 1984. Meanwhile, New Delhi's overtures to Washington provoked insecurity in the Kremlin, even as Gandhi attempted to assuage Soviet concerns by recognizing the Vietnam-backed government in Cambodia that replaced the murderous Khmer Rouge, thereby angering China.

In the mid-1980s, key leadership changes transformed the diplomatic landscape. Brezhnev died in 1982, followed by Gandhi's assassination at the hands of her Sikh bodyguards in 1984. Rajiv Gandhi's inauguration following his mother's death coincided with Mikhail Gorbachev's ascendance in the Soviet Union. Improving relations with the United States topped the younger Gandhi's ambitions when he took office, and he scored some major successes. In 1985, Reagan indicated a willingness to help India produce light combat aircraft, marking the first instance of substantial military cooperation between India and the United States since the latter suspended military aid in 1965. Washington and New Delhi simultaneously concluded a "memorandum of technical cooperation," allowing for the United States to export computers to India. Washington followed this up with a promise to provide India with jet engines for aircraft, which Radchenko calls "an agreement widely heralded as a breakthrough for Indo-US military relations."[105]

Despite these breakthroughs, Washington's approach to New Delhi remained marred by suspicion of the South Asian giant as little more than a Soviet pawn.[106] Gorbachev, spurred to action by American inroads with one of the Soviet Union's most important strategic partners, stepped up support for India's regional policies. Regarding India as the cornerstone of a newly revitalized Soviet foreign policy, he envisioned a global strategic partnership with New Delhi as "a model of interstate relations for the future." Though wary of the younger Gandhi, the Kremlin continued to provide India with military hardware and, despite its own mounting economic woes, extended India a credit exceeding all previous loans combined. In 1986, Moscow and New Delhi forged an ambitious program of cooperation in the realms of science and technology, and adopted a joint "Declaration of Principles of a Nuclear-Weapon-Free and Non-Violent World," which represented a significant shift away from the power political foundations of the Soviet-Indian partnership. Meanwhile, Gorbachev initiated a dramatic shift in the Soviet approach to security in South Asia, proposing an all-Asia forum to include China. Rather than seeking to block Chinese power as usual, the Kremlin enlisted Beijing in a program of collective security aimed at thwarting American designs on the region. In his 1987 Vladivostok speech, Gorbachev challenged the United States to start withdrawing forces from Asia. When the United States refused, the Soviets began to withdraw troops unilaterally from Chinese borders.[107]

Under Rajiv, India initially raised its international profile, effectively playing the Soviet Union and the United States off one another to win the best possible terms from both. Perhaps due to overconfidence, he soon stumbled into a regional foreign policy blunder that cost India dearly, and ultimately cost Rajiv his life. In 1987, India, which had taken the lead in mediating an ethnic conflict on the island of Sri Lanka, concluded a settlement calling for the deployment of Indian peacekeeping forces on the island. Those forces quickly found themselves mired in a quagmire that would last more than two years. Rajiv, distracted by domestic unrest and under suspicion of corruption, let the crisis fester. Not only did this mistake damage India's role in the region, it frustrated officials in both Washington and Moscow, who saw Rajiv's efforts to assert India as a regional power broker as threatening to their own interests.

While Rajiv sought to establish India's regional hegemony at Pakistan's expense, Gorbachev was increasingly committed to improving Soviet-Pakistani relations with an eye toward ending the costly war in Afghanistan. Following the 1988 Geneva Accords that charted steps for a cessation of hostilities, the Soviet Union all but abandoned India in favor of Pakistan, without whose cooperation Moscow had no hope of cutting its losses in Afghanistan. Moreover, Gorbachev shifted from a posture of confrontation to one of cooperation with the United States, rendering impotent India's balancing act between the two powers. "Prime Minister Rajiv Gandhi over-played his hand," writes Radchenko. "In the mid-1980s, as he set out to improve relations with both Moscow and Washington, India briefly punched above its weight; in the end, neither the Soviet Union nor, especially, the US, valued their relationship with India above their respective regional and global priorities."[108]

The Afghan settlement, which excluded India from a major international agreement in its own sphere of interest while including Pakistan, dealt a crippling blow to India's great-power ambitions. By the end of his five-year stint in power, which began with an ambitious program to establish India as a leading regional and global power, Rajiv seemed to lack a foreign policy strategy altogether. India's relations with its neighbors were as strained as ever, and the prime minister no longer had the ear of Reagan or Gorbachev, both of whom were pursuing an increasingly collaborative international agenda that did not involve India. In 1989, Rajiv suffered a resounding electoral defeat, only to be killed two years later by a Tamil Tiger suicide bomber for his role in the Sri Lankan intervention.[109]

As the Soviet Union approached collapse, its relations with India continued to wither. Trade relations diminished, military cooperation seized up, and political scandals abounded. Nonetheless, the demise of the Soviet Union proved catastrophic to South Asia's largest, most populous country. It triggered an economic crisis that forced New Delhi to seek help from the

International Monetary Fund (IMF), which, in turn, inspired a set of "Look East" policies that would ultimately propel India's long-overdue economic takeoff.[110] Post–Cold War India has continued to maneuver between the United States, China, and Russia to establish itself as a major military and economic power. Its first test of a "real" nuclear bomb in 1998 punctuated New Delhi's great-power ambitions while adding fuel to the ongoing arms race with Pakistan. That regional rivalry largely defined, and ultimately transcended, India's Cold War.

India's signal contribution to the Cold War was nonalignment. Nehru's ambition to spearhead a coalition of nonaligned countries in Africa and Asia was basically stillborn, as its constituents proved incompatibly diverse and all too inclined toward alignment. But he had much greater success in steering India among competing international blocs to win the widest possible swath of support for its economic development strategy, its bid for regional hegemony, and its aspirations to great-power status. Nehru and his successors succeeded in drawing substantial economic and military aid from both the United States and the Soviet Union. Development aid emerged early on as a primary vehicle through which the superpowers competed for India's favor, transforming it into a laboratory for the competition between modernization and development models that would take off globally in the 1960s. As India's perceived significance as a bulwark against the expansion of Chinese communist power in Asia grew, especially in the wake of the Sino-Soviet split, both Washington and Moscow tolerated its refusal to pick sides in the Cold War. New Delhi leveraged its position as a regional counterweight to China to secure military aid that, combined with the American military commitment to Pakistan, added fuel to the fire of the Indo-Pakistani conflict. And by playing on its nonaligned status to become a nuclear power with relative impunity, India guaranteed that the arms race with Pakistan would outlive the Cold War.

3

Egypt

The Crush of Arab Nationalism

Egypt, though not a formal colony, entered into the Cold War system as it broke free from a state of de facto British imperialism that it had endured since the late nineteenth century. After World War II, Soviet and American eyes were trained on the Middle East as a site of critical oil reserves and strategic bases. On top of those strategic considerations, the 1948 creation of the state of Israel, and the subsequent emergence of Arab nationalism led by Gamal Abdel Nasser, would spur decades of superpower competition in the region. Whereas Washington—and to a lesser extent Moscow—filtered Middle Eastern politics through a Cold War lens, regional states proved much less concerned with the ideological conflict between communism and liberal democracy than they were with rivalries between conservative and Nasserite Pan-Arab regimes and the vicissitudes of the Arab-Israeli conflict. As the United States replaced Britain as the dominant Western power in the Middle East amid Soviet efforts to make its own inroads there, superpower interventions would intensify and transform those regional conflicts—and the states involved—in enduring ways.

Britain initiated its military occupation of Egypt in 1882. Previously a province of the Ottoman Empire, the country had fallen deeply in debt to European creditors amid a midcentury push for modernization in education, industry, and transportation that included the construction of the Suez Canal. Egypt experienced a brief economic boom when the American Civil War vaulted global demand for cotton. But that bubble burst quickly, and by 1878 soaring debt to Europeans provided a pretext for British and French authorities to impose control over Egyptian finances. In 1881 a group of Egyptian army officers led by Col. Ahmed Urabi, frustrated with increasing foreign influence and court corruption, staged an uprising under the slogan "Egypt for Egyptians." The uprising precipitated a rash of antiforeign riots in Alexandria, a port city with a robust European population, to which Britain responded with a military invasion. The onslaught, ostensibly to protect resident Europeans, quashed Urabi loyalists and established de facto British rule over Egypt.[1] For more than thirty years thereafter, British troops occupied Egypt while it remained under formal Ottoman suzerainty.

When World War I erupted in 1914, pitting Britain against the Ottoman Empire, the former declared martial law in Egypt and claimed it as a protectorate of the British Empire, ending centuries of Ottoman control. Seeking to defend the strategically vital Suez Canal and fortify Egypt as a wartime base, Britain dispatched a large contingent of troops that disrupted daily life, strained the country's resources, and ultimately contributed to the emergence of a vibrant independence movement. That movement, like many others in the colonized world, was buoyed by US president Woodrow Wilson's lofty wartime rhetorical commitments to making the world safe for democracy, ensuring self-determination, and defending the rights of small nations. As Erez Manela has shown, the Egyptian press reported widely on Wilson's pronouncements, encouraging the public to embrace the promise that it implied for their own country's autonomous future.[2] By late 1918, a group of Egyptian politicians led by Sa'd Zaghlul that had initially seen merit in gradualism—lobbying at first for no more than an enlarged role in their country's administration—began to embrace the far more ambitious aim of complete self-determination.[3] Zaghlul's group organized a new party, the Wafd, which set out to rally public opinion behind the goal of independence. Confident that it would have the sympathy and support of Wilson and the United States, Zaghlul's delegation set its sights on traveling to Versailles, where it could plead directly with the US president to include Egyptian independence in the peace settlement.

Wafd ambitions, though, were to be thwarted at every turn. British officials, who concluded that Egyptian self-determination posed a direct threat to the security of their empire, sought to suppress Zaghlul's movement and prevent his delegation from reaching Versailles. In March 1919, British troops arrested Zaghlul and three other leading members of the Wafd and exiled them to the Mediterranean island of Malta. Far from silencing Egyptian demands for independence as intended, this inspired popular demonstrations throughout the country, culminating in a series of violent clashes that

would become known as the 1919 Revolution.[4] Washington ignored the protestors' appeals for US support. Rather than come to their aid, the United
States extended formal recognition to the British protectorate in Egypt, a
move it had resisted throughout the war in the name of neutrality, and in the
hope of distancing US policy from the Allies' expansionist war aims. Presaging the dynamics of the early Cold War in the Middle East, American officials were persuaded to do so in part by British foreign secretary Lord Arthur
Balfour's warnings that Egyptian nationalists were in fact Bolshevik agents
bent on stirring up a Holy War. "Having invoked the specters of Egyptian
chauvinism, Bolshevism, and Islamic fanaticism in one fell swoop," writes
Manela, "Balfour concluded that it was of the utmost importance for the
United States to recognize the protectorate immediately."[5] In bowing to British pressure, Wilson weakly insisted that he remained committed to self-
determination for Egypt but that it should be achieved through an orderly,
gradual reform process rather than by revolution. This was consistent with
Wilson's approach to the entire non-European world, where he had no intention of extending the principle of self-determination to peoples whom he and
a majority of his countrymen deemed "either inherently or developmentally
. . . unfit for self-government."[6]

Zaghlul and his associates were released from prison just in time to head
to Versailles to plead their case. Undeterred by Washington's decision to recognize the protectorate, they spent nearly a year in Paris—long after the
peace conference ended—seeking international support for Egyptian independence. Although their efforts failed in the face of the Allies' stark political
compromises at Versailles and Wilson's retreat from his bold vision for a new
liberal international order, Egyptian nationalists had embraced the principle
of self-determination as their fundamental objective. There was no going
back. Until his death in 1927, Zaghlul would lead Egypt in building the
most dynamic nationalist movement in the Arab world. In 1936, his successors persuaded Britain to sign a treaty promising the sixteen-year-old King
Farouk that it would withdraw from Egypt within two decades, setting up
the crisis that would develop over the disposition of the Suez Canal as that
clock expired in 1956.[7]

Until World War II, American missionaries and private oil firms took
much more of an interest in Egypt—and the Middle East as a whole—than
did American diplomats. "Egypt is a charming place to be stationed," mused
the American minister to Cairo, William J. Jardine, in 1932. "As I see it there

is not much going on here of tremendous consequence to my government. . . . [I]t appears to me to be quite a sideshow."[8] World War II, however, shined a light on the importance of the Middle East as a strategic location, a critical site for military bases, and a source of increasingly valuable petroleum. Viewing the region as vital to Britain's fight against the Axis powers, the United States once again skirted its commitment to self-determination—which Franklin D. Roosevelt had reaffirmed with the 1941 Atlantic Charter—to sanction its ally's imperial presence in Egypt. When British forces rolled into Cairo on February 4, 1942, surrounding King Farouk's royal palace and forcing him to install a pro-Allied government led by prime minister Mostafa el-Nahhas, FDR turned a deaf ear to the king's pleas for support.

By the war's end, officials in Harry Truman's new administration had come to regard the Middle East as a region of great strategic import, just below western Europe in its emerging defense hierarchy. US national security, they concluded, depended on unfettered access to Middle Eastern petroleum reserves that could satisfy the nation's ever-increasing demands for oil, and fuel military operations in the event of war. US officials were also preoccupied with denying the Soviet Union—with which the Anglo-Americans seemed on an inevitable collision course—access to the Middle East and its seemingly limitless cache of oil. To this end, Washington aimed to support and capitalize on Britain's entrenched regional power. "Even more important than the region's oil repositories," writes Melvyn Leffler, "were its airfields, on which U.S. and British strategic plans depended."[9] The retention of Egyptian bases, from which Anglo-Americans could strike more than three-quarters of Soviet refineries in the Middle East, became a paramount objective. But Britain's hold on the region was slipping, leaving Washington to grapple with its willingness to take over as the dominant Western power.

In late February 1947, Britain forced Truman's hand by announcing its imminent withdrawal of funds for Greece and Turkey, a move precipitated by its own struggles with postwar economic recovery. Secretary of State Dean Acheson later recalled the imperative to convince Congress—which was under the control of fiscally conservative Republicans—to authorize funding for the United States to replace British aid, invoking stark Cold War language that cast communism as a rapidly spreading contagion:

> Soviet pressure on the Straits, on Iran, and on Northern Greece had brought the Balkans to the point where a highly possible Soviet

breakthrough might open three continents to Soviet penetration. Like apples in a barrel infected by one rotten one, the corruption of Greece would infect Iran and all to the east. It would also carry infection to Africa through Asia Minor and Egypt, and to Europe through Italy and France. . . . The Soviet Union was playing one of the greatest gambles in history at minimal cost. . . . We and we alone were in a position to break up the play. These were the stakes that British withdrawal from the eastern Mediterranean offered to an eager and ruthless opponent.[10]

On March 12, 1947, in making his pitch for Congress to authorize $400 million in military and economic aid for Greece and Turkey, Truman warned: "If Greece should fall under the control of an armed minority, the effect upon its neighbor, Turkey, would be immediate and serious. Confusion and disorder might well spread throughout the entire Middle East."[11] By adding broad rhetorical flourishes committing the United States to defending free peoples everywhere against the forces of totalitarianism, the president laid the groundwork for an expanded and militarized containment policy that would fuel a problematic global pattern of Cold War interventionism. As for the Middle East, the Truman Doctrine paved the way for deeper American involvement and set the precedent for the Eisenhower Doctrine a decade hence.

Meanwhile, just as Truman responded to the confluence of Soviet encroachment and British retreat by ramping up its commitment to defending Western interests in the Middle East, he made the fateful decision to support the creation of a Jewish state in Israel, a move that would immeasurably complicate regional dynamics. Truman was sympathetic to the Zionist project on humanitarian grounds, sensitive to growing political pressure from his Jewish constituents, and eager to preempt Soviet influence in Israel. He flouted warnings from his advisors that US support for Israel would only antagonize Arabs, thereby threatening US oil interests and access to bases in the region. Truman's first move was to support the 1947 UN plan to partition the British mandate of Palestine into separate Jewish and Palestinian states. When Britain formally terminated its mandate in May 1948, prompting Palestinian Jews to declare independence for Israel, Truman responded almost instantaneously to extend de facto recognition to the new state. The Soviet Union followed three days later with formal recognition. Stalin, hoping to prevent Israel from aligning with the West, dispatched the first official diplomatic mission to Tel Aviv and thumbed his nose at the UN embargo on arms exports to the region by directing weapons to the new state via Czechoslovakia and Yugoslavia.[12]

Israel faced an immediate military challenge from a coalition of Arab states, prominently featuring Egypt, that had long been antagonistic toward the notion of a Jewish state in Palestine. The ten months of fighting that ensued proved disastrous for the Arabs, who were forced to cede not only the territory recommended by the 1947 UN partition plan to comprise a Jewish state but almost two-thirds of the proposed Palestinian state as well. Nearly 700,000 Palestinians were forced from their homes, generating a refugee crisis that would compound territorial disputes to fuel an intractable Arab-Israeli crisis spanning decades. The UN cease-fire resolution that took effect on January 7, 1949, and the Israeli-Egyptian armistice signed on February 24, 1949, were but the first of many pauses to a conflict seemingly impervious to mediation.

Support for Israel wrought profound consequences for the future of US policy in the Middle East. As Salim Yaqub argues, many Arabs conceived of Israel as "a creation of Western imperialism designed to re-enslave the Arab world just as it was on the verge of gaining true political liberty."[13] By casting its lot with Israel, the United States invited some Arab critics to include it, for the first time, in the nefarious company of their imperialist adversaries. And the ongoing Arab-Israeli conflict would prove to be a deep and persistent complication for American strategists, as the US national security paradigm of West versus East chafed against the grain of regional politics that centered on the Arab-Israeli dispute.

In May 1950, in the hope of keeping a lid on the simmering Arab-Israeli conflict, Britain, France, and the United States issued the Tripartite Declaration. To ward off an arms race, they pledged to regulate arms sales to the Middle East. And they vowed to prevent the violation of existing demarcations by any means, including force if necessary. As Philip Zelikow writes, "By issuing this declaration, not only were the three powers trying to restrain those in the region, they were also trying to regulate each other."[14] Meanwhile the outbreak of war in Korea alarmed Truman's administration, heightening its sense of urgency to develop a more robust strategy for preventing Soviet encroachment in the Middle East. Anglo-American officials drew up plans for a Middle Eastern Command (MEC) that would enlist regional partners in a defense system—under a British supreme commander—to flank the Soviet Union's southern border from Greece to Iran. But Egypt scuttled the plan before it was even launched. In October 1951, Egypt's infamously pro-British prime minister el-Nahhas, who had been removed from his post in 1944 only to be reinstated in 1950, had come around to sharing with many of his compatriots the view that British imperialism posed a far greater threat to Arab autonomy than did communism. Cairo lashed out at what seemed to be the latest scheme to reimpose Western control over the Middle East, flatly rejecting the MEC proposal and demanding that British forces withdraw from the military base straddling the Suez Canal.

There was overwhelming support among the Arab public for Egypt's defiant stance, ensuring that other Arab states would also decline to participate in both the MEC and the slightly retooled Middle East Defense Organization (MEDO) that British and American diplomats concocted in an effort to salvage their regional defense plans. These events further undermined American faith in Britain's ability to protect the region against Soviet aggression. A December 1951 NSC report pointed to "the rapidly declining ability of the U.K. to maintain and defend Western interests in parts of the Middle East," signaling the imminent "decline of the U.K. as a world power."[15] As Peter Hahn writes, the failure of the MEC-MEDO concept convinced State Department officials that it was "no longer safe to assume, automatically, that Britain can and should be considered the principal protector of Western interests in the Middle East."[16]

The tide was, indeed, turning against UK influence in Cairo. Britain's ongoing military control of the Suez Canal after World War II was a festering wound on the Egyptian body politic. After the war, London had pledged to remove its troops within three years, only to renege. El-Nahhas's revocation in 1951 of the defense treaty that permitted British forces to remain in the Canal Zone set off a rebellion that would culminate in a coup against him. British forces crushed an initial armed uprising, but outrage at el-Nahhas's historic complicity in British imperialism was enough to force Farouk to replace him. Chaos ensued as four prime ministers cycled through in quick succession before a group calling themselves the "Free Officers" intervened with a mutiny that would reshape the political landscape of the Middle East.[17]

Just before dawn on January 23, 1952, an Egyptian army cabal staged a bloodless coup against King Farouk. The group's thirty-four-year-old leader,

Gamal Abdel Nasser, installed the well-known liberal Gen. Mohammad Naguib as prime minister and established a nine-member Revolutionary Command Council to govern the country. En route to the coup, Nasser's clique had easily abolished potential revolutionary rivals in the weak Muslim Brotherhood. When the panicked Farouk reached out to his British and American patrons for help to reverse the coup, he was met with cold shoulders. London and Washington initially welcomed the new regime, hoping it would be better able to address Egypt's considerable internal political and economic woes while staving off communist advances. Truman was heartened by the new government's expressed desire for friendly relations with the United States and, even more, by its immediate crackdown on communist activities that prompted Moscow to denounce it as a reactionary regime.[18] It would not take long, however, for Nasser's nationalistic and Pan-Arab commitments to muddy the waters for Washington. The Eisenhower administration that replaced Truman's in early 1953 would find itself at ever greater odds with Cairo.

By late 1954, Nasser emerged from behind the curtain to supplant Naguib and assume the mantle of Egyptian—and Pan-Arab—leadership. Nasser, the son of a postal clerk from Alexandria, came of age steeped in the nationalist and anticolonial fervor of interwar Egypt. He participated in anti-British demonstrations before joining the Egyptian army in 1937, at the age of nineteen. During his rapid ascent through the military ranks, he grew increasingly troubled by Egypt's impotence in the face of foreign powers. Nasser shared with a great many of his countrymen a sense of national humiliation in response to Britain's bald use of force to control Egyptian politics through the compulsory coup in 1942, after which he began meeting clandestinely with a group of other officers—later known as the Free Officers—to discuss army reform. That humiliation deepened by the end of the decade, as he served with the Egyptian army in Palestine, giving him a front-row seat to his superiors' incompetence, dishonesty, and lack of basic preparation and communication with other Arab armies. Following the catastrophic events in Palestine, the Free Officers concluded that the entire Egyptian government must be radically reformed or possibly overthrown. Nasser's participation in the 1948 war against Israel—where he fought alongside Christian as well as Muslim Palestinians—deeply informed the development of his political project as Arab, rather than Muslim.[19] Elected in 1950 as president of the Free Officers' executive committee, Nasser's leadership was crucial to planning for Farouk's ouster.

As Nasser took charge of Egypt's military dictatorship in 1954, he also took the public stage, beginning to articulate with captivating oratorical flair the Pan-Arab philosophy that would soon establish him as the most formidable figure in Arab politics and throw a significant curveball at the Middle Eastern Cold War. He articulated a vision of social justice, progress, development, and dignity for the Egyptian people, a project that could only be pursued by liberating Egypt from the chokehold of British domination that dated back to 1882.[20] In the words of Laurie Brand, "Ensuring sovereignty, striving for social justice, and, as regional politics evolved, leading a transnational Arab people or community (umma) all became central to Egypt's mission and definition as constructed and practiced between 1952 and 1970."[21] Nasser pursued swift domestic political transformations, replacing the existing liberal government with a strongly socialist and populist military-backed executive, implementing land reform, and establishing a system of state-owned factories.[22] In foreign policy, he set out to secure Egyptian autonomy.

When Eisenhower's newly appointed secretary of state, John Foster Dulles, traveled to Cairo in May 1953, Nasser was quick to inform him that British imperialism, rather than Soviet subversion, posed the greatest threat to regional stability.[23] In his incendiary 1954 treatise *Egypt's Liberation: The Philosophy of Revolution,* Nasser pledged to promote revolution across the Arab and Muslim worlds and in Africa. Core to Nasser's emerging Pan-Arab philosophy was the belief that Arab people were one, sharing a common destiny, and in need of a cohesive policy to combat the imbricated threats of Zionism and Western imperialism. To achieve this, alongside an ambitious program of economic and social justice comprising Arab socialism, Nasser was determined to pursue a policy of nonalignment in the Cold War. Reflecting the strong influence of India's Jawaharlal Nehru, Nasser espoused "positive neutrality," implying that Arabs, far from passive pawns subject to the superpowers' geostrategic whims, would actively shape their own destinies by strategically avoiding alignment with either Cold War bloc while seeking support from both.[24] His participation at the Bandung Conference in 1955, where he rubbed shoulders with China's Zhou Enlai and stood alongside Nehru and Yugoslavia's Joseph Broz Tito as one of the three leading exponents of neutralism, fueled distrust among American observers who saw neutralism as a gateway to alignment with the communist bloc.

Such fears, though rooted in an underestimation of Arab nationalists, were not entirely unfounded in light of Moscow's reorientation toward the

Middle East after Stalin's death. Whereas Stalin had all but ignored the region, dismissing its leaders as reactionary Anglo-American pawns, his successor, Nikita Khrushchev, deemed it ripe for socialist, anti-Western revolution.[25] In the summer of 1955, after Khrushchev's emissary Dmitri Shepilov returned from a reconnaissance mission to the Middle East, a Soviet official explained the Kremlin's policy shift as follows: "From now on we will support the Arab nationalists. The longer-term target is the destruction of the established relations of the Arabs with Europe and the United States, creation of the 'oil crisis'—this will generate problems for Europe and will make it more dependent on us."[26]

Dwight D. Eisenhower's administration, which replaced Truman in January 1953, anticipated such challenges. The new president and his secretary of state, John Foster Dulles, remained bent on creating an alliance system in the Middle East that could serve as a bulwark against Soviet encroachment. The White House encouraged Britain to collaborate with the Northern Tier states of Turkey, Iraq, and Pakistan in forming what would be known as the Baghdad Pact, signed into existence in February 1955. But Nasser immediately railed against the pact, refusing to join while marshaling a robust propaganda campaign to discredit it across the Arab world. "The Egyptian government," writes Jonathan Alterman, "took Iraq's inclusion in this 'Baghdad pact' as proof of a Western design to split the Arab world and assert its control over weaker individual states."[27] Britain's decision to join that April, against American advisement, cemented Nasser's hostility toward the alliance. To undercut the appeal of the Baghdad Pact, Nasser would form a rival alliance with Syria and Saudi Arabia. American officials, surprised by Nasser's vitriolic reaction to the Baghdad Pact, refrained from joining and urged a moratorium on additional Arab membership, both moves that rankled their allies in London.[28]

Growing concern over Soviet assertiveness in the Middle East, a threat greatly exacerbated by the simmering Arab-Israeli conflict, motivated Eisenhower and Dulles to redouble Anglo-American efforts to broker an Arab-Israeli settlement through Project Alpha, a peace initiative that had been stalled since late 1954. The goal was to tackle nettlesome territorial disputes and security concerns, and to address the problem of Palestinian refugees, with the inducement of American aid dollars. But Israel refused to budge on territory, and Nasser declined to participate, learning of the terms just days before Israel launched a devastating attack against an Egyptian outpost in the Gaza Strip.[29] In February 1955, in retaliation for an Egyptian raid that had killed an Israeli cyclist, Israel struck Egyptian military installations in Gaza, killing thirty-seven and wounding many more. A UN Security Council resolution censuring Israel did little to placate Egypt. Nasser became more active in training Palestinian fighters, fedayeen, to launch raids into Israel, and he sought resources to help build up his army. Consistent with the logic of positive neutrality, Nasser approached the United States with a request for heavy arms, threatening to turn to the Soviet Union if refused. Rather than reject his appeal out of hand, the Eisenhower administration offered to sell him arms at full price, payable in hard currency.

Burned by this proposal, more humiliating than an outright denial, Nasser contacted the Kremlin sometime that spring about acquiring Soviet arms. Moscow, intent on countering what it saw as a threatening US-Israeli partnership and eager to encourage Egypt's commitment to neutralism as a means of blocking Western influence in the Middle East, proved receptive to Cairo's overtures.[30] In September 1955 Khrushchev and Nasser made a deal valued publicly at $86 million. The Soviet Union would direct military hardware to Egypt via Czechoslovakia in exchange for 100,000 tons of cotton. The deal sent shock waves through Washington where, as Douglass Little writes, it seemed clear that "the Kremlin intended to leapfrog over the Northern Tier into the heart of the Middle East, an action that would call into question the concept of perimeter defense on which the Baghdad Pact and America's approach to regional security in the Middle East was predicated."[31] And, according to Philip Zelikow, "The Soviet arms deal seemed, at a stroke, to destroy the West's Tripartite Declaration system of trying to regulate the Middle Eastern arms race."[32] Nasser relished turning the tables on the Americans. Upon learning of the arms deal, Washington immediately dispatched Deputy Secretary of State for Middle Eastern Affairs George V. Allen to Cairo. Nasser made him wait hours for a hearing. "The Allen trip," writes Nasser biographer Robert St. John, "convinced Nasser, his advisers, and the Arab public that the West was panicky. This caused delight in a large part of the Middle East."[33]

In December 1955, to counter this audacious Soviet move and preserve some Western influence in Cairo, the United States offered to join with Britain and the World Bank to offer economic and technical assistance for construction of the Aswan High Dam. Plans for the $1.3 billion project that would harness the Nile River for both irrigation and electricity generation emerged shortly after the 1952 coup, as the new regime was "thinking big" in its approach to domestic development. Egyptian foreign minister Mahmoud Fawzi first pitched the idea to Dulles during the secretary's 1953 trip to Cairo in terms that demonstrated a nuanced grasp of the Cold War logic underpinning US development assistance. He explained that Egypt's internal weakness made it vulnerable to domestic subversion and foreign aggression, and that only by addressing its social and economic problems could it rally against the political threat of communism. Dulles was unmoved, replying simply that "the new Administration's policies will be based on the Communist threat," which he perceived to be mainly external.[34] Eisenhower and Dulles made few commitments but dangled the prospect of US aid—military and economic— in an attempt to press Egypt to reach a settlement with Britain over the Suez Canal Zone and to lure Cairo into a mutual defense agreement with the United States. By the time Nasser made a deal for Soviet arms, both sides had given up on finding a mutually agreeable military arrangement. But US support for the Aswan Dam project, deemed feasible and necessary by a recent World Bank study, seemed to offer Egypt an opportunity to address dire economic and social crises and avoid an overreliance on the Soviet bloc. It could also give Washington a chance to preserve the possibility of a working relationship with Cairo, without which its entire schema for containing communism in the Middle East would be scrapped.

Nasser was infuriated to learn in early 1956 that Washington was making the release of its $200 million aid package contingent on an Egyptian peace settlement with Israel. Ongoing conflict between Israel and Egypt, and the influence of Zionist political forces in the United States, led Nasser to conclude that Western aid for the dam would not be forthcoming. In March 1956, frustrated by Nasser's intransigence on the Israel question, by his recognition of the PRC and his refusal to break with the Soviets, and by his incendiary support for a revolt against the pro-Western king of Jordan, Britain and the United States concocted the Omega Initiative, designed to isolate Nasser politically.[35] He was far from shocked, then, when Dulles informed his government on July 19 that the United States was withdrawing its funding on the grounds that the Egyptian economy could not support the project. But he was enraged by the intentionally humiliating way Washington conveyed the message, having distributed the terms of the rejection to journalists before the official meeting, depriving Egypt of the opportunity to prepare a response. The American move, it seems, was designed intentionally to undermine Nasser's domestic political position. Six days later, probably feeling under the gun to assert his government's strength, he delivered an impassioned speech on the fourth anniversary of the Free Officers' revolution announcing his impromptu decision to nationalize the Suez Canal.

The move struck a tremendous popular chord. "Rejecting financing of the Aswan High Dam," writes Alterman, "was intended as a humiliation. Abdel Nasser used it as an opportunity to assert his independence."[36] It was a transformative moment, not only for Egyptians, but for viewers across the Arab world. In their eyes, Nasser was doing so much more than simply nationalizing a vital economic asset. As Tarek Osman writes, "He was asserting national pride; standing up against the imperialist powers that had dominated the region for decades; emotionally freeing millions of oppressed Arabs and Egyptians; through his actions—and thus in his person—effecting the rebirth of Egyptian (and Arab) dignity."[37]

Nasser's decision to nationalize the Suez Canal from the primarily French-and-British-owned Universal Suez Canal Company, through which three-quarters of the western European oil supply flowed, set off one of the most fraught confrontations of the Cold War. The United States, Britain, and France immediately denounced the move, calling for an international conference to address the crisis. Egypt refused to dispatch a formal delegation to the Suez Canal Conference, held in London August 16–23, but Nasser did send his cabinet chief, Ali Sabri, as an observer. The next month, a delegation led by Australian prime minister Robert Menzies traveled to Cairo to negotiate with Nasser over the contents of the London conference, only to find him unyielding in his commitment to nationalizing the canal and placing it under Egyptian management. To Menzies's entreaties for a regime of international control, Nasser replied: "If I accept your position, problems will arise with the Egyptian people, and if I do not accept it, there will be problems from your side. Thus, it appears to me that we will have problems in any event, and if the case, we will simply face up to our own problems."[38] As the UN Security Council debated the issue for the first half of October, Nasser began to sense victory. He believed that, with every passing day, the likelihood of war diminished, especially given assurances that both the United States and the Soviet Union opposed a military solution to the conflict.[39]

As it turned out, it was not victory Nasser sensed, but the calm before the storm. In late October, rumors began to circulate about an impending British and French attack, perhaps involving Israel. In fact, Israel had already secured approval from London and Paris for a joint operation. Despite

Eisenhower's warning to Israeli prime minister David Ben-Gurion that the use of force at this time would "endanger the peace and growing friendship between our two countries," Israel launched the Suez War on October 29, under the cover of night.[40] Taken by surprise and outgunned, having not yet consolidated arms from the recent Soviet deal into its arsenal, the Egyptian army was almost immediately overrun. With Egyptian ground forces overwhelmed and the air force grounded, Britain and France stepped in to issue a prearranged ultimatum demanding that Israeli and Egyptian troops retreat to ten miles from their respective sides of the Suez Canal. This gave Israel, currently forty miles to the east of the canal, license to advance another thirty. As expected, Nasser rejected the ultimatum. He appealed to the Soviet Union for support, but the Kremlin, wary of provoking a wider confrontation and bogged down with an existential crisis in Hungary where a student-led movement sought to overthrow the pro-Soviet regime, demurred. Nasser then called the US ambassador to request military assistance, denying that he had first approached the Soviets. On the evening of October 31, as Egypt desperately sought help staving off the Israeli advance, British warplanes launched an attack on Cairo while French jets targeted Egyptian troops in Suez. Facing the reality of tripartite aggression, Nasser addressed the Egyptian people during a prayer ceremony on November 2, pledging that he would never surrender and announcing preparations to go underground and fight a guerrilla war against occupying forces.

Meanwhile, international opposition to British and French operations, especially from the United States, stymied the effort to subdue Nasser's Egypt. London and Paris had gravely underestimated Washington's opposition to the use of military force to solve the Suez Crisis and thereby failed to anticipate the rapidity with which it would move to halt their aggression. The United States was concerned about potentially devastating effects of Anglo-French actions on the western European oil supply, borne out by ARAMCO's Saudi-inspired decision during the crisis to halt all shipments to Britain and France. Even more important for Eisenhower, who was shocked and outraged by his allies' intemperance, was the way this crisis fit into the larger Cold War competition with the Soviet Union. There was the very real possibility that the Soviet Union might intervene directly, pulling the United States into a major conflagration, especially should the conflict drag out past the resolution of the Soviets' own crisis in Hungary. Moreover, the Kremlin was poised to take advantage of widespread anger over the invasion—in the

Arab world and beyond—delivering it unnecessary political dividends and depriving the West of opportunities to capitalize on the propaganda coup that otherwise would have resulted from the violent crackdowns taking place simultaneously on the streets of Budapest.

The Eisenhower administration, concerned that Anglo-French actions imperiled US global standing, took to the UN to oppose the tripartite attack, even taking the rare Cold War–era step of voting alongside the Soviet Union. When Britain and France deployed their veto powers to block action in the Security Council, the United States introduced to the General Assembly a bill demanding the immediate cessation of hostilities and calling for an Israeli troop withdrawal. The resolution passed overwhelmingly, alongside a Canadian measure providing for a United Nations Emergency Force (UNEF) to oversee the canal zone following a cease-fire.[41] Khrushchev, meanwhile, made threats about sending Soviet forces—and perhaps even using nuclear weapons—to solve the conflict. Although this may have been bluster, it prompted Eisenhower to step up financial pressure on Britain to force a quick resolution. On November 6, faced with nearly unanimous international opprobrium, coupled with Washington's refusal to send emergency oil ship-ments while blocking London's request to borrow aid from the IMF, Britain agreed to an unconditional cease-fire. France and Israel were left with no choice but to follow suit. Britain and France, having relinquished whatever remained of their dominance in the Middle East, withdrew their forces from the Sinai by December 1956. Israeli troops dragged out the process, finally completing their exit in March 1957.

The Suez Crisis and its resolution transformed the Middle East politically and diplomatically. It delivered the swan song of British dominance, leaving the NATO set to assume that Washington would inherit the role of protecting Western interests and preventing Soviet advances in the region. With Khrush-chev riding high on the wave of prestige generated by his role in opposing tri-partite aggression against Nasser—just as the British retreat generated a vacuum of foreign influence in the Arab world—the Eisenhower administra-tion's anxieties about the Soviet threat mushroomed. Eisenhower and Dulles also fretted about the tremendous boost to Nasser's power and influence in the Arab world generated by his unlikely victory in the Suez Crisis. Although American officials claimed most of the credit for that triumph, they were wary of Nasser's ascendance redounding to the Soviet advantage. Even independent of Soviet inroads, the popular appeal of Nasser's revolutionary

Egyptian president Gamal Abdel Nasser waves to cheering countrymen as he is driven through a street in Cairo, July 28, 1956, to his office after a train trip from Alexandria. Egyptians, obviously pleased with Nasser's decision to nationalize the Suez Canal, marched in huge crowds, shouting anti-Western, pro-Russian slogans, when their president arrived in the capital. (AP Photo)

pan-Arabism threatened to undermine the conservative Arab regimes on which Washington so heavily relied to protect and advance Western interests in the Middle East.

In the immediate wake of the cease-fire, Eisenhower and Dulles hoped to press the advantage they believed the United States had earned in the Middle East, having proved itself a fair and just power by stepping up to oppose its own allies' aggression against Egypt. But relations with Nasser soured almost immediately. Nasser "saw the revolutionary fervor that he had unleashed as an unstoppable political tsunami."[42] He launched vitriolic attacks on "regressive regimes" in the region—Saudi Arabia, Jordan, and Iraq—condemning their overreliance on the West. According to Salim Yaqub, American officials believed that US action "had almost single-handedly rescued the Egyptian leader from oblivion, and now Nasser was repaying the United States by attacking its friends, courting its enemies, and obstructing a reasonable settlement of the crisis."[43] This rift provided the backdrop for a major new US diplomatic initiative in the Middle East aimed both at challenging Soviet advances and deepening and exploiting existing divisions in the Arab world, with an eye toward breaking Nasser's undisputed leadership of revolutionary Arab nationalism. On January 1, 1957, Eisenhower previewed the plan to a bipartisan group of twenty-nine congressional leaders. In that meeting, he and Dulles specifically invoked the Truman Doctrine, in which his predecessor a decade prior had implored Congress to authorize funds for the United States to replace British power in Greece and Turkey for a goal no less vaunted than protecting free peoples from the forces of tyranny. "To keep Russia out [of the Middle East] has been British policy for the last hundred years, and they have succeeded pretty well up to the present time," explained Dulles. "Now they are finished, and it is a good deal like the situation was in Greece and Turkey." Should the United States shirk its responsibilities, "the area will probably fall under Soviet control, and that will be a very great disaster."[44]

On January 5, 1957, Eisenhower went public with what would become known as the Eisenhower Doctrine in a "Special Message to the Congress on the Situation in the Middle East." He asked Congress to authorize US military action and economic aid to protect the territorial integrity and political independence of countries in the Middle East that came under threat of "overt armed aggression from any nation controlled by international communism."[45] Despite significant resistance from Democrats, Congress approved the doctrine in early March by votes of 72 to 19 in the Senate and 350 to 60 in the House. Eisenhower and Dulles's first order of business was to strengthen conservative Arab regimes like Iraq, Saudi Arabia, Lebanon, and Libya. By providing them with economic and military aid, along with explicit security guarantees, the administration hoped to lure them into open alliance with the United States, thereby isolating Nasser and his allies in the region.

Western governments were generally receptive to the Eisenhower Doctrine, although Britain privately complained that it was too little, too late. The Soviet Union predictably railed against it, coming out a week later with its own policy that called for international powers to pledge noninterference in the internal affairs of Middle Eastern states, to withdraw troops from the region, to dismantle military bases, and to supply unencumbered economic aid to foster development in the region. Nasser was, at first, reluctant to issue an outright denunciation of the Eisenhower Doctrine. He feared that doing so would rule out completely the prospect of future economic aid from the United States, rendering him solely dependent on the Soviet Union, an outcome anathema to the fundaments of positive neutrality. Washington, likewise, continued to pursue an ambivalent relationship with Nasser, maintaining economic pressure while avoiding a complete diplomatic rupture, in the hope that he would moderate his anti-Western stance.[46] It soon became clear, though, that the emerging battle lines in the Middle East pitted US-backed conservative Arab governments against Nasserite revolutionary movements and regimes. The Soviet-American rivalry mapped onto those conflicts poorly, making the Eisenhower Doctrine an awkward fit for American policy in the region.

Throughout 1957, political crises in the Arab world exacerbated the divide between pro-Western conservative and Nasserite liberal regimes, to the distinct advantage of the latter, while also laying bare divisions within the Arab Left and ultimately dooming the Eisenhower Doctrine. The most pivotal of these was in Syria, where the government announced in mid-August that it had just thwarted a US-backed coup attempt. This accusation, which is supported by available evidence, precipitated a complete break in US-Syrian diplomatic relations and accelerated the radicalization of Syrian politics that had begun during the Suez Crisis, when the attack on Egypt coincided with revelations of a CIA plot to overthrow the Syrian government. In addition to these covert attempts at Syrian regime change, Washington was overtly campaigning for an anti-Syrian coalition in the region. Eisenhower and Dulles, writes Yaqub, "believed that Syria would soon become a base for Soviet sponsored subversion of neighboring Arab countries, especially Jordan and Lebanon."[47] Nasser, for his part, had little sympathy for Syrian communists, but his overriding goal was to prevent the consolidation of a US-backed conservative Arab bloc. In mid-October, he dispatched 1,500 Egyptian troops to Syria aimed at preventing hostile intervention by conservative forces. This move was enough to prevent a US-sponsored attack, but the removal of that threat unraveled the temporary unity generated by the Syrian crisis among the Arab Left. By the end of the year, both Nasser and Syrian Ba'thists were deeply concerned about the growing Soviet influence in Syria. For Nasser, such reliance on the Soviet Union not only threatened positive neutrality, it undermined his own political influence among the Arab Left.[48]

On February 1, 1958, Egypt and Syria announced their political merger into the United Arab Republic (UAR), a move that was significant but short-lived, as the UAR would fall apart in 1961. Nasser was convinced that the formation of the UAR would cement his position as the leader of the Arab world while continuing to distance Egypt from both Moscow and Washington.[49] He predicated Egypt's attachment to the UAR on Syrian officials dissolving all political parties and requiring that all military officials withdraw from politics or resign their commissions. The result was a crippling blow to Syrian communists, compounded by the Soviet Union's pragmatic decision to recognize the UAR, preserving good relations with Syria and Egypt at the expense of defending local communists. US State Department officials celebrated the initiative's dampening effects on Arab communism but feared it would fuel Nasser's domination of the Arab world, further weakening conservative US allies in the region. On February 25, in the hope of drawing Egypt away from Moscow's orbit, the State Department formally recognized the UAR. The United States proceeded to resume private sales of military supplies, aircraft, and wheat to the UAR, restarted cultural exchanges, assisted with economic development programs, and offered military training for UAR troops. This US-Egyptian diplomatic thaw was aided by a coincidental settlement between the Suez Canal Company and the Egyptian government, which allowed Washington to release Egyptian assets held in US banks since 1956.[50]

In the spring and summer of 1958, a series of events redrew the lines of Middle Eastern politics and signed the death warrant of the Eisenhower Doctrine, advancing Washington's accommodationist trend toward Nasser. On July 14, as Eisenhower dithered over whether to intervene on behalf of Lebanon's embattled conservative president, Camille Chamoun, a new crisis erupted in Iraq. An independent Nasserite movement known as the Free Officers, led by Abd al-Karim Qasim, overthrew the conservative Hashemite monarchy, assassinating King Faisal. An enraptured mob then captured and killed Prime Minister Nuri al-Said on the streets of Baghdad. The coup was greeted with a wave of popular enthusiasm across the Arab world, sending shivers down the spines of the conservative Arab leaders aligned most closely with Washington. Eisenhower considered but rejected the option of attempting to reverse the coup in Iraq but decided it was imperative for the United States to respond to Chamoun's appeals for intervention in Lebanon, lest Washington lose international credibility by failing to support a stalwart ally. Eisenhower dispatched thousands of US Marines to Lebanon, provoking harsh criticism but no retaliation from the UAR and the Soviet Union. Eventually, with help from the UAR, the Soviet Union, and Great Britain, Washington managed to prevent the crises in Lebanon and Iraq from metastasizing throughout the region.

Yet the summer of 1958 proved a moment of reckoning for US Middle East policy. Even as US Marines landed in Lebanon, Eisenhower lamented to Vice President Richard Nixon, "The trouble is that we have a campaign of hatred against us, not by the governments but by the people." By early October, a White House task force concluded that the Eisenhower Doctrine "must now be considered out of date."[51] US officials were forced to acknowledged that their efforts to polarize the Arab world along ideological lines was working decidedly against Washington's interests.[52] The Eisenhower administration therefore abandoned its policy of building up conservative Arab rivals in an effort to isolate Nasser, turning instead to a more accommodationist approach to the Pan-Arab leader. Although never openly renouncing the Eisenhower Doctrine, the administration effectively replaced it in November 1958 with NSC 5820/1. The new policy distinguished between vital interests in the region—preventing communist encroachment and preserving Western access to oil—and secondary interests, including the preservation of Western transit rights and military bases, resolution of the Arab-Israeli conflict, and economic and social development aimed at promoting political stability and friendly relations with the West.[53] Officials in Washington were encouraged by Nasser's own moves to crack down on communists in the UAR. Tensions between the UAR and the Soviet Union, however, did not disrupt the flow of military aid from Moscow to Cairo, and Washington's reciprocal increase in arms sales to Israel ensured ongoing suspicion between Nasser and Eisenhower.

President John F. Kennedy, during his brief time in office, largely continued the policy of Nasserite accommodation that Eisenhower initiated. Friendship between Egypt and the United States was hampered, however, by ongoing US support for Israel, revelations of an Israeli nuclear reactor, tensions over a simmering conflict in Yemen, and what Nasser considered to be baldly neocolonialist American actions in the Congo. Lyndon Johnson's ascension to the presidency in November 1963 dealt a crippling blow to already fragile US-Egyptian relations. LBJ, a longtime supporter of Israel and harsh critic of Nasser, lambasted his Egyptian counterpart for stirring up trouble in the Congo, supporting the Vietcong in Vietnam, criticizing US-backed regimes in Iran and Saudi Arabia, and goading the newly formed PLO to attack Israel. When a mob burned down a US Information Agency library in Cairo, for which Nasser refused to apologize, LBJ seized the opportunity to cut off aid to Egypt.[54]

Far from humbled, Nasser redoubled his support for many of the Third World revolutionary forces that Washington was determined to quash. He invited Cuba's Che Guevara to Egypt to discuss plans to overthrow the US-backed regime in the Congo, allowed the Vietcong to open a diplomatic office in Cairo, and unveiled a "Blueprint for the Liberation of Palestine" involving revolutionary Arab action against Israel. In 1964, as ties between Cairo and Washington frayed, the Soviet Union implemented a strategy designed to penetrate more fully into the Arab world. The Kremlin had come under new leadership that October, as Leonid Brezhnev replaced Khrushchev. Brezhnev, with support from the Soviet military, breathed new life into Khrushchev's courtship of Egypt, which had been set back in the late 1950s as a result of Nasser's opposition to communists in Syria and Iraq, coupled with a steady stream of mutually antagonistic polemics between Moscow and Cairo. The Soviet-Egyptian relationship turned a corner in 1961 with the collapse of the UAR, which allowed for an ideological thaw. Nasser faced grave economic challenges at home and a reduced threat of communist penetration into the region as Damascus and Baghdad swung back to anti-communist leadership. Both developments facilitated a Soviet-Egyptian rapprochement, especially in the context of LBJ's enmity. Soviet military assistance to Cairo increased steadily between 1964 and 1967, reaching its peak surrounding the Six-Day War in June 1967.[55]

In 1966, troubled by Israel's military buildup, and especially its furtive nuclear weapons program, a group of Arabs including Egypt, Syria, Jordan, and the PLO began to prepare for a confrontation. Palestinian commandos staged raids into Israel from the West Bank while Syrians pleaded with the Kremlin to fast-track shipments of weapons and aircraft. On April 7, 1967, Israel finally responded to a steady spate of provocations, shooting down six Soviet-supplied Syrian MiGs in a dogfight near the Golan Heights. As tensions built, Nasser joined the fray, warning Israel against invading Damascus and, fatefully, expelling UN troops from the Sinai. He replaced the UN Emergency Force, which had policed the Israeli-Egyptian border since the resolution of the Suez Crisis in 1957, with his own troops and closed off the Straits of Tiran to Israeli shipping. Washington publicly urged Tel Aviv to be patient while the United States mustered a response. But in the wake of the Tonkin Gulf incident, Congress was especially wary of direct intervention in the Middle East. Through backchannel communications, LBJ's administration encouraged swift Israeli retaliation.

As the sun rose on June 5, Israeli jets launched a devastating surprise attack on the grounded Egyptian air force before moving unopposed to occupy the Gaza Strip and the Sinai. Jordan and Syria then entered the war in Egypt's defense, only to be trounced in a similar fashion. Before the cease-fire went into effect on June 10, Israel wrested control of the West Bank from Jordan and the Golan Heights from Syria. The Six-Day War was a devastating defeat for Israel's Arab foes. Egypt, Syria, and Jordan lost huge swaths of territory, and the Palestinians of the West Bank and Gaza found themselves living under enemy occupation or forced into refugee status.[56] The war proved as transformative for the region's geopolitical landscape as it was for its borders.

In the immediate term, the Six-Day War intensified the Cold War in the Middle East. In its aftermath, the United States was pitted more squarely against Egypt than it had ever been. The clash shattered the uneasy state of coexistence that had defined the relationship between Cairo and Washington between 1952 and 1967. A humiliated Nasser salved his pride by euphemistically referring to the war as "the setback," but he was all too aware of Egypt's dire postwar state. Egypt's trouncing—largely a result of his inept leadership—dealt a serious blow to his ego, his reputation, and the appeal of Arab nationalism.[57] Deprived of the leverage that once enabled him to play the superpowers off one another, he severed diplomatic ties with the United States in the hope of courting support from the Soviet Union that he so desperately needed to rebuild Egypt's military, economy, and infrastructure.[58] Moscow was frustrated with Nasser, whose crushing defeat forced the Soviet Union to intervene more directly into the Middle East, most notably to prevent the resurgence of Saudi Royalist forces in Yemen. While this heightened Soviet-American tensions, Kremlin officials' concern over losing influence in the Middle East—especially as the Americans increased their support for Israel—led them to grit their teeth and bolster Cairo's defenses.

Moscow, embarrassed by the rapid collapse of the Soviet-supplied Egyptian army, immediately severed diplomatic ties with Israel and initiated an operation to resupply Egyptian military equipment. Nasser's obsession with reversing the losses suffered in 1967 led him to undertake a series of low-level provocations against Israel that would precipitate what is known as the War of Attrition, thus forcing the Kremlin's hand. In 1970, Israel retaliated against stepped-up Egyptian artillery attacks and commando raids along the Suez Canal with an onslaught of aerial attacks deep into Egyptian territory, reaching as far as Cairo. Moscow, increasingly anxious about the survival of Nasser's government, responded with the unprecedented decision to provide Egypt with a robust air defense system, including a sizeable dispatch of the first overt Soviet military forces to the Middle East. The initial deployment consisted of eight thousand Soviet technicians and pilots, a number that would double by the end of the year.[59] Moscow would also supply Egypt with modern anti-aircraft guns, surface-to-air missiles, and MiG fighter jets.[60]

As the Arab-Israeli conflict became more deeply entangled with the Cold War—an outcome Washington had long sought to avoid—the United States also found itself increasingly on the hook for supplying the Israeli military. President Richard Nixon, who replaced LBJ in January 1969, was determined to continue supporting Israel but also sought to avoid inflaming Arab opinion. As the War of Attrition escalated over the summer of 1970, pitting Soviet and Israeli fighter pilots against each other in dogfights over the Suez Canal, Nixon's administration stepped up efforts to achieve a diplomatic solution.

The Nixon administration was divided between Secretary of State William Rogers, who was eager to broker an Arab-Israeli peace deal involving European powers and the Soviet Union, and National Security Advisor Henry Kissinger, who harbored a deep distrust of the Soviets and a personal sympathy for Israel. Kissinger, who privately discouraged Israel from entertaining State Department proposals, managed to scuttle Rogers's initial plan. But as fighting intensified and casualties mounted over June and July 1970, a second peace deal known as Rogers II found better reception. The new proposal called for a cease-fire and peace negotiations led by UN mediator Gunnar Jarring. It also affirmed UN Resolution 242, passed in November 1967, which called for Israel's withdrawal from Arab land in exchange for Arab states' recognition of Israel's right to a peaceful and secure existence. Fatefully, it provided no indication of which should occur first. On July 23, Nasser announced Egypt's acceptance of Rogers II, with Jordan quick to follow. Israel put up fierce resistance to the plan but finally assented on July 31. A cease-fire went into effect on August 7.[61] But Nasser's acceptance of Rogers II sparked outrage across the Arab world, and evidence of Egyptian violations surfaced almost before the ink was dry. This was the state of play on September 28, 1970, when Nasser died of a heart attack on the way home from an Arab League summit at age fifty-two.

A national plebiscite the next month confirmed Anwar Sadat as Nasser's successor. Although most Egyptians viewed his tenure as transitional, he began to establish his authority in mid-1971 with a reform project known as the Corrective Revolution. Aimed at establishing his own legitimacy while reversing what he viewed as the excesses of Nasserite politics, he initiated a suite of economic reforms and purged the government of pro-Soviet and left-leaning elements. He sacked and imprisoned Vice President Ali Sabri, who had close ties to Soviet officials, and Sharawy Gomaa, who led the secret police. These moves portended a major diplomatic reorientation away from the Soviet Union and toward an alliance with the United States and eventual rapprochement with Israel. In a February 4 speech, Sadat publicly signaled his willingness to renew the Egyptian-Israeli cease-fire, and to reopen the Suez Canal, which had been closed since 1967, in exchange for a partial Israeli withdrawal from the Sinai. Privately, he made it clear to Nixon and Kissinger that he wanted the United States to take the lead on brokering a deal. Rogers, returning from a visit to the Middle East in May 1971, recounted Sadat's pledge that, if a settlement could be reached, "I promise, I give you my personal assurance, that all the Russian ground troops will be out of my country within six months."[62] Israel, however, rejected Sadat's overture, and Kissinger demurred.

In 1971, the same month as Sadat's pledge to kick Soviet troops out of Egypt, Cairo and Moscow concluded a treaty of friendship and cooperation; far from signaling a rapprochement, however, the treaty proved to be a red herring. The Soviets, with growing concern over the political trajectory of Nasser's successor, proposed the treaty as a means of harnessing Egypt to the Soviet bloc. Sadat saw it more narrowly as a vehicle for extracting from Moscow the offensive weapons he sought in preparation for an attack on Israel to reclaim the Sinai. But the Kremlin, unwilling to risk the fragile process of Soviet-American détente that was simultaneously underway, refused the Egyptian request. In July 1972, Sadat responded by expelling nearly twenty thousand Soviet military advisors from Egyptian soil, justifying the move in terms of Egyptian sovereignty. "I don't want a Soviet soldier to fight my battle for me," he stated. "Give me weapons and leave me to act, it's not your business."[63]

The Soviets reacted somewhat desperately, agreeing to supply Egypt with the weapons that it had previously withheld.[64] The United States, for its part, declined to seize the opening Sadat had created. Kissinger, who led Nixon's Middle East policy, dismissed Sadat as a lightweight and devoted little attention to reestablishing ties with Egypt.[65] His vision of regional security instead hinged on Israel, which, in keeping with the Nixon Doctrine, he expected would serve American objectives by containing both Soviet communism and Arab nationalism. Nixon, meanwhile, was preoccupied with his reelection campaign and loath to undertake any serious diplomatic moves in the Middle East. Nixon and Kissinger refused even to meet with Sadat's national security advisor until February 1973. "By then," writes Yaqub, "Egypt's determination to break the cease-fire was nearly unstoppable."[66] Egypt's economic crisis, fueled by lost revenues from the Sinai oil fields and Suez Canal transit resulting from its failure to secure an Israeli withdrawal, had become untenable.[67]

Over the summer and fall of 1973, Nixon came under increasing international pressure to stave off armed conflict in the Middle East. Brezhnev, during a June summit meeting in the United States, urged Nixon to do something about the volatile Arab-Israeli impasse. Nixon, by then consumed with the growing Watergate scandal, claimed he could not commit to the Soviet proposal to develop a set of joint principles for resolving the dispute. Hope was all but dead that the superpowers could prevent a clash. On October 6, 1973, during the Yom Kippur holiday, Egypt and Syria launched a surprise joint offensive against Israeli forces in the occupied territories of the Sinai and Golan Heights. The Arab armies, benefiting from an airlift of Soviet supplies, made startling advances in the war's early days. Kissinger was by then single-handedly in charge of US policy in the Middle East as Nixon floundered through the Watergate fiasco. He aimed to respond in a way that would simultaneously enable the Israelis to repel the attack and regain the offensive, forestall a crushing defeat of Egypt and Syria, and prevent the Soviet Union from gaining political influence in the Middle East. To those ends, he arranged for a massive airlift of arms to Israel while preparing to take the lead in negotiating an end to the fighting. The enhanced arsenal enabled Israel to gain the upper hand but also sparked outrage in the Arab world, prompting some oil-producing states to announce an embargo of oil to Western countries, coupled with a price hike from the Organization of the Petroleum-Exporting Countries (OPEC). On October 20, as Kissinger was en route to Moscow to broker a peace, Sadat signaled his willingness to accept a narrow cease-fire, which the UN passed two days later as Resolution 338. Both Israel and Egypt agreed to the terms immediately on October 22, followed the next day by Syria.

It was only after the warring parties' formal acceptance of the cease-fire that the crisis entered its most dangerous phase. Despite having agreed to the terms, Israel remained determined to destroy or capture Egypt's invading army. Sadat, in hopes of inspiring superpower cooperation to Egypt's benefit, pleaded with both the United States and the Soviet Union to send troops to enforce the cease-fire. Although Brezhnev was game for a joint operation, Nixon and Kissinger not only rejected the idea of cooperation but threatened that a unilateral Soviet intervention would "produce incalculable consequences which would be in the interest of neither of our countries."[68] To lend gravity to the threat, the United States placed its troops and nuclear forces worldwide on high alert, generating heightened signal traffic for Moscow's consumption. The crisis receded quickly, as the Soviet Union ignored Washington's gratuitous flexing of muscles and Sadat withdrew his request, calling instead for an international peacekeeping force excluding the superpowers. Both the White House and the Kremlin embraced the new proposal, which would become UN Security Council Resolution 340. It reaffirmed the cease-fire, required combatants to revert to the October 22 cease-fire lines, and authorized the deployment of a UN peacekeeping force. On October 28, Egyptian and Israeli military officers sat down in the Sinai for the first direct talks between the two countries in a quarter century.[69]

The 1973 war, though a military defeat for the Arabs, was nowhere near the humiliation suffered in 1967. Indeed, Sadat never set out to achieve victory on the battlefield; instead, he aimed to marshal a credible military performance that would force the United States to take seriously Egyptian diplomatic overtures. This required some deception, as Syria's Assad never would have agreed to the joint operation had he realized the limited scope of Sadat's military objectives. But the gambit proved remarkably successful. Egypt and Syria, though ultimately defeated, put up a strong fight. Israel, which since 1967 had dismissed the Arabs as too weak to go to war, lost its aura of invincibility as a surge of pride coursed through the Arab world. The Arab states had demonstrated their ability to disrupt regional and world stability, jolting Western powers to take Arab actors seriously in renewed efforts to resolve the Arab-Israeli conflict. Moreover, international pressure was growing for a settlement involving a complete Israeli withdrawal to pre-1967 borders in exchange for Arab recognition. This time Soviet bloc and Third World voices were joined by some of America's own allies, many of which depended heavily on the uninterrupted flow of oil from the Middle East. More than ever, Arabs were starting to believe that peace on acceptable terms might be in reach.[70]

According to Jason Brownlee, the October 1973 crisis "brought two U.S. strategic imperatives into focus: preventing another Arab-Israeli war and maintaining reliable ties with Gulf oil exporters."[71] To those ends, Kissinger entered into an intensive process of "shuttle diplomacy," organized a five-power conference in Geneva including the United States, the Soviet Union, Israel, Jordan, and Egypt, and restored diplomatic relations with Egypt. Between late 1973 and late 1975, Kissinger made no fewer than eleven trips to the Middle East, working to end the Arab oil embargo, secure the disengagement of forces in the Golan and the Sinai, and reduce the likelihood of another major Arab-Israeli war. Yet, he aimed to do so in a way that sidelined the Palestinian issue and prevented Israel from being forced to retreat to pre-1967 borders, which he and his Israeli counterparts agreed were indefensible. He also feared that Israel might block US pressure to relinquish occupied territory, thereby embarrassing Washington. He proceeded, then, with an approach to Middle East diplomacy marked by characteristic Kissingerian deception, courting Arab leaders with an eye toward reaching a settlement that would neutralize the Arab threat while securing Israel's advantage. Kissinger's so-called step-by-step approach involved mediating separate negotiations between Israel and each of its principal Arab foes, a process that would create an illusion of progress to placate the Arabs and quell international outcries while enabling Kissinger to manipulate individual Arab states in a manner designed to preclude further Israeli withdrawals.

Key to this was Sadat. It was becoming increasingly clear that he wanted to detach from the Soviet sphere and align more closely with the United States. He was eager to end his country's dispute with Israel and devote desperately needed attention to rebuilding Egypt's military and infrastructure, for which access to US capital would be critical. He therefore hinted at a willingness to pursue a separate agreement with Israel that would return most or all of the Sinai to Egypt, even if it did not include any guarantees regarding the disposition of other Arab claims. "For Kissinger," writes Yaqub, "a tantalizing prospect was coming into view: an Egyptian-Israeli deal that not only eased international pressure for the 1967 borders, but dramatically reduced Soviet influence in the Middle East."[72] The Geneva Conference that opened on December 21, 1973, was essentially a ruse designed by Kissinger to divert Soviet attention from Sadat's defection while lending an aura of credibility to a bilateral Egyptian-Israeli agreement.[73] Israel, Egypt, and the United States largely skirted the official proceedings in Geneva, as Kissinger shuttled back and forth between Egypt and Israel. Sadat, perhaps too eager to make a deal, made unexpected concessions, withdrawing the bulk of Egypt's forces in exchange for a small slice of the Sinai. On January 15, 1974, Sadat and Israel's Golda Meir signed the disengagement agreement. This was followed by a similar deal between Syria and Israel for the Golan, brokered by Kissinger primarily to sideline Arab concerns about the bilateral Egyptian-Israeli deal and make way for future progress. Nixon, hoping to distract himself from Watergate while soaking up the glow of diplomatic success, traveled to the Middle East in August 1974 for what would be his diplomatic swan song. Kissinger had by then established himself as the master of US policy in the Middle East, a role he would continue to play under Nixon's inexperienced successor, Gerald Ford.

In the spring of 1975, as talks for a second Sinai agreement resumed, Sadat's position seemed to be softening even further. Sadat had not abandoned Nasser's embrace of Arab unity, but he shifted his rhetoric to emphasize Arab economic cooperation over political unity, with an eye toward shoring up Egypt's domestic stability.[74] His ability to compromise with Israel, however, was limited by his determination to avoid a complete rupture with his Arab allies, who abhorred the prospect of a bilateral Egyptian-Israeli deal. Kissinger warned Ford on March 18, "Sadat is conceding more than I ever thought possible, but if he goes beyond a certain point he will be destroyed."[75] Kissinger implored Israel's new prime minister Yitzhak Rabin to settle on the terms Sadat was offering, lest Egypt be pushed past the breaking point. Rabin put up stiff resistance but finally acquiesced in exchange for $1.5 billion in US military assistance and a pledge to post two hundred American civilian observers in the Sinai desert.[76] The Sinai II agreement signed by Egypt and Israel on September 4, 1975, called for additional troop withdrawals, a UN-monitored buffer zone, and the reopening of the Suez Canal to Israeli cargo ships. It was met with dismay throughout the Arab world, which rightly saw it as yet another obstacle to ever reclaiming lost territories. "What few historians have grasped," writes Yaqub, "is that Kissinger *deliberately* designed the [Middle East peace] process to enable Israel's indefinite occupation of Arab land, a function it served in later decades, whatever his successors' intentions."[77] Although Sinai II relegated a comprehensive settlement of the Arab-Israeli conflict to the back burner, it permitted Egypt to reclaim its eastern oil fields, which generated about $1 billion in revenue annually, and to collect about $500 million in tolls from the Suez Canal in 1976, both critical to addressing the nation's deepening economic woes.[78]

By the time Jimmy Carter assumed the US presidency in January 1977, Sadat's regime was embroiled in a domestic political crisis stemming from the fallout of his own failed economic reforms. As the Egyptian president bungled through what Brownlee has called "the greatest period of social unrest Egypt had seen in twenty-five years," he blamed riots on Soviet agents and communist holdovers from the Nasser period.[79] Growing more authoritarian by the day, he rolled back a spate of earlier reforms, criminalized strikes and demonstrations, and limited election eligibility to government sponsored parties. Carter's administration, which espoused a new human rights–based foreign policy, turned a blind eye to Sadat's domestic abuses, deeming it critical to step up support for his government—including an increased supply of arms—to ensure that Egypt would act to keep regional Soviet clients in check while continuing efforts to broker an Arab-Israeli peace.

One of Carter's first moves in office was to launch the most ambitious presidential initiative to date in pursuit of peace in the Middle East. Generally sympathetic to Arab claims and determined to tackle the Palestinian issue, he called for an international conference at Geneva that would, he hoped, include Palestinian Liberation Organization (PLO) representatives in negotiating a comprehensive settlement. But Carter faced what turned out to be insurmountable stumbling blocks en route to the Geneva conference, which never materialized. In May 1977, the right-wing Likud bloc won the Israeli elections, ushering in Menachem Begin as Rabin's successor and stiffening Tel Aviv's already significant resistance to Carter's scheme. That fall, an unexpected controversy arose over a joint Soviet-American statement of principles for the Geneva conference. The otherwise boilerplate document included a Soviet-supplied clause calling for a resolution to the Palestinian problem that respected "the legitimate rights of the Palestinian people."[80] Israelis and American Jews lambasted Carter's team for inviting the Soviets to play a major role in the Middle East after they had been effectively sidelined in the wake of the October 1973 War. Meanwhile, Sadat had his own concerns about the Geneva forum, especially as it threatened to undermine Egypt's negotiating autonomy by committing it to a unified Arab bloc that would grant Syria or the Palestinians veto power over its decisions. Begin, who sensed Sadat's reticence, reached out cloak-and-dagger style to engage the Egyptian leader in direct talks toward a bilateral agreement. In mid-November 1977, the world watched in shock as Begin invited Sadat to Jerusalem to address the Knesset, and Sadat immediately accepted. He explained that it was his duty "to exhaust all and every means in a bid to save my Egyptian Arab people and the entire Arab nation [from] the horrors of new, shocking and destructive wars."[81] Carter's administration was forced to accept that the Geneva conference, trumped by Begin and Sadat's bilateral talks, would have to be tabled indefinitely.

By early 1978, the Israeli-Egyptian talks stalled. Sadat's goal was to negotiate on the Sinai without Arab meddling, but he also hoped to secure a final agreement that would commit Israel to withdrawing eventually behind the 1967 lines, enabling him to save face among his Arab neighbors. Begin would have none of it. Carter, who sympathized with Arab claims, attempted to move the needle in Tel Aviv with no success. To break the deadlock, Carter issued an invitation to the Egyptian and Israeli leaders to join him at the presidential retreat at Camp David, which both were eager to accept. At the Camp David meeting, September 5–17, Begin and Sadat rarely met face-to-face, leaving the US president to mediate the talks. Once again, Begin proved as unyielding as Sadat was flexible. As Carter's administration noted, the Egyptian leader's autocratic tendencies made it relatively easy for him to make diplomatic concessions without fear of domestic political backlash.[82] Against his own instincts, the American president resigned himself to extracting whatever small concessions he could get from the Israelis, as long as Sadat was willing to go along.

The Camp David Accords, signed at a White House ceremony on September 17, 1978, consisted of two agreements: "A Framework for Peace in the Middle East" and "A Framework for the Conclusion of a Peace Treaty Between Egypt and Israel." The first outlined a three-year plan for transitioning the West Bank and Gaza from occupied territories to self-governing districts under Palestinian authority with Israeli security guarantees, but critically left out any reference to Israeli settlements. The second committed Israel and Egypt to sign a peace treaty within three months, guaranteeing the normalization of Egyptian-Israeli relations while Israel conducted a phased withdrawal from the Sinai. It also placed limits on troop deployments at the border, authorized UN peacekeeping forces on Egyptian soil, and secured Israeli shipping rights through the Suez Canal and the Straits of Tiran.[83] When Sadat and Begin were jointly awarded the Nobel Peace Prize for the effort, Carter penned in his diary, "Sadat deserved it, Begin did not."[84]

The January 1979 Iranian Revolution—which toppled Washington's key ally in the Persian Gulf—dealt a stinging blow to US security and prestige, lending urgency to Carter's quest to secure the Egyptian-Israeli treaty outlined at Camp David. Secretary of Defense Harold Brown opined that, of US allies in the Middle East, "Egypt came the closest" to being a possible replacement for Iran.[85] Unlike Iran, however, Egypt was devoid of oil wealth, making it dependent upon outside resources that Washington would only be able to deliver after a peace treaty was signed. Washington thus lured Sadat to the negotiating table with promises of the substantial military and economic aid that would flow into Egypt once a deal was complete. On March 26, Sadat and Begin met again at the White House to sign the Egyptian-Israeli peace treaty. Camp David—and the ensuing treaty—dealt a staggering blow to the Arabs. Not only had their most powerful regional ally officially removed itself from the fight to reclaim Israeli-occupied territories, the Carter administration had reneged on its promises to support Arab efforts to do so diplomatically. A number of Arab states responded by severing diplomatic relations with Cairo. The Arab League expelled Egypt, relocating its headquarters from Cairo to Tunis and initiating a boycott of any Egyptian companies that dealt with Israel. For Egypt, the treaty represented the culmination of two of Sadat's long-term projects: extricating the nation from the Arab-Israeli conflict and transferring its Cold War allegiance from the Soviet bloc to the United States. "Cairo became a full-fledged client of Washington," writes Yaqub, "its share of U.S. military and economic aid second only to Israel's."[86] Camp David—and the Egyptian defection it heralded—dealt a sharp blow to Moscow's strategic position in the Middle East. But a series of upheavals taking place outside the Arab world obscured this reality from American strategists.

The Iran Hostage Crisis that began in early November 1979, followed shortly thereafter by the Soviet invasion of Afghanistan, sowed panic in the Carter administration over the apparent vulnerability of American allies and interests in the Middle East. In his last State of the Union address on January 23, 1980, Carter blasted the Soviets for "endangering the free movement of Middle East oil." In a section of the speech that would become known as the Carter Doctrine, he pledged that "an attempt by any outside force to gain control of the Persian Gulf region will be regarded as an assault on the United States of America, and such an assault will be repelled by any means necessary, including military force."[87] Sadat proved eager to help the United States implement the new doctrine. He publicly backed the anti-Soviet mujahideen in Afghanistan and, with support from the CIA, surreptitiously provided them old Soviet-supplied Egyptian weapons stockpiles. Egypt also dispatched troops to Pakistan to join Saudi Arabian forces in a deployment to Afghanistan. Sadat invited the

Egyptian president Anwar Sadat and US president Jimmy Carter share a laugh during the speech of Israeli prime minister Menachem Begin after the signing of the peace treaty between Israel and Egypt at the White House in Washington, March 26, 1979. (AP Photo)

United States to use Egyptian airbases, which Carter utilized in April 1980 to launch an unsuccessful and, ultimately, humiliating attempt to rescue hostages from Iran. The outbreak of the Iran-Iraq War in 1980 only further cemented the US-Egyptian military alliance. Carter officially proclaimed neutrality in that conflict, while Sadat made moves to assist both sides in the hope of keeping them bogged down and free from Soviet influence. In October 1980, foreshadowing the near-term future of Middle East politics, a State Department memorandum mused, "If we have to hunker down with Egypt and Israel and face a hostile Middle East, a sustained, smoldering conflict in the east that keeps Iraq bogged down and the Arabs bickering among themselves may at least provide the easiest circumstances in which to face this prospect."[88]

Such conditions, however, were not advantageous for Sadat, whose support for US strategic initiatives in the Middle East only compounded the political woes he faced at home. The Egyptian economy remained in tatters, and, in the wake of his accommodation with Israel, public approval for Sadat dipped to an all-time low. His regime's support for the mujahideen, calculated in part to assuage criticism from the Muslim Brotherhood and other Islamic groups, failed to dampen their outrage. During the 1981 Autumn of Fury, Sadat cracked down on dissidents, jailing hundreds before he was assassinated during a parade held in remembrance of the 1973 war.[89] It was no small irony that Sadat, who had appealed to Islam and morality throughout his tenure to challenge his opponents on the Left while courting the religious Right, was gunned down by members of the Islamic Jihad.[90] Americans were shocked and saddened by Sadat's demise, but the new Ronald Reagan administration that had taken over for Carter in January 1981 was heartened to see his successor, Hosni Mubarak, condemn terrorism as a "criminal deviation" and continue the thrust of Sadat's diplomacy unabated.[91] Mubarak justified his rule in terms of continuity with Nasser, while furthering Sadat's efforts to move the country away from the revolutionary icon's commitment to socialism and Arab nationalism. He reaffirmed Egypt's commitment to peace with Israel and cemented Cairo's position as a client of the United States, driving the final nail into the coffin of Soviet power in the region.

Reagan, a dyed-in-the-wool Cold Warrior, was inclined to view the Middle East through an anti-Soviet prism, even as Moscow languished, intraregional conflicts rose to the fore, and anti-American terrorist organizations gained steam. His secretary of state, Alexander Haig, set out to ensure Soviet containment in the Middle East by arming and aiding a "consensus of strategic concerns," comprising friendly regional powers including Egypt, Israel, Saudi Arabia, Turkey, and Pakistan. Almost immediately thereafter, Israel's 1982 invasion of Lebanon unleashed the massacre of hundreds of Palestinian refugees, highlighting the new regional balance of power marked by decreased Arab leverage, a dearth of Soviet influence, and unchecked US dominance. Reagan dispatched US Marines to intervene in the Lebanese civil war, the first direct US military intervention in the Arab world since Eisenhower's 1958 foray into Lebanon. Washington was no longer inclined to rein in Tel Aviv, nor was it afraid of provoking Soviet interference. But the intervention only fueled anti-American sentiment, revealed the central flaws of the strategic consensus that failed to take into account intraregional rivalries, and undermined Reagan's political will to broker an Arab-Israeli settlement.[92]

Throughout the 1980s, Mubarak was able to win favor with Washington by continuing to support the Afghan mujahideen, while maneuvering Egypt back into the good graces of its Arab neighbors by backing Baghdad in the grueling eight-year Iran-Iraq War. By 1988, Mubarak had restored diplomatic relations with nearly all Arab governments. Two years later, the Arab League returned to Cairo. Meanwhile, the Pentagon and the Egyptian army grew closer, punctuated in 1987 by Egypt's inauguration as one of the United States' "major non-NATO allies" (MNNAs), which earned it preferential treatment in acquiring American military technology.[93] The US-Egyptian military alliance reached its crescendo in the first Iraq War, as President George H. W. Bush's good friend Mubarak rallied Arab League members in support of US operations against Iraq and sent Egyptians to join Saudi forces in a liberated Kuwait City, thereby avoiding the appearance of US occupation. Cairo's efforts paid off in spades, earning it forgiveness of nearly $14 billion in debt owed to the United States and a number of Arab states that had been hanging over the Egyptian economy like a sword of Damocles.

In the post–Cold War era, the United States and Egypt remained close partners in the fight against Islamic terrorism. Washington, which relied heavily on Mubarak's willingness to share intelligence and to repress individuals and groups with ties to terrorist organizations, encouraged his undemocratic tendencies in a pattern Brownlee has labeled "democracy prevention."[94] The alliance flourished until the early 2010s, when the Egyptian public joined in a region-wide explosion of public opposition to oppressive regimes known as the Arab Spring. The 2011 uprising in Egypt had deep roots, representing a rejection of the stark military control of society initiated under Nasser and continued by Sadat and Mubarak, with American sanction. Subsequent repression of these popular uprisings only begot a series of long and devastating regional conflicts sometimes referred to as the Arab Winter.

Though based in regional, religious, and ethnic rivalries that transcend the Cold War, these conflicts cannot be understood without attention to the superpower interventions of that era. Over four decades, the United States and the Soviet Union intentionally pitted Middle Eastern powers against one another while funneling unimaginable quantities of military hardware to their regional allies. "In turn," writes Lorena De Vita, "by exploiting the Cold War divide between East and West and flirting with the superpower that could offer more, most local regimes did not have to bother with democratic accountability, transparency, or the rule of law."[95] Superpower meddling, which did not stop with the fall of the Berlin Wall, thwarted the development of democratic systems, leaving the Middle East to hash out its conflicts with massive foreign-supplied arsenals.

4

The Congo

A Moral Defeat in the Heart of Africa

From 1960 to 1965, the Congo emerged as the first Cold War hot spot in sub-Saharan Africa. The resource-rich country, bordered by nine territories in central, southern, and east Africa, held great political, economic, and strategic importance for the colonial and Cold War powers, as well as for the white-minority regimes in southern Africa and Third World members of the UN.[1] It became a target for significant foreign intervention by the UN, Belgium, the Soviet Union, the United States, a cohort of mercenaries from white-minority African countries, and even Cuban revolutionaries. The Congo Crisis, and its resolution with the establishment of Joseph Désiré Mobutu's US-backed military dictatorship in 1965, had lasting ramifications for the future of postcolonial Africa, the trajectory of the United Nations, and the fate of the nonaligned movement. It shaped both Soviet and American strategies for the Third World, particularly with regard to Africa, and contributed to the growing rift between Beijing and Moscow as they vied for revolutionary primacy in the postcolonial world. Cuba's involvement further signified the fragmentation of the communist bloc. The Congo Crisis was a key chapter in the Cold War. It was also a pivotal act in an ongoing national tragedy.

Amid the late nineteenth-century scramble for Africa, the Congo first came under Belgian King Leopold II's personal control in 1885. Leopold II, who never bothered to set foot in his prized colony, ran the Congo Free State as a corporate moneymaking venture focused on extracting ivory and rubber. It became notorious for a string of atrocities committed by colonial officials against the local population, inspiring Joseph Conrad's *Heart of Darkness* and Arthur Conan Doyle's *The Crime of the Congo,* among other harrowing literary works. In 1908, following an intense propaganda war between the king and his critics, most notably Roger Casement and the Congo Reform Association, Leopold II was forced to relinquish his colony to Belgian control. The Belgian Congo persisted in much the same form, but with a veneer of "civilizing mission," until the rather abrupt transition to independence in 1960.

The Congolese independence movement developed late but gained steam rapidly once it appeared in the late 1950s. A small but growing middle class referred to as *évolués* (French for "developed" or "evolved") that had been largely assimilated to European values and patterns of behavior began to demand independence, and it quickly became obvious that its members would not be appeased by vague promises and half measures. Among this new cohort of anticolonial leaders, Patrice Lumumba and Joseph Kasavubu stood out.[2]

Lumumba was tall, handsome, charismatic, and impulsive, and his political flame was as brilliant as it was brief. Leftist French philosopher Jean-Paul Sartre referred to him as "a meteor in the African firmament."[3] Born in Kasai in 1925, Lumumba attended Catholic and Protestant missionary schools before moving to Stanleyville to become a postal clerk. From there, the colonial post office sent him to Léopoldville for training, where he discovered an unquenchable thirst for knowledge and a newfound obsession with the French revolution. In the mid-1950s, just at the dawn of Congo's nationalist movement, he dove headlong into political life. He juggled a number of board positions and chaired Stanleyville's Association of Évolués, a post that he leveraged to become the city's most influential Congolese. Known for getting by on just a few hours of sleep a night, he attended meetings and published political analyses at a feverish rate, even starting his own periodical, *L'Écho Postale*. His ambition, charm, and energy were matched by his dashing physical appearance—the commanding, bespectacled young man with a beard and bow tie had a habit of telling people what they wanted to hear. This quality facilitated his path to power but would also contribute to his undoing, as US officials later deemed him too wily and duplicitous to entertain as a viable leader for postcolonial Congo.

Lumumba's place in Congo's nationalist pantheon was secured following a 1955 conversation with Belgium's King Baudouin. As rumor had it, Lumumba ran into the king at a garden party, where he commanded his attention for a full ten minutes, explaining some of the problems plaguing the native population. It seemed that if anyone could solve them, it would be Lumumba. Even his subsequent prosecution for forgery and embezzlement from the post office did not stall his meteoric rise. He served a twelve-month prison term before a number of his supporters paid back the stolen funds, securing him early release. He then took a job with a beer company, which he used to promote political organization in working-class neighborhoods where he "brought beer and promised freedom."[4]

It was not until a December 1958 trip to Accra that Lumumba's political philosophy began to crystallize. In Kwame Nkrumah, who had just led Ghana to become the first country in sub-Saharan Africa to gain independence, Lumumba found a revolutionary mentor. Nkrumah's Pan-Africanism mapped perfectly onto Lumumba's instinctive drive to assert the rights and dignity of Black people and to denounce the colonial exploitation that suppressed African heritage and progress. Attracted to the communist commitment to equality and support for national liberation, he made overtures to the Soviet Union prior to independence, but his sights remained set on independence for the Congo and autonomy for Africa. By the time Lumumba became committed to the urgent cause of liberation, he was far from alone among his countrymen.

Kasavubu stood in stark contrast to Lumumba. Born into a noble family of Bas-Congo in 1925, he studied for the priesthood—the highest level of educational attainment available to native Congolese under Belgian rule—before deciding that his calling lay elsewhere.[5] Like much of his political cohort, he moved to Léopoldville during World War II to take a post as a low-level civil servant in the colonial administration. As part of the new Black political elite, his ruminations on social and racial issues led him to his trademark slogan: "a travail égal, salaire égal" (the same work, the same wages).[6] Put off by both communism and Pan-Africanism, this was about as radical as Kasavubu would get.

In 1955, Kasavubu was appointed chairman of the Alliances de Bakongo (Abako), a regional tribal association that would evolve into an overtly political, anticolonial organization during his tenure. In response to an ill-conceived Belgian proposal to grant independence in stages over a thirty-year period, the Abako published a prescient rebuttal, declaring: "The time is ripe, and therefore they must grant us that emancipation this very day rather than postpone it for another thirty years. History knows no belated emancipations, for when the hour has come, the people will no longer wait."[7] At the time, Kasavubu's Abako was the most unrelenting advocate for Congolese independence. But the future Congolese president had a very different vision for the Congo than did Lumumba; rather than a strong centralized government, he imagined a loose confederation of mini-states. These two competing visions would not be reconciled, nor even really addressed, prior to independence, an oversight that would lead the country almost immediately down the path to civil war.

In December 1957, when Belgium finally made a nod to native political participation by allowing the boroughs of a few large cities to elect their own mayors and city councils, Kasavubu's political climb gained a boost. With 80 to 85 percent of eligible voters showing up at the polls, he was elected mayor of one of Léopoldville's boroughs. Accepting his new post, he delivered one of the most impassioned speeches of his career, decrying the inadequacy of Belgium's shallow nod to democracy and independence and demanding "general elections and internal autonomy."[8]

Kasavubu articulated what many of his countrymen were feeling, but he was no Lumumba. A timid and mediocre speaker, he lacked the future prime minister's charisma and flair for oratory, and he could never command the same type of loyal following. Yet the plump, understated Kasavubu possessed political skills Lumumba lacked. Patient, plodding, and self-controlled, he was able to conceal his opinions and intentions as he worked quietly to obtain power. As the Congo rushed headlong toward independence, fate would align these polar opposite political stars before setting them at odds.

As the decade wore on, agitation for independence gained steam. On January 4, 1959, it finally boiled over following a soccer match at King Baudouin Stadium on a blazing-hot day in Léopoldville. Enraged by Belgium's stalling on the question of independence, the entire city erupted in convulsions of violence and looting. It was a critical turning point. On January 13, King Baudouin announced Belgium's intention to "lead the people of Congo in prosperity and peace, without harmful procrastination but also without undue haste, toward independence."[9]

Yet Belgian politicians remained divided among themselves over the Congo question, which resulted in a series of missteps that ultimately hastened the march to independence. The liberal minister of the Congo, Maurice Van Hemmelrijck, had barely introduced reforms designed to speed up the colony's transition to self-rule before he was forced to resign. His replacement, August de Schryver, immediately rescinded the reforms, provoking a rash of riots throughout Congo in the fall of 1959. In December, de Schryver finally agreed to hold a roundtable meeting to discuss the future of the Congo. The conference, devoted to hashing out the terms of Congolese independence, opened in Brussels on January 27, 1960, and lasted for almost a month. It turned out to be a stunning defeat for Belgium and a rousing victory for the Congolese delegation that achieved almost all of its aims. A date certain for independence was set for June 30, 1960, less than six months away. Although Belgium's bid to maintain some form of guardianship was defeated, it still expected to maintain a modicum of informal control. But the Belgians would soon find out just how wrong they were.

The roundtable conference took place at a critical moment in the history of African decolonization. Britain had declared 1960 the Year of Africa, with no fewer than seventeen countries standing at the precipice of independence. As the Congo—the richest, largest, and most strategically important colony in sub-Saharan Africa—joined those ranks, the question was not whether but how the Cold War would grip the continent. The United States viewed the Congo as one of many left-wing threats in the Third World, but a critical one due to the country's immense natural wealth. The Congo's resources included diamonds, gold, copper, cobalt, and uranium, which had fueled the first nuclear bomb used in combat against the Japanese city of Hiroshima.[10]

With long-standing ties to European colonial powers, solidified in the postwar years through NATO, US policy was governed by a desire to prevent revolutionary changes during the transition to independence. Thus, while rhetorically committed to anticolonialism, Washington's economic and strategic interests were served by maintaining the status quo. Above all, the United States aimed to protect Western business interests and access to raw materials in the Congo and other former colonies, which required blocking Soviet efforts to displace them. Officials in Washington were deeply wedded to the belief that the Soviet Union was an imperialist power bent on deploying tactics of trickery, deception, and bald exploitation of hapless postcolonial leaders to bring as much of the world as possible under communist enslavement. On final analysis, this rigid view would distort their perception of the Congo's unique political realities and enable them to justify policies that leftist critics in Africa and the Soviet bloc decried as neocolonial.

The evolution of Soviet policy toward the Third World in the latter half of the 1950s, as the pace of decolonization accelerated, only fueled American paranoia. After Premier Nikita Khrushchev emerged from a drawn-out power struggle in 1955 to succeed the late Joseph Stalin, he reoriented Soviet policy in the Third World to more actively support national liberation movements. Between 1957 and 1960, he forged connections with the West African states of Guinea, Ghana, and Mali as part of a larger project to establish the Soviet Union as the natural ally of the continent's emerging neutralist figures and to promote "noncapitalist development."[11] In 1960, the Soviet Union decided to "considerably expand" its relations with African peoples, primarily in the form of cultural exchange and information gathering.[12]

Moscow clearly had its sights trained on the Congo as a golden opportunity to make inroads into the region that was just emerging from the exclusive grips of Western colonial power. Khrushchev also understood the strategic value of gaining access to critical raw materials in the Third World that had been wrested from Western control. Moscow first established back-channel contacts with Lumumba in mid-1959. Although it was clear to Khrushchev that the Congolese firebrand was neither a communist nor a Marxist, he did respond favorably to Soviet suggestions for implementing a planned, centralized economy. Moreover, his determination to break "foreign monopolies" lined up perfectly with Khrushchev's vision for Africa, guaranteeing him Soviet support once he took office.[13]

Lumumba's leadership of postcolonial Congo was secured in May 1960, through countrywide elections set at the roundtable conference. Votes were divided among a large number of political parties, almost all of which were regional and ethnic in nature. Lumumba's Mouvement Nationale Congolais (MNC)—the only truly national party in the mix—garnered a plurality of the votes. Belgium was therefore left with little choice but to cede the post of prime minister to Lumumba, who set up his new government with the more moderate Joseph Kasavubu as president.

Given the hasty move toward independence, neither Belgian colonial officials nor Congolese nationalists had a clear plan in place for the new government.[14] Several disparate political organizations comprising the Congo's nationalist movement agreed on the goal of liberation, but little else. Would there be a strong centralized government or a loose confederation of ethnic states? The Fundamental Law (Loi Fundamentale) penned by Belgians would be the law of the land, but it left many questions unanswered about the Congo's political organization and economic system. Faced with these daunting hurdles, the new government was handicapped by a shortage of qualified, experienced administrative personnel that resulted from restrictive colonial-era

August 10, 1960, on arrival in Léopoldville after visits to North African heads of state, Congolese premier Patrice Lumumba is greeted by his children and an unidentified person. (AP Photo/Babout)

policies designed to limit Africans' educational attainment and to keep them a safe distance from the halls of power.[15]

Belgium expected that, despite Congo's nominal independence, Brussels would continue to run the country by proxy through friendly African leaders. King Baudouin kicked off the independence day ceremony with an ill-advised speech that revealed his expectation for a gradual, conservative transition that would preserve the trappings of Belgian authority in the Congo. Praising Belgium for rescuing the colony from Arab slavery and setting it on the path to civilization, he urged "his" Congolese: "Don't compromise the future with hasty reforms, and don't replace the structures that Belgium hands over to you until you are sure you can do better. . . . Don't be afraid to come to us. We will remain by your side, train you with the technical experts and administrators you will need."[16] The king seemed utterly oblivious to the outrage his condescension would spark.

Next up to the podium was the new president, Kasavubu, who gave an innocuous address pledging Congolese goodwill and parroting the message that little would change in the newly independent Congo. But then Lumumba, who had not been scheduled to speak, approached the lectern. He delivered an impassioned speech that, according to Belgian sociologist Ludo De Witte, made the Belgians' "blood run cold."[17] Independent Congo's first prime minister painted a harsh but honest picture of life under Belgian colonial rule, vowing to "put an end to the humiliating bondage forced upon us." Lumumba pointed to forced labor, racism, exile from native lands, political and religious persecution, and violence as hallmarks of Belgium's "regime of injustice, oppression, and exploitation," a regime that, despite the so-far bloodless transfer of power, he credited Congolese nationalists with overthrowing through just and noble struggle. He called for national unity and proclaimed Congo's independence to be "a decisive step towards the liberation of the whole African continent."[18]

Africans in the audience interrupted Lumumba's speech with applause no fewer than eight times and stood at the end for an impassioned ovation. The Belgians were shocked, their belief in their colonial endeavor as a civilizing mission shaken and their expectation for a seamless continuation of Belgian domination by proxy undermined. Lumumba, whom Brussels had tried to bar from office in the first place, cemented his former colonial master's enmity. The Americans, who even prior to this speech held a dim opinion of Lumumba as an impetuous, untrustworthy dope smoker whose personal failings would render him vulnerable to communist exploitation, grew even more concerned over his dangerous radical tendencies and intemperate character.[19]

Its disquiet with Lumumba notwithstanding, Belgium proceeded on the assumption that its role in postcolonial Congo would resemble that of the colonial days. Almost immediately, however, it would be confronted with a very different reality. On July 5, 1960, just five days after the independence ceremony, Belgian-born army general Émile Janssens convened a meeting with nearly two hundred noncommissioned officers in Léopoldville. Upon entering the room, he strode to the blackboard and wrote, "Before Independence = After Independence."[20] Janssens's tone-deaf arrogance poured salt on wounds opened by Belgium's failure to take any meaningful steps to Africanize the army in the lead-up to independence. As he spoke, the army had yet to promote a single Congolese soldier to officer rank.[21] Later that same day, Black soldiers at the Thysville barracks, ninety miles south of the capital, launched a full-scale mutiny in protest against poor pay and mistreatment by overbearing white officers.

Lumumba tried to calm the mutiny by announcing immediate promotions—including the fateful elevation of Joseph Désiré Mobutu to army chief of staff—and the Africanization of the army, which he renamed the Armée Nationale Congolais (ANC). But it was too little too late. Frustration, fueled by Lumumba's own rhetoric, boiled over in response to the lack of real changes accompanying independence. Workers began to strike in solidarity with the soldiers, and violent protests quickly spread to the streets in hot spots around the country, pitting Black civilians against white.

On July 9, Lumumba learned that Belgium was sending forces to the Congo under the pretext of protecting European citizens and restoring order.[22] Realizing the urgent need to secure outside help to put a halt to Belgian intervention, he made immediate overtures in his and Kasavubu's name to the African American UN undersecretary Ralph Bunche. Bunche, a brilliant Harvard PhD and winner of the 1950 Nobel Prize for his role in Middle Eastern peace negotiations, was, like Lumumba, a radical critic of colonialism and racial inequality. In his Nobel acceptance speech, he seized the opportunity to call for "an acceleration in the liquidation of colonialism."[23] Under different circumstances, the two men might have been allies. But, as Crawford Young writes, "Confronting the Congo Crisis, Bunche and Lumumba were embedded in radically different institutional matrices."[24] Bunche's loyalty was to the UN and to its general secretary, Dag Hammarskjöld, with whom he shared the vision of rallying the emergent Afro-Asian majority in the General Assembly to establish the organization as the vanguard of decolonization and postcolonial development projects. To Bunche, Lumumba came across as a dangerous demagogue with intolerable communist leanings, as nettlesome "riffraff" not unlike Africa's leading neutralists, Nkrumah and Guinean president Sékou Touré. Over the next few months, Lumumba, desperate to save his country but ill-equipped both temperamentally and institutionally to manage the ever-deepening crisis, grew furious with a spate of UN actions that seemed to align with the interests of Belgian colonialists and American anticommunists at the expense of his nationalist project.

The trouble really began with two key events of July 11 that crushed any hope of limiting the Belgian intervention or channeling it into a UN-directed peacekeeping effort. First, Belgian troops landed at the port city of Matadi, ostensibly to protect European citizens and aid in their evacuation. This prompted resistance from Congolese garrisons and intensified violent conflict. Second, Moise Tshombe, leader of the Confédération d'Associations Tribales du Katanga (Conakat), announced that the mineral-rich province of Katanga, threatened by a communist insurgency, was seceding from the Congo. Belgium, which retained strong financial interests in Katanga via mining industry giant Union Minière du Haut-Katanga, supported the secession. Knowing that the international community hoped to see the Congo remain united, Brussels stopped short of offering formal recognition to independent Katanga. Belgian forces did, however, help disarm Lumumba's troops, establish a new Katangan army—the Gendarmerie Katangese—and even collaborated with Katangan officials to set up a new central bank.[25]

Yet the common view of Tshombe as nothing but a Belgian stooge is oversimplified. Tshombe led Conakat in asserting a series of ethnohistorical arguments to justify Katangan independence, which the secessionists considered necessary to secure the benefits of the region's mineral wealth for its rightful residents.[26] Conakat, established at the same time as Lumumba's MNC, proposed an alternative to Congolese nationalism that focused on a version of the regionalism and ethnic consciousness that Kasavubu favored. Although Tshombe accepted some elements of Pan-Africanism, especially its rejection of white paternalism and its celebration of Blackness, he spurned the notion that the colonial borders imposed by Belgium should dictate the boundaries of postcolonial Congo. He argued instead for the creation of a loose confederation of autonomous states, the boundaries of which would be determined by shared kinship, language, and history.[27] As historian Ryan Irwin has noted, Tshombe's position "that incorporation into the Congo was a greater threat to CONAKAT's supporters than collaboration with Belgium" challenged prevailing thinking about decolonization by "upending the implicit binary between freedom and colonialism."[28] For Tshombe, self-rule in collaboration with Belgium was preferable to Katanga's subordination to the central government Lumumba established in Léopoldville.

Economic control was at the heart of the clash, which soon became an international crisis. The secession secured Katanga's wealth for Conakat's supporters while depriving the new government in Léopoldville of more than half of its annual revenue, as well as a significant chunk of its foreign exchange earnings. And it shattered Lumumba's vision of national unity. The day after Tshombe's announcement, Lumumba sent a telegram to the UN accusing Belgium of launching a hostile intervention and requesting military aid "to protect the national territory of the Congo against the present external aggression which is a threat to international peace."[29] As would become his standard practice in foreign correspondence, he attached Kasavubu's name to the note. Twenty-four hours later, to clarify the request, he sent a second missive indicating that the purpose of their request was "not to restore the internal situation in Congo, but rather to protect the territory against acts of aggression committed by Belgian metropolitan troops."[30] As historian Lise Namikas writes, "The wording suggested that they wanted to convince the world that imperialist aggression, not tribal division, was at the root of the problems in the Congo and that aggression had to be stopped as quickly as possible."[31]

Belgium, in an effort to combat the perception that it was engaged in a thinly veiled imperial reconquest, defended its actions in Cold War terms. Yet whereas Brussels claimed that Tshombe best represented Western interests against the growing communist threat in the Congo, US president Dwight Eisenhower's administration saw the Cold War implications of the conflict differently. Although deeply troubled by Lumumba's communist ties and seemingly untrustworthy behavior, Washington was even more fearful of a pattern of political fragmentation in Africa that would render the continent vulnerable to communist infiltration. If the Congo was deprived of its richest province, the rest of the country would be plunged into the very state of darkness and despair that American officials expected the Soviet Union to exploit. As historian Madeline Kalb writes, US Ambassador to the Congo Clare Timberlake "believed that anarchy in the Congo would have repercussions far beyond the immediate crisis: it would play directly into the hands of the Russians by providing an opportunity for radical forces to take over and undermine Western interests in this rich and strategic part of Africa."[32] Washington was especially concerned with preventing the Soviets from gaining access to Katanga's rich uranium deposits. The United States therefore sought to end the secession of Katanga and restore the Congo's integrity while simultaneously exploring ways to remove Lumumba from power to make way for a regime friendly to Western interests. Having ruled out the possibility of sending its own troops to the Congo, Washington worked through the UN to achieve the former objective and would rely increasingly on the CIA to pursue the latter through covert operations.

On July 14, the UN Security Council issued a resolution calling on Belgian forces to withdraw and providing for a UN peacekeeping mission in the Congo. Britain and France, colonial powers appalled by the prospect of international intervention into the process of decolonization, abstained from the vote. Both the United States and the Soviet Union supported the resolution but for very different reasons. In the summer of 1960, the United States enjoyed a dominant position in the UN organization and held sway over its decision-making process. Washington, which had once been skeptical of the UN, adopted a much more favorable view of the organization after its critical role in resolving the Suez Crisis. The State Department was newly inclined to "let Dag do it."[33] Furthermore, the Americans held unique advantages in this case, as their representatives including Ralph Bunche, Andrew Cordier, and Heinz Wieschhoff dominated a select group known as the Congo Club, members of which were privy to top-secret details about the situation in the Congo. Washington thus viewed the UN as a vehicle to pursue its own aims in the Congo without having to commit US troops or prestige.

Soviet interests in the UN were as marginalized as American interests were privileged. Beyond its veto power, the Soviet Union exerted little influence over the Security Council. But Khrushchev aimed to challenge the balance of power in the organization by establishing Moscow as the dominant global opponent of colonialism and imperialism, a move that could dramatically enhance Soviet prestige in the Third World. He hoped the Congo Crisis might offer him an opportunity to win over the emerging Afro-Asian bloc in the UN—which had recently swelled to occupy 46 out of 99 votes—thereby reorienting the balance of forces away from the United States and its allies and toward the socialist bloc.[34] Khrushchev was thus determined to work through the organization to reach an international solution to the brewing crisis in the Congo that would avoid conflict with the United States, minimize American gains, and restrict the involvement of the Soviet Union's increasingly antagonistic Chinese ally in the crisis.

In the first of many Soviet failures at the UN during the Congo Crisis, Khrushchev's bid to attach a series of amendments to the July 14 resolution fell flat. As a result, the final text was riddled with milquetoast language that stopped well short of condemning Belgian aggression. The resolution pledged the UN only to a limited peacekeeping operation, while taking sharp jabs at Lumumba, indicating that the mission's primary task would be not to expel Belgian troops but to restore order, an action that was only made necessary by his government's failure to do so.

Snubbed by the UN, Lumumba wasted no time in reaching out to the Soviet Union. Once again including Kasavubu's name, he sent a public telegram that read: "Given the threats to the neutrality of the Republic of the Congo from Belgium and various Western nations conspiring with her against our independence, we ask you to watch the Congo situation closely. We might be led to ask help from the Soviet Union if the Western camp does not stop its aggression against our sovereignty." This overture, intended more as a form of pressure and propaganda than a plea for direct Soviet intervention, provoked an immediate response from Khrushchev, who made a vague pledge of Soviet aid "that might be needed for the victory of your rightful cause."[35] While the Soviets attached themselves to the UN operation, they immediately asserted independence from it and left the door open to take unilateral measures in the future. However, as Irwin notes, "The hitch . . . was that Moscow did not actually have the ability to intervene in the Congo; Khrushchev's flair for dramatic prose elided the fundamental asymmetry of the superpower game in the early 1960s."[36] Over the coming months, Khrushchev talked loudly but carried a small stick. His efforts to secure cooperation from other leftist African leaders to maximize Moscow's leverage in the Congo fell flat, and the meager aid he could provide would amount to far too little, too late.

Meanwhile, Khrushchev became increasingly antagonistic to the UN, which he came to see as an instrument of US imperialism in the Congo. The United Nations Operation in the Congo (UNOC) opened on July 15 with the arrival of the first of 19,825 UN troops assigned to the country. Whatever understanding existed between the superpowers dissolved almost immediately, as the security force proceed to prioritize the protection of white lives and the stabilization of the political situation in the Congo to Western advantage. On July 17 Lumumba, incensed by the lack of attention to Belgian aggression, delivered to Bunche an ultimatum signed by himself and Kasavubu. He insisted that his government would be obliged to call upon the Soviet Union for help if the UN proved "unable to discharge the mission we have entrusted to it."[37] He gave the UN a seventy-two-hour timetable to complete the withdrawal of Belgian troops. That afternoon the prime minister took to the airwaves to clarify that he acted not out of sympathy with socialist dogma but rather in service of building a strong Congo and laying the groundwork of the liberation of Africa.

Lumumba secured a promise of Belgian troop withdrawal by July 23, which was largely hollow as the former colonial power continued to act unilaterally and unopposed in Katanga. Meanwhile, his rash ultimatum backfired in almost every sense. His efforts to distance himself from communist ideology rang hollow in American ears. Washington's dismay over Lumumba's impetuous behavior, exacerbated by his apparent orientation to the Soviet Union, hardened the Eisenhower administration's opposition to the prime minister and encouraged it to begin thinking seriously about how to remove him from power. Khrushchev, meanwhile, proceeded cautiously, announcing an increase in economic and humanitarian aid rather than offering direct support for Lumumba's government. In Léopoldville, the Senate rejected Lumumba's ultimatum and opposed the possibility of unilateral Soviet intervention. And regionally, the UN African bloc met on July 18 to express its unanimous opposition to Lumumba's threat to call Soviet troops to the Congo.[38]

Desperate for any foreign support he could muster and still naively believing he could play the Soviets and Americans off one another to his advantage, Lumumba decided to go to the United States to plead his case with both the UN and the Eisenhower administration. In late July, he arrived in New York to meet with Hammarskjöld, who quickly refused his request for the UN to open operations against Belgian forces in Katanga. Although Hammarskjöld reported to the Eisenhower administration that Lumumba's demands were clear-sighted, not irrational, the meeting seemed to solidify a brewing rift between the head of the UN and the leader of the Congo, whose personalities proved as incompatible as their goals. As historian Sergey Mazov writes: "Lumumba believed that Hammarskjöld was working mainly for Western interests and that he could not be trusted. Hammarskjöld judged Lumumba as a political self-destroyer without good sense."[39]

Having failed to make headway at the UN, Lumumba made his way to Washington, where he met with even greater disappointment. Since he did not follow diplomatic protocol to arrange meetings in advance, he was denied access to Eisenhower, who went on vacation in Newport, Rhode Island, to keep his distance. Instead, he met with Secretary of State Christian Herter and Undersecretary of State Douglas Dillon to appeal for help persuading the Belgians to withdraw from Katanga, for economic and technical aid for his government, and for small aircraft to aid the ANC's military effort. Herter shot down each of these requests, simply informing Lumumba that all US aid would be channeled through the UN.

Reflecting on Lumumba's visit, Dillon bemoaned his "irrational, almost 'psychotic' personality." Pointing to everything from his frenetic demeanor and his unreasonable demands to his ill-conceived request that a top State Department official arrange for a blonde call girl to visit his hotel room, the undersecretary deemed him "someone you couldn't work with at all."[40] In truth, the last nail in the coffin of US cooperation with Lumumba had been hammered before he set foot in the United States. Policymakers in Washington, who had been highly skeptical of Lumumba's erratic behavior and communist ties from the start, ruled out any possibility of working with him after the July 17 ultimatum. They drew the line formally at a National Security Council Meeting on July 21, where top US officials reached the conclusion that reconciliation with Lumumba was impossible. CIA director Allen Dulles concluded, "In Lumumba we are faced with a person who is a Castro or worse." It was, in Dulles's estimation, "safe to go on the assumption that Lumumba has been bought by the Communists," although his communist tendencies "fit with his own orientation."[41]

Dulles, Herter, Secretary of Defense Thomas Gates, and others agreed that there was very little immediate threat of the Soviet Union sending troops to the Congo but that figures like Lumumba, whom the Soviets could exploit to do their bidding, posed a much more significant danger. The American ambassador in Léopoldville, Clare Timberlake, branded the Congolese prime minister with the derogatory nickname "Lumumbavitch."[42] In a briefing to Dulles, CIA station chief in the Congo, Lawrence Devlin, summed up US fears: "If the Soviets achieved their objective of influencing and eventually controlling Lumumba, they would use the Congo as a base to infiltrate and extend their influence over the nine countries or colonies surrounding the Congo." This, he warned, would give the Soviets "an extraordinary power base in Africa," control over the continent's wealth of raw materials, dramatically increased sway over the Third World, and enhanced influence within the UN.[43] Although American officials correctly identified Soviet designs on Congo, they seriously overestimated Moscow's capacity to exert its power in Africa, and especially miscalculated its ability to control leftist figures like Lumumba, who was, in fact, fiercely independent.

Yet there was more to Americans' scorn for Lumumba than his drift toward the communist bloc. Top US officials regularly maligned his personality, describing him as everything from "a little flighty and erratic" to "just not a rational being," "definitely a dope fiend," "crazy," "insane," and even "a sorcerer." As Thomas Borstelmann has argued, many of these assessments were rooted in a deep-seated racism that permeated the halls of Washington. Lumumba was threatening not only for his ties to communism but also because of the peril to the existing racial order that he so clearly symbolized. Especially among white southerners who were busy defending the color line at home, his government was seen as responsible for Black sexual violence against white civilians in Congo, and his request for a blonde hooker riled up additional fears of racialized sexual transgressions. This, combined with his condemnations of the Belgian colonial administration that the United States had praised throughout the 1950s, read as a boundary-crossing lack of gratitude when viewed through the lens of early-1960s racial thinking in the United States.[44] "By coming to America," writes Namikas, "Lumumba in a sense forfeited his stature as a foreign leader and found himself lost in a sea of racism for which he was not prepared."[45] The discourse of imperialism as a civilizing mission—repackaged in the Cold War language of modernization and development—involved racial epistemologies that led US and UN officials alike to conclude that Congolese politicians, unprepared for self-rule, would be easily duped and co-opted by communist agents. This made them all the more determined to eliminate left-leaning, Soviet-backed political figures like Lumumba to make way for Congolese politicians who would advance Western interests.

Thus, a deflated Lumumba returned to Léopoldville following his unsuccessful visit to the United States with little choice but to turn to the Soviet

Union for help expelling Belgian troops from Katanga. In the coming weeks, his deepening clash with the UN would further cement his alignment with Moscow. On August 2, following intense negotiations, Belgium agreed to let UN troops into Katanga, and Hammarskjöld announced that they would arrive on August 6. But when Bunche arrived for advance negotiations, Tshombe informed him that the entry of UN forces into his province would mean war. Although Bunche and Hammarskjöld saw this as a bluff, they agreed to postpone the troop deployment, sparking outrage from Lumumba's cabinet and the Soviet Union, as well as from Ghana's president, Kwame Nkrumah; Guinea's Sékou Touré; and Egypt's Gamal Abdel Nasser. Although these three paragons of neutralism agreed to redirect forces to the Congo to help oust the Belgians, they remained committed to working through the UN wherever possible. Even Nkrumah, the African politician most ardently supportive of Lumumba's government, sent a message to Hammarskjöld indicating his intention to stand by the UN for the foreseeable future. Due to the Afro-Asian bloc's growing frustration with the organization's alignment with Western interests, Khrushchev saw an opening for the Soviet Union to challenge US power. But he failed to recognize the extent to which neutralist figures depended on the UN to bring stability and autonomy to Africa and the Congo.[46]

Lumumba, however, infuriated by Hammarskjöld's decision to negotiate directly with Tshombe, was prepared to make a complete break with the UN. In mid-August, stopping short of demanding the immediate departure of all UN forces, he called for the withdrawal of all non-African troops. The next few days brought a spate of government attacks against white UN personnel in the Congo, provoking Hammarskjöld to announce that he would withdraw the entire UN mission at once if Lumumba did not put a stop to what he condemned as clearly racial attacks. The United States, fearing that a UN withdrawal would force a direct clash with the Soviet Union in the Congo, reacted with alarm. Devlin sent an urgent message to Washington indicating that the CIA station and the US embassy in Léopoldville agreed that the Congo was "experiencing [a] classic communist effort [to] take-over [the] government." Timberlake added that he would hate to stand by and watch this play out "under [the] noses of an impotent UN military force."[47] The Eisenhower administration thus reached the conclusion that it must take a more independent approach, largely though covert operations, to pursue its aim of preventing a communist takeover in the Congo.

The National Security Council met again on August 18 to deliberate on the Lumumba problem. Although the discussion centered on finding the best path to promote Western interests and halt Soviet advances in the Congo, there was consensus on one point: Lumumba must go. Participants avoided any overt mention of assassination, but Robert Johnson, the note taker at the meeting, later recalled Eisenhower saying something that sounded very much like an assassination order.[48] The United States reached this decision independently while Belgium was already far along the path to developing its own assassination plans.

Back in the Congo, Lumumba's power was eroding precipitously. On August 8 the prime minister declared a state of emergency, arresting a number of his enemies in an effort to crack down on demonstrations throughout the country. That same day, the diamond-rich province of South Kasai followed Katanga's lead and announced its independence. Desperate, Lumumba ordered the ragtag ANC to Kasai, where it unleashed a series of massacres that claimed thousands of civilian lives. A livid Hammarskjöld went so far as to suggest that Lumumba's regime was guilty of genocide. Khrushchev, meanwhile, broke from the UN organization to initiate a limited program of unilateral assistance to Lumumba's government in the form of planes, trucks, and advisors. To that point, he had been reluctant to take such a step without the support of key African leaders. But by late August, with Lumumba's government hanging in the balance, Khrushchev proceeded with unilateral aid to Léopoldville over African leaders' pleas for him to cooperate with the UN.[49]

Although Soviet support for Lumumba remained insignificant, the United States read it as a chilling sign of Moscow's aggressive designs on Africa. "In those days," recalls Devlin, "when everything was measured in Cold War terms, we were convinced that we were observing the beginning of a major Soviet effort to gain control of a key country in central Africa for use as a springboard to control much of the continent."[50] Thus, at an August 25, 1960, meeting, the NSC set in motion a plan to depose Lumumba. The next day, Dulles sent this message to the CIA station in Léopoldville: "In high quarters here it is the clear-cut conclusion that if (Lumumba) continues to hold high office, the inevitable result will at best be chaos and at worst pave the way to Communist takeover of the Congo with disastrous consequences for the prestige of the UN and for the interests of the free world generally. Consequently we conclude that his removal must be an urgent and prime objective and that under existing conditions this should be a high priority of our covert action."[51] On September 1 the NSC Special Working Group for the Congo authorized Project Wizard, which provided Kasavubu with funds to use in the anti-Lumumba program that both the United States and Belgium pressed him to pursue.

On September 5 Kasavubu, who had remained in the shadows throughout the Congo's tempestuous first summer of independence, went on the state radio station to announce his decision to fire Lumumba and six other ministers, a decision that challenged the new Fundamental Law that Belgium had drafted for Congo leading up to independence. He instructed the ANC to relinquish its arms and submit to a period of formal UN training, and charged Senate leader Joseph Ileo with setting up a new government. Kasavubu was following a CIA "how-to" paper that, according to Devlin, laid out "step-by-step the actions he should take before dismissing Lumumba and what he should do in the aftermath."[52]

Lumumba, unsurprisingly, refused to walk away without a fight. Later that same evening he took to the airwaves to announce Kasavubu's dismissal, asking the UN and the international community to refrain from interfering in the Congo's internal affairs. Overnight the Council of Ministers released a statement dismissing Kasavubu for having violated the Fundamental Law. Two days later the Chamber of Representatives voted overwhelmingly to declare both ousters null and void. The Senate then repealed Kasavubu's attempt to dismiss Lumumba. The almost farcical political deadlock in Léopoldville showed no obvious path to resolution within the existing political order.

With the Congolese government stuck in limbo, UN forces sprang into action. On September 6 they shut down the radio station in Léopoldville to keep Lumumba off the air and seized control of the area's major airports to prevent him from recalling loyal forces from the provinces to the capital. Eisenhower spoke out the next day to condemn Soviet military aid to Lumumba's government, claiming that, "motivated entirely by the Soviet Union's political designs in Africa," it threatened the UN's collective mission in the Congo.[53] Hammarskjöld, too, questioned the legality of Moscow's provision of military aid to the Congo, to which Khrushchev replied by attacking the general secretary personally for working openly "to the advantage of the colonizers, thus compromising the UN."[54] He demanded that the UN immediately reopen the state radio station, withdraw its troops from

Congolese airports, and dismiss the UNOC command. Despite his tough rhetoric, though, Khrushchev accepted the precariousness of Lumumba's domestic political position and understood that his failure to win the support of key African leaders rendered the Soviet position in the Congo fairly impotent. He appeared to be pulling back from the policy of unilateral military aid to the Congo.

On September 14, the ANC's chief of staff, Col. Joseph Mobutu, put an end to the political deadlock between Kasavubu and Lumumba, announcing on air that he was taking power and "neutralizing the head of state, and the two rival governments now in office, as well as both houses of the Parliament."[55] He called in ANC forces to disperse a Senate meeting and occupy the Parliament. Kasavubu was allowed to stay in place as a figurehead, and Lumumba was placed under house arrest. Prior to his military career, Mobutu worked as a journalist. He made friends with Lumumba amid the rioting for independence that took place in Léopoldville, a factor that may have contributed to his selection as the first head of the ANC.[56] Yet his loyalty was not to Lumumba but to a stable Congo, an objective that would become highly perverted over the course of his rule. Mobutu, who was hand-picked by the CIA for his leadership qualities and his anti-Soviet orientation, met with Devlin the night before his takeover to gain assurances that the United States would support his new government. He immediately made good on his Cold War promises to Washington. At his first press conference following the coup he announced the Congo's termination of diplomatic relations with the Soviet Union and ordered all Soviet bloc personnel out of the country within forty-eight hours.

Khrushchev learned of Mobutu's coup aboard the *Baltika,* as he made his way across the Atlantic Ocean to attend the Fifteenth Session of the UN General Assembly. With little recourse left to influence events within the Congo, he launched a vicious rhetorical attack against Hammarskjöld for his spinelessness in the face of American imperialist pressure. "I spit upon the UN," he fumed. "It is not our organization!" Meanwhile, on September 16, his representative to the UN vetoed a resolution regarding the organizations' future activity in the Congo on the grounds that the exclusive role it carved for the UN would give way to neocolonial trusteeship. This was the first time the Soviet delegation vetoed a resolution that had broad support from the Afro-Asian bloc.[57] Days later, the Soviet delegation abstained from a vote in the General Assembly on a resolution promoting the continuation of vigorous

UN activity in the Congo; a resolution that had been proposed by the Ghanaian representative on behalf of sixteen Afro-Asian nations. The resolution was easily adopted 70–0, with 11 abstentions including the Soviet bloc.

Khrushchev's attack on Hammarskjöld backfired. As Kalb writes, "One of [Khrushchev's] chief reasons for coming to New York was to court the new African heads of state and to start building a socialist-neutralist alliance which would form a numerical majority in the General Assembly." But the Soviet veto and subsequent abstention on two key votes pertaining to the Congo "had isolated him from the very people he was trying to reach."[58] Instead of falling in line with the Soviet Union, the Afro-Asian bloc in the UN redoubled its support for the general secretary.

Despite these setbacks, Khrushchev refused to admit defeat in the Congo and remained determined to push forward with his plan to win over the Afro-Asian bloc. In a fiery speech before the General Assembly he blasted the current configuration of the organization's executive machinery, claiming that Hammarskjöld, chosen by the Western powers, represented their bias, a fact that had become particularly glaring in the Congo, where he had "virtually adopted the position of the colonialists."[59] The Soviet premier went on to propose that the position be abolished and replaced by a three-person executive council—a troika—representing the world's three major blocs: Western, socialist, and neutralist. Again, however, Khrushchev miscalculated. The nonaligned leaders he courted saw the troika as a threat to the survival of the UN, which, as Nkrumah stated, held "the responsibility of keeping the Cold War out [of] Africa."[60] To shore up his position, Hammarskjöld made the case to Afro-Asian members of the UN that the organization had acted impartially in the Congo. This required that he detach himself from the United States, at least publicly, not only to dispute Khrushchev's claim that he was little more than America's neo-imperial patsy but to distance himself from Washington's persistent presentation of the Congo Crisis in Cold War terms that seemed to validate Khrushchev's claims of anticommunist bias.

Back in the Congo, Lumumba spent the weeks following his ouster under house arrest in his Léopoldville residence. The UN, guaranteeing his protection as long as he remained under house arrest, sent a contingent of Ghanian blue helmets to camp out in his garden. By early October, a standoff emerged between these UN guards and a group of soldiers that Mobutu sent to arrest the former prime minister. Officials in Washington, Brussels, and Léopoldville agreed that Lumumba, because of his charismatic leadership and nationalist appeal, was as great a threat in captivity as he was in office. Mobutu's lack of legality remained a significant problem. With Lumumba in captivity, he was unable to obtain parliamentary approval to set up a new government. Thus, the United States and Belgium doubled down on their efforts to develop independent assassination plans to neutralize his influence.

With Lumumba in isolation, Antoine Gizenga took over as the official representative of his regime. By all assessments, Gizenga lacked the charisma to command widespread support in his own right, but as a proxy for the falsely imprisoned Lumumba he posed a grave threat to Mobutu and his Western backers. In early November he departed Léopoldville for Stanleyville, the capital of the eastern province of Orientale and the heart of Lumumba's movement. Declaring himself deputy prime minister, he set up a rival government under which he intended to reunite the Congo. Just a few months into its experiment with independence, the Congo was divided into four parts with competing governments in Katanga, Kasai, Léopoldville to the West, and Stanleyville to the East, each replete with its own army and rival foreign allies.

Although the governments of Katanga and Kasai were regional, the leaders of Léopoldville and Stanleyville each claimed sovereignty over the Congo in its entirety. Both regimes sought international recognition, making counterclaims to legitimacy that led to yet another tense international showdown at the UN headquarters in New York. On November 24, after weeks of tense diplomatic wrangling and heated debate in which the United States rolled out every pressure tactic it could muster, the UN General Assembly elected to seat Kasavubu and Mobutu's delegation as the official representative of the Congo with a vote of 53 in favor, 24 opposed, and 19 abstentions. It was yet another defeat for the Soviet Union, although this time it at least found itself in a respectable minority.

With this devastating international trouncing, Lumumba realized he could no longer count on UN protection. So, the night of November 27, amid torrential tropical rains, he escaped house arrest by climbing into the back seat of a Chevrolet, curling up under the feet of other passengers, and being driven past the guards posted at his gate. Mobutu soon learned of his escape and vowed to catch him before he could reach Gizenga and reinvigorate the opposition government. Lumumba's convoy made painfully slow progress, in part due to heavy rains and roadblocks, but also because he

insisted upon making frequent stops along the way to speak with his supporters. On December 1, Lumumba and his retinue were intercepted by ANC
forces as they tried to cross the Sankuru River. He was flown immediately to
Camp Hardy at Thysville, the site of the army mutiny that ignited the Congo
Crisis months before. According to foreign journalists, when he arrived at the
base, he had trouble getting out of the car and his face bore marks of beatings. With his hands tied and his trademark glasses missing, someone stuffed
a piece of paper in his mouth. Printed on it was the text of his famous independence day speech.[61]

The news of Lumumba's arrest brought the UN Security Council back
into session on December 7. Hammarskjöld, in keeping with previous statements on the matter, maintained that the Congolese authorities had the right
to arrest Lumumba, and insisted that the principle of noninterference in internal affairs—upon which UN intervention in the Congo was predicated—
limited its ability to intervene. So it was that the Congo's first prime minister
was officially a prisoner of Mobutu's regime and denied any international
protection. In Namikas's estimation, "It was one of the greatest abdications
of responsibility of [Hammarskjöld's] career."[62] His inaction, and the neo-
imperialist sympathies it implied, provoked an immediate international outcry. Nasser announced that Egypt was withdrawing from the UNOC, and a
number of pro-Lumumba African states quickly followed suit. Khrushchev
railed against Hammarskjöld and the UN, accusing the West of a plot to
"snuff out" Congolese independence.[63]

By the end of 1960, though, Moscow's ability to affect the situation in
the Congo was extremely limited, and the Soviet leader's bark far exceeded
his bite. Marginalized in the UN, which Khrushchev had come to see as a
bald agent of Western imperialism in the Congo, he resorted to withholding
Soviet assessments to pay for the UNOC in the hope of hamstringing the
operation. In the long term, this move created a budget crisis in the UN that
severely curtailed its operations for well over a decade, but it had few short-
term effects on UN activity in the Congo.

In the meantime, Khrushchev responded with great caution to Gizenga's
increasingly fervent cries for "direct Soviet interference" in support of the
Stanleyville regime. Recognizing that he had been outplayed by the West,
Khrushchev resorted to blustery rhetoric but refrained from taking any
actions that would further jeopardize peaceful coexistence. Throughout the
crisis he had maintained that Soviet military aid to the Congo was dependent

on support from other African countries, and their reluctance provided useful cover for Moscow's failure to intervene on any meaningful scale. Sudan refused a modest request to transfer East German aid to the Congo, consisting of food and medical supplies, through its territory. And a shipment of Soviet arms and ammunition sent to Ghana at the end of the year, intended for Gizenga's government, never made it to Stanleyville. US financing for Nkrumah's ambitious hydroelectric system, the Volta River Project, was enough to convince him, for the moment, to turn his back on the Soviets and support the American position in the Congo.[64] This was a prime example of the American strategy of using development aid to lure postcolonial countries into its orbit, and it served not only to bring Ghana closer and weaken Soviet influence in Africa but also to deprive Gizenga's rebel government of crucial regional support.

Even without significant Soviet aid to Gizenga's government, Mobutu's struggle to establish order continued. On January 12, the soldiers at Thysville started another revolt, and demonstrations in support of Lumumba spread throughout the country. Troops loyal to the deposed president controlled nearly half the country while Mobutu's ANC was almost useless. Devlin concluded, "Refusal to take drastic steps at this time will lead to defeat of [US] policy in Congo."[65] Belgium reached a similar assessment. Desperate to secure a regime in Léopoldville with which it could do business, Belgian officials decided to dispose of Lumumba before he could escape and mount an insurmountable challenge to Mobutu. On January 17, with Brussels' sanction, the ANC transferred Lumumba and two other political prisoners—Maurice Mpolo and Joseph Okito—to Katanga, where they were handed over to Tshombe's forces. The three prisoners were beaten mercilessly on the flight to Elizabethville, then brutalized throughout the day as they awaited their fate in an abandoned mansion near the airport. After nightfall, they were loaded into the back of a car and driven to a secluded spot where a shallow well had been dug just hours before. In attendance were a few uniformed Black policemen, Tshombe and his small entourage, and four Belgians. One by one, the prisoners were led to the edge of the well where a barrage of bullets from a firing squad mowed them down. At 9:43 p.m. on January 17, 1961, Lumumba was the last of the three prisoners to crumple backward into the pit. The world would not learn of his murder for several weeks.

Who, ultimately, was responsible for Lumumba's assassination? Ludo De Witte may have the best answer to this question: "The Belgians and the

Congolese actually killed Lumumba, but without the steps taken by Washington and the United Nations during the preceding months, the assassination never could have been carried out."[66] The United States, in an effort to forestall what it perceived to be Lumumba's plans to steer the Congo into the Soviet orbit, facilitated his ouster, then proceeded to plan for his assassination. As early as September, the CIA was considering a range of options, including an elaborate plot to poison the recently deposed prime minister's toothpaste. Although Washington played no direct role in the eventual assassination, it had long been angling for just that outcome, a fact it made clear to both Mobutu and Tshombe. The UN, for its part, undermined Lumumba's legitimacy through a peacekeeping intervention that baldly served the interests of Belgium and the United States, then facilitated his murder by refusing to protect him from the wrath of Mobutu's military junta. Hammarskjöld, like his American and Belgian counterparts, believed that the Congo's future stability depended on removing Lumumba from the scene.

It would take three weeks for the world to learn of Lumumba's fate. When the news broke on February 13, convulsions of grief and outrage reverberated around the globe. Rioting erupted in Eastern bloc cities from Warsaw, Moscow, and Belgrade to hubs of the nonaligned movement in Bombay, Jakarta, and Havana. Lumumba's martyrdom contributed to the emergence of a coordinated nonaligned faction in Africa, as a group of neutralist leaders including Nasser, Touré, and Nkrumah met in Casablanca the same month to form the African Charter of Casablanca, a precursor to the Organization for African Unity (OAU).[67] Chinese officials pulled together more than a half million people to protest. And African Americans registered their dismay with rallies and demonstrations, including one at the UN headquarters in New York during which a small group attempted unsuccessfully to disrupt a Security Council meeting. To many, the martyred Lumumba had become a symbol of the "black man's humanity struggling for recognition."[68]

Lumumba's assassination coincided with an important transfer of power in the United States, as John F. Kennedy succeeded Eisenhower in the White House on January 20, 1961. During his campaign, the new president had sharply criticized Eisenhower's inadequate Third World policy, and particularly condemned his failure to manage the Congo Crisis. Yet he, too, was uncertain about what to do in the Congo, and upon taking office he set up a Task Force to explore policy options. From the beginning, Kennedy spoke out more forcefully than the outgoing administration had against Tshombe and the Katangese secession. Yet he shared Eisenhower's determination to keep American troops out of the fray and continued to rely heavily on the UN and the CIA to carry out American policy.[69]

Moscow, having suffered a devastating blow to its prestige with Lumumba's murder and facing the harsh reality of its "relative inferiority in power-projection capabilities," realized by early 1961 that it needed to cut its losses in the Congo. Khrushchev was inclined to ratchet down East-West conflict over the issue.[70] To boot, he could not muster much enthusiasm for Gizenga, whom he considered an unreliable ally at best. And the Afro-Asian bloc was putting tremendous pressure on the UN to end the Katangese secession. Taken together, these factors persuaded the Soviet Union to abstain from voting on—or vetoing—a February 21 UN resolution authorizing the UNOC to take Katanga by force if necessary.

Kennedy, meanwhile, set out to buy time for the UN to find a workable resolution to the Katangan issue and to establish a more moderate government to replace Ileo's faltering regime in Léopoldville. An unexpected opportunity to unite the Congo's fractured politics presented itself when Gizenga, whose persistent pleas for increased Soviet military aid went unanswered, made a somewhat desperate appeal to the United States. The rebel leader fervently denied any communist leanings and presented himself as a neutralist, seeking only to do what was best for his country. This played perfectly into Washington's hands, as the United States was working with Kasavubu and the UN to plan for a July conference at Lovanium University, just outside of Léopoldville, at which parliament would be charged with electing a new government capable of bringing the elusive quality of unity to the Congo. Kennedy's Congo Task Force struck a compromise with Kasavubu to name the pro-Western Cyrille Adoula prime minister, with Gizenga agreeing to accept the post of deputy prime minister. Gizenga likely accepted the post to avoid being cut out of the new power arrangement altogether, but, despite officially dissolving his rival regime after Lovanium, he gave no indication that he intended to leave Stanleyville or cooperate with Adoula. Moscow, however, along with most of the international community including the Afro-Asian bloc, recognized Adoula's government as the legitimate successor to Lumumba's. On September 24, 1961, the official Soviet diplomatic mission arrived in Léopoldville, accompanied by others from the Soviet bloc.

The Lovanium agreements were an important step in bringing stability to the Congo. But as long as Katanga's secession continued, the new regime remained vulnerable, and its prospects for creating a unified government were limited. Tshombe's last-minute withdrawal from the talks at Lovanium prompted Hammarskjöld to abandon his last-ditch attempt to bring him to heel diplomatically. The UN launched a series of offensives in the fall of 1961 to regain Katanga, subdue the local army, and drive out the white foreign mercenaries who were helping to keep the secession alive. This first round of UN operations failed, as Tshombe and his mercenaries regrouped to Northern Rhodesia with support from Prime Minister Roy Welensky, bringing UN forces to the verge of defeat.

Kennedy walked a fine line in his support for UN operations in Congo, his credibility pulled in several directions at once. In aligning with the Afro-Asian bloc clamoring for UN action to end Katanga's secession, he drove a wedge between the United States and its NATO allies, particularly Britain, France, and, of course, Belgium. What Kennedy regarded as a critical move to restore order to the heart of Africa, they regarded as an egregious overstep by the United Nations, as it used force to interfere in what they argued was a localized crisis of decolonization. Meanwhile, JFK faced criticism from domestic political rivals who agreed with the European argument that Tshombe provided a necessary bulwark against communism. These same critics shuddered at the prospect of getting dragged into a drawn-out African conflict. Kennedy himself was furious about UN military bungling, both because the organization had failed to consult the United States on key decisions, and because the impending UN defeat threatened to pile onto the damage to his—and his country's—international prestige on the heels of the Bay of Pigs debacle just six months earlier.

A tragic accident on September 18 changed the dynamics in Congo entirely. En route to Katanga for a hard-won meeting with Tshombe, Hammarskjöld's plane crashed into the side of a mountain in Ndola, just across the border in Northern Rhodesia. Although no evidence has ever emerged to suggest foul play, conspiracy theories abound due to the timing and circumstances of the UN general secretary's demise. The gravity of Hammarskjöld's death at this critical turning point in Congo's history can hardly be overstated. Suddenly leaderless, the UN negotiated an immediate cease-fire with Tshombe.

After a politically fraught process, U Thant was selected to replace Hammarskjöld. Although committed in the long run to ending the Katangese secession, he accepted the cease-fire in the short term and worked throughout

1962 to end the secession diplomatically, to no avail. Finally, in late December, Kennedy threw US support behind a final mission to topple Tshombe's government. Operation Grand Slam succeeded in less than two weeks. On January 21, 1963, UN troops marched into Kolwezi, forcing Tshombe to flee and dispersing the mercenaries that had enabled him to stay in power.

While Washington and the UN worked to end the secession, Gizenga had been arrested, his rebellion in Stanleyville neutralized, and the secession on South Kasai brought to an end. The country that was once divided into four rival governments was now down to one, but its prospects remained as precarious as ever. Three years of civil war left a trail of ethnic rivalries, economic woes, and physical dislocation that compounded the already profound problems of decolonization that the Congo faced from its inception. The country would tackle its future challenges without interference—or help—from the UN. In June 1964, eager to wash its hands of the crisis that had riven the organization for four years, the UN finally withdrew its troops from the Congo.

Kennedy, too, was hoping to take a step back from the Congo. Fearful of being saddled with responsibility for the country as the UN phased out its presence, he aimed to support the development of a self-sufficient regime in Léopoldville. Mobutu, who promised Kennedy during a May 1963 visit to the United States that he could keep order in the Congo with the help of US aid, emerged during this period as a key figure. His fateful relationship with Washington, initiated under Eisenhower and cemented by Kennedy, would largely dictate the course of Congolese politics for the next three decades. In the immediate term, his assurances encouraged JFK to commit bilateral military aid and advisors to an ANC retraining program, an act that set the United States on a collision course with Congo's next postcolonial clash. But before that clash could take place, Kennedy was assassinated, leaving his successor, Lyndon Johnson, to deal with the fallout. LBJ was ill-equipped to deal with any foreign policy crisis, much less one in Africa. Unlike his predecessor, who saw the continent as a primary battle ground in the Cold War struggle for Third World hearts and minds, Johnson "tried to keep Africa off the agenda."[71] Yet, in short order, as he sought to put out what seemed to be an annoying brush fire, he would considerably deepen Washington's investment in the Congo's long-term stability.

Moscow, meanwhile, was licking its wounds. Khrushchev's Africa strategy, with the Congo at its core, had failed on multiple levels. Lumumba's assassination symbolized its inability to help an allied regime survive, much less thrive, a fact that was only further highlighted by Gizenga's downfall. Tshombe's defeat, accomplished without Soviet input, eliminated Moscow's last trump card to win international support for its policy in the Congo. And on November 21, 1963, Adoula's government expelled the entire Soviet diplomatic mission—for the second time in just over two years—leaving Moscow with no formal presence in the country. Perhaps most critically, Khrushchev's bid to win over Afro-Asian allies in the UN fell short, as his most promising prospects consistently supported US-backed UN policies in contravention to Soviet maneuvers. Key neutralist figures like Nkrumah and Touré moved away from the Eastern bloc and toward the West in response to carefully calculated US development aid projects like the Volta River Project in Ghana. With its shortcomings in the realms of both military aid and propaganda laid bare, the Soviet Union turned its attention away from the Congo but left the door cracked open just wide enough to allow for one last burst of activity there.

The final act of the Congo Crisis opened in 1964 with a Lumumbist rebellion, comprising two closely related movements, that started in the east and quickly spread across nearly half the country. Lumumba's close associate Pierre Mulele kicked off the revolt in Kwilu. His compatriots Christophe Gbenye and Gaston Soumialot led the Conseil National de Libération (CNL), proclaiming the People's Republic of the Congo. Referring to themselves as Simbas, the rebels promoted a vague leftist ideology, inspired by Mao's writings, which Mulele had devoured during a brief exile in China following the collapse of Lumumba's government. Devoid of a coherent ideological platform, their slogans were more anti-imperialist and anti-American than they were communist. The rebels relied on hero worship of Lumumba to unite their followers.[72] Aside from rhetorical support from Beijing, they lacked meaningful foreign backing. But the Simbas were emboldened by the magical belief that ritual behaviors combined with drugs ingested the night before battle would turn their enemies' bullets into water, rendering them invincible. ANC soldiers, who shared this belief, ran scared at the sight of crazed rebels charging with an array of antiquated weapons at their disposal. Although it was poorly organized, ill-equipped, and prone to indiscriminate violence and pillaging, the Lumumbist movement spread like wildfire, laying bare the Léopoldville regime's impotence in the countryside.

The rebellion lured the Cold War superpowers into conflict over the Congo one last time. When U Thant predictably denied UN help putting down the rebels, LBJ gradually stepped in to assume a more active role in combat operations in the Congo than either of his predecessors had been willing to undertake. The Soviet Union, nursing wounds from its previous failures in the country, was reluctant to intervene on behalf of the rebel movement. But the simmering Sino-Soviet rivalry would force its hand. By 1963, Mao openly condemned the Soviet Union for forsaking national liberation movements in favor of peaceful coexistence with the West. With China openly backing the Simbas and stepping up its game in Africa more generally, Moscow was convinced to provide the rebels with token amounts of aid.

Back in Léopoldville, Kasavubu and Adoula competed for control of the central government. Kasavubu gained the upper hand by securing parliamentary approval of a new constitution that negated the Lovanium agreement. In early July, he pushed Adoula out of the government to make way for Tshombe, whom he invited to form a transitional government. There is no evidence to suggest that the United States knew or approved of Kasavubu's plans to revive Tshombe's political career in this way. But the former leader of Katanga's secessionist movement and key player in Lumumba's murder did have strong support in Belgium, and he brought with him a Rolodex of mercenary support. The mercenaries deployed to Katanga by white minority–rule African states gradually dissolved in 1962 as Conakat's defeat at the hands of the United Nations became inevitable. However, they regrouped to eastern Angola and northern Rhodesia and, in 1962 and 1963, Tshombe paid for a mercenary force to be built up and maintained for future use in Congo. In 1964, he was able to recall these troops from exile to help suppress the Lumumbist Simba rebellion in eastern Congo.[73] While keeping a tight lid on its involvement with mercenary forces in the hope of avoiding a public relations disaster, LBJ's government recognized Tshombe's government immediately.

Less than a month after Tshombe took office, the CNL Simbas took Stanleyville, raping, maiming, and murdering anyone they suspected of having ties to the West. They took hundreds of Europeans and the staff of the US consulate hostage, prompting Belgium and the United States to initiate large-scale military operations: Operation Ommegang and Operation Dragon Rouge, respectively. The United States enlisted support from anti-Castro Cuban refugees, whom the CIA and the Defense Department trained to conduct aerial missions using US aircraft.

The crisis reached its crescendo on November 18, when Simba forces marched the American hostages to Lumumba's monument in Stanleyville and began preparing them for ritual sacrifice. LBJ hesitated at first, hoping to buy time for Operation Ommegang—a Belgian-led military force composed of Cuban exiles, the Katangan gendarmerie, white mercenaries, and ANC soldiers—to reach Stanleyville. But on November 23, he decided he could wait no longer. Johnson authorized a hostage rescue mission that eventually freed two thousand Europeans as well as the American consulate staffers. The Simbas responded by opening fire on their hostages, killing approximately one hundred Europeans in the process. The number of Congolese killed in the operation has never been determined.[74]

While Johnson claimed that the airdrop of paratroopers was purely a humanitarian operation, it was in fact a military operation aimed above all at defeating the rebels. Washington's pretense of concern for the Congolese was flimsy, at best. "The need for the rescue," writes Namikas, "showed the ineffectiveness of the administration's crisis management and the failure to find real solutions."[75] By and large, though, few in the United States questioned the humanitarian smokescreen. LBJ faced criticism from some in the African American community for his support for Tshombe and his use of white mercenaries. Internationally, protests against America's brazen intervention into the Congo's civil conflict erupted throughout Africa, Asia, and the Soviet bloc. By this time Khrushchev had been replaced by Leonid Brezhnev, whose Politburo adopted a much more cautious approach to national liberation movements. Even so, Moscow continued its policy of condemning Western aggression in the Congo and quietly supporting the rebels.

After the American intervention, rebel leaders scattered across the east, and Léopoldville gradually gained ground, but the civil war raged on. The United States supported the ANC's campaign against the rebels, proving its willingness to supply military aid to embattled African regimes. The Soviet Union and China competed to court rebel leaders and their allies, while the Simbas received a temporary boost from an unlikely source. In the spring of 1965, the Argentine Marxist revolutionary Che Guevara arrived in the Congo with a small force of Afro-Cubans to aid Simba guerrilla leader Laurent-Désiré Kabila. But Guevara, who saw Africa as imperialism's soft underbelly, quickly became disillusioned with the rebel's weak leadership.[76] He grew frustrated with what he would later describe as a disorganized movement, marked by internecine quarrels and little will to fight for the ultimate cause of national liberation. Making things even more difficult, white mercenaries operating with the support of the CIA and its team of anti-Castro

Cuban pilots kept him under close surveillance and thwarted his moves at every turn. Eight months after setting foot in the Congo, stricken by dysentery, asthma, and intense disdain for his Congolese comrades, Guevara returned to Cuba with his tail between his legs.

The final months of 1965 brought ANC successes in the antirebel campaign but also a growing rivalry between Kasavubu and Tshombe. Kasavubu pulled a familiar trick, dismissing Tshombe just as he had dismissed Lumumba, and naming Everiste Kimba to replace him as prime minister. But he was once again stymied by parliament, which, in its first session since the summer of 1963, blocked Kimba's nomination. Unfazed, Kasavubu renominated Kimba over Tshombe's objections. On November 24, 1965, Mobutu repeated his own bit of history, announcing that he would end the impasse by taking over control of the country in what amounted to his second bloodless military coup in five years. Some evidence suggests he made this move at US urging, and it was certainly to Washington's relief. Mobutu immediately canceled elections and declared himself president for five years of a "regime of exception."[77] He would, in fact, rule a bungling US-backed dictatorship for more than thirty years, bringing great suffering to the people of the Congo and contributing to regional instability that would erupt into staggering violence after the end of the Cold War. But for the moment, the international community, weary of five years of crisis in the Congo, issued a muted response. Even Nkrumah was willing to give Mobutu a chance. Of course, the Soviet Union condemned the coup, but in bland terms that conveyed its resignation to American ascendance in the Congo. The US victory was pyrrhic, attained only by marrying itself to Mobutu's abusive regime.

Few episodes highlight the interconnections between the Cold War and decolonization as clearly as the Congo Crisis. The intervention of former colonial powers, the superpowers, and the UN into the crisis infused the Congo's civil conflict with ideological and military characteristics that subverted the country's—and indeed much of Africa's—political and economic development. It significantly increased the tension between the communist bloc and the West while also laying bare the divisions within each of those camps. Controversy over UN intervention in the Congo revealed deep international conflicts over the role of peacekeeping missions in the decolonization process and uncovered the challenges those missions would face. Although the Congo Crisis helped transform the UN from an instrument of American influence to a more independent international organization, it also made clear that the

On August 4, 1970, US president Richard Nixon points out one of Washington's landmarks from the balcony overlooking the South Lawn of the White House to Lt. Gen. Joseph Mobutu, president of the Congo Republic (*left*) and his wife. US First Lady Pat Nixon stands in the background at right. (AP Photo)

organization would not be able to manage Africa's crises of decolonization, especially given the budget crisis generated by Soviet nonpayment.[78] The memory of the Congo Crisis hamstrung UN peacekeeping operations for decades, as Soviet and American delegates would not agree on another major mission until the 1980s, by which time the Cold War was on the wane.

Soviet and American diplomats' mutual misunderstanding of each other's intentions and capabilities was one of many hallmarks of the Cold War on display in the Congo. Each viewed the other as an imperialist power bent on world domination and saw itself as acting defensively to stave off predatory aggression. The Soviet Union concluded that the United Sates was determined to establish neocolonial control in the Congo and saw its own support for legitimate African nationalists like Lumumba and his comrades as a means of gaining influence on a continent from which it had been excluded under the old imperial order. Washington, meanwhile, concluded that the Soviets were scheming to manipulate vulnerable local leaders like Lumumba as part of a broader plan to takeover of the Congo en route to dominating all of Africa. American officials thus considered their intervention into the Congo Crisis to be a defense not only of Western interests but of the future of democracy in Africa. As was all too common in the Cold War, the United States relied on this worldview to justify a series of policies that quashed democratic development in favor of strongmen who could exclude communist influence.

As a result, American soft power took a serious hit. American policymakers misapprehended African and Asian fears of neocolonialism, fears that became a harsh reality with the Congo Crisis and Lumumba's assassination. Committed to presenting the Soviet Union as the greatest neocolonial threat, they failed to recognize the extent to which their own anticommunist policies came off as neocolonial machinations in ways that not only diminished US prestige in the Third World but also drove nonaligned leaders to depend more deeply on Moscow. This had direct ramifications for how nonaligned figures viewed American involvement elsewhere in the Third World, most notably in Vietnam. As Robert Rakove has argued, "Rising disenchantment with U.S. policies in Africa spurred a growing willingness in 1964 to describe Washington's growing entanglement in South Vietnam as a colonial project."[79] Thus, the global antiwar movement that would erupt surrounding the US war in Vietnam was shaped significantly by actions carried out in the Congo.

Although they may not have always succeeded, both Washington and Moscow were intensely aware throughout the crisis of the need to limit their own liability and protect their own credibility and prestige. This was not only to avert open conflict with each other, as they simultaneously pursued peaceful coexistence and adversarial policies in the Third World, but also to avoid damaging their larger Cold War projects. Characteristically, Moscow and Washington displayed during the Congo Crisis an overriding preference to work through proxies or with the cover of international support in an effort the prevent the Cold War from turning hot in the heart of Africa. Above all, the United States worked to persuade the United Nations to do its bidding. At times it turned to Belgium and other NATO allies, only intervening directly through Operation Dragon Rouge when it seemed impossible to obtain its objectives any other way. Moscow, for its part, made every effort to secure the cooperation of African leaders in its interventions into the Congo and to win the support of the

Afro-Asian bloc in the UN. Moreover, whenever possible it sought to channel material aid through bloc allies like Czechoslovakia and East Germany.

The lack of strategic parity between the Soviet Union and the United States in the Congo was also typical of the larger Cold War. In the post–World War II era, the United States built a sprawling system of military bases around the world that the Soviet Union could not rival. Its close relationship with Belgium, a NATO ally, and its history of economic, cultural, and missionary involvement with the Congo lent Washington a great deal of influence from the outset, influence that was enhanced greatly by its strong hand in the UN decision-making process. Washington invested significantly more capital in support of its objectives in the Congo than Moscow was able to muster. The Soviet Union's ability to project its power was inferior in all respects, and its leaders acted cautiously throughout the crisis. Moscow, which offered only token assistance to Lumumba and his revolutionary successors, failed to win the support of the Afro-Asian bloc in the UN and fell short in its efforts to rally regional support for Congolese leftists. The end result was a decisive victory for the United States with the installation of pro-Western General Mobutu in 1965. Yet Soviet intervention in the Congo cannot be deemed a total failure. Khrushchev succeeded in weakening Western popularity in much of Africa, and his ability to keep the Americans at bay for five years without a major military or economic commitment enhanced Soviet prestige in the decolonizing and postcolonial world.[80]

Ironically, then, the key lesson that the Soviet Union took away from this foray into Congolese affairs was the need to ramp up its conventional military power in the Third World, where the strategic dispersal of economic and technical aid no longer seemed sufficient.[81] Indeed, with UN activism curtailed, both Cold War superpowers would thenceforth rely much more heavily on channeling direct military to aid strongmen as they pursued their objectives in decolonizing and postcolonial countries.[82] The Congo Crisis was thus a key turning point in the militarization of the superpower conflict in the Third World, where Cold War ideologies and weapons would fuel increasingly violent conflicts in the coming decades.

The consequences of Cold War intervention in the Congo Crisis had profound ramifications not just for the Congo but for all of Africa. Mobutu, who renamed the country Zaire in 1971, ruled his military dictatorship with an iron fist and served as a template for the military dictatorships that would dominate postcolonial Africa's political landscape. Clinging to power by stoking fear in the hearts of his enemies, Mobutu brutally executed his former Lumumbist rivals. He is rumored to have murdered Tshombe, who reportedly died of a heart attack in his prison cell at the age of forty-eight, a claim many find incredible. In the early days of his thirty-year rule, Mobutu's army quashed idealistic student movements so violently that they would never return, and implemented repressive cultural policies that included banning Western music and clothing in an effort to enforce a "traditional" Zairian culture. His regime profited mightily from the skyrocketing price of copper during the Vietnam War, but rampant corruption, gross mismanagement of the national economy, and Mobutu's own flamboyant excesses crippled Zaire. Mobutu found his country subject to IMF stabilization plans in the 1970s, and by the 1980s he faced much more extreme structural adjustment plans. But these interventions did little to curb the nation's rampant inflation and staggering national debt.

Through these trials, the United States refused to abandon its strongman in the Congo. Mobutu provided a bastion of noncommunism in a sea of communist and socialist experiments, including those in Angola, Congo-Brazzaville, Uganda, Tanzania, Zambia, and elsewhere farther afield in Africa. As one CIA official put it, "Mobutu is a bastard, but at least he's our bastard."[83] In the decades following the Congo Crisis, the United States, the Soviet Union, and, to an increasing extent, China and Cuba would stoke Africa's violent conflicts, supplying rival factions with immense firepower and ideological rigidity. Mobutu managed to cling to power until 1997, when Rwanda ousted him during an invasion designed to stop cross-border raids by Hutu militias entrenched in Zairian refugee camps. Within a year of his successor, Laurent-Désiré Kabila, taking the reins, the country was swept up in the Great African War, involving nine countries and twenty-five armed groups. A formal ceasefire in 2003 did little to stem the conflict, which by 2008 resulted in more than 5 million deaths and more than 2 million refugees. The Cold War in Africa, inaugurated by the Congo Crisis, halted the region's political and economic development, saddling it instead with kleptocratic military dictatorships and leaving it a state of perpetual underdevelopment and semi-permanent war. Africa's process of decolonization, swept up as it was in the Cold War, has yet to be completed. The continent remains in many ways subject to the cultural, political, racial, and economic power imbalances between North and South that were established during the colonial era and then reinforced by superpower intervention in postcolonial crises.

5

Vietnam

Cold War Crucible

Vietnam was the site of the Cold War's greatest, most violent, and most prolonged collision with decolonization. Over the course of thirty years, militarized conflict in Indochina claimed the lives of approximately 55,000 French, 58,000 Americans, and as many as 4 million Vietnamese. This does not count the Cambodians—maybe more than 2 million—who died in the Khmer Rouge genocide that grew largely out of conditions generated by the war in Vietnam. The fighting began as a war for independence—to wrest Vietnam free from the grips of French imperialism—but soon developed also into a Cold War proxy war. Mao's 1949 victory in the Chinese Civil War, and the ensuing outbreak of war in Korea the following year, transformed Southeast Asia into a top strategic priority for both Moscow and Washington. The United States, assuming from retreating French imperialists the burden to prevent the spread of communism, ensured that Vietnam's anticolonial war would morph into the Cold War's hottest battleground.

The Vietnam War was the most significant—and bloody—conflict between the United States and the communist camp, but it also spelled the undoing of communist solidarity in the Third World.[1] Competition for leadership of Vietnam's revolution would fuel the Sino-Soviet split, putting the final nail in the coffin of an alliance that had always been marked more by conflict than friendship. The United States suffered a humiliating loss in Vietnam—one that undermined the faith of its public in American power and virtue—but simultaneously took advantage of fragmentation in the communist camp to undertake a major strategic realignment. With its diplomatic credibility and prestige in tatters, Washington made overtures to both China and the Soviet Union, enabling it simultaneously to check Soviet power and advance Soviet-American diplomatic initiatives, including critical nuclear arms control agreements. Meanwhile, Hanoi's victory seemed to signal to the rest of the decolonizing world that a model for independence without submission to superpower direction was, indeed, possible. It was a David and Goliath story that fundamentally transformed geostrategic configurations and revolutionary paradigms.

It all began on September 2, 1945, as Vietnam's revolutionary icon, Ho Chi Minh, clambered to the podium in Hanoi's Ba Dinh Square to deliver a declaration of independence for the new Democratic Republic of Vietnam (DRV). His speech was the centerpiece of an independence day celebration that followed a swift campaign to overthrow Japanese occupation forces waged by the Viet Minh, the dominant nationalist organization among many that had proliferated across Vietnam in recent decades. Anticolonial activism kicked off in the 1910s and 1920s with a vibrant movement known as the Reform Generation. Its leading lights, Phan Boi Chau and Phan Chu Trinh, decried the dehumanization of their countrymen under French rule and called for wholesale reform of exploitative and brutal French colonial practices. Although Trinh's calls for gradual, moderate reforms of the existing system contrasted with Chau's embrace of violent and immediate anticolonial resistance, both demanded an end to corvée labor, reforms to abusive penal systems and tax codes, and greater educational and economic opportunities for Vietnamese people. Both of these influential early critics of French colonialism subscribed to Herbert Spencer's notion of social Darwinism, which seemed to offer a powerful explanation for the weaknesses in traditional Vietnamese society that had rendered it vulnerable to French domination.[2] By the 1930s, social Darwinist thinking, and the Reform Generation itself, would give way to more radical anticolonial movements. But those movements, too, drew heavily on Western thought, particularly Marxism-Leninism.

Ho was at the vanguard of this new wave of radicalism. A sojourner who spent much of his early life outside of Vietnam, he had participated as a founding member of the French Communist Party in 1921. For Ho, the great appeal of communism was its avowed support for anticolonial movements. Indeed, he only turned to the Soviet Union and its revolutionary model after being spurned in 1919 by President Woodrow Wilson, the great American exponent of self-determination, at the Versailles peace conference. By the summer of 1923, Ho made his way to Moscow to become a low-level employee of the Comintern before heading to China, where he would stay until forced out by Chiang Kai-shek's forces in 1927. All the while, his over-riding commitment was to Vietnam's independence movement. Convinced that undeveloped colonial countries were not ready for socialism, he envisioned a two-stage revolution, first nationalist and antifeudal and then socialist. Moreover, he remained committed to a united front approach designed to include as many nationalist elements as possible in pursuit of independence.

In 1925, Ho took the lead in founding the Revolutionary Youth League, the precursor to the Vietnamese Communist Party (VCP), established in 1930. The VCP's initial party program eschewed the radical class struggle advocated by the Comintern, earning Ho a healthy dose of scorn and suspicion from the Kremlin that he would never really shake. Moscow considered him too "petty bourgeois" and nationalist, and insufficiently dedicated to class struggle.[3] The VCP would soon change its name to the Indochinese Communist Party (ICP) on Moscow's orders, largely as a means of subordinating Ho's nationalist ambitions, but his penchant for united front politics would, time and again, undermine the trust of his communist patrons.

Meanwhile, as Vietnamese anticolonial movements across the board suffered brutal crackdowns at the hands of French colonial administrators in the early 1930s, the ICP gained ascendance over its rivals like the more conservative Viet Nam Quoc Dan Dang (VNQDD). This was due not only to persistent activism outside the country but also to effective political organizing in colonial prisons. Faced with a wave of violent resistance in 1930, French administrators clamped down on rebels, locking up record numbers of Vietnamese political prisoners. Yet, far from accomplishing the goal of crushing anticolonial resistance, Party cells thrived in poorly policed common areas where prisoners festered, enabling them to build strength while waiting out this dark, repressive period. Imprisonment enabled a generation of Vietnamese communists to build revolutionary solidarity, establish prestige, and swell their ranks with fellow-convicts who, infuriated by the injustices of the colonial legal system, were ripe for conversion. By the second half of the decade, as France embraced Popular Front politics, political prisoners were released in droves. As a result, historian Peter Zinoman writes, "the years between 1936 and 1939 were among the most exuberant periods of anticolonial activism in the history of French Indochina."[4]

During World War II, Ho dug into the deep well of anticolonial fervor to organize the Viet Minh, a party led by communists but comprising a range of nationalists, including student activists and members of the

VNQDD. This ostensibly united front organization originated across the Chinese border, where it met in the waning years of the Pacific War with members of the American Office of Strategic Services (OSS), the precursor to the CIA, to collaborate on fighting Japanese forces in Indochina. In March 1945, Japanese occupation forces staged a coup to oust Vichy French colonial administrators whom they had left in place for most of the war. When Japan was driven to surrender just five months later, the well-organized Viet Minh were quick to capitalize on its retreat. Seizing control of administrative offices in Hanoi and other parts of northern Vietnam, the party immediately built goodwill by distributing rice to peasants suffering in the throes of a great famine. Ho, maneuvering as ever to build widespread support for his new government, downplayed the Viet Minh's communist associations, going so far as to dissolve the ICP. A necessary move to consolidate DRV power, this would only reinforce Moscow's suspicion of Ho, with grave consequences for his government's diplomacy and composition in coming years.

This juncture in Vietnam's revolution points to a distinctive quality of Ho Chi Minh's: his elusiveness. Throughout his life, he carefully cultivated an enigmatic image in service of political expediency, making it nearly impossible to put a finger on the real Ho. To his foreign patrons, he presented himself as an internationalist committed to class struggle and socialist revolution. To his countrymen, he was as an austere man of the people, an avuncular Confucian devoted to the cause of national independence and the reclamation of Vietnamese tradition. As Hanoi's communist leaders radicalized over the ensuing decades, they would rely upon these conflicting but convenient myths of their revolutionary father to legitimize their rule at home while also courting much-needed diplomatic support.

As he declared independence for Vietnam, Ho's hopes for international support were not confined to the communist camp. The slight, goateed paragon of Vietnamese nationalism eschewed the Western suits and ties worn by most of his colleagues that day, sticking instead to what would become his trademark ensemble of a faded khaki jacket, high white collar, and white rubber sandals.[5] Yet his sartorial choices by no means signaled a rejection of Western influence. The opening lines of his speech borrowed heavily from the American "Declaration of Independence" and the French "Rights of Man and the Citizen" in equal parts homage and diplomatic appeal. Contrasting the principles of life, liberty, and the pursuit of happiness to more than eighty years of French colonial oppression, Ho challenged leaders in

Paris and Washington to live up to their stated ideals by respecting Vietnam's newly claimed autonomy. Listening in the audience were four of the OSS officers who had helped the Viet Minh defeat Japanese forces. The Viet Minh had asked one, Archimedes Patty, to join them on the platform. He declined, but as he listened from the front row, it seemed at times as if Ho was speaking directly to him.[5]

By no means was Washington's hostility toward Ho and the Viet Minh a given at this point, communism notwithstanding. Throughout the war, President Franklin Roosevelt's talk of self-determination and trusteeship for Indochina, among other colonial possessions, had boosted the hopes of Vietnamese nationalists. With World War II just coming to a close, concerns about a brewing conflict between the Soviet Union and the United States did not yet extend to Southeast Asia. However, FDR's successor, Harry Truman, did not share the wartime president's passion for the cause of anticolonialism. Under this new leadership, the dynamics of the emerging Cold War in Europe, and its implications for Washington's relationship with critical French and British allies, would prevent the United States from responding to Ho's calls to support Vietnamese independence. Ho's declaration thus signaled the beginning rather than the end of struggle, the opening salvo en route to three decades of revolution and war in Vietnam.

France emerged from the national humiliation of World War II determined to reassert its imperial grandeur. Nowhere was more critical to that project than Indochina, the nation's most economically valuable colony—a rival to Britain's jewel in the crown, India—which entitled it to a major role in Far Eastern affairs.[6] Troubled by America's rhetorical commitment to anticolonialism, French officials teamed up with their British counterparts to dissuade Washington from meddling with their imperial holdings and to persuade it to actively support their war against the Viet Minh. Scornful as they were of French imperialism, American officials were far more concerned with the postwar disposition of Europe. Rising tensions with the Soviet Union over the postwar settlement made the United States reluctant to do anything that would alienate France, which it saw increasingly as an important ally in reconstructing a vibrant, noncommunist western Europe as a bulwark against Soviet expansionism. Moreover, the intensification of China's civil war encouraged Washington to seek stability in other parts of Asia.[7] Therefore, as France marched to war with the Viet Minh, the United States withheld formal support but would not stand in its ally's way. For the next few years, Washington would sit uncomfortably on the fence, torn between its commitment to anticolonialism on one hand and the North Atlantic alliance on the other.

As per the agreement reached at the Potsdam Conference (July 17–August 2, 1945) Britain was charged with accepting Japan's surrender in southern Vietnam, while China oversaw the process in the north. Not only did the British contingent bring with it a detachment of French troops, it refused to deal with the DRV-affiliated committee that had taken power in the south.[8] Shortly upon arrival, French forces unleashed a spate of violence aimed at reclaiming control of Vietnam. They quickly drove most of the resistance into the countryside. While his southern revolutionary counterparts called for war, the ever-cautious Ho sought to stave off a violent conflict by entering into negotiations with French representatives in Hanoi. Foreshadowing what was to come for the next three decades, the key sticking point was the fate of southern Vietnam, the French colony of Cochinchina. DRV negotiators wanted nothing less than national unification and complete independence, whereas France was determined to retain control of the south. Ho reached a preliminary accord with his French counterpart, Jean Sainteny, in March 1946, but the settlement collapsed before the year's end. In November, while Ho worked desperately to find a diplomatic solution, French forces seized the northern port city of Haiphong. By mid-December, the Vietnamese were committed to fighting a war.

Ho and his comrades retreated to their cave at Pac Bo in northwestern Vietnam, along the Chinese border, to coordinate the "Resistance Against French Colonial Aggression." Their strategy followed closely on Mao's "people's war" doctrine, incorporating a three-pronged strategy of military action, political action—or propaganda—and diplomatic action. In the short term, Viet Minh military activity made little dent in France's superior military strength, but it just managed to stave off defeat, buying time to make progress on the other two fronts.[9] By 1948, the war ground to a stalemate that would persist for several years. The French, with their superior firepower, controlled the cities and a number of fortified posts throughout the countryside, while the Viet Minh laid claim to the rural areas in between.

Faced with domestic political and economic crises, France was pressed to fight its increasingly unpopular *sale guerre* (dirty war) on the cheap. Seeking to break the stalemate without provoking additional domestic political backlash at the war's cost in francs and French lives, Paris pursued a policy known as *jaunissement* (yellowing). Especially in the deep south, where early Viet Minh efforts to consolidate control after the August Revolution had devolved into campaigns of terror and violence against localized nationalist groups like the Hoa Hao, Cao Dai, and Binh Xuyen, France found a number of willing Vietnamese partners to aid the fight against the Viet Minh. By exacerbating a low-level civil war that existed in southern Vietnam even prior to the outbreak of war between France and the DRV, these alliances set the stage for nationalist conflict that would continue after France's eventual departure.[10] For the time being, the stalemate persisted.

Desperate for Washington to bankroll its war, France carried out a sustained diplomatic campaign to convince the United States that the regional threat posed by Ho's communist forces demanded a response calibrated to the Cold War. Britain, motivated by concern for the fate of its own nearby colony in Malaya, joined forces with France to persuade leaders in Washington that the war in Indochina was not an elective one of colonial reconquest but a necessary front in the struggle against Soviet expansion. Not only did they need to convince American officials that Indochina was of strategic importance in the context of the Cold War, they had to overcome American objections to France's baldly imperialist intentions there. In 1949, to this end, France negotiated with Vietnam's former emperor Bao Dai to reach the Élysée Accords, which promised eventual independence to Vietnam, Laos, and Cambodia under the canopy of the French Union and put Bao Dai in charge of the newly formed State of Vietnam (SVN). The so-called Bao Dai solution served several purposes. It created an alternative government to Ho's with which France could claim to negotiate in good faith. It appealed to noncommunist Vietnamese nationalists who sought independence but not under uncontested DRV authority. And, perhaps most importantly, it presented to the United States the possibility of supporting France's war in Indochina without falling in line with the forces of imperialism that the tides of history were turning so rapidly against. While the Bao Dai solution did lay the groundwork for later US aid to France's war effort, Washington recognized the former emperor for the puppet he was and continued for the time being to steer clear of direct involvement in Indochina.

DRV diplomats also encountered one frustration after another. Most significantly, Soviet leaders, wary of Ho's revolutionary mettle and reluctant to alienate left-leaning French leaders, withheld support for the Viet Minh.[11] It was not until January 1950, when the newly ascendant People's Republic of

China (PRC) announced its formal diplomatic recognition of the DRV, that the Soviet Union followed suit. The self-proclaimed world leader of socialist revolution would not be upstaged. "Chinese communists," writes historian Christopher Goscha, "probably played the determining role in saving Vietnamese communists from international marginalization at this critical juncture."[12] And they also made the first move to transform Vietnam into a central focus of the Cold War. It was the Chinese and Soviet diplomatic recognitions of the DRV that pushed the United States to pull the trigger and recognize Bao Dai's SVN. Within a few months the floodgates of Southeast Asia's Cold War would burst open.

Truman initiated direct US involvement in Vietnam against the backdrop of a fresh wave of anticommunist hysteria on the home front, spurred by a junior senator from Wisconsin. Joseph McCarthy punched above his weight in the Senate by exploiting fears arising from the twin shocks of 1949: the Soviet Union's successful nuclear test and the "loss" of China to Mao's communist forces. Over the summer of 1950, the outbreak of war in Korea seemed to validate McCarthy's apocalyptic predictions about rapid Soviet military advances in the face of American weakness, not to mention the alleged complicity of Truman's State Department. Facing a Cold War that seemed to be spiraling out of control at home and abroad, Truman adopted a new national security strategy: NSC-68. This new doctrine expanded the focus of Washington's containment strategy from key strategic sites in Europe to the entire world and shifted its methods away from economic manipulation to military might. By the middle of 1950, following this new strategic outlook, the United States was firmly committed to opposing the DRV on Cold War grounds. As historian Mark Lawrence has put it, by this time, "the period of possibility," during which the United States could have avoided direct involvement in Vietnam, came to a close, as "patterns of thought laid in place in 1950 drove American policy uninterruptedly to 1965 and beyond."[13]

In the short term, the internationalization of the First Indochina War did little to disrupt the stalemate on the ground. Washington steadily increased its support for France's war. Meanwhile, with Chinese backing, the DRV made a dramatic shift from guerrilla tactics to conventional warfare. For the first time, Hanoi's forces employed mass-combat methods to score unexpected victories against the French. But overall, the battle lines did not change; with the influx of aid, materiel, and advice from China and the

United States, they simply grew bloodier and more destructive. In 1951, as Bao Dai's SVN instituted a draft, pitting it directly against DRV recruitment efforts, the conflict became more deeply marked by internecine violence. That same year, the DRV shifted deeper into the communist camp, as Ho publicly admitted it had been a mistake to dissolve the ICP and announced the formation of the Vietnam Workers' Party (VWP) to supplant the Viet Minh. Desperate as he was to secure full support from both China and the Soviet Union, Ho also worried about the deepening civil war, the internationalization of the conflict, and the radicalization of the Vietnamese revolution that followed on China's involvement. Perhaps even more deeply concerned about the prospect of direct American military intervention in Vietnam, Ho sought a diplomatic solution to the war.

Paris was also quickly growing weary of the fighting. Faced with domestic political crises and unrest in their prized Algerian colony, French officials who just a few years earlier had worked assiduously to convince the United States that Indochina was too strategically important to let go were coming to see it as a domestic political and economic liability. In October 1953, newly elected Prime Minister Joseph Laniel announced his intention to seek an "honorable exit" from Indochina, which would involve accepting a negotiated settlement. The big powers, inspired by the Korean armistice and the promise of improved superpower relations stemming from Stalin's death— and his successors' "peace offensive"—agreed to host an international conference on Indochina following the talks about Korea that were already scheduled to take place in Geneva the following spring.

DRV military officials, far from biding their time until the negotiations could begin, embarked on a series of bold military initiatives in late 1953 designed to outmaneuver France's aggressive new military strategy known as the Navarre Plan. President Dwight D. Eisenhower's administration had agreed to pay $385 million to implement the brainchild of Gen. Henri Navarre, which called for strengthening SVN armed forces, pacifying Cochinchina, and preventing enemy incursions into neighboring Laos, all in preparation to annihilate the Viet Minh by attacking their strongholds in the North. DRV forces, led by Gen. Vo Nguyen Giap, had other plans. Giap and his troops focused their efforts on the valley of Dien Bien Phu in northwestern Vietnam, where the French had established a garrison designed to choke off DRV cross-border operations. In November 1953, French forces began parachuting into the valley, where they would soon number 12,000 strong.

As soon as the big powers confirmed that the Geneva Conference on Indo-china would open the following May, DRV officials turned their full attention to destroying the garrison in the hope of claiming a clear military victory that would carry over to the negotiating table. "The remote, heretofore unimportant valley," writes historian Pierre Asselin, "suddenly became the fulcrum on which the DRVN's prospects for success in Geneva—and in the Indochina War—rested."[14]

Chinese assistance figured heavily into DRV capabilities at Dien Bien Phu. No longer tied up with the war in Korea, Beijing diverted significant materiel and advisory support to Giap's contingent. Many of the small arms and artillery supplied by the Chinese were of US vintage, captured from rival nationalist forces in the Chinese Civil War and from South Korean and United Nations forces in the Korean War. This, combined with a detachment of specialized technicians, advisors, and artillery crews sent to train Viet Minh forces in the new weapons, and a pair of Chinese generals to consult with Giap on strategy, boosted Vietnamese prospects considerably. Equally critical was the work of more than a quarter million *dan cong* (patriotic workers) conscripted to supply and sustain the 45,000 Vietnamese troops deployed to take down the French garrison. They hauled up the mountain surrounding the valley everything from food and water to heavy artillery weighing nearly 5,000 pounds each.

Giap's initial strategy, "lightning battle, lightning victory," called for an all-out assault on the French designed to bring them to their knees in as little as three days. However, he was forced to reconsider at the last minute when one of his men, possessing information about the timing and nature of the attack, was captured. He shifted to a new strategy of "steady attacks, steady advances." This approach would take longer but seemed more likely to yield the victory he had promised Ho. On March 13, Giap launched his assault, scoring swift victories against the French but at the calamitous cost to his own forces of 2,000 killed and 7,000 wounded. To avoid such an unsustainable casualty rate, he pursued a "protracted war" approach, ordering his troops to encircle French forces slowly while defending themselves with the heavy artillery the *dan cong* had previously delivered to the mountain ridges surrounding the valley.

France was on the ropes. Desperate, Paris sent army chief of staff Paul Ély to Washington to plead for American intervention in the form of Operation Vulture, a massive aerial assault on the Viet Minh positions and supply lines.[15] The United States, which by this point was footing nearly 80 percent of the war's cost, was deeply invested in French success in Indochina. Yet Eisenhower reacted coolly to Ély's proposal. Having just extracted American troops from Korea and announced his New Look strategy, which was designed to reduce defense spending by ramping up nuclear deterrence, he was reluctant to commit US troops once again to combat halfway around the world. He therefore agreed to intervene only in concert with other powers, especially Britain, and with congressional approval. However, neither the Brits nor his own legislative body assented to this "United Action." On April 8, then, Washington relayed to Paris its decision to stay out of the battle at Dien Bien Phu. Secretary of State John Foster Dulles supposedly softened the blow by offering two nuclear weapons for use against the Viet Minh. Whether or not this was true, the bombs never materialized.[16]

On May 7, 1954, the day before the Geneva Conference on Indochina opened, French forces at Dien Bien Phu surrendered to the Viet Minh. In military terms, the victory was indecisive, as the balance of forces across Vietnam remained stalemated, if not slightly favorable to the French. But it delivered a striking psychological advantage to Ho's delegation at Geneva. The Viet Minh had just dealt a humiliating defeat to France in the eyes of a rapt international audience and ensured that Paris would negotiate an end to the war that no longer had its people's support. Yet the Viet Minh victory came at great human cost. Giap's forces suffered approximately 7,900 killed and more than 15,000 wounded, not counting the thousands of *dan cong* who died from disease and malnutrition. "No other war of decolonization in the twentieth century," writes historian Christopher Goscha, "ever reached the level of deployable violence demonstrated in this valley floor between March and May 1954."[17] Viet Minh morale was at low ebb. The battle had taken its toll on Vietnamese communist leadership, provoking a rash of infighting, and on Viet Minh fighting forces, who were exhausted physically and psychologically. Remarkable as it was, the Vietnamese victory at Dien Bien Phu was nowhere near as glorious as Vietnam Workers' Party (VWP) propaganda would later make it out to be.

Battle-weary DRV officials were, like their French counterparts, eager to negotiate an end to the fighting. On top of concerns about morale and fighting strength, Ho shared with his Chinese and Soviet patrons concerns about provoking the United States to enter into a wider conflict. Ho, cautious as ever, entered the Geneva Conference bent on reaching a deal with France.

His DRV delegation, headed by like-minded Pham Van Dong, met with representatives from Britain, France, the Soviet Union, the PRC, the SVN, and the pro-French governments of Laos and Cambodia. The United States dispatched a delegation but, citing its refusal to negotiate directly with the PRC representatives, declined to participate formally. With both sides desperate to negotiate a cease-fire, but neither willing to bend on key provisions, the talks immediately stalled.

It would take more than two months to hash out the Agreement on the Cessation of Hostilities in Vietnam, signed on July 21, 1954. The settlement divided the country at the seventeenth parallel, established a demilitarized zone between the two halves, provided for a period of regroupment, and called for nationwide elections two years hence. An International Control Commission (ICC) was established to oversee the implementation of the cease-fire, which called for the withdrawal of French forces and prohibited the introduction of any new foreign troops in Indochina. Although historians have long argued that Ho was forced by his Chinese and Soviet allies to accept what many saw as an unfavorable settlement, recent research suggests instead that it was his overriding fear of American intervention that tipped the scales.[18] At the time, DRV officials earnestly hoped that the elections provision provided a path to reunify the country peacefully under communist rule. Ominously, however, the SVN refused to sign the accord. Washington, which was not a party to the agreement, promised to abide by its terms but made public its objection to the formula. Motivated by the domino theory, which predicted that the collapse of one Southeast Asian country to communism would spread the contagion to neighboring countries in rapid succession, Eisenhower's administration was unwilling to let South Vietnam fall.

Perhaps one of the most fateful events in Vietnam's recent history was Bao Dai's decision, amid the Geneva negotiations, to appoint Ngo Dinh Diem as the SVN's first postwar prime minister. While the former emperor made his selection autonomously, it was heavily influenced by the United States. Eisenhower's State Department and the CIA, which had reached the conclusion that Diem was the only available noncommunist nationalist capable of running a viable postarmistice government, made clear that Washington's desperately needed support for the SVN would hinge on him getting the job. To be sure, this strong US endorsement was the product of Diem's own deft maneuvering in US religious and political circles, as well as his brother Ngo Dinh Nhu's ascendance within southern Vietnam's nationalist scene.

During the early years of the French War, the austere, morally uncompromising Diem was a prominent *attentiste* (fence sitter), one of a group of Vietnamese nationalists who, faced with the unpalatable option of aligning with the Viet Minh or rallying to the colonial regime, refused to pick a side. He remained politically active at home until the dramatic events of 1950 drove him to leave the country in pursuit of foreign support for his vision of an independent, noncommunist Vietnam. In the United States, with the help of Michigan State University political scientist Wesley Fishel, he ingratiated himself with a host of important religious and political figures who would prove instrumental in his rise to power. A group that would become known as the Vietnam Lobby was impressed by his proven commitment to the unique combination of anticommunism, anti–French imperialism, and Catholicism. Citing his "unquestioned integrity" and his "sincerity, nationalism and honesty," his American backers maintained that Diem stood alone above other nationalist alternatives whom they deemed politically naïve, unpredictable, childlike, and dangerously vulnerable to the lure of neutralism.[19] Meanwhile, back in Vietnam, Nhu maneuvered within a fragile noncommunist nationalist coalition to position his brother to take the helm.[20] By the time the Geneva Conference opened, Bao Dai was boxed into a corner, outmaneuvered by the Ngos at home and abroad. Although Diem owed his position largely to Washington's influence, he was not the American puppet that he has long been considered. In fact, his vision for nation-building in Vietnam, and the steps he took to enact it, contrasted so sharply with that of the United States that historian Edward Miller has aptly termed the partnership a "misalliance."[21] But before that clash could develop, Diem had to overcome seemingly insurmountable obstacles to consolidate his control over the newly created South Vietnam.

The new prime minister returned home to Vietnam in June 1954 to a site of near anarchy. The SVN, a weakly defined political entity created hastily during wartime to serve France's immediate political needs, lacked the organizational structure necessary for effective governance. Meanwhile, three politico-religious organizations, the Hoa Hao, Cao Dai, and Binh Xuyen controlled approximately one-third of the territory and population below the seventeenth parallel. The Binh Xuyen crime syndicate held a monopoly over vice industries in the Saigon-Cholon capital district, running prostitution rings, opium dens, and gambling at Cholon's famed Grande Monde Casino. Owing to its wartime alliance with French forces, the Binh Xuyen had also recently purchased the rights to operate the capital district's police and security detail, giving the organization near total control over the densely populated commercial hub surrounding Diem's palace gates. The Hoa Hao and Cao Dai, meanwhile, operated as "states within a state," with their own administrative structures, taxation systems, and armies that had grown considerably during the war due to payments supplied by France in exchange for defense against the Viet Minh. To add insult to injury, the Vietnamese National Army (VNA), which rested under the control of Francophile Gen. Nguyen Van Hinh, was hostile to the new prime minister. Diem, who sought to consolidate total control at the expense of his rivals, would clash almost immediately with a coalition comprised of Hinh, Hoa Hao, Cao Dai, and Binh Xuyen leaders, and an array of other noncommunist nationalists, all of whom angled to exert influence relative to their current strength in the new southern government.

At first, Diem's stubborn refusal to accommodate his rivals seemed likely to doom his administration. Throughout his first year in office, US officials maintained their commitment to Diem not because of a deep faith in his abilities but out of respect for his strength of character and because they believed no viable noncommunist nationalist alternative to him existed. This was, in part, due to their faith that a devout Catholic like Diem would never brook the sort of accommodation with communists to which they suspected his Buddhist counterparts would be susceptible.[22] Washington made its decision to "sink or swim with Ngo Dinh Diem," but for a time it appeared likely that he would be more of an anchor than a life raft. As he took a series of bold moves to divide and conquer his enemies and eliminate the remnants of French power in Vietnam, Washington began to second-guess the wisdom of supporting him. US officials pressed him to compromise, but he consistently did the opposite, forcing conflicts rather than ceding political power to what he saw as corrupt, unsavory elements. In early 1955, after provoking an armed clash with the Binh Xuyen, he seemed particularly on the ropes. Amid the Battle of Saigon, facing serious pressure from France as well as pleas from the US ambassador to Saigon to consider replacing Diem, John Foster Dulles came close to pulling the plug on his government. At the last minute, however, Diem pulled out an improbable eleventh-hour victory, breaking his enemies and driving Binh Xuyen forces from the capital.

Washington thereafter hailed Diem as a "miracle man." He had entered the Battle of Saigon on the brink of collapse and emerged from it with what appeared to be nearly uncontested control over southern Vietnam. For the next eight years, the US commitment to Diem would be unflappable. For his part, Diem took from the episode a series of lessons that would influence his approach to governance and future crises. First, he recognized just how dependent was the United States on his success. Second, the rectitude of his natural inclination to attack rather than negotiate with political rivals seemed confirmed. Finally, and fatefully, he concluded that he could resist American pressure to compromise and reform, even as his government brutally suppressed opposition movements.[23]

Following on his triumph in the Battle of Saigon, Diem doubled down on his efforts to eliminate what he referred to as the "sources of demoralization" in Vietnamese society. Underpinning his nation-building vision was the arcane philosophy of Personalism, borrowed from French interwar Catholic philosophers and imported to Vietnam by his brother Nhu. Despite—or perhaps because of—hours of dry, impenetrable sermons on the subject, Diem was unable to render it meaningful to his constituents. Clearer was his "triple enemy" formula, which pointed to communism, colonialism, and feudalism as overlapping categories of social degradation to be eliminated before any meaningful nation-building program could commence. To this end, on July 20, 1955, he announced the Denounce the Communists campaign designed to root out and destroy communists and the remnants of French colonialism and feudalism that abetted them. Bao Dai and the remaining Hoa Hao, Cao Dai, and Binh Xuyen forces fell squarely in these crosshairs, as did a number of other nationalist figures who refused to bow to his total control over South Vietnamese politics.

Diem's anticommunist crusade would become increasingly authoritarian, violent, and divisive in the coming years. To establish his uncontested authority and evade the requirement for countrywide reunification elections set out by the Geneva Accords, Diem staged a referendum to depose Bao Dai in October 1955. In what was clearly a rigged outcome, he won 98.5 percent of the vote, after which he proclaimed himself president of a new Republic of Vietnam. Diem then justified his refusal to participate in talks with the DRV to prepare for a countrywide vote on the grounds that North Vietnam's communistic slave state was incapable of putting on a free and fair election. The United States, although slightly embarrassed by the baldly undemocratic nature of Diem's own referendum, let out a sigh of relief, knowing that the elections that would have surely brought Ho and the VWP to power over a united Vietnam would not take place.

Relief was the opposite of what VWP officials experienced. After signing the Geneva Accords, communist officials in Hanoi held out hope that the terms would enable them to reunify Vietnam without further bloodshed. But by the summer of 1956, Diem's refusal to participate in countrywide elections called into question the "North-first" policy that the Politburo's moderate leadership had pursued since the cease-fire. Weary of fighting and eager to pursue political and economic transformations that were put on hold as the August Revolution spiraled straight into war with France, North-firsters like Ho, Giap, and VWP general secretary Truong Chinh prioritized socialist development in the North while renouncing violence and authorizing only "political struggle" among stay-behind cadres in the South. This approach was reinforced by the desire of key allies to avoid further conflict with the Western powers in Asia. As China and the Soviet Union turned their attention to domestic matters, North Vietnamese officials followed suit.[24]

The North-first strategy proved somewhat of a disaster in the short term. Hanoi's land reform program spiraled out of control as individual cadres pursued ruthless and indiscriminate methods to wrest property from land-owners for redistribution to previously landless and impoverished peasants. The poorly executed policy provoked widespread hardship and resentment and, most catastrophically, fueled the exodus of more than a million people from North to South, at least half of whom were Catholic. The United States, reveling in the political boon offered by this mass migration, encouraged refugees to flee and facilitated their movement.[25] Ho backtracked, apologizing for the regime's excesses and instituting a "Rectification of Errors" campaign, but the debacle fueled a wave of purges against Party moderates and emboldened a group of militants who would take charge of the Party in the critical years leading up to war with the United States.

Chief among these militants was Le Duan, a southerner himself who was one of an estimated 10,000 Party cadres who decided after the Geneva Agreements to remain below the seventeenth parallel and struggle for reunification. Disappointed and frustrated by what he perceived as Hanoi's betrayal of the revolution in the South, he stepped up pressure on the VWP after the July 1956 deadline for countrywide elections had passed. Convinced that violent struggle was the only way to combat the American imperialists and their South Vietnamese lackeys, he implored the Politburo to authorize a militant approach. A few weeks before the Party's Central Committee meeting scheduled for December 1956, he sent a carefully worded tract to Hanoi, "The Path to Revolution in the South," in which he made a case for abandoning the current line and resuming armed struggle in the South. His goal was to score a swift victory before the United States could marshal its forces to resist. Hanoi, not entirely deaf to Le Duan's appeal, authorized southern communists to conduct targeted assassinations against "reactionary traitors" and to carry out terror bombings of institutions associated with Diem's government and its American backers. Although this fell far short of what Le Duan wanted, it represented a tacit acknowledgment by the Politburo that political struggle alone had proven insufficient to achieve the Party's goals in the South.[26] Fatefully, DRV leaders decided at that point to recall Le Duan to Hanoi, appointing him acting general secretary of the Party.

This small shift in 1956 augured a much larger change in course that unfolded over the remainder of the decade. The Party's slow but steady movement toward the resumption of armed struggle in the South occurred under the shadow of Moscow's policy of peaceful coexistence, a policy that emboldened Eisenhower's administration to step up its aid to Saigon even as it pursued détente with Moscow. Existing fissures within the Politburo between moderates and militants were exacerbated by deepening divisions within the Sino-Soviet camp, as Moscow sent dangerous signals that it was willing to accept the permanent division of Vietnam, while an increasingly radicalized Beijing denounced Soviet "revisionism." Le Duan and other advocates of armed struggle in the South naturally gravitated toward China, whereas moderate North-firsters like Ho and Giap tended to favor the Soviet Union.

While Ho's contingent continued to hold sway over the Politburo, a major policy statement issued in 1959, known as "Resolution 15," signified an important tilt in Le Duan's direction. Alarmed by the growing strength of Diem's military, the Army of the Republic of Vietnam (ARVN), and its heightened violence against communist cadres and their sympathizers below the seventeenth parallel, VWP officials determined that the balance of forces in the south had reached a crisis point. While maintaining the primacy of Northern concerns, they acceded to a resolution calling for more aggressive action in the South aimed at motivating workers, peasants, and petty bourgeoisie to rise up against Diem's government. Asselin has called the resolution "one of the pivotal policy statements in the course of events that propelled Hanoi into the Vietnam War," for it "ended Hanoi's policy since 1954 of benign neglect of the South and the revolutionary situation there."[27]

The Party's operational guidelines for implementing Resolution 15 were slow in coming and tempered significantly the belligerent language of the resolution itself. In part, this reflected reluctance on the part of moderates to instigate armed struggle in the South, but it was also indicative of Hanoi's need to build up its own economy, armed forces, and foreign support to prepare for a successful reunification fight. Equally important was the DRV's conviction that international support for the cause of Vietnamese reunification, particularly among Afro-Asian and Western audiences, depended on the image of the southern resistance as an indigenous, self-sustaining movement to liberate South Vietnam from the American imperialists and their RVN lackeys. In terms of critical big power support, Chinese aid and influence had increased throughout 1959, while Moscow continued to discourage its allies from taking any action—such as a new aggressive approach in South Vietnam—that could increase Cold War tensions. Hanoi was, moreover, loath to take any action that would give the United States a justification for deploying its own forces to Vietnam.

Southern revolutionary activity therefore increased, albeit moderately. The response from Diem's administration, however, was far from moderate. His crackdown on the upsurge in insurgent activity stymied any possible success among his opposition and virtually guaranteed a more vigorous policy from Hanoi. In May 1959, Saigon promulgated Law 10/59, which assigned the death penalty to anyone who "commits or attempts to commit . . . crimes with the aim of sabotage, or infringement upon the security of the state."[28] Tantamount to all-out war on the southern insurgency, the law provided the RVN with the pretext to round up thousands of dissidents and suspected dissidents, including student activists, politico-religious leaders, and anyone suspected of so much as sympathizing with the communists. The result was devastating for southern revolutionaries, forcing Hanoi's hand.

In forging a response to the southern crisis, VWP leaders had to wade through a complex and delicate diplomatic situation within the communist bloc. Hanoi had close relationships with China and the Soviet Union and depended heavily on both. While China provided critical aid and advice during the French War, the Soviet Union supplied most of the hardware and technical expertise behind the North-first strategy. Hanoi's leaders believed success in any future conflict would require support from both powers. At this stage, however, China and the Soviet Union jointly condemned increased militancy in the South. And even more critically, a deepening Sino-Soviet rivalry threatened to force Hanoi to pick a side. Moscow was furious with Hanoi's gambit in Resolution 15, which risked provoking war with the United States, thereby threatening to derail Khrushchev's policy of peaceful coexistence. Beijing, on the other hand, now openly avowing the inevitability of war between the socialists and capitalist camps, advised Hanoi to restrain itself in the South while it worked to develop its northern "rear base." In short, Beijing was unwilling to match its belligerent rhetoric with tangible support for Vietnam's liberation movement.

Yet while neither of the communist giants supported Hanoi's more aggressive approach in the South, they could agree on little else. The Sino-Soviet conflict intensified throughout 1960 over Mao's condemnation of Soviet revisionism and his encouragement of militant national liberation movements. Beijing openly defied Khrushchev's policy of peaceful coexistence by sending assistance to communist forces fighting the British in the Malayan "Emergency," marking an end to the PRC's policy of "leaning to one side" (i.e., the Soviet Union) and opening up an earnest competition between the two communist powers over the leadership of world revolution.[29] With Mao and Khrushchev unleashing increasingly vitriolic personal attacks on each other, Vietnamese communist leaders found it increasingly difficult to remain above the fray, especially as hostility within the communist bloc aggravated mirrored tensions within VWP leadership. Hanoi, however, was determined to mediate the Sino-Soviet dispute in an effort to salvage international communist solidarity and, most importantly, preserve its special relationship with both of Vietnam's communist patrons. Ho's efforts to mend the breach were unsuccessful but may have contributed to Khrushchev's announcement in January 1961 that the Soviet Union intended to increase assistance to Third World national liberation movements in order to "use postcolonialist momentum [to] break into the 'soft underbelly of imperialism.'"[30]

The timing of this announcement was propitious, coming as it did just weeks after Hanoi's decision to form the National Front for the Liberation of South Vietnam (NLF). In December 1960, a group of sixty revolutionaries met in Tay Ninh province, near the Cambodian border, to establish the NLF. The organization, intended to unite all of Ngo Dinh Diem's southern opponents, was open to anyone regardless of political affiliation. It was, in fact, conceived and dominated by the VWP in Hanoi. Consistent with its commitment to presenting the southern insurgency as homegrown, for both the purposes of recruiting a broad-based coalition of anti-Diem forces and presenting to the world an image of heroic struggle against foreign invasion, the communists concealed their overweening role.[31]

This is not to say that no spontaneous southern resistance existed. In fact, historian David Hunt has documented that news of the NLF's existence took months to reach some parts of the South, where it "came as an afterthought to revolutionaries who were already deciding on their own what sort of liberation they were striving to achieve."[32] The bitter repression carried out by Diem's government in the mid- to late 1950s alienated not only embattled communists and politico-religious figures but also a host of rural peasants who suffered at the hands of RVN policies. Diem's rural resettlement program, which moved people off their ancestral lands and into agrovilles, proved particularly galvanizing.

The Saigon government also faced growing criticism from urban moderates who were shut out of political life under the Ngo family's insular, nepotistic rule.[33] While the NLF worked to coordinate the South's revolutionary insurgency, a group of eighteen notable noncommunist nationalists, including several former government officials, published the Caravelle Manifesto, demanding real reform from the RVN. That statement of grievances, published in the spring of 1960, charged the government with requiring of its officials "blind submission to the leaders" and blamed Diem's repressive policies for provoking "the discouragement and resentment of the people."[34] Then, on November 11, his own ARVN staged an abortive coup attempt. Rather than prompting Diem to reform, however, these attacks only spurred him to double down on his authoritarian approach to governance and ramp up the apparatus of his already repressive police state in an effort to quash the mounting insurgency in the face of his deteriorating domestic political standing.

The deepening crisis in South Vietnam occurred against the backdrop of John F. Kennedy's election as president of the United States. JFK, the youngest man ever voted into the office, slid in with the slimmest electoral margin in US history. Yet he was no ignoramus on the situation in Vietnam, having taken a special interest in the matter for over a decade. Kennedy, writes historian Fredrik Logevall, "was more informed about the issues on the ground than virtually any senior Democrat in Washington."[35] He recognized the myriad perils, including Diem's liabilities, Hanoi's strengths, and the limits of American power. But as a dedicated anticommunist, he took it as a given that the United States would hold the line against Ho Chi Minh's forces in Vietnam. His refusal to renege on Washington's commitment to Diem, however, followed a slightly different logic than the domino theory that drove his predecessor. Kennedy recognized the increasing centrality of the Third World to the Cold War and was loath to suffer losses there that could drive decolonizing and postcolonial countries into the communist camp. He was afraid not of a geographically contiguous cascade of red dominos but of the harm to American credibility that would result from abandoning a close ally like South Vietnam, a "psychological domino theory," in the words of Jonathan Schell.[36]

To chart his course through choppy international waters at the very peak of the Cold War—and its collision with decolonization—Kennedy chose as his top advisors several leading lights of higher education and industry. The "best and the brightest" who would lead the United States down the garden path to war in Vietnam included Secretary of State Dean Rusk, Secretary of Defense Robert McNamara, and National Security Advisor McGeorge Bundy. This trio, known retrospectively for their hubris, presided over a gradual escalation of American military involvement in Vietnam under JFK. After Kennedy was struck down by an assassin's bullet in November 1963, they would stay on under President Lyndon Johnson to oversee the escalation and Americanization of a war they believed to be, in equal parts, unwinnable and unavoidable.

A series of international events in 1961 served to heighten the importance of Vietnam for Kennedy and his advisors. Khrushchev's January 1961 speech proclaiming support for wars of national liberation, followed by increased support for insurgents in Laos and Congo, as well as stepped-up aid to Cuba and North Vietnam, was principally a reaction to Chinese criticisms of Soviet revisionism. But it signaled to Washington renewed hostility in the Third World, where Soviet advances contrasted starkly with Kennedy's failed gambit to invade Cuba through the Bay of Pigs in April 1961. Kennedy's debacle in Cuba was compounded by events in Laos, where communist forces seemed poised to win a three-way civil war. As Eisenhower handed over the keys to the Oval Office, he warned Kennedy that Laos would "be the loss of the cork in the bottle'" that would lead to the erosion of US influence in most of the Far East.[37] Unpersuaded of Laos's strategic importance, and skeptical of American prospects for success there, Kennedy opted to negotiate a neutralist government for Laos. This decision to negotiate a settlement for Laos only made Kennedy and his team more inclined to pursue a military solution in Vietnam, where they would come under increased pressure to prove their resolve in the global fight against communism.[38]

First, Kennedy needed more information. In October 1961, he dispatched a team, headed by Gen. Maxwell D. Taylor and Walt W. Rostow, to assess the situation in Vietnam and make policy recommendations. Both unabashed hawks, Taylor and Rostow concluded that the only remedy for the desperate political and military situation they encountered was to step up training and material assistance for RVN forces. In a top-secret memo for the president, they also advised sending an 8,000-person military task force to South Vietnam. McNamara and the Joint Chiefs of Staff (JCS) considered this recommendation woefully inadequate and pressed Kennedy to send 200,000 troops, to show that "we mean business."[39] The president also listened to a more dovish set of advisors who urged him to negotiate a way out of the Vietnam debacle rather than staking US prestige on a battle where prospects appeared grim.

Kennedy's decision in fall 1961 was to avoid a decision. He rejected the alternatives of seeking a negotiated settlement and deploying combat forces, instead opting for a middle-of-the-road approach. He increased US economic and military aid to South Vietnam. More significantly, he raised the number of US advisors to 3,000—exceeding by a fair bit the level allowed under the Geneva Accords—and, for the first time, authorized them to participate in combat operations. These measures, he knew, were not enough to tip the scales in South Vietnam. Intended as stopgaps to buy time, Kennedy's gradual increases in Washington's military commitment to South Vietnam made it that much more difficult for him, and his successors, to avoid a larger war as the crisis mounted in coming years.

In the short-term, Kennedy's policies seemed to be working. By early 1962 the ARVN appeared to have seized the military advantage, but its success was an illusion. Vietcong guerrillas, operating in stealth, simply retreated to undetectable bases following engagement, making their real strength impossible to gauge. Optimistic assessments of US–South Vietnamese progress also focused on the new strategic hamlet program, a counterinsurgency measure designed to protect peasants by relocating them into new villages the NLF supposedly could not infiltrate. The hamlets went a step further than agrovilles by fortifying village borders with barbed wire and bamboo stakes. In actuality, this served more to imprison peasants, who had been moved unwillingly from their ancestral homes, than to insulate them from stealth NLF forces, which often moved freely within the hamlets. Thus, a marquis program designed to win support for the government in Saigon only stirred up resentment, delivering easy converts to the NLF. This was but one of many signs that Diem was losing the political battle in South Vietnam.[40]

Kennedy, hoping he could somehow find a way to both preserve a non-communist South Vietnam and withdraw US forces, refused to see the writing on the wall. In July 1962, he considered progress against the Vietcong so promising that he asked McNamara to initiate plans for a phased withdrawal of US advisors. The plan called for withdrawals to begin at the end of 1963, if the war continued to go well. In January 1963, the Battle of Ap Bac delivered the first unmistakable sign that the war was, in fact, not going well for Washington and Saigon. On the advice of American military advisor Lt. Col. John Paul Vann, the ARVN set out to attack a group of guerrillas concentrated near the village of Ap Bac in the Mekong Delta. ARVN forces significantly outnumbered the enemy, boasting superior weaponry and US helicopter support. But when it came time to fight, they refused to leave the protection of their armored personnel carriers to initiate battle with the NLF. ARVN forces ended up firing on each other, suffering more than 450 casualties, while the guerrillas escaped with only three dead. The debacle highlighted the ARVN's weakness and low morale while simultaneously shining a light on NLF strength and military prowess. A crushing defeat for South Vietnam covered heavily by American journalists, the Battle of Ap Bac called into question the Kennedy administration's optimistic claims about the state of the war. Indeed, it raised nagging questions about the very viability of the South Vietnamese government. That spring and summer, Diem's situation would go from bad to worse.

While Diem's government was under serious assault from the NLF insurgency in the countryside, it was the so-called Buddhist Crisis that brought him down. Widespread protests against RVN repression—particularly religious repression toward South Vietnam's majority Buddhist population—were sparked by an incident in Hue on May 8, 1963. As a procession assembled to celebrate Vesak day, participants were angrier than they were celebratory. They were there to protest Saigon's decision to deny a petition to fly the colorful international flag of Buddhism—following a law banning the display of religious flags—just one week after Hue had been festooned with Catholic flags in celebration of Diem's brother Ngo Dinh Thuc's silver anniversary as archbishop. The demonstration turned violent when heavily armed RVN security forces unleashed a series of explosions and fired a volley of bullets into the crowd. Following the resulting melee, police discovered the bodies of seven protestors, as well as two who had been seriously injured and would soon succumb. The victims were between the ages of twelve and twenty.

The incident sparked immediate controversy. Saigon officials sought to deflect blame by claiming that the deaths were the result of a communist bomb attack, a claim that never gained traction outside of Diem's inner circle. Nationwide demonstrations, many of them among students, sprang up to protest government oppression and brutality. After June 11, the movement galvanized around Buddhist monk Thich Quang Duc's dramatic self-immolation outside Xa Loi pagoda in Saigon. Malcolm Browne's disturbing photograph of the event, one of the most iconic images of the Vietnam War, spread quickly around the world. Onlookers in the United States and elsewhere naturally interpreted the image of the burning bonze as a dramatic response to Diem's religious persecution. Nhu's wife, Tran Le Xuan—better known as Madame Nhu—compounded the image crisis with her cavalier references to monk "barbeques." Throughout the crisis, Washington steadily increased its pressure on Diem to negotiate with the Buddhists' Intersect Committee, and eventually pressed him to get rid of Nhu and his wife, who seemed bent on making the situation worse.

Diem would not listen. At grave personal and political cost, Diem misapplied lessons from the Battle of Saigon. He believed that US officials would once again tolerate his decision to disregard their advice and pursue a brutal crackdown on his enemies, just as they had in 1955. In late August 1963, on the flimsy premise that it was necessary to thwart an imminent communist attack on Saigon, he declared martial law across the country and initiated a series of pagoda raids to destroy his Buddhist opposition. Although the movement's key leaders were imprisoned or forced into hiding, these draconian measures did little to slow the pace of antigovernment demonstrations. Equally troubling to the United States were rumors circling that Diem was seeking a deal with Hanoi. In this desperate context, anti-Diem figures within the Kennedy administration, including the newly dispatched ambassador to Saigon, Henry Cabot Lodge, signaled to a cabal of ARVN generals that the United States would not stand in the way of his ouster. When they finally launched their coup on November 1, 1963, they did so with confidence in

Thich Quang Duc, a seventy-three-year-old Buddhist monk, self-immolates in protest against government persecution before thousands of onlookers in Saigon, Vietnam, on June 11, 1963. (AP Photo/Malcolm Browne)

Washington's tacit support.[41] The next day, Diem and Nhu's bodies were found in the back of an armored vehicle. They had been shot point-blank in the head with their arms tied behind their backs, belying claims by their captors that they had committed suicide.

Diem's ouster represented a key turning point in the Vietnam War. It offered the United States a clear opportunity to walk away from the rapidly deteriorating situation in South Vietnam rather than double down on a commitment to the military junta that had just assassinated its longtime ally. Kennedy did not immediately seize this chance. Just three weeks later he, too, would be gunned down on the streets of Dallas. His successor, Lyndon Baines Johnson, was ill-versed in foreign policy. He was brash and domineering but insecure in the face of Kennedy's coterie of the "best and brightest." Yet he kept them on, and they urged him to stay the course. Johnson felt boxed in by three presidents before him who had made—and then deepened—a commitment to maintaining a noncommunist South Vietnam.

He was unwilling to shoulder the burden of changing tack, of being the one to "lose" Vietnam. He believed his own personal credibility, that of the Democratic Party, and that of the United States would be unable to absorb the hit.[42] As the situation in Vietnam spiraled downward rapidly under his watch, Johnson seemed determined to dispatch with the crisis in such a way that it did not interfere with his domestic political plans for his Great Society program. This meant slipping deeper into the morass without ever committing fully to the fight. In the face of a newly resolute North Vietnamese enemy, his fatalism would spell disaster.

In late 1963, with Saigon and Washington reeling, Hanoi seized the initiative. Already emboldened by the Battle of Ap Bac, VWP militants jumped on the Saigon coup to stage "a coup of a different kind." Shocked by the sudden turn of events in Saigon, the VWP Central Committee immediately convened the Ninth Plenum to discuss recent developments in the South. While Diem's removal was not unwelcome, the emergence of a US-backed military regime in his place raised new concerns. A debate emerged within the VWP over whether to wait and see what happened or to launch a full invasion of the South before the new regime could establish itself.

True to form, Le Duan led the charge for war. His militant faction prevailed over moderate objections, voiced most vehemently by Giap, that North Vietnam's armed forces were not yet prepared for large-scale combat. The result was Resolution 9, a virtual declaration of war against South Vietnam, which called for the initiation of "mass combat operations" aimed at destroying the strategic hamlet program and annihilating Saigon's armed forces before the United States could introduce sufficient military force into South Vietnam to turn the tide. After equivocating for nearly a decade since the Geneva Accords, Hanoi decided to launch major war to achieve southern liberation and national reunification. "For Hanoi," writes Asselin, "it constituted a point of no return that eventuated the onset of war against the United States a little over a year later."[43]

With this major shift in North Vietnam's strategy came an equally momentous change in leadership. Discredited by the outcome of the Ninth Plenum, Ho and his moderate faction were shoved aside by the ascendant bloc of Party militants. By early 1964, Le Duan had established himself as the paramount leader in Hanoi, a position he would occupy throughout the coming war. His first act was to purge the Party of those he considered "revisionists," "pacifists," and "rightist deviationists." The "campaign against modern revisionism" was aimed at eradicating the influence of Khrushchev's policy of peaceful coexistence in North Vietnam's cultural and political spheres. Party members, writers, artists, and intellectuals, according to historian Martin Grossheim, were forced not only to renounce revisionism but "to depict sanitized versions of the war as a sacred and heroic struggle for the reunification of the country and not dwell on the ugliness of war."[44] At the same time, Hanoi intensified its pro-Chinese propaganda, praising Beijing for its revolutionary culture, compared with the dangerous bourgeois revisionism emanating from Moscow and Eastern Europe.

As the VWP geared up for war, an August 1964 incident in the Gulf of Tonkin—in the South China Sea off the coast of North Vietnam—dimmed Le Duan's hopes of defeating ARVN forces before the United States could intervene in full force. On August 2 and 4, two US destroyers reported being fired on by North Vietnamese patrol boats. In the first incident, with some provocation, North Vietnam volleyed three torpedoes at the *Maddox* and missed. The second attack on the *Turner Joy* was likely not an attack at all, although its captain returned fire without hitting anything. Johnson used these events as a pretext to trot out a resolution his national security team had previously drafted requesting congressional authorization on the use of force. The Gulf of Tonkin Resolution, which passed easily on August 7 with only two senators voting no, served not only as the green light for retaliatory air strikes but as a blank check for Johnson to escalate the war in Vietnam in coming months.

Despite a campaign promise that he would not send American boys to do the fighting that Asian boys should do for themselves, Johnson was forced to reconcile that position with the fact that South Vietnam was failing fast without American military intervention. The military junta that ousted Diem was unstable, undergoing a series of coups before Nguyen Van Thieu eventually came to power in 1965. Meanwhile, the NLF was gaining significant ground on the ARVN, which suffered from cripplingly low morale and high rates of desertion. Civil unrest continued, as Buddhist monks organized hunger strikes, protest marches, and immolations. Over the summer of 1964, as Johnson contemplated his options in Vietnam, he was unable to stir up significant international support for military escalation to stave off South Vietnamese defeat. His "More Flags" campaign was a flop. At home, key Democratic figures also warned against escalation, providing LBJ with an option to avoid war that he ultimately chose not to take.

Johnson's hand was forced by the DRV, which stepped up its military activity in fall 1964, not only in response to American aggression but as a function of increased support from both the Soviet Union and China. Although Moscow had scaled back its aid to North Vietnam following the Ninth Plenum—and in reaction to Hanoi's tilt toward China—it shifted course following the Gulf of Tonkin incident. "With the confrontation between the United States and the DRV," writes historian Lien-Hang T. Nguyen, "rendering aid to the fraternal socialist cause was mandatory."[45] Khrushchev's ouster in October 1964 seemed to signal that the Soviet Union would end its policy of peaceful coexistence, and his successor, Leonid Brezhnev, made a concerted effort to repair relations with Hanoi. In turn, for the time being, Le Duan and his fellow militants in the Politburo called off their attacks on revisionism and returned to a position of neutrality in the Sino-Soviet split. This reorientation in Hanoi's relations with Moscow, combined with China's first successful nuclear test, increased Hanoi's confidence that it could obtain the foreign support necessary to achieve victory. In fall 1964, then, Hanoi dispatched the first People's Army of Vietnam (PAVN) troops down the Ho Chi Minh Trail, and soon began making plans for a major offensive. The most significant event in the resulting campaign took place on February 7, 1965, as Vietcong guerrillas attacked a US airbase in Pleiku in the Central Highlands. This proved the last straw for Johnson and the Americans, who responded with a massive escalation. In February 1965, the American war in Vietnam began in earnest with Operation Rolling Thunder, a program of sustained air strikes against North Vietnam, followed shortly by the landing of US ground troops in Danang.

In early 1965, both Johnson and Le Duan were hoping for a quick victory. What they got instead was a steady increase in levels of violence, leading to a stalemate. The head of the American military mission to Vietnam, Gen. William Westmoreland, implemented an attrition strategy known as search-and-destroy, aimed at killing enemy forces faster than they could be replaced. Recent scholarship by Nick Turse suggests that American soldiers, in preparation to execute this strategy, were systematically indoctrinated with dehumanizing racialized ideas about Vietnamese people and encouraged by their commanding officers to "kill anything that moves."[46] Through search-and-destroy, coupled with the sustained bombing of North Vietnam's infrastructure and unrelenting aerial assaults on South Vietnam with bombs, napalm, and toxic defoliants like Agent Orange, Washington sought to bring Vietcong forces to their knees. In the war's early years, American officials derived false optimism from high—often manipulated and inflated—body counts that proved a poor measure of military progress.

Hanoi, meanwhile, had a strategy of its own that thwarted America's far superior firepower. Consistent with their approach to the French war, North Vietnamese strategists simultaneously pursued three "modes of struggle." The first mode, military struggle, was aimed at destroying the ARVN and mitigating the effectiveness of foreign troops. In response to Westmoreland's search-and-destroy tactics, communist forces adopted a protracted war approach, launching small surprise operations on US and ARVN troops while evading detection via underground tunnel systems, by retreating across the Cambodian border, and by hiding in villages in plain sight among civilians. The second mode, political struggle, consisted of a propaganda campaign within Vietnam to recruit fighters and political supporters while fueling opposition to the regime in Saigon. Hanoi's political struggle was aided considerably by the damage inflicted by American bombs, which, although intended to attrit communist forces, actually served as an incomparable recruiting tool for both the PAVN and the NLF. Through the third mode, diplomatic struggle, Hanoi sought international support for its own war effort and aimed to stir up international opposition to America's "imperialist" intervention and the corrupt Saigon regime. The Politburo directed its diplomatic messages especially at the communist camp and allies in the Afro-Asian bloc and Latin America, but it also made successful overtures to leftists in Europe and the United States in an effort to isolate its enemy diplomatically. As Asselin puts it, Hanoi "aimed to defeat the United States by using circumstances outside Vietnam to deny Washington the ability to win."[47] This diplomatic prong turned out to be critical to North Vietnam's success.

Equally crucial was Hanoi's deft handling of its key international patrons amid deepening Sino-Soviet acrimony. Despite improvements in relations with Moscow, leaders in Hanoi remained ideologically closer to their comrades in Beijing, who supported North Vietnamese militarism in South Vietnam and fully backed Hanoi's refusal to negotiate a settlement that amounted to anything short of total victory. Sino-Soviet tensions only fueled PRC support for Hanoi's war, as Asia's communist giant sought to demonstrate its superior revolutionary mettle over the Soviet Union. Beijing therefore contributed significant military and economic aid to North Vietnam and sent tens of thousands of troops to join the fight. At the same time, the Sino-Soviet rivalry also motivated the Kremlin to back North Vietnam, lest China's criticisms of Soviet "revisionism" be proven right. Moscow, frustrated with North Vietnam's lean toward Beijing and worried that the fighting in South Vietnam would derail peaceful coexistence, continued to encourage Hanoi to negotiate a settlement. But it also ramped up aid to the DRV. Thus, while the Sino-Soviet rivalry posed a challenge for North Vietnamese diplomats, they ultimately benefited from their ability to play the two sides off one another. This is a prime example of a small satellite state manipulating the contours of the Cold War to seize the upper hand in its dealings with superpower patrons.

Aid from both the PRC and the Soviet Union enabled North Vietnam to match American escalations, which contributed to a cycle of increasing lethality in South Vietnam but failed to tip the military balance on the battlefield. Between 1965 and 1967, the United States dropped more than a million tons of bombs—as well as copious amounts of napalm and environmentally catastrophic defoliants like Agent Orange—on South Vietnam while North Vietnam and the NLF stepped up assaults on American and ARVN troops, all to little effect. By the summer of 1967, Le Duan made the fateful decision to launch an offensive designed to break the stalemate that had developed over two years of destructive warfare.

North Vietnamese planning for the Tet Offensive, to be unleashed in early 1968, was highly contentious. VWP leaders confronted war weariness after two years of costly fighting against the world's mightiest superpower, internecine political strife, and an increasingly tense diplomatic environment amidst the deepening Sino-Soviet split. Against hearty objections from VWP moderates, Le Duan's militant faction forged ahead with a plan to launch massive attacks on South Vietnam's cities and provincial towns with the aim of inspiring a General Offensive–General Uprising (GO-GU). Officials in Beijing, who had watched with concern as Hanoi drew closer to Moscow over the preceding two years, saw this not only as a premature move but a wholesale rejection of Mao's doctrine of guerrilla warfare. The Soviet Union, meanwhile, ramped up pressure on Hanoi to negotiate with Washington, a move that prompted Le Duan's faction within the Politburo to launch a purge of Party moderates. This "Revisionist Anti-Party Affair," the largest purge in VWP history that cut off the Soviet Union's "eyes and ears" in Hanoi, was intended to send a message to Moscow while placating Beijing.

Planning for the Tet Offensive, then, stemmed from a combination of factors including pressure to break the stalemate on the battlefield, Le Duan's desire to silence moderate pro-Soviet voices in the VWP (most notably Ho Chi Minh and Vo Nguyen Giap), and Hanoi's efforts to maneuver between key Cold War allies. The latter had become an especially delicate dance, as the VWP sought to retain the support of the world's preeminent communist powers, now in open breach, without bending to the will of either.

As historian Lien-Hang T. Nguyen has written, "The General Offensive and General Uprising was a risky strategy with little chance of success."[48] Yet, having eliminated his detractors, Le Duan forged ahead. The ARVN, having agreed to a duplicitous request from the DRV for a cease-fire over the Tet holiday, was caught unprepared and outmanned. Beginning just after midnight on January 30, 1968, communist forces attacked thirty-six of forty-four provincial capitals and five of six major cities in South Vietnam, including the brief but dramatic capture of the US embassy in Saigon. Vietcong occupation of the US embassy lasted just eight overnight hours, but its political significance can hardly be overstated. The image of Americans being forced out of their own embassy in the South Vietnamese capital—amid an enemy offensive no one saw coming—gave lie to official Johnson administration reports that the United States had been making progress toward victory. Washington's public relations nightmare was compounded by a well-timed photograph taken by Associated Press photographer Eddie Adams, depicting ARVN Gen. Nguyen Ngoc Loan shooting a bound Vietcong soldier point-blank in the head in the middle of Saigon. As that photograph circulated around the world next to images of the embassy under fire, trusted CBS Evening News anchor Walter Cronkite went on air to bemoan the stalemate revealed by the Tet Offensive. In ever-greater numbers, Americans began to question not only whether their military could win in Vietnam but whether it was even worth fighting to save such a ruthless ally. Across the globe, countercultural opposition to America's war in Vietnam sprang up like wildfire.

In diplomatic and political terms, Tet was a catastrophic failure for the United States, a turning point from which its war effort would never recover. In the immediate term, however, it amounted to a military victory for the United States and its ARVN ally, and an unmitigated disaster for the Vietnamese resistance on the battlefield. Following critical defeats in January, Le Duan ordered his forces to launch second and third waves of attack that only further weakened Hanoi's military position. The anticipated general uprising

On February 1, 1968, South Vietnamese Gen. Nguyen Ngoc Loan, chief of the National Police, fires his pistol into the head of suspected Vietcong officer Nguyen Van Lem (also known as Bay Lop) in Saigon, early in the Tet Offensive. The photo showed the war's brutality in a way Americans had not seen before. Protesters saw it as graphic evidence that the United States was fighting on the side of an unjust government. (AP Photo/Eddie Adams, File)

never transpired, and the southern communist infrastructure was destroyed in the fighting. It would take the Vietnamese resistance three years to recover fully from losses incurred during the disastrous offensive.

The aftermath of Tet occasioned strategic reconsiderations by all sides and led to the negotiating table. Johnson, who was suffering from various health problems that had him considering retirement even before Tet, decided to announce on March 31, "I will not seek, and I will not accept, the nomination of my party for . . . President." Hoping to pursue peace unencumbered by domestic political considerations, he invited VWP leaders to meet in Paris to negotiate an end to the war. Hanoi, crippled in its ability to pursue total military victory and unsure of the support it could expect from Beijing, accepted the invitation. North Vietnam's strained relationship with China resulted from the waning Cultural Revolution, the deepening Sino-Soviet split, and the resulting thaw in Beijing's relations with Washington.[49] While the decision to open negotiations was a first step in Hanoi's strategic shift away from China and toward closer alignment with the Soviet Union, Moscow remained highly suspicious of VWP leaders following the 1967 purges. As VWP diplomats sat down for the first time with the Americans to negotiate an end to the war, Hanoi faced serious challenges on all three of its strategic fronts: military, political, and diplomatic.

In January 1969, the hawkish Republican Richard Nixon replaced LBJ as president, amid growing public opposition to the war. While pursuing back-channel diplomacy aimed at averting a settlement in Paris, he campaigned on the promise of a secret plan to end the war. That plan seems to have consisted of ramping up military and diplomatic pressure on the enemy while generating the appearance of drawing down the American commitment. His first move was to implement a strategy known as Vietnamization, by which the United States would reduce its own troop levels in Vietnam and turn over to the ARVN increasing responsibility for fighting. At the same time, he stepped up pressure on enemy forces by illegally expanding the war across South Vietnam's border into neighboring Cambodia and Laos, where he hoped that massive bombing campaigns and covert incursions would destroy the southern revolutionary command center and disrupt Hanoi's ability to supply the resistance with personnel and equipment via the Ho Chi Minh trail. The invasion of Cambodia would turn out to be especially catastrophic, as it helped turn the tide in Cambodia's civil war, fueling the rise of the murderous Khmer Rouge regime.

Vietnamization, combined with the post-Tet reality that the brunt of anti-American fighting in the South was borne by regular PAVN forces from the North, threatened the VWP narrative that the war in South Vietnam was one of resistance against an invading imperialist power and its illegitimate lackey. To combat the appearance of a more conventional civil war, in which North Vietnam was the invading force, Hanoi decided to expand the neutered NLF's political and diplomatic responsibilities and, in June 1969, announced the formation of a Provisional Revolutionary Government of Southern Vietnam (PRG). The goal was to create a southern political alternative to Thieu's RVN that could help rally domestic and international support for resistance forces. This occurred against the backdrop of revolutionary icon Ho Chi Minh's death in September 1969, which itself dealt a serious blow to Hanoi's propaganda strategy, as much of the world continued to associate Vietnam's liberation struggle with the moderate Ho rather than the militant Le Duan, who had, in fact, been calling the shots for years.

Nixon, meanwhile, had some diplomatic tricks up his sleeve. He aimed to exploit Sino-Soviet conflict to advance American objectives through "triangular diplomacy." By the late 1960s, China had begun to see the Soviet Union as an even greater threat to its security than its traditional American rival. This opened the door for Nixon and his national security advisor, Henry Kissinger, to pursue parallel tracks of rapprochement with China and détente with the Soviet Union, with an eye toward driving a deeper wedge between the former allies and compelling them both to pressure North Vietnam to accept peace on American terms. Nixon, however, seriously overestimated their influence on North Vietnam. The rapid deterioration of Hanoi's relationship with Beijing led to stronger ties between North Vietnam and the Soviet Union, but to Moscow's chagrin, VWP leaders continued to resist direction from the Kremlin. Le Duan's Politburo, viewing negotiations primarily as a diplomatic tool to communicate its commitment to peace while putting pressure on the United States to scale back its demands, continued to push for total victory.

After Nixon took office, it quickly became evident to South Vietnamese president Nguyen Van Thieu that the United States' days in Vietnam were numbered. As the United States improved its relations with China, its commitment to South Vietnam waned, causing Thieu to fear that Washington would go behind his back to strike a secret deal with Hanoi. Yet Nixon, motivated largely by fear of domestic political backlash, sought "peace with honor," a deal that would lead to a "decent interval" between the departure of US troops and North Vietnam's inevitable domination of the South. Nixon and Le Duan proved equally determined to conclude the war on their own terms and to pull out all the stops in pursuit of that end. It therefore took all of Nixon's first term in office—and several major escalations of the level of violence unleashed on Vietnam—to reach an agreement.

From almost day one of his presidency, mounting bad press piled on Nixon, putting increasing pressure on his administration to extricate the United States from its theretofore longest and most divisive war. The My Lai Massacre, which occurred in March 1968 and was exposed in late 1969, broadcast an image to the world of lawless American soldiers savagely murdering innocent women and children. This fed right into North Vietnam's propaganda that depicted its resistance war as a patriotic struggle against brutal foreign invaders. It served as an important recruitment tool for the NLF and as a critical element of diplomatic appeals to gain foreign sympathy. Similarly, Nixon's secret bombings and incursions in Cambodia and Laos elicited condemnation from a growing antiwar movement in the United States and around the world but also sent a chilling message to VWP leaders about just how far Nixon was willing to go to bring them to their knees.

By early 1972 Nixon's overtures to both China and the Soviet Union had borne fruit, and North Vietnam faced the very real prospect of diplomatic isolation if it maintained its refusal to budge on its negotiating terms. VWP leaders were especially stung by Beijing's about-face, because of the dangers posed by geographic proximity as well as the betrayal of the long history of Sino-Vietnamese wartime cooperation. True to form, however, Le Duan responded to this diplomatic noose not by giving in but by getting tough. In the spring of 1972 he decided to try once again for a general offensive in the South, launching the Easter Offensive aimed at destroying and demoralizing the ARVN, tipping the military balance in South Vietnam in favor of resistance forces, influencing the US presidential election, and disrupting Soviet-American rapprochement by derailing the Moscow summit scheduled for that May. Nixon responded with a massive bombing campaign against North Vietnam and Northern supply lines into the South. Even as bombs rained down on their DRV ally, Moscow and Beijing continued apace with their diplomatic overtures to Washington, issuing little objection. The Easter Offensive was a catastrophe for Hanoi militarily, politically, and diplomatically. The VWP faced a level of war weariness and low morale in the North that it had never seen before. Total victory, for the first time, took a back seat to ending the war.

Still, it would take several more rounds of negotiation—and massive outbursts of violence—to reach a deal. A key sticking point in the talks had been Hanoi's refusal to allow the South Vietnamese president to stay in power. Faced with pressure from both China and the Soviet Union, North Vietnam decided in fall 1972 to drop the demand for Thieu's removal. Signaling for the first time Hanoi's willingness to accept a two-stage solution—first settling military issues with the United States before allowing Vietnamese parties to determine the fate of the two Vietnams—VWP negotiator Le Duc Tho delivered to Kissinger a draft settlement that served as the basis for an agreement. But Thieu refused to accept the terms, and Nixon proved unwilling to turn his back on the longtime US ally in the midst of his campaign for reelection. Furious with Washington's volte-face, Hanoi refused to reopen the talks. But just days later, Nixon won reelection by a landslide, changing the DRV's calculus. Le Duan feared the lengths to which Nixon, unencumbered by domestic political constraints, would go to win in Vietnam. The two sides thus returned to the negotiating table in November. They were able to agree on five of six proposed changes, but Hanoi resisted the wording of a proposed change to the disposition of the demilitarized zone (DMZ). When negotiations again ended in failure, Nixon the "mad bomber" once again turned to a massive aerial assault on North Vietnam referred to as the Christmas Bombings. Le Duan caved, announcing on December 26 his willingness to resume negotiations. Both Kissinger and Tho came to the table under clear orders to bring the war to an end. Tho made a series of critical concessions in exchange for Kissinger's promise to withdraw all US troops from South Vietnam and to suspend fighting indefinitely. The Paris Peace Agreement, signed in January 1973, essentially set Vietnam back to where it was prior to the American war. When Kissinger and Tho were awarded a Nobel Peace Prize jointly for their role in negotiating an end to the war, Tho refused to accept it. The DRV had not yet achieved its objective of reunifying Vietnam under communist rule; negotiating an American exit did not amount to peace.

American military involvement in Vietnam ended with the Paris accords, but the civil war continued. Thieu, who never had any intention of sticking to the agreement, was the first to violate its terms. North Vietnamese leaders, recognizing the futility of trying to abide by the agreement, responded by renewing large-scale combat operations. By this point, Hanoi operated largely in a diplomatic vacuum, as both China and the Soviet Union scaled back support in 1973 and the international community quickly lost interest once the struggle against Western neoimperialism was resolved. At the same time, VWP leaders were emboldened by the United States Congress, which voted to cut off funds for future combat operations in Indochina and then passed the War Powers Act, which limited presidential powers to make war without congressional authorization, thereby relieving the DRV of any concern about a renewed American war. After almost two more years of fighting, Vietnamese troops entered Saigon, seizing the capital and reunifying the country under what would be renamed the Socialist Republic of Vietnam (SRVN). The chaos that followed, including a steady stream of evacuees being transported by helicopter from the roof of the besieged US embassy in Saigon, served as an image of American humiliation and failure in the eyes of the world.

Indeed, the war in Vietnam—both the way it was conducted and the way it ended—dealt a devastating blow to US credibility. Americans questioned their country's power to influence developments abroad and, more devastatingly, doubted its moral authority to do so. Following on the Nixon Doctrine by which the United States insisted that its allies would be responsible for the burdens of their own defense, US officials were reluctant to send American troops into combat lest they relive the humiliation of the Vietnam War. To many in the Third World, the self- proclaimed "leader of the free world" had, in fact, proven itself to be a bastion of neo-imperialism and inhumane savagery. In 1977, Jimmy Carter rode to the White House determined to restore the moral core of American foreign policy by decentering Cold War competition with the Soviet Union to make room for a focus on human rights. To many Americans this reeked of defeatism, a sign that what Ronald Reagan would call the "Vietnam Syndrome" must be overcome.

As the United States faced down its own divisions, SRVN leaders confronted the challenge of governing a reunified Vietnam ravaged by decades of warfare and internecine strife. The task of integrating southern Vietnam into the sociopolitical and economic order of the country was mighty, and the policies pursued to that end were largely disastrous. As many as one million people associated with the former southern regime were sent to reeducation camps, where they languished for anywhere from a few months to many years, subjected to hard labor, starvation, and harsh beatings. A refugee crisis ensued as millions of Vietnamese fled by boat from southern Vietnam to refugee camps in Thailand and then ports farther afield. New Economic Zones set up throughout southern Vietnam proved wholly ineffective at both developing the southern economy and reintegrating southerners into the socialist body politic. Likewise, literary works like Bao Ninh's *The Sorrow of War* painted a bleak picture of a postwar northern Vietnam beset by corruption, frustration, even nihilism as wartime sacrifices yielded little reward.[50] Political scientist Tuong Vu writes, "Drunk with pride in their success in war, Vietnamese leaders set highly unrealistic goals and employed draconian tactics in their quest to develop socialism 'in five, ten years.'"[51] North Vietnam's leadership proved much more successful at waging war than governing in a time of peace.

Almost as soon as its own war ended, Vietnam found itself embroiled in conflicts with neighboring Cambodia, and subsequently China. After 1975, Vietnam's Cold War was much more about Sino-Vietnamese and Sino-Soviet rivalries than it was about conflict with the United States, which dramatically reduced its military presence on the Southeast Asian mainland following defeat in Vietnam.[52] Hanoi's late-1978 intervention to remove Pol Pot and his genocidal Khmer Rouge regime, which had been provoking Vietnam with a steady stream of cross-border raids, inspired the pro–Khmer Rouge Chinese to invade Vietnam in early 1979. Beijing, which supported the Khmer Rouge largely as a regional counterweight to the Soviet-backed government in Hanoi, wanted to teach Vietnam a lesson. China and Vietnam, allies in the long struggle against US militarism, had become enemies engaged in the first-ever wars fought between communist-led states.[53] Washington, eager to punish Vietnam and unwilling to jeopardize its fragile new relationship with China, gave tacit support to the genocidal Khmer Rouge regime and praised China's actions in Vietnam. The Third Indochina War, or Sino-Vietnamese Border War, lasted only four weeks but had profound, long-lasting implications not only for regional politics but for revolutionary movements the world over.

These internecine struggles among Asia's communists sent shock waves across the Third World, where leftists assumed that socialist states would never fight each other. Chinese aggression against Vietnam was especially troubling, as Vietnamese revolutionaries had been elevated to almost divine status within the pantheon of national liberation. Cuba's Che Guevara summed up the luminescence of the Vietnamese revolutionary model at the 1966 Tricontinental Conference in Havana: "How close and bright would the future appear if two, three, many Vietnams flowered on the face of the globe, with their quota of death and their immense tragedies, with their daily heroism, with their repeated blows against imperialism, forcing it to disperse its forces under the lash of the growing hatred of the peoples of the world." Chinese aggression against Vietnam, not to mention its new friendship with the United States, seemed to signal that Beijing was no longer a reliable ally for socialists in the Third World. Meanwhile, revelations of atrocities committed by its Khmer Rouge ally did irreparable damage to the reputation of socialism in the Third World.

In the post–Vietnam War era, with communist solidarity in tatters, the Cold War took on an entirely different cast. No longer a bipolar contest between the democratic capitalist West and the socialist East, it became a fragmentary, multisided competition. While China and the Soviet Union were bogged down in competition for the revolutionary vanguard, Cuban and Vietnamese revolutionaries developed alternative models for national liberation. Cuba positioned itself as an active player in distant liberation struggles, sending troops, advisors, and medical staff and asserting itself as an important voice in strategic conversations with Moscow and Beijing, while Vietnam held itself up as a role model. Vietnamese revolutionaries stood for the potential of small Third World nations to achieve independence on their own terms, within the communist sphere but unbeholden to its giants. That example would motivate a new brand of ethno-religious revolutionaries that emerged in the Middle East during the final decade of the Cold War, changing its terms entirely.

Vietnam, meanwhile, found itself increasingly isolated diplomatically and economically in the final decade of the Cold War. While the United States led an effective trade embargo against its former enemy, Hanoi's alliance with the Soviet Union became unstable as the superpower staggered toward extinction. Finally admitting the failures of its postwar economic development policies, Vietnam in 1986 introduced a series of market-oriented reforms known as *doi moi* (new life). Shortly thereafter, Hanoi made cautious moves toward rapprochement with China, although that relationship remains tense even today due to regional power struggles that transcend Cold War structures. Meanwhile, the collapse of the Soviet Union and the end of the Cold War paved the way for Vietnam and the United States to reestablish formal diplomatic relations in 1995, which has led to increasingly close strategic and economic ties. Indeed, in a twist no one would have seen coming in the 1960s, Vietnam is now one of Washington's closest security partners in Asia; partners in opposing Chinese expansionism.

6

Angola

A Tangled Web in Southern Africa

Angola, the richest and most strategic of Portugal's colonies, emerged as a critical proxy conflict during the last wave of decolonization, elevating Africa to the forefront of superpower competition in the final chapter of the Cold War. It gained independence in the mid-1970s, as a coup on the home front finally compelled Portugal to relinquish control of its colonies in southern Africa. That coup resulted in no small part from the strain of more than a decade of war aimed at retaining those same colonies. By the time Portugal stepped aside, Angola was riven by fighting among three rival nationalist groups that that would devolve into a civil war lasting into the next century. The scope, duration, and brutality of that war would be the direct result of foreign interventions led by South Africa, Cuba, the United States, the Soviet Union, Zaire, and China, and featuring a host of other actors in more minor roles.

The calculations underpinning these foreign interventions constituted a tangled web of regional security concerns and shifting Cold War logics that were emblematic of the post–Vietnam War era in which they took place. Angola, a major producer of oil, diamonds, and coffee, boasted significant Western—including American—business investments that guaranteed a level of outside interest. Nonetheless, the United States' initial reaction to the Portuguese coup and its effects on southern Africa was one of yawning disinterest. This was, in part, because Secretary of State Henry Kissinger—then the undisputed captain of American foreign policy—deemed Africa a strategic backwater. Moreover, he sought to limit US interventions in the Third World, which, in the wake of recent events in Vietnam, seemed only to squander American power and prestige. But he and President Gerald Ford would conduct an about-face in response to a Soviet-sponsored Cuban intervention in support of Angola's Marxist faction.

In 1965, Cuba launched a revolutionary program in Africa that reached its climax in Angola. In the words of Piero Gleijeses, the premier chronicler of Cuba's decades-long intervention in Africa, "Angola was, by far, the most important foreign policy initiative of the Cuban revolution."[1] Castro capitalized on the Sino-Soviet split to lure a wary Soviet Union into supporting its Angolan adventure. The Kremlin, in the wake of the Vietnam War, felt the tide of history was turning in the direction of socialist revolution. Although they stepped up support for Third World revolutionaries, Soviet leaders initially were not convinced that Angola was the right place to act. Ultimately, however, concerns over Chinese challenges to the Soviet position in southern Africa—coupled with a desire to avoid alienating its enthusiastic socialist partner in the Caribbean—led Moscow to follow Cuba's lead. The Cuban case for direct intervention was strengthened by South Africa's military invasion, which gave Moscow political cover for its own involvement.

South Africa, panicked by the collapse of its regional security buffer following the coup in Lisbon, opposed Angola's Marxist faction not out of ideological enmity but in response to its support for movements that opposed white-minority regimes in the region, including its own government and its colony in Namibia. Cuban and Soviet involvement threatened Pretoria by bolstering the fortunes of those Black African nationalist fronts. To Pretoria's advantage, though, Havana and Moscow's moves prompted the United States to authorize a robust program of covert aid to South Africa and Zaire's Angolan allies. For Kissinger and his fellow right-wingers, Angola suddenly seemed to offer a perfect opportunity to demonstrate America's ability and resolve to resist communist aggression in the Third World.

It would not be that easy. Congress, acting on its growing distrust of executive power in the realm of foreign policy, would take action to halt Washington's covert aid program. Combined with Cuba's escalation of the war, this doomed South Africa and its Angolan allies to defeat. The 1975–1976 war in Angola—which brought a Marxist regime to power in Luanda—contributed to the collapse of Soviet-American détente, fueled the neoconservative commitment to reassert American power with force, stoked Cuba's revolutionary flames, and emboldened Black African nationalist movements across the region to press their advantage against South Africa. Pretoria would not take this lying down, and its allies in Angola would not accept defeat. A civil war therefore raged in Angola for nearly two more decades, fueled by foreign interventions that shifted with the geopolitical winds of the late Cold War. The story of the Angolan civil war—one of deep human tragedy rooted in the predations of Portuguese colonialism—in many ways tells the tale of Cold War interventionism from the Vietnam War to the collapse of the Soviet Union.

Portugal's colonization of the topographically and ethnically diverse territory in southwestern Africa that would eventually comprise Angola was a drawn-out process. Beginning in the fifteenth century with forays into the region by Portuguese explorers, the gradual expansion of metropolitan control occurred over centuries. It was not until the last decade of the nineteenth century, amid the Scramble for Africa, that Angola's colonial status was formalized through an Anglo-Portuguese agreement. Despite Lisbon's protestations in the first half of the twentieth century that its colonial project reflected a unique, race-blind, utopian Lusotropicalism that bound Portuguese and Africans together as one, historian David Birmingham argues that "Portugal's colonial territories became sources of resource wealth, coerced labor, and national pride." Its African colonies in particular "remained racially stratified, repressive police states well into the 1960s."[2]

By early 1961, conditions in Angola were ripe for rebellion. The colony's white settler plantations had taken to conscripting native laborers into near slave conditions, often shipping them far from home, to places where rival ethnic groups resented their presence. Colonial policies sowed division between Angolans of different ethnic, racial, regional, economic, and religious status. While the vast territory of Angola consisted of several regions with distinct social and economic problems, they were all poised to rise up in opposition to Portugal's exploitative rule. This provided the backdrop to the 1961 February Uprising in Luanda that kicked off Angola's struggle for independence. Although several exiled rebel groups claimed credit for organizing the failed putsch, one historian suggests it was likely a more impromptu eruption of violence among a group of urban youth who sought to free their rabble-rousing friends from the secret police.[3] No matter its provenance, the small but fateful uprising spooked white settlers and unleashed a movement for Angolan independence that would take well over a decade to realize.

The following month, a much greater paroxysm of violence shook northern Angola as white settlers unloaded their guns on a group of demonstrators who were marching peacefully to a coffee plantation office to demand their unpaid wages. The Portuguese vigilantes, inspired by exaggerated accounts of Black-on-white violence over the border in Congo, likely believed they were about to be ambushed. Their gunfire unleashed a series of attacks and counterattacks, spearheaded by a guerrilla organization that would soon reconstitute itself in exile as the Front for the National Liberation of Angola (FNLA).

Portugal, governed by António Salazar's fascist dictatorship since 1932, remained impoverished and poorly industrialized by European standards. Yet it clung to illusions of grandeur stoked by its significant African possessions, including Guinea-Bissau, Mozambique, Angola, and the islands of São Tomé and Príncipe off the coast of central Africa. Unlike France, Britain, and Belgium, it did not have the option of relinquishing formal political control of its colonies while establishing neocolonial relationships that would retain the economic benefits of imperialism. "Without the cheap labor and raw materials that resulted from a harsh forced labor regime," writes Elizabeth Schmidt, "Portugal's industries would not be profitable."[4] Thus, as the "winds of change" swept across much of the continent, Portugal was determined to crush nationalist uprisings in its own African colonies. Salazar issued weapons to white settlers and dispatched a Portuguese conscript army to Angola. Tens of thousands died in the ensuing struggle, inaugurating a protracted colonial war that would eventually help bring down the fascist government in Lisbon. Thousands of Angolans fled across the border to the Congo, where they would remain in exile for the next fourteen years, plotting to liberate their country.[5] Three rival nationalist groups emerged to compete for primacy in the armed struggle, and ultimately for control of the postcolonial state: the FNLA and the Movement for the Liberation of Angola (MPLA), both formed in the mid-1950s, were joined in 1966 by Jonas Savimbi's Union for the Independence of the Totality of Angola (UNITA). Each claimed to represent both the whole of Angola and particular ethnicities, regions, and classes within the vast colony.

The FNLA, founded in 1962 through the merger of two northern regional parties, would remain the largest of Angola's anticolonial movements throughout the 1960s. The movement's uncontested leader was the rigid, authoritarian Holden Roberto, who ultimately proved more interested in personal power than he was in the fate of Angola.[6] A descendant of Kongo Kingdom royalty who grew up across the border in the Belgian Congo, he founded the Union of Peoples of Angola (UPA) in 1954. Throughout the late 1950s, Roberto burnished his nationalist and Pan-African credentials with trips to the UN and the All-African People's Congress of Ghana, where he rubbed shoulders with the likes of the Congo's Patrice Lumumba and Kenya's Tom Mboya. He then returned to Kinshasa to organize a band of guerrillas that, in mid-March 1961, launched an incursion into Angola, taking the lead in the incipient armed struggle against Portuguese colonial rule. "The FNLA ideology," writes Odd Arne Westad, "was a strong African-nativist nationalism—anti-Communist and anti-Western in equal amounts."[7] The peasant-based movement was heavily dependent on support from ethnic Bakongo in the north; indeed, it started as a separatist movement and only later shifted its focus to independence.[8] FNLA efforts to broaden support in the preindependence years were hampered by its members' abiding suspicions of more privileged whites, *mestizos* (mixed-race Angolans), and *assimilados* (the term for Black Angolans who had assimilated into Portuguese language and culture). In regional and international terms, the FNLA owed its survival to Zaire's long-standing grant of sanctuary and support, secret links to the US Central Intelligence Agency (CIA), limited aid from the People's Republic of China (PRC), and support from South Africa.

The MPLA, founded by a group of Marxist Angolan intellectuals in the late 1950s, would be led throughout the 1960s and 1970s by the Afro-Socialist medical doctor and mild-mannered poet Agostinho Neto. The movement's stronghold was among the Mbundu in north-central Angola, including the capital city of Luanda.[9] It also enjoyed the support of urban intellectuals, *mestizos, assimilados,* and a small number of Portuguese settlers.[10] Though the MPLA, with its Marxist bent, would later obtain backing from Cuba, the Soviet Union, and other socialist bloc countries, by no means was it submissive to Moscow's ideological direction. Indeed, it was very much a product of Angola's unique circumstances and steered by Neto's own life experiences. A Black African born to a Methodist minister in a village about forty miles south of Luanda, the future MPLA leader leveraged his Western education to earn a scholarship from the American Methodist Church to study medicine in Lisbon. As a student in Portugal, his association with the outlawed Communist Party put him in the crosshairs of the secret police, landing him in a Portuguese prison. The newly formed Amnesty International chose Neto as one of its first prisoners of conscience, perhaps a factor in securing his release. In 1959, with his new Portuguese bride in tow, Neto returned to Angola, where he joined the underground MPLA, a nascent anticolonial movement that had been formed just three years prior. Within a year, his political activities once again led to his arrest by colonial officials, sending him first back to a Lisbon prison, then to house arrest, and eventually into exile in Zaire, where he took up leadership of the movement's armed struggle against Portugal.[11]

In 1966, two years after a falling-out with Roberto led him to quit the FNLA, Jonas Savimbi formed UNITA, the last of Angola's three major nationalist organizations. The southern-based movement claimed to represent Angola's largest ethnic group, the Ovimbundu, thereby posing a formidable challenge to the FNLA.[12] Savimbi was a confident, charismatic, master of self-presentation; a consummate networker. He was one of few Ovimbundu with significant international ties. He studied in Portugal and Switzerland, ditching his medical studies in favor of a course in politics at the University of Lausanne, although he still "called himself 'Doctor' in the way the honorific title was used in Portugal to denote any university graduate."[13] Within Angola, he leveraged his connections to Swiss and American missionary churches and to the Benguela railway to mobilize popular support for a guerrilla movement that emphasized self-sufficiency. His diplomatic approach was entirely pragmatic, aimed at securing his own personal success and survival, and that of UNITA. Savimbi initially adopted a Maoist ideology to court Chinese support but later abandoned it as he pursued closer ties with the United States. In the early 1970s he entered into secret negotiations with Portuguese army officers and, in the postindependence era, aligned with South Africa.

Throughout the 1960s, amid these nationalist challenges, and in the face of the continent's rapid decolonization, officials in Salazar's government remained convinced that they could hold onto their African colonies, including the anticolonial hotbeds of Mozambique, Angola, and Guinea-Bissau. In 1961, leading anticolonial movements from the three colonies founded the Conference of Nationalist Organizations of the Portuguese Colonies (CONCP), and in 1966 they participated in the Tricontinental Conference in Havana, which focused on the liberation of peoples in Africa, Asia, and Latin America. In Angola, however, rebel forces made little headway, and Portugal's armed forces were able to contain the war to the sparsely populated east. This relative stability on the battlefield, combined with support from NATO allies who were determined to bolster Portugal's faltering economy against the prospects of a communist takeover, led politicians and business elites in Lisbon to believe they could secure a solid future for white hegemony in southern Africa, where Portugal had strong ties with Ian Smith's white-minority regime in Rhodesia and the apartheid state of South Africa.[14]

John F. Kennedy provided tacit support for Portugal's colonial wars in Africa that, at first glance, seems surprising. Kennedy, who considered colonialism a grave diplomatic liability for the Western alliance and prioritized building relationships with African nationalist leaders, initially resisted Portugal's appeals for help putting down the March 1961 rebellion in Angola. But Salazar possessed a trump card in the form of control over US access to a strategically critical military base in the Azores Islands. Portugal first granted the United States access to the base in 1944 through an agreement that would come up for renewal every few years. Implicit in the deal, which included a provision for the United States to restore full Portuguese sovereignty over East Timor, was an understanding that "the Portuguese colonial empire would be tolerated at least in the short term."[15] Upon first taking office, Kennedy's administration made some attempts to distance the United States from Portuguese colonialism, voting in favor of UN Security Council resolutions urging colonial reforms in Lisbon, adopting a new policy of refusing to sell Portugal weapons for non-NATO purposes (namely the African theater), and even making overtures to Angolan nationalists, particularly Holden Roberto. By mid-1962, however, the United States began an about-face, retreating to the familiar territory of accommodating Portuguese colonialism. Salazar's threats to dislodge American forces from the North Atlantic took on new urgency amid the October 1962 Cuban Missile Crisis—just two months before the latest base agreement was set to expire—as Portugal refused to guarantee unimpeded US access to the Azores even as Washington stared into the looming abyss of nuclear war with the Soviet Union. This, combined with congressional pushback against Kennedy's anticolonial policies, divisions within his own administration, and European support for Portugal's war effort, meant that the United States would not stand in the way of Salazar's struggle to retain his African colonies. This general trend continued under Lyndon Johnson, who relegated Africa—especially Portuguese Africa—to the periphery of his strategic concerns.[16] From the Kennedy through Nixon administrations, "American weapons, tanks, planes, ships, helicopters, napalm, and chemical defoliants were used against Africans in the Portuguese colonies, while American military personnel trained thousands of Portuguese soldiers in counterinsurgency techniques."[17]

The year 1968 brought leadership changes to both Lisbon and Washington that would bear greatly on Angola's future. Marcelo Caetano took the helm as Portugal's prime minister, replacing the seventy-nine-year-old Salazar—who had ruled since 1932—following a brain injury the elderly dictator sustained in a bathtub accident at home. From the more "liberal" wing of Lisbon's fascist regime, Caetano promised constitutional reforms yet failed to make any substantive changes to Portugal's colonial policies. He continued the wars in Angola, Mozambique, and Guinea-Bissau, but in the context of a vastly improved relationship with the United States. Newly elected President Richard Nixon and his national security advisor, Henry Kissinger, brought to the White House a much more favorable attitude than their democratic predecessors toward the white regimes in southern Africa. To Nixon and Kissinger, the stable continuation of white-minority rule was vastly preferable to the instability wrought by Africa's violent anticolonial movements. An entente ensued between Nixon and Caetano, as the former refrained from UN votes pertaining to Portugal and relaxed its arms policy to allow for the diversion of some types of equipment to Africa, and the latter committed to resume stalled talks on the Azores, agreeing in 1971 to extend US rights for another three years.[18]

Just as the diplomatic context improved for Portugal's colonial crusaders, the domestic political outlook dimmed. "By the 1970s," writes Candace Sobers, "Portugal's simultaneous colonial wars on Guinea-Bissau, Mozambique, and Angola were sapping the metropole's resources and straining its social fabric."[19] As casualties mounted, Portuguese young men were expatriating themselves in increasing numbers to avoid the draft. Junior officers grew convinced that they would be unable to reap the benefits of wartime grifting that had fattened the previous generation. And Portugal's business class, ever more resentful of stratospheric war taxes, came to the conclusion that it would be better served by shifting its focus away from Africa and toward Europe.[20]

On April 25, 1974, a group of young officers calling themselves the Armed Forces Movement (MFA) staged a bloodless coup in Lisbon, ousting Caetano and dismantling Portugal's authoritarian regime. Although the strain of the ongoing colonial wars in Africa was not the sole reason for the coup, it was a key contributing factor. Former general António de Spínola, whom Caetano had recently sacked for advocating a political solution to the colonial wars, took the helm of Portugal's new provisional government. He would move immediately toward decolonization but not quickly enough for a group of leftist MFA leaders who, on July 27, 1974, forced him to sign Law 7/74—also known as the Decolonization Law—which promised rapid progress toward independence for all of Portugal's African colonies.[21] "The major Portuguese Government objective in Angola," noted the US National Security Council, "was to get out with honor, if possible, but in any case to get out."[22] Guinea-Bissau was granted independence almost immediately, followed soon after by Mozambique. Angola was, as one Portuguese military officer put it, "the most difficult case," due to a host of unique demographic, economic, and political circumstances.[23]

Chief among those circumstances was the weak and divided insurgency. "The three Angolan guerilla movements," writes historian Piero Gleijeses, "had fought one another as bitterly as they had the Portuguese."[24] In the words of historian Jeremy Ball, "the conditions for independence in 1974 were disastrous," in no small part due to Portugal's abject failure to plan for a transition of power to Angolans.[25] Consumed by what amounted to a civil war within an anticolonial struggle, neither the MPLA, the FNLA, nor UNITA had established consistent control over any substantial portion of the population. Neither had they developed formidable political branches capable of taking over the operations of an independent state. The nature and composition of the three rival groups only compounded Angola's underlying ethnic, racial, and socioeconomic tensions. And the MPLA, once the most effective fighting force of the three, had been decimated in the early 1970s by a series of Portuguese operations and was, by the time of the Portuguese coup, militarily weak and wracked with internal division between three rival factions. Neto's group, headquartered in Tanzania, faced serious challenges from Daniel Chipenda's Zambia-backed "Eastern Revolt," as well as the Congo-based "Active Revolt" led by "the father of Angolan nationalism," Mario de Andrade.[26]

In the months following the coup in Lisbon, which came as an unwelcome surprise to Nixon and Kissinger, the United States evinced little interest in the fate of Portuguese Africa. Nixon's administration, distracted by the Watergate scandal and subject to intense congressional pressure on foreign policy matters following revelations of its complicity in the 1973 Chilean coup, had little domestic political room to maneuver.[27] And, in line with the Nixon Doctrine, the duo had oriented their foreign policy toward reining in, not expanding, Washington's Third World interventionism. Believing that

American power had been badly damaged by unnecessary foreign interventions like the disastrous one currently unraveling in Vietnam, their goals were to nurture détente with the Soviet Union, protect vital American interests, and conscript regional "policemen" to fight far-off battles in lieu of sending American soldiers. Moreover, considering a spate of recent setbacks to Soviet policy in Africa—from Mobutu's victory in Zaire to the downfall of prominent radical leaders in Algeria, Ghana, and Mali—Nixon and Kissinger believed the communist threat to the continent had been neutralized.[28] Though certainly concerned about the fate of regional allies like South Africa and Zaire, they saw little reason to intervene forcefully in Angola's decolonization process.

Nixon and Kissinger's lackluster response to the decolonization of Portuguese Africa was, in part, due to Moscow's lukewarm support for the MPLA. Though inspired by the US failure in Vietnam to adopt a more activist approach to the Third World—especially in Africa—the Soviet Politburo found Neto difficult to trust. Moscow first backed the MPLA in 1970, but the relationship quickly hit turbulence. Soviet officials found Neto to be an inept communicator, poorly organized, and largely responsible not only for the factionalism within the MPLA but also for the organization's inability to collaborate with the FNLA.[29] On top of this, Neto's desperate decision to seek aid from the PRC in 1972, after the Soviets cut him off, instilled in Moscow a lasting suspicion that the MPLA was really pro-Chinese.[30] This tapped into Moscow's abiding fear of being outmaneuvered by Beijing for influence over left-wing African liberation movements. Indeed, when the Soviet Union resumed aid to the MPLA after Caetano's overthrow, it was driven primarily by a desire to combat perceptions that it was less willing and able than the Chinese to support national liberation movements on the continent.[31] Initially, however, Moscow made aid to the MPLA contingent upon Neto uniting the organization's rival factions. "Finally," writes Gleijeses, "after Neto had regained control of the movement, the Soviets relented, accepting that unity was a chimera."[32] In December 1974, despite its reluctance to get sucked into Angolan affairs, the Kremlin drew up plans for supplying Neto's MPLA with weapons and stockpiles of ammunition.

Just a few weeks later, on January 15, 1975, Roberto, Neto, and Savimbi met in Portugal to sign the Alvor Agreement, which recognized the MPLA, the FNLA, and UNITA as "the sole and legitimate representatives of the people of Angola."[33] The accord established a provisional tripartite government for Angola with a Portuguese high commissioner who would rule until November 11, 1975, at which point Portugal would transfer power peacefully to Angolan nationals. This orderly plan had little to do with reality on the ground. As Gleijeses observes, "The Transitional Government took over on January 31 in an atmosphere of deep mistrust."[34]

Although the FNLA boasted a much stronger military than its rivals, the MPLA had a more substantial base of popular support. Roberto therefore decided to press the FNLA advantage by provoking a war. Chipenda—Neto's defeated MPLA rival who was now in cahoots with Roberto and Mobutu—sent forces to Luanda to establish a presence in the capital, with the aim of asserting his right to participate in the postindependence government from which he was excluded by the terms of the Alvor Agreement. Meanwhile, FNLA troops attacked the MPLA in the north, with the ultimate goal of taking Luanda and positioning the FNLA to assume power on the day of Angola's independence.

The FNLA was emboldened by support from a convoluted team of international bedfellows. Roberto had long benefited from the sponsorship of Zaire's Mobutu, to whom he was related by marriage. FNLA fortunes therefore improved mightily in the early 1970s, as Zaire reconciled with the PRC, opening the possibility of Chinese aid to the FNLA. Chinese support, although short-lived and ultimately ineffectual, contributed to Roberto's aggressive posture.[35] So, too, did American aid, as the secretive Forty Committee—a top-level US government review board assigned to vet covert operations—met a week after the Alvor proceedings to approve modest covert aid to Roberto in the sum of $300,000. "The U.S. government still had no overarching strategy concerning Angola," writes historian Tiago Moreira de Sá, "and was simply reacting, on the one hand, to intelligence that the USSR was sending arms to the MPLA and, on the other, to Mobutu's pleas for aid."[36] FNLA aggression inaugurated a renewed state of war and ushered in a period of increasing foreign intervention into Angola's messy decolonization process.

At the start of 1975, while the MPLA remained politically and administratively superior to the FNLA, it was at a distinct military disadvantage. Before the provisional government took power on January 31, the MPLA initiated a plan to transform its ragtag forces into a regular army, the Popular Armed Forces for the Liberation of Angola (FAPLA).[37] In mid-May, after several months of intermittent fighting and abortive cease-fires, FAPLA regained the initiative on the battlefield. In light of Washington's decision to support their enemies, Soviet leaders concluded it was their "moral internationalist duty" to increase aid to their allies in Angola.[38] An influx of military hardware to the MPLA, first, from Yugoslavia—the MPLA's most stalwart international supporter throughout the 1960s and early 1970s—and then from the Soviet Union, had steadily erased the FNLA advantage.[39] Moreover, the MPLA capitalized on popular resentment of FNLA brutality to recruit heavily among the population in and around Luanda. Following another brief, futile cease-fire on June 7, FAPLA managed to expel FNLA forces from Luanda and began attacking FNLA strongholds in the north. Soviet bloc military aid, it appeared, had enabled Moscow's allies to best Mobutu and Kissinger's anticommunist clients. This turning of the tide in Angola's internal struggle suddenly delivered the country top billing in the Cold War, setting the stage for independent decisions undertaken in Washington, Pretoria, and Havana to intervene on a massive scale in Angola's civil war.

In July 1975, contravening National Security Council advice that he himself had recently solicited, Kissinger began lobbying Gerald Ford's administration to adopt an offensive policy toward Angola. The failure of the FNLA/UNITA offensive against the MPLA, evidence of increasing Soviet involvement, and pressure from allied governments in the region all contributed to the new Ford administration's decision to step up US intervention.[40] Appeals from Zaire's Mobutu and Zambian president Kenneth Kuanda persuaded Kissinger that their regimes—and with them the system of pro-American stability that prevailed in southern Africa—would be threatened by an MPLA victory in Angola.[41] "Kissinger," argues historian James Meriwether, "began offering a 1970s' African version of the domino theory. If Angola went communist, then so would go Zaire, then Zambia, Tanzania, Rhodesia, and eventually South Africa."[42] Moreover, as Gleijeses notes, Soviet meddling in the conflict meant that "a vital interest was indeed at stake: prestige."[43] Should Washington stand by while the Soviets tipped the scales in favor of a Marxist ally in Africa, the United States would lose face with the FNLA and UNITA's international supporters, which included China, England, France, South Africa, Zaire, and Zambia, among others. Kissinger was especially concerned that, coming on the heels of America's humiliating retreat from Vietnam, the Soviet Union might take American inaction in Angola as a sign of weakness, a failure of American resolve to resist communist expansion, and an invitation for the Kremlin to promote revolution more vigorously throughout the Third World. On July 18, over strong opposition from both the State Department and the CIA, the Ford administration authorized a robust program of covert aid to the FNLA and UNITA. Operation IAFEATURE consisted of three types of aid—totaling more than $30 million over the next few months—including funding to train, equip, and transport troops, money for the purchase of military equipment to be channeled through Zaire, and additional resources to recruit mercenary advisors to Roberto and Savimbi's armies.[44]

Just as the United States launched IAFEATURE, South Africa took its first steps toward what would soon become a major—albeit secretive—direct military intervention in Angola. US and South African intelligence agencies worked together closely during this period, as both countries funneled funding, weapons, and supplies to UNITA and the FNLA. South African officials acted in a desperate attempt to redress the catastrophic blow to the country's regional security buffer wrought by the prior year's coup in Lisbon. Once protected from hostile regimes to its northern flank by a kindred white-minority colonial administration in Portuguese Africa, Pretoria now faced a new leftist regime in Mozambique alongside a regionally destabilizing civil war in Angola that threatened to yield a Marxist-dominated postcolonial government. Its other key ally in the region, Ian Smith's Rhodesia, was on the ropes, as was its own colony of Namibia, where a liberation movement led by the Marxist South West Africa People's Organization (SWAPO) gained steam.[45] All of these trends were exacerbated by increasing Soviet and Cuban involvement in Angola, which enabled Moscow and Havana to widen their influence among leftist movements in the region and invited SWAPO to expand its operations across the Angolan border.[46] Roberto and Savimbi, who would officially join forces in August and declare war on the MPLA in September, lobbied South Africa for support. Savimbi, whose UNITA fielded by far the weakest military of the three Angolan liberation movements, largely avoided the fighting while working behind the scenes to forge an alliance with Roberto and garner South African backing. Pretoria devoured his poetic appeals to democracy, free elections, and unity, and especially his promises of a postwar modus vivendi with South Africa based on the principle of noninterference and the creation of a regional anticommunist bloc.

On July 14, 1975, in an effort to forestall what appeared to be an otherwise certain MPLA victory, South Africa's Prime Minister John Vorster approved the provision of more than $14 million worth of weapons to Savimbi and Roberto's forces. His assent was predicated on the condition that the weapons be purchased abroad to obscure Pretoria's involvement. South African officials understood all too well the international backlash they would incur for meddling in Angola's decolonization and recognized that evidence of collusion with the apartheid state would undermine their Angolan allies' credibility in African nationalist circles.[47] It was with utmost secrecy, then, that a small patrol of South Africa Defense Force (SADF) troops first entered Angola the next month, initially with the narrow goal of protecting the Cuenene hydroelectric project that powered South Africa's uranium mines in Namibia. Over the next two months the SADF launched raids on SWAPO camps in Angola, and across the border into Namibia, before clashing directly with FAPLA troops. Just days after that first skirmish, on October 14, 1975, Vorster launched Operation Savannah, a full-scale military incursion into Angola. The covert operation, led by a Zulu column, entered the country via Namibia. Its objective was to eliminate FAPLA forces in southwestern and central Angola en route to capturing Luanda by November, in time for the FNLA and UNITA to accept the scheduled transfer of power from Portugal. "With the South African invasion," writes Gleijeses, "the second phase of the Angolan war began. Foreign troops would take center stage as a bush war entered into an East-West crisis."[48]

Confounding American intelligence assessments, Cuba—with indispensable Soviet support—soon entered the fray, staging a massive airlift of troops to aid the MPLA in its resistance to the SADF/FNLA/UNITA offensive. In 1959, when Fidel Castro led the Cuban Revolution, he was not yet a confirmed Marxist, nor was he a presumed foe of the United States. Enmity quickly developed between Havana and Washington, however, largely over a series of socialist economic policies that harmed American business interests on the island. President Dwight Eisenhower's cautious optimism toward the new regime devolved into a determination to overthrow its leader. Soon after moving into the White House, JFK oversaw the famously disastrous Bay of Pigs coup attempt, then dug in his heels to punish Castro with crippling sanctions and an often-comical array of covert assassination plans. While this wedge drove Cuba deeper into alliance with the Soviet Union, Khrushchev's retreat from the October 1962 Cuban Missile Crisis convinced Castro that he could not count on the Kremlin to guarantee Cuban security. Capitalizing on the Sino-Soviet split to join Beijing in criticizing Soviet revisionism without risking Soviet support, Castro developed his own Third World revolutionary movement aimed both at spreading Cuban ideology and securing the island against an American attack. Castro first charged Che Guevara with exporting the Cuban revolutionary model to Latin America and the Caribbean. But the Latin American strategy ran into trouble almost immediately, prompting Castro and Guevara to turn their attention to Africa, where they saw an opportunity to strike at the soft underbelly of American imperialism, promote socialism in newly independent states, and pay back "a debt to Cuba's African ancestors," whose "blood runs through our veins."[49] Cuba's revolutionary adventures in Africa began in 1962, with minor support for the Algerians, followed by a much more robust commitment to Congolese and Angolan rebels in 1965. That mission ended in failure, prompting Castro to moderate his approach to the continent. A year later, though, Castro dispatched a contingent of doctors and military instructors to support rebels in Guinea-Bissau, where they remained until 1974. This was Cuba's longest and most successful intervention in Africa prior to the introduction of Cuban troops into Angola in November 1975.[50]

Recent improvements in Havana's relationship with Washington and the West contributed to US officials' dismissal of prospects for Cuban intervention in Angola. Kissinger, however, underestimated Castro's revolutionary fervor. Cuba's deployment, after months of equivocation, coincided with Roberto's last-ditch effort to take Luanda before the deadline for Portuguese withdrawal. Despite South Africa's intervention, support from Zaire, and substantial American military aid to the FNLA and UNITA, the MPLA had been steadily gaining ground. In mid-October, FNLA forces en route to the capital launched an attack on the MPLA that, with the help of about forty Cuban instructors, succeeded in pushing the FNLA back to Quifangondo, where they held the line. According to Gleijeses, this was the first time Cubans participated in the fighting, though another set of advisors would again do so five days later.[51] It was through this direct Cuban combat experience that Castro learned of the well-masked South African invasion. On November 2–3, Cuban and South African forces met for the first time, resulting in an MPLA rout. The shock of SADF presence in Angola prompted Castro to move up his timeline for Operation Carlotta, a Soviet-backed plan to dispatch Cuban combat troops to Angola after the MPLA declared independence. Instead, on November 4 he gave the green light for Carlotta to commence immediately. Just three days later, a battalion of 652 Cuban special forces boarded planes bound for Luanda, followed by an artillery regiment traveling by sea. The planes landed on November 9, and Cuban reinforcements lined up behind FAPLA at Quifangondo, ready to intervene should Roberto's forces succeed in penetrating its defenses.[52]

Having examined Cuban and Soviet sources extensively, historians now agree that Cuban officials made the decision to send troops on their own, without consulting the Soviet Union, whose leaders were then presented with a fait accompli.[53] Havana and Moscow had been collaborating for months to supply Neto's forces through Congolese territory, but Moscow resisted Castro's pleas to intervene militarily before Neto could declare independence, after which he could legally request the presence of foreign troops. In early November, however, when Soviet leaders learned of Cuba's intervention, they quickly jumped on board. Their earlier concerns about setting back the process of détente with the United States dimmed in the face of an imminent MPLA defeat. Moreover, the South African intervention gave them cover to intervene more openly, without provoking the ire of other African allies.

On November 11, MPLA forces squared off against the FNLA and UNITA in pitched battle at Quifangondo. That evening, in what one journalist has called "one of the most unusual acts of decolonization ever witnessed in Africa," the Portuguese high commissioner held a ceremony at the governor's palace in Luanda—at which no Angolans were present—to transfer sovereignty to "the Angolan people."[54] He then lowered the flag and drove off in a limousine, washing Portugal's hands of nearly five centuries of colonial rule. Right around midnight, Neto took the stage in Luanda to announce independence for the People's Republic of Angola. The FNLA and UNITA, for their part, announced an alternative Democratic People's Republic of Angola headquartered in Huambo. Meanwhile, the battle for control of the country raged on, with foreign armies en scène, poised to tip the scales.

The MPLA prevailed at Quifangondo without the help of Cuban special forces. Immediately, though, it faced the far greater challenge of staving off a Zulu column, which was advancing rapidly from the South. On November 23, Cuba's decisive victory over SADF at the Battle of Ebo proved a key turning point. The South Africans, unsettled by their bloody defeat, halted their offensive, giving the Cubans breathing room to build up their forces. Back in Washington, desperate to stave off their allies' defeat at the hands of Soviet-backed Cuban forces, the Ford administration approved an additional $7 million for IAFEATURE, bringing the total of US aid to $31.7 million. This depleted the CIA Contingency Reserve Fund for fiscal year 1975, requiring additional appropriations to be approved by Congress. In a move that would prove pivotal for the trajectory of the Angolan War, Ford attempted to bury in the 1976 Defense Appropriation Bill an allocation of $28 million for IAFEATURE.[55]

Ford's attempt to secure congressional funding for covert operations in Angola came just weeks after the Western press broke news of South Africa's invasion, and "the stench of U.S. collusion with Pretoria was in the air."[56] With the wounds of Washington's failures in Vietnam still fresh, conditions were ripe for liberals in Congress to challenge executive authority in foreign policy that, they claimed, had gone unchecked for most of the Cold War. They charged that successive administrations had sacrificed American ideals of democracy, human rights, and, self-determination on the altar of anticommunism, ceded control of foreign policy to the military, and shrouded diplomacy in a cloud of secrecy that worked only to subvert the democratic process. The 1973 War Powers Act was a significant step toward reasserting congressional power in foreign policy, but Ford's request for IAFEATURE funds gave legislative critics of US Cold War foreign policy an opportunity to exercise the power of the purse directly to veto Washington's misadventure in Angola. On December 19, 1975, the Senate passed the Tunney Amendment to the Defense Appropriations Act of 1976 by a vote of 54 to 22, cutting off funds for the current operation. The next June, Congress would pass the Clark Amendment to the US Arms Export Control Act of 1976, making permanent the ban on private aid to groups engaged in military or paramilitary operations in Angola. In the waning days of 1975, Washington's foray into the Angolan War ground to a halt. "The two amendments," writes Robert David Johnson, "represented the high point of congressional revolt against the anti-Communist ethos of the Cold War and executive authority in foreign policy."[57]

South African forces were hardly in a position to weather the withdrawal of American support. During the last two months of 1975, Cuban forces had successfully repelled repeated SADF attempts to penetrate their defenses and push forward to Luanda. Now Cuba and the Soviet Union, emboldened by Ford's legislative defeat, started pouring additional troops and weapons into Angola. On January 14, a diplomatically isolated Vorster ordered South African troops to withdraw. "Bereft of the South African shield," writes Gleijeses, "UNITA and the FNLA promptly crumbled."[58] With Roberto and Savimbi in retreat and Cuban troops continuing to pour into the country, the MPLA quickly swept up previous enemy strongholds. In mid-February, as the anti-MPLA capital of Huambo fell to Neto's army, the OAU and most African

A Cuban soldier who fights for the MPLA in the Angolan civil war drives a tractor with MPLA forces on a nationalized farm around January 21, 1976. (AP Photo)

states recognized an independent, MPLA-led People's Republic of Angola. A growing number of Western countries followed suit the next month, as SADF completed its withdrawal. However, as historian Christopher Saunders claims, "South Africa remained in a virtual, though undeclared, state of war with Angola for the next decade and more."[59]

On March 31, 1976, in the first of five UN resolutions over the next five years to censure South Africa for its direct involvement in Angola, the UN Security Council voted 9–0 to condemn South African aggression and demand that it compensate Angola for war damages. The United States, France, Italy, and Japan abstained from the vote, as did China, whose leaders unleashed a torrent of criticism against "Soviet social-imperialism and its Cuban mercenaries" for their "towering crimes" against Angola.[60] Although China had withdrawn its support in late October as news of the SADF invasion went public, the uncomfortable truth was that each of these powers found themselves in bed with South Africa's pariah apartheid state and on the losing side of a proxy war against Cuba and the Soviet Union.

Cuba's military intervention was decisive in preventing the MPLA from succumbing to Roberto and Savimbi's SADF-backed forces. This, Castro's greatest of successes in Africa emboldened him to broaden the island nation's revolutionary program on the continent, with the lofty goal of liberating it from American and Chinese influence. In the coming years, Cuban revolutionaries pursued a series of smaller military operations and training missions, alongside substantial technical assistance and student exchange programs. For more than a decade, tens of thousands of Cubans armed with Soviet weapons remained in Angola to defend the MPLA regime. Castro, having learned from the Angolan War the value of deference, was careful thereafter to coordinate Cuba's Africa strategy with the Kremlin and to pay obeisance to his Soviet benefactors.[61]

For Soviet premier Leonid Brezhnev, claims historian Odd Arne Westad, "Angola became a benchmark for 'active solidarity with the peoples of Africa and Asia' and evidence that the Soviet Union could advance socialism in the Third World during a period of détente with the United States."[62] Brezhnev remained adamant, as historian Raymond Garthoff put it, "that east-west détente was not an endorsement of the status quo in the world."[63] Indeed, the Soviet Politburo believed détente was "creating favorable conditions for the struggle for national liberation and social progress."[64] Therefore, just as signs of weakness began to appear in the Soviet economy— and in no small part to distract attention from them—Moscow adopted a more optimistic, adventuristic approach to the Third World. This included continued backing for Cuban forces in Africa and increased support for the South African ANC, especially after the summer of 1976, when a massive uprising— and subsequent brutal repression—of Black schoolchildren at Soweto seemed to confirm Soviet suspicions that the country was ripe for revolution.[65]

In Pretoria, the Angolan loss not only raised the threat of Soviet support for South Africa's regional foes, it augured an ominous shift in the region's racial power dynamics. In the words of one South African analyst: "In Angola Black troops—Cubans and Angolans—have defeated White troops in military exchanges, and that psychological edge, the advantage that the White man has enjoyed and exploited over 300 years of colonialism and empire, is slipping away."[66] The South Africans were desperate to defend their apartheid regime, and control of their Namibian colony, in the face of greatly diminished regional security and heightened international scorn. With the MPLA in charge of Angola, SWAPO and the ANC had a permanent sanctuary from which to coordinate operations against Namibia and South Africa, respectively.

"The most important aspect of the Angola episode from the standpoint of American leaders," in historian Raymond Garthoff's assessment, "was concern over setting a precedent that might encourage bolder and more active Soviet efforts to extend its influence," especially using what they described as Cuban surrogates.[67] In liberal political circles, revelations about IAFEATURE—and strong suspicion of US collusion with South Africa—raised unprecedented anti-interventionist sentiments that threatened to restrain US policymakers in the future. For neoconservatives, Washington's failure to prevent a communist victory in Angola—and the role of Congress in blocking the funding necessary to do so—raised alarm bells about America's dwindling power and waning resolve to engage in the Cold War struggle for influence in the Third World. Right-wing Americans would soon join critical Chinese voices in decrying the country's post–Vietnam War capitulationism. For American officials who rejected Brezhnev's view that conflict over the Third World could be compatible with efforts to reduce East-West tensions, the events in Angola constituted a breach of trust that doomed the already wounded project of détente. Foreign intervention in the Angolan War also elevated Africa—formerly viewed as a strategic sideshow—to the forefront of American concerns, where it would remain for the duration of the Cold War.

In Angola, the transition from war to state-building was not a smooth one. The MPLA government in Luanda brought to the job far greater war-making than administrative experience. The years following independence laid bare the challenges of postcolonial governance amid a host of challenges. These included ongoing rural-urban divides, internal ethnic and ideological conflicts, economic dysfunction caused in part by the abrupt Portuguese withdrawal, regional struggles between Black African nationalist leaders and apartheid South Africa, and the increased salience of Cold War ideological and military conflicts to the affairs of southern Africa. Perhaps most press-ingly, Portugal's rapid withdrawal of industrial capital led almost immedi-ately to high rates of urban unemployment, just as rural peasants began flocking to depressed cities with dreams of prosperity that would soon be dashed. This created an urban powder keg that Neto's rivals within the ruling clique would seek to explode.

The first serious challenge to MPLA leadership came not from a foreign army but from a disaffected faction of the ruling party that began by mobi-lizing underprivileged urbanites into seemingly innocuous activities like study groups and football clubs. On May 27, 1977, former MPLA central committee member Nito Alves, along with key members of the army, the police, and the administration, leveraged this discontent to marshal a coup attempt in Luanda.[68] The MPLA quickly put down the rebellion and elimi-nated Alves and his clique, but the episode revealed cracks in the regime's hold on power. The government responded with a program of vicious repri-sals against anyone rumored to be involved with the plot, and borrowed from the Portuguese colonial playbook to mobilize security forces to suppress any future dissent.[69] Although Alves, in the months leading up to the uprising, had managed to curry favor with Moscow, Soviet officials ultimately deferred to the Cubans. Having hitched its star to Neto—who would succumb to cancer in a Moscow hospital just two years later—and established an ongo-ing presence in the country, Cuba "played a decisive role in defeating the revolt."[70] The Soviet-Cuban mission in Angola thus found itself bound to an increasingly tyrannical government that was about to confront a much big-ger internal challenge brewing in the countryside.

Camped out in the central highlands, Savimbi maneuvered to seize con-trol of widespread disaffection among the rural populace to revive UNITA as the chief organ of resistance to the Luanda government. Savimbi's approach turned out to be ruthless and deeply inhumane. "The objective of UNITA," writes Birmingham, "was to impoverish zones under government control by indiscriminate robbing, killing, and burning." Survivors—men, women, and children—were forcibly relocated to "liberated zones" and, in many cases, recruited to become the next generation of guerrilla fighters. Ostensibly car-ried out in the name of Ovimbundu peasants, Savimbi's antigovernment strategy placed rural members of the ethnic group in the crosshairs of UNITA and MPLA violence. Government forces, "assuming all free peasants to be potential UNITA sympathizers, adopted the same arbitrary and inhumane strategy as its colonial forebearers," herding them into barbed-wire villages—akin to South Vietnam's strategic hamlets—designed to cut them off from rebel influence. Rebel and government forces alike engaged in scorched-earth tactics aimed at starving out the enemy that ultimately resulted in a famine so deep it "caused the death of half a million children in the 1980s."[71]

This cruelty was cooked up at home, but its scope and duration expanded immeasurably throughout the 1980s as a result of foreign intervention into Angola's "war of destabilization." Between 1976 and 1981, Pretoria undertook only limited operations in the country aimed at facilitating UNITA's ability to retain its strongholds. In 1978, the tide began to shift toward more robust South African intervention as defense minister P. W. Botha was promoted to replace Vorster as prime minister and, within months, approved a more proactive role for the SADF.[72] Botha rejected Vorster's recent attempts to secure white-minority rule at home by pursuing détente with neighboring Black nationalist regimes, instead reverting to a more militaristic approach to defeating regional foes. This was aimed particularly at Angola, which, with support from Cuban forces, had been giving aid and sanctuary to South Africa's enemies, notably SWAPO and the ANC.

Pretoria was motivated less by the ideological struggle between communism and capitalism than by the pressing need to defend its Namibian colony and its own government from the rising threat of left-wing Black liberation movements. But the permanent presence of Soviet-sponsored Cuban forces in Angola gave Botha an easy pretext for his decision to ramp up support for UNITA and intervene directly in Angola. Cuban participation in the war against Savimbi's forces, though limited in the early 1980s, also helps explain Western—especially US—support for South African maneuvers despite the potential taint of association with the apartheid regime.[73] As long as Pretoria could reasonably claim that it served as a bulwark against Soviet expansionism Africa, it would have a winning formula for courting American support.

In 1981, Ronald Reagan gave Washington's nod of approval for South Africa's renewed intervention in Angola. This was demonstrated most clearly when the United States vetoed a proposal before the UN Security Council to condemn Pretoria for a recent incursion into the country. As the newly elected Republican president replaced Jimmy Carter in the White House, he proceeded to thrill neoconservatives by inaugurating a fierce revitalization of the Cold War aimed at supporting Third World anticommunist "freedom fighters" in "low intensity conflicts" designed not only to halt but to roll back the tide of communism. At first glance, this seems a stark departure from Jimmy Carter's foreign policy, which, in the name of restoring morality to American foreign policy, emphasized human rights over traditional Cold War considerations. In fact, the peanut farmer from Georgia viewed human rights—albeit an earnestly held priority—not as a replacement for Cold War competition but as a tool for besting the Soviet Union, especially in the Third World, where the United States had been losing one high-profile battle after another, to the great detriment of its prestige and morale. The second half of Carter's presidency was dominated by what his national security advisor, Zbigniew Brzezinski, described as "a rising arc of crisis" across much of the Third World—including southern Africa, the Horn of Africa, Iran, and Afghanistan—that fueled a resurgence of Soviet-American conflict.[74] Within Carter's cabinet, the hawkish Brzezinski gained ascendance over dovish Secretary of State Cyrus Vance and began to dictate an increasingly aggressive approach to the Soviet Union and its allies. For southern Africa, this meant that Carter rejected proposed sanctions against Pretoria—aimed at shifting its policies toward Rhodesia and Namibia—on the logic that "the problem was not South Africa, but Cuba and the Soviet Union and that, therefore, sanctions would have struck the wrong target."[75] Thus, as Westad claims, Reagan's foreign policy "signified a change in method rather than in aims in American Third World policy."[76]

For southern Africa, Reagan initially pursued a policy of "constructive engagement," spearheaded by his assistant secretary of state for African affairs, Chester Crocker. "Recognizing that the nature of the South African system prevented the United States from pursuing its interests without political costs," writes historian Flavia Gasbarri, "Crocker proposed a policy that combined diplomatic pressure with calls for reform."[77] This entailed working closely with South Africa as a regional ally to combat Cuban and Soviet influence while encouraging it—through dialogue rather than economic pressure—to reform its domestic and foreign policies. To resolve the chain of conflicts that beset southern Africa, Crocker conceived of a linkage strategy aimed at persuading South Africa to grant independence to Namibia in exchange for the total withdrawal of Cuban troops from Angola. Crocker reached out to both Pretoria and the MPLA government led by Neto's successor, José Eduardo dos Santos, to open talks aimed at settling southern Africa's interwoven crises. Meanwhile, according to Kathryn O'Neill and Barry Munslow, the Reagan administration "was happy to give the green light for South Africa to confront the Angolan government and its regional allies."[78]

By the mid-1980s, constructive engagement seemed dead in the water. From the outset, Botha's government proved stubbornly resistant to Crocker's linkage formula on the grounds that a Namibian government under SWAPO leadership—virtually guaranteed to follow independence—was anathema to South Africa's regional security, with or without the withdrawal of Cuban forces from Angola.[79] Moreover, "the South Africans wanted the Cubans to leave Angola, but not too soon," as their presence was the primary factor preventing Reagan from pressing for Namibian independence and compelling him to veto UN sanctions against South Africa.[80] By the middle of the decade, however, Botha's brutal campaign of repression against protestors at home and increasingly bold military attacks against South Africa's neighbors sparked outrage in the United States, leading Congress to pass the 1986 Comprehensive Anti-Apartheid Act (CAAA) over Reagan's veto. In late 1985, faced with overwhelming domestic political pressure, Reagan anticipated congressional action by imposing limited sanctions against South Africa, to which the CAAA added considerably. Washington's leverage with Pretoria had reached low ebb.

Meanwhile, "a fresh upsurge in the Cold War confrontation in the first half of the 1980s hindered Crocker's diplomatic efforts to address the regional turmoil."[81] By mid-decade, Reagan's support for the Afghan mujahideen had morphed into to a much broader policy of support for "freedom fighters" around the world.[82] In July 1985, in the context of renewed Cold War interventionism, hawks in the administration secured the repeal of the Clark Amendment, which had, for the past decade, barred the United States from aiding private groups engaged in military or paramilitary operations in Angola. Gleijeses perfectly distills the irony: "The same Congress that was imposing sanctions on South Africa against Reagan's wishes had embraced UNITA, Pretoria's protégé."[83] The repeal of the Clark Amendment opened the floodgates for Reagan to initiate a legal program of aid to UNITA, which he justified in an October 24, 1985, speech to the United Nations General Assembly, later dubbed the Reagan Doctrine. He named Angola as one of five countries where the United States was committed to aiding anticommunist movements in their struggles against Soviet oppression.[84] From 1986 on, US aid began flowing to UNITA through Zaire, increasing quickly from $15 million to $50 million annually.[85] Unsurprisingly, Reagan's decision to resume large-scale aid to Savimbi led MPLA officials to abandon bilateral negotiations with the United States.

Just as Reagan ramped up Washington's support for UNITA in the name of fighting communism, the Soviet Union's new general secretary, Mikhail Gorbachev, embarked on a sustained effort to resolve proxy conflicts around the world in an effort to revive the corpse of détente. In 1985— motivated by an urgent need to end Soviet involvement in Afghanistan, which had revealed the limits of his country's ability to influence foreign proxies, spurred domestic and international opposition, and crippled the Soviet economy—Gorbachev called for a radical restructuring of Moscow's foreign policy. He began to articulate a diplomatic reform program known as "New Thinking," designed to ratchet down the hyperideologized Cold War competition to make way for the Soviet Union to invest in its desperately needed domestic reform program. The success of Perestroika, Gorbachev knew, would require some level of cooperation with the West. Yet, though he understood that the Soviet Union needed to scale back defense spending and support for revolutionary commitments abroad, "he wanted to do so in a way that did not reduce the international status of the Soviet Union or its position as a global superpower."[86] To that end, he extended a strategic diplomatic olive branch to Reagan, conscripting America's die-hard Cold War president into the joint pursuit of solutions to ongoing proxy conflicts across the Third World, a topic that would constitute a key focus of the two leaders' discussions for the remainder of Reagan's term. As the Cold War marched to its conclusion, Reagan and Gorbachev increasingly shared the perspective that Third World conflicts constituted a persistent but unnecessary driver of superpower rivalry.

According to Westad, Pretoria took Soviet-American détente, together with renewed US support for UNITA, as "a renewed license to attempt to topple the MPLA regime."[87] Botha and his governing clique of right-wing militarists believed their chances of retaining control over Namibia depended on destroying the government in Luanda and defeating the Cubans. This, they reasoned, would also enable South Africa to eliminate ANC bases inside Angola, en route to its larger objective of crushing the party outright. The MPLA, for its part, aimed to annihilate UNITA as a prerequisite to national reunification, domestic reform, and normalization with the United States.

This impasse peaked in the fall of 1987, as the South Africans instigated a head-to-head clash with Cuban forces in southern Angola, near Cuito

Cuanavale. The SADF, hoping to deliver a final blow to UNITA and its allies with minimal casualties, gravely underestimated Castro's commitment to victory in Angola. Not only did Cuban forces blunt the South African offensive, they escalated the conflict considerably.[88] From January to March 1988, Castro sent 15,000 new troops to Angola to launch a counterattack, threatening South Africa with the prospect of a Cuban invasion of Namibia. This impetuous escalation of Cuban involvement in southern Africa horrified Castro's Soviet allies, with whom relations had strained since Gorbachev took power. Cuban suspicions of Gorbachev's softening toward the United States were not unfounded. "While dismayed by Castro's actions," writes Westad, "the Americans and the Soviets worked together to make use of the momentum for negotiations that the Cuban leader had created by his willingness to confront the South Africans."[89]

In July 1987, Washington and Luanda had opened a new round of negotiations, based on their shared acceptance of a plan to link Namibian independence with the withdrawal of Cuban troops from Angola. These talks quickly stalled over disagreements about the proposed order and timing of these events.[90] Subsequent rounds of negotiations went nowhere, as Pretoria and Havana dug in their heels amid the raging Battle of Cuito Cuanavale. But in the lead-up to a diplomatic summit scheduled to take place in New York in July 1988, the ground began to shift. South Africa, facing mounting battlefield losses against Castro's forces, dwindling domestic political support for the war, and deepening international condemnation, dropped several of its key demands. No longer did it require the simultaneous withdrawal of Cuban and South African forces, nor did it insist that the MPLA reconcile with Savimbi. As the talks concluded, Cuban, Angolan, and South African representatives agreed to a statement of formal principles, including the staged and total withdrawal of all Cuban troops and a pledge to set a date for the implementation of UN Resolution 435, a 1978 document that called for South Africa to accept "the independence of Namibia through free elections under the supervision of the United Nations."[91] Throughout the summer and fall, negotiations continued between South African, Cuban, and Angolan representatives, first on Sal Island Cape Verde, then in New York and finally in Geneva. By early August, the parties reached a provisional peace agreement and committed to a cease-fire. That December, the United States presided over the signing of the 1988 Tripartite Accord, which called for South African, Cuban, and Soviet military disengagement from Angola as well as

Angolan president José Eduardo dos Santos (*left*), Gabon president Omar Bongo (*center*), and UNITA rebel leader Jonas Savimbi (*right*) meet the press on Thursday, August 10, 1995, after a meeting aimed at salvaging Angola's peace treaty in Franceville, Gabon. Savimbi accepted an offer to become vice president in dos Santos's new government of national reconciliation. (AP Photo/Joao Gomes)

Namibian independence.[92] In September 1988, South Africa completed its troop withdrawal, followed by the departure of Cuban forces, the last of which boarded a plane for Havana in May 1991. On March 21, 1990, following UN-monitored elections, SWAPO established an independent Namibian government.

The removal of all foreign troops from Angola ended the paradigm of Cold War intervention in the region, just as the sun was setting on the Cold War itself. Yet, the 1988 peace agreement failed to resolve the civil war that raged on between UNITA and the MPLA. In December 1990, following two years of unsuccessful diplomatic efforts led first by Zaire and then by Portugal, Washington and Moscow took charge of the peace process. Their joint efforts led to the May 1991 Bicesse Agreement between Savimbi and dos Santos, which spelled out the details of a cease-fire and plans for national elections. Savimbi, whose Cold War patronage ended in 1990 as the United States pulled the plug on covert funding for UNITA, only grudgingly accepted the cease-fire. Angola held elections in September 1992, following what Birmingham has called "a year of blissful peace." However, when Savimbi lost at the polls, he prepared once again to go to war. UNITA, using heavy equipment purchased with diamonds from former Soviet bloc countries, set out to destroy what he saw as disloyal Angolan cities. This marked a departure from previous phases of the conflict in which fighting was relegated to the countryside. UN-led negotiations produced yet another cease-fire in 1994, but again it failed to hold. In 1998, war erupted anew, beginning an especially cruel denouement to Angola's civil war that finally drew to a close in 2002, after Savimbi was killed—and secretly buried—by government forces.

Angola's protracted civil war, fueled by foreign intervention, weapons, and funding, took an astronomical toll on a country that, while nominally independent for nearly three decades, had never known peace. At least a half million Angolans perished in the fighting, and nearly 4.5 million more were displaced. Child soldiers, conscripted into the conflict on all sides, had been subjected to unspeakable trauma.[93] Both the economy and the nation's infrastructure were virtually destroyed. Homes and bridges lay in ruins, and fertile farmlands strewn with landmines were rendered unusable. Millions of citizens lacked access to water and basic medical care, much less a coherent national identity or functioning political system.[94] Angola would face the enormous task of rebuilding devoid of influence from the Cold War international system and South Africa's apartheid government, both of which its civil war had outlasted.

7

Iran

A Case of "Occidentosis"

Although the shah's Iran stood as a stalwart ally of the United States for most of the Cold War, crises there bookended—and in many ways shaped—the superpower conflict. The 1946 Azerbaijan Crisis, precipitated by the Soviet Union's support for separatist movements and its ultimate refusal to withdraw troops in keeping with wartime agreements, informed Washington's perceptions of Moscow's aggressive intentions in the Middle East and beyond, contributing to the logic of the emerging strategy of containment. It also drew the United States directly into Iranian affairs and persuaded the shah that Iranian security could only be secured by a massive arms buildup to stave off Soviet encroachment. Sitting on critical oil reserves at a strategically vital site in the Persian Gulf, Iran became a cornerstone of US security in the region. By 1953, so essential was a friendly Iranian regime to American policymakers that the Eisenhower administration authorized the first CIA-backed coup against a foreign government there, ousting Mohammad Mosaddeq in an episode that would become a blueprint for future covert operations in the Third World.

The US-Iranian relationship reached its peak during Richard Nixon's administration in the early 1970s. But even as the shah became a guardian of the United States' immediate interests in the region, Washington's support for and association with his brutal authoritarian rule, and his willingness to compromise Iranian sovereignty in the name of security, poisoned the Iranian people not only against his regime but also against his American backers. Long simmering anti-Americanism came home to roost with the Iranian Revolution in 1978–1979, the rise of Ayatollah Khomeini's Islamic Republic, and the ensuing hostage crisis. The United States, once Iran's closest ally, would be branded "the Great Satan." Not only did the revolution sound the death knell of American primacy in Iran, it introduced into the international system a homegrown Third World ideological alternative to communism and liberal democratic capitalism: revolutionary Islam.

Iran, though not formally colonized, struggled to reclaim its sovereignty that had been curtailed over generations by colonial powers. The Iranian teacher, writer, and anthropologist Jalal Al-i Ahmad described his country's sickness of "Occidentosis" as follows: "We have been unable to preserve our historico-cultural character in the face of the [Western] machine and its fateful onslaught."[1] That onslaught was initiated by Britain and Russia, which, throughout the nineteenth century, were locked in competition to draw Iran into their respective spheres of influence. The United States, hewing to its traditional policies of isolation and nonentanglement, avoided being lured into this European contest, earning Washington no small measure of goodwill with Iranian nationalists. In 1907, amid a constitutional revolution within Iran that birthed the parliament (Majlis), the two great powers chopped the country's nascent sovereignty at the knees with the Anglo-Russian Convention, which carved Iran into spheres, with a Russian zone in the north and a British zone in the south. Following the 1921 Persian coup d'état that ushered in the Pahlavi monarchy, Moscow and Tehran concluded a Soviet-Iranian treaty that canceled all of the Soviet Union's existing territorial and financial claims and eliminated Iran's standing obligations. The new treaty, which Moscow signed with the goal of preventing White Russian forces that fled the country during the Bolshevik Revolution from launching counterrevolutionary attacks from Iranian territory, enabled Tehran to maneuver more freely within the international system.[2]

From 1925 to 1941, Reza Shah Pahlavi ruled Iran. He was "a shrewd and ruthless dictator who eliminated all rivals while at the same time working to protect his country's independence and modernize its military."[3] In international relations, he relied on a traditional Persian approach to balancing (*movazeneh*) predatory powers against one another in order to protect Iranian interests. During World War II, his overtures to Germany as a bulwark against Russian and British encroachment backfired. On August 25, 1941, following on the heels of Germany's attack on the Soviet Union, British and Soviet armies invaded Iran to check German influence and to secure critical access to oil fields and transportation routes. The Anglo-Russian invasion thrust Iranian politics into chaos, forcing Reza Shah into exile in South Africa. His twenty-one-year-old son, Mohammad Reza Shah Pahlavi, just managed to claw his way to the Peacock Throne amid a gaping political vacuum. When the United States entered the war a few months later, dispatching tens of thousands of troops to Iran to join the occupation, the shah—picking up on his father's efforts to balance Iranian foreign relations—welcomed the rising power of the United States as a potential check on persistent British and Soviet imperial ambitions in his country.[4]

Despite hitching its wagon to the Anglo-French occupation, President Franklin Delano Roosevelt's administration was determined to steer its own course in Iran. To preserve its diplomatic autonomy, the United States refused to sign the January 1942 Tripartite Treaty between Iran, Britain, and the Soviet Union that committed the occupying powers to respect Iran's sovereignty and to withdraw forces from the country within six months of the war's end. The new shah and his advisors, whose fears of national dismemberment were little allayed by British and Soviet pledges to adhere to Atlantic Charter principles, pressed for greater American involvement in their country. At the December 1943 Tehran Conference, Churchill, Stalin, and Roosevelt all signed the Declaration of the Three Powers Regarding Iran, which recognized Iran's contribution to the war effort and pledged to uphold the country's sovereignty and territorial integrity. Almost before the ink could dry, however, the three Allied powers found themselves embroiled in competition for oil concessions that would invigorate the forces of Iranian nationalism.

In an effort to lure Washington into greater involvement with Iranian affairs, the shah's regime encouraged the United States to pursue oil concessions in Iran. The move sparked a diplomatic crisis with grave ramifications for Iranian politics and foreign policy. Churchill deeply resented American encroachment into a traditionally British domain, while Stalin, furious that the Soviet Union was left out, demanded similar concessions of his own. Majlis leader Mohammad Mosaddeq, who rejected the foreign policy of balancing, lambasted the shah for precipitating what he claimed should have been a predictable diplomatic imbroglio. In December 1944, Iran's parliament sought to diffuse the crisis by forbidding foreign oil concessions until after the occupation, at which point parliamentary approval would be required. Far from extinguishing the diplomatic flames, this measure infuriated the Soviets, who saw it as a boon to Britain, the only power that currently held oil concessions in the country. The Soviets, with support of the

Tudeh Party—Iran's communist party with close ties to the Kremlin—set out to oppose Mosaddeq, whom Stalin had come to view as pro-British. "This competition over oil in the mid-1940s," writes historian James Bill, "represented the earliest origins of the Cold War between the United States and the Soviet Union."[5]

With Japan's surrender on September 2, 1945, the deadline for Allied forces to pull out of Iran was set for March 2, 1946, following the terms of the Tripartite Treaty and the Tehran Declaration. It soon became clear, however, that Stalin had no intention of withdrawing Soviet troops. Immediately following World War II, Soviet policy toward the Middle East was driven by two primary objectives. Moscow's first goal was to project Soviet power in the territory beyond its southern border, and the second was to weaken or eliminate Western—particularly British—influence in that same area.[6] In Iran, the Kremlin was determined to preserve access to oil fields in Baku; to protect its Iranian proxy, the Tudeh Party; and to establish a Soviet oil concession in the northern part of the country commensurate with the British concession in the south. To those ends, the Soviet Union sponsored the creation of two secessionist movements in Iranian Azerbaijan: the Azerbaijani Democratic Party and the Kurdish Democratic Party. The Red Army proceeded to block Iranian military forces from entering the province, facilitating a swift victory for the rebels.

Iran's septuagenarian prime minister, Ahmad Qavam, emerged as a key figure in the Azerbaijan Crisis. Responding to Soviet pressure, the shah appointed him to his fourth nonconsecutive term as prime minister in January 1946. Far from kowtowing to the Kremlin, though, Qavam played a masterful political game that ultimately secured the Red Army's retreat without ceding Iranian ground—or oil—to the Soviets. In February and March, Qavam traveled to Moscow for talks with Stalin aimed at resolving the crisis. Meanwhile, the deadline for troop withdrawals came and went, prompting Truman to send a sharply worded telegram to Moscow, making clear that the United States would not tolerate the ongoing presence of Soviet forces in Iran. While Qavam negotiated with Stalin, he quietly backed the Iranian contingent that was, with strong US encouragement, arguing its case at the United Nations in New York. Stalin was on the ropes, facing the unsavory prospect of a direct military confrontation with the United States, humiliation in the halls of the UN, and international isolation. Armed with a pledge from Qavam to secure for the Soviets a majority stake in a joint Soviet-Iranian oil company in northern Iran, he finally agreed to withdraw Soviet troops from Azerbaijan by early May. But in October 1947, with the Red Army occupation in the rearview mirror, the Majlis voted 102–2 against the Soviet oil concession. Qavam, too, turned on the Soviets, enlisting US support for an Iranian military operation in northern Iran to crush the separatists, while joining forces with the shah to crack down on Tudeh activity in urban centers. When asked by the Soviet ambassador in Iran for a message to assuage Iranian communists, Stalin replied: "Tell [the Tudeh] it is none of our business. We cannot interfere in the domestic affairs of Iran."[7]

The Azerbaijan Crisis was a formative experience for all parties involved in Iran's Cold War. For the Soviets, it was a humiliating defeat at the hands of a poor, weak country, a defeat that instilled in Stalin an enduring pessimism about the prospects of projecting Soviet power in the Middle East. In the immediate aftermath of the crisis, the Soviet Union conducted a "war of nerves" in Iran, consisting of propaganda attacks and threats of intervention. To make the threat credible, the Red Army posted large numbers of troops just across the border from Iran and, in October 1948, attacked an Iranian border post and briefly invaded Iran.[8] Historian Malcolm Byrne has concluded, based on Soviet bloc records, that early US intelligence estimates of Kremlin intentions were correct. Stalin, it seems, lacked a coherent strategic vision, instead responding to crises on a case-by-case basis. Moscow was attuned to the dangers of provoking Britain and the United States on the periphery, proving "grasping and opportunistic, but flexible in proportion to the degree and nature of the resistance encountered."[9]

The Azerbaijan Crisis was one of the critical early Cold War encounters that informed this assessment, which rested at the heart of Washington's emerging containment strategy. Soviet actions in Iran demonstrated to American officials that the Kremlin harbored baldly aggressive, expansionist designs beyond the bounds of the Iron Curtain, and that it could not be trusted to honor its international commitments but that it could be expected to back down in the face of stalwart resistance from the United States. Moreover, Soviet actions in Azerbaijan seemed to confirm the Truman administration's suspicions that the Kremlin was unlikely to risk open warfare, preferring instead to rely on infiltration, cooptation, and subversion in areas outside its existing sphere of influence.[10]

Beyond its contribution to American Cold War understandings of Soviet capabilities and intentions, the Azerbaijan Crisis marked the first time the

United States was drawn directly into Iran's political affairs. Thereafter, the United States would steadily increase its involvement in Iran, which American strategists deemed critical both for its geostrategic position and its oil reserves. The United States would steadily tighten its relationship with Mohammad Reza Shah over the next quarter century. The shah was among a generation of Iranian nationalists whose politics were forged in the cauldron of Azerbaijan. Consumed with memories of the Soviet Union trying to "nibble away pieces of our territory" in 1946, he concluded that a weak Iran would always be vulnerable to Soviet aggression from without and communist subversion from within.[11] In the years to come, he would lobby successive American administrations unrelentingly for the high levels of military backing and support he believed were necessary to protect Iran from Soviet encroachment.

To the shah's great frustration, US support for Iran would consistently fall short of his demands, only reaching the levels he desired under Richard Nixon's administration in the 1970s. After World War II, London and Washington agreed that the defense of the "Northern Tier"—countries stretching from Turkey in the west to Pakistan in the east that served as a buffer against Soviet expansion into the Persian Gulf and Indian Ocean—would fall primarily to the United Kingdom. Britain's 1947 default in Greece and Turkey, leading to the Truman Doctrine, focused US attention more squarely on the region, but, throughout the 1940s, US officials continued to view Iran as "vital to the security of the United States," but not so critical as to warrant the highest levels of American support.[12] Washington supplied modest development aid under the 1949 Four Point Program and established a Military Assistance Advisory Group in Iran in 1950, but resisted the shah's pleas for more military aid on the assumption that the real communist threat to his regime emanated from internal political subversion rather than external military aggression.

Indeed, the Iranian regime faced no shortage of domestic threats. A February 4, 1949, assassination attempt against the shah, carried out by a shadowy figure with ties to the Tudeh Party, gave him the pretext he needed to declare martial law and outlaw the Tudeh, arresting nearly five hundred members and fellow travelers, closing dozens of left-leaning newspapers, and driving Iranian communists deep underground.[13] US officials, concerned with the growth of communist power in Iran following the assassination attempt, pressured the shah to install a new prime minister, the strong military figure Haj

Ali Razmara. Yet, even in the face of a steep Iranian recession the following year that drove people into the arms of the subterranean Tudeh, and toward the broad-based radical reform movement known as the National Front, American aid to Iran remained but a trickle. The shah was left with no option but to fund Iran's military and development programs through oil revenue. Popular demands to nationalize the Anglo-Iranian Oil Company (AIOC) reached fever pitch just as Razmara took office. On March 7, 1951, upon failing to secure ratification of a supplemental agreement between Iran and the AIOC that would have modestly increased the Iranian share of the profits, Razmara was assassinated by a radical Islamist.

On April 26, led by Mohammad Mosaddeq, the Majlis passed a resolution to nationalize the AIOC. This prompted Razmara's successor to resign, at which point parliament nominated Mosaddeq to replace him. Facing an overwhelming tide of public support for both nationalization and Mosaddeq's appointment, the shah had little choice but to approve both.[14] Mosaddeq, a staunch opponent of Razmara's, opposed the *movazeneh* policy embraced by both the shah and his father, insisting that Iran should refuse to compromise its sovereignty in the name of balancing. He played a leading role in blocking the Soviet oil concession in 1944 and was now going one step further toward independence by expelling Britain from Iranian oil fields.

The AIOC nationalization briefly stitched together a heterodox alliance of Iranian nationalist forces—from the radical Left to the religious Right—behind Mosaddeq, but it also sparked a diplomatic crisis that would eventuate the prime minister's downfall when that coalition fractured. Officials in London feared that the loss of Iranian oil revenue would cripple Britain's weakened postwar economy and that the humiliation at the hands of the Majlis would undermine the credibility of British power throughout the empire. Determined not to stand down, London retaliated by imposing economic sanctions on Iran and lobbying for an international boycott against Iranian oil exports. The Anglo-Iranian standoff generated a crisis for Truman administration officials, who viewed it as a double-edged threat to American Cold War interests, undermining efforts to reconstruct Europe's postwar economies while also imperiling the project of containing communism on the periphery.

British officials, who concluded early on that the only way to resolve the crisis would be to topple Mosaddeq, deployed Secret Intelligence Service (SIS) agents to sabotage Mosaddeq's political base. Washington was equally

On Sept. 27, 1951, Iranian prime minister Mohammad Mosaddeq rides on the shoulders of cheering crowds in Tehran's Majlis Square, outside the parliament building, after reiterating his oil nationalization views to his supporters.
(AP Photo, File)

critical of Britain for stubbornly resisting Iranian demands, and the National Front, which it deemed a "demagogic," "non-productive" organization under the leadership of the "fanatically nationalistic" Mosaddeq.[15] The Truman administration, which saw the resolution of the oil crisis as the key to improving Iran's relations with the West, resisted British appeals for direct intervention and rejected outright the notion of sponsoring a coup, committing the United States instead to seeking an equitable solution. "Truman's concern was to keep Iran in the Western camp," writes historian Roham Alvandi, "not to preserve Britain's stake in Iranian oil."[16]

Throughout 1952, however, American concerns over the prospect of Iran slipping into the Soviet orbit deepened. Despite its failure to gain ground at the ballot box, the Tudeh continued to agitate, and the US embassy noted significant communist infiltration of the armed forces and penetration of government ministries. Iran struggled with growing fiscal and trade problems as the oil crisis dragged on, exposing Mosaddeq to a barrage of domestic political opposition from all sides, and contributing to deep fissures within the ideologically diverse National Front. In the face of strong parliamentary opposition to his politics, Mosaddeq resigned briefly over the summer, only to be reinstated following a disastrous interregnum by Qavam that spurred massive protests to which government security forces responded with violent suppression. For nervous American observers, the instability of Iranian politics raised the specter of a communist takeover.[17]

In October 1952, having learned of SIS-backed plots against him, Mosaddeq broke off diplomatic relations with Britain. London transferred its intelligence assets—and full responsibility for protecting Western interests in Iran—to the United States. By then, both Washington and the Soviet Union had their own extensive covert psychological warfare operations up and running within Iran. The CIA operation employed Iranian agents primarily for the purpose of discrediting the Soviet Union and the Tudeh. In November 1952, the Truman administration shot down a British proposal to mobilize SIS and CIA intelligence assets in an effort to oust Mosaddeq. It was not until President Dwight D. Eisenhower was inaugurated in January 1953 that plans for a coup began to materialize.

Even before they took office, Eisenhower and his secretary of state, John Foster Dulles, concluded that the loss of Iran to the free world was all but inevitable should the United States fail to remove Mosaddeq from power. In mid-February 1953, US and British officials met to confirm their mutual interest in a coup. The next month, a showdown between Mosaddeq and the shah exposed the fragility of the prime minister's regime and highlighted his increasing reliance on the Tudeh. Sometime in March, fearing that an imminent collapse of Mosaddeq's regime could lead to a communist takeover, Eisenhower gave the CIA a green light to turn its Iranian political action network against Mosaddeq and to begin drawing up plans for his overthrow. The agency sent $1 million to the station chief in Tehran for the express purpose of bringing down the prime minister.[18] Early in the summer, a Tudeh resurgence comprising the largest rallies since it was outlawed in 1949, coupled with a series of friendly overtures between Moscow and Tehran, prompted Eisenhower to issue formal authorization for a coup on July 11.

The initial scheme involved bribing and manipulating the Majlis to vote Mosaddeq out of office. But in early August the prime minister anticipated the move and rigged a referendum—earning 99 percent of the vote—to dissolve the existing parliament and replace it with a new one.[19] The CIA then turned to its backup plan, which called for agency-backed anti-Mosaddeq military units to seize power. On August 15, an imperial guard pulled up to Mosaddeq's home to deliver a decree removing him from power only to discover that he had been tipped off. His own loyal forces arrested the messengers and spread across Tehran to round up those suspected of participating in the plot. The shah fled the country the next day, as Mosaddeq loyalists took to the airwaves to announce that the coup had been thwarted. But the CIA had still more tricks up its sleeve. It paid some Iranian citizens to stage anti-Mossadegh rallies and others to wreak havoc posing as Tudeh members in an effort to stir up opposition to the party. By midday on August 19, huge crowds had assembled in Tehran to attack pro-Mosaddeq and pro-Tudeh positions throughout the city. They ransacked Mosaddeq's home, forcing him to flee. By the end of the day, anti-Mosaddeq forces subdued the loyalists and seized control. The CIA's hand-picked prime minister, Fazlollah Zahedi, broadcast a statement over Radio Tehran announcing he had replaced Mosaddeq, who surrendered the next day. On August 22 the shah returned from his brief—somewhat embarrassing—exile to reinstate the monarchy.

What do we make of Eisenhower's choice to proceed with the coup? And how do we assess its effects? Eisenhower's decision to authorize Mosaddeq's ouster was rooted in a broad-based assumption that chaos and political disorder, if left unchecked, would leave the gate open for the Soviet Union to seize strategically important places like Iran, most likely through local communist proxies. Dulles and Eisenhower enshrined covert operations as a central feature of their national security strategy aimed at forestalling such outcomes. In Iran, they feared that the politically embattled Mosaddeq could become a tool of the Tudeh, which was itself an extension of the Kremlin. Soviet bloc records make clear, however, that officials in Moscow had nothing but contempt for Mosaddeq, whom they regarded as a reckless American patsy with a long history of favoring Britain and the West. "The Soviet leaders," argues Vladislav Zubok, "refused to take Mosaddeq for what he really was: a radical Iranian nationalist, a corruption-free visionary, a supporter of constitutional monarchy, and a believer in the possibility of absolute independence for his country from foreign influence."[20] Soviet and Iranian evidence also indicate that Mosaddeq rejected an alliance with the communists during the pivotal period in August 1953.[21] Political scientist Mark Gasiorowski has argued that the Tudeh "did not pose an immediate threat in early 1953," concluding, "If the coup against Mossadegh was intended to prevent a communist takeover, it was premature at best."[22] While perhaps not urgently necessary to prevent a communist takeover at the time, the coup did enable the United States to usher Iran squarely into its own Cold War camp, where it would remain for nearly a quarter century, serving as a lynchpin of American strategy in the Middle East and the Northern Tier. But at what cost?

The CIA operation to topple Mosaddeq was the first of its kind. Hailed within US intelligence and policymaking circles as a success, it established a model for the agency to deploy in other cases, including the 1954 overthrow of Guatemalan president Jacobo Árbenz, the 1961 assassination of Congolese prime minister Patrice Lumumba, and less successful attempts to depose Cuba's prime minister, Fidel Castro.[23] Yet the coup in Iran, and each of those subsequent coups, eventuated a host of unintended consequences. While covert maneuvers to remove communist—or otherwise undesirable—leaders sometimes met with success, they often bound the United States to dictatorial clients. And Washington's insistence that those clients comply with American prescriptions for internal security, economic development, and foreign policy only riled up domestic political opposition that they would then be compelled to suppress, often violently. That violence and repression, in turn, would be associated with the United States. Its meddling in the internal affairs of fledgling democracies earned the United States a reputation for duplicity and subjected it to charges of neoimperialism across the Third World. While American audiences made little of US involvement in the Iranian coup until decades later, it was a formative experience among Iranian and Third World nationalists, for whom it was common knowledge.

The coup against Mosaddeq linked the shah more closely to the United States, initiating a patron-client relationship that would endure in some form until the 1978–1979 Iranian Revolution. Thereafter, Washington supplied Iran with levels of military and economic aid that stabilized his power while freeing him from the constraints of Iranian domestic politics, which only encouraged his dictatorial tendencies. Taken together with the widely acknowledged CIA involvement in the coup, his ruthless suppression of opposition groups, whether they be religious, nationalist, or communist, and his obeisance to Washington's Cold War strategic priorities "quickly tarred the shah in Iranian eyes as a treacherous client of the United States."[24] Leading Iran scholar James Bill writes, "The 1953 intervention aborted the birth of revolutionary nationalism in Iran that would burst forth twenty-five years later in deeply xenophobic and extremist form." By ensuring Iran's Cold War alignment with the United States, he argues, the coup and the subsequent tightening of the relationship between Washington and the shah alienated Iranian nationalists of all political stripes, "paving the way for the incubation of both leftist and rightist extremism."[25]

For the rest of the decade following Mosaddeq's ouster, the association deepened between the shah and the United States, which increasingly appeared determined to assume Britain's prior mantle of chief-meddler in Iranian affairs. An early contribution to this pattern was the negotiation of an oil agreement in 1954 that resolved the ongoing Anglo-Iranian oil crisis and increased Iranian oil revenue dramatically, while failing to wrest control of the country's oil completely free from foreign powers. The agreement guaranteed Iran's ownership of its own oil reserves and industry but assigned control over operations to a consortium of foreign companies. Under the agreement, Iranian oil revenues soared from $10 million in 1954 to $285 million in 1960, underwriting a level of economic stability that enabled the shah's regime to survive.[26] But it also preserved significant profits for the British and paved the way for the five major American oil companies to put down stakes in Iran. Iranians, including the shah, were universally displeased with the arrangement, but, with no better option on the table, the Majlis ratified the agreement in late 1954.

Having resolved the oil crisis and stabilized the economy, the shah set out to consolidate control with an iron fist and the help of expanded American economic and military aid. Following a forty-day trial in military court at the end of 1953, Mosaddeq was sentenced to three years in jail, after which he lived under house arrest until his death in 1967. The shah proceeded to all but destroy the Tudeh inside Iran's borders, cripple the United Front, and neutralize the religious Right. In 1957, American military and intelligence advisors, alongside Israelis, assisted Iran in creating a modern intelligence agency, the State Information and Security Organization, known by its Persian acronym SAVAK. The organization, which would develop into a notorious instrument of torture and repression, emerged as "the centerpiece and dreaded symbol of the shah's new system of control."[27]

Between 1953 and 1960, the Eisenhower administration channeled more than $1 billion in aid to Iran with the goal of shoring up the shah's government in the face of internal and external threats. On face value, this raised the hackles of Iranian nationalists who saw it as a bald play to gain control over the country's policies. Moreover, the country lacked the bureaucratic capacity to administer such voluminous aid, resulting in a scourge of corruption during what came to be known as Iran's "decade of decadence."[28] Huge infusions of US aid were regarded by many as both the source of this corruption and the bedrock of the shah's repressive, undemocratic policies. Under US aid, it seemed, the Iranian rich grew richer and more debauched, while the poor benefited little. Moreover, middle-class Iranians grew critical of the military focus of US aid, arguing that millions were being wasted on the construction of a police state while the Iranian people remained desperate for social, economic, and educational development programs that never materialized.

Even in the face of growing domestic political backlash over the corrosive effects of exorbitant US aid, the shah insisted that the US purse strings were too tight. Drawing lessons from the Azerbaijan Crisis, he maintained that it was critical for Iran to build up its armed forces in preparation for a Soviet invasion. Eisenhower and Dulles, meanwhile, clung to the conviction that the threat of a communist takeover in Iran stemmed not from external attack but from internal subversion. The shah, they concluded, did not need the additional military aid he so desperately sought. Washington's ultimate refusal to join the Baghdad Pact in 1955 further strained US-Iranian relations, as it cost the shah politically to join the unpopular alliance while leaving him without a formal security guarantee from the United States. His sense of vulnerability intensified in 1958, as the bloody overthrow of the Hashemite monarchy in Iraq coincided with an uptick in antiregime activity at home. In this context, the shah initiated secret talks with the Kremlin in the hope of diffusing the Soviet threat and reducing his dependence on the United States. Eisenhower's administration caught wind of the talks and quashed them with an offer for a bilateral defense agreement, which Washington and Tehran formalized in February 1959. The agreement came on the heels of Iran refusing to sign a nonaggression pact with the Soviet Union, which accused the United States of scheming to turn Iran into its own private military base.[29] Yet the US-Iranian relationship remained on the rocks. Eisenhower worried about the stability of the shah's increasingly unpopular government, while the shah, with good reason, harbored doubts about the US commitment to his regime.[30]

By the time President John F. Kennedy was inaugurated in January 1961, opposition to the shah's corrupt and repressive regime threatened to erupt in revolution. The new president rode to office on a wave of fear that the United States was losing ground in the Cold War, in part due to what he considered his predecessor's failed policies in the Third World. He saw an urgent need to take action to secure Iranian stability and alignment with the West but believed that US support for economic development and political reform, not ever-increasing arms sales, would be key to halting communism in its tracks. JFK formed an Iran task force charged with translating academia's modernization theory—a program for staged development aimed at preventing the perversions of communism—into a policy prescription for Iran. The opportunity to implement its recommendations came in May 1961. Following a teachers' riot, the Kennedy administration pressured the shah to replace the ineffectual caretaker prime minister Ja'far Sharif-Emami with the reform-minded Ali Amini. US officials made clear that the continued flow of American aid to Iran depended not only on Amini's appointment but also on the shah removing himself from personal participation in Iranian politics.[31]

With the help of a $35 million US aid package, Amini's government set about implementing a program of "controlled reform," manipulated from above in order to prevent revolution from below. The Kennedy administration, explains political scientist David Collier, hoped that "incorporating democracy from the bottom up whilst enacting social and economic reforms from the top down would allow for a stable and controlled transition to democracy."[32] Parliamentary elections were thus postponed while the new prime minister pursued sweeping reforms, including an anticorruption campaign, broadening the cabinet to include opposition members, and land reform. To US advisors, the latter of these was the most critical. According to a Ford Foundation report, two-thirds of the country's population were peasants who owned no land and held little wealth. Should the Soviet Union move to exploit popular discontent stemming from these stark socioeconomic inequalities, the report concluded, the West would be at real risk of losing Iran, and perhaps the entire Middle East, behind the Iron Curtain.[33]

Amini's reform program showed some early signs of success but ultimately collapsed in the face of growing discontent with the regime's refusal to hold elections. As thousands took to the streets of Tehran in protest, the shah deployed military forces against them, pinning the blame on his prime minister. The Kennedy administration looked with equal alarm at a recent thaw in Soviet-Iranian relations that was, from the shah's perspective, "partially intended as a not-so-subtle warning to the United States not to take him for granted or push him too far."[34] In 1962, the shah assured Moscow that he would no longer permit US military bases on Iranian soil, the first assurance of its type from a country aligned with the West.[35] The gesture was mostly symbolic now that the United States had ICBMs, but it contributed to JFK's willingness to abandon Amini in favor of a return to the shah's heavy-handed tactics. Embattled in the Iranian public sphere, thrown under the bus by the shah, and abandoned by his US backers, Amini resigned on July 18, 1962.

This brief reformist interlude under Kennedy's administration proved the last time any US president would seriously reconsider the policy of support for the shah's regime until his overthrow in 1979. Given the concomitant failures of the Alliance for Progress, JFK's signature development project in Latin America, the president was inclined to move away from modernization theory in favor of another pillar of his foreign policy approach: counterinsurgency. In Amini's absence, then, JFK looked to the shah to crush opposition forces and restore order in Iran. In January 1963, the shah co-opted the mantle of reform to unveil his own "White Revolution," a six-point reform program that included many of the elements Washington had demanded of Amini. Rather than preparing for a phased transition to democracy, however, the shah sought to assuage American critics and silence domestic political opposition as he worked to restore his authoritarian grip on Iran. When he staged an egregiously rigged referendum returning 99.9 percent of the vote in favor of his reform program, the White House applauded. Although the shah's reform program did accomplish some much-needed economic and social change, it signaled the death knell of Iranian hopes for democratization. The popular appetite for freedom of the press, free and fair elections, and broader political participation did not disappear but was forced underground as the shah cemented his dictatorial position with full American backing.

The shah's ability to silence his opponents was put to the test in the spring of 1963, as a crisis erupted that would have grave, but long-delayed ramifications for Iranian politics. A number of Iranian Shia religious scholars (mullahs), led by the Ayatollah Ruhollah Khomeini, began delivering sermons warning that the White Revolution posed a fundamental threat to Islam and castigating Iran's close ties to the West. Following Khomeini's June 3 sermon, in which he condemned the shah as an enemy of Iran, the police arrested him along with several other mullahs, sparking a massive wave of protests across the country. After five days of unrest, the shah ordered his forces to shoot to kill, with weapons that rioters could easily recognize as

American-made. Although the number of casualties is hotly debated, the figure was in the hundreds, with scores more arrested. To quell further unrest, the shah placed Khomeini under house arrest and set out to establish a government ministry charged with overseeing all religious activity in Iran. "The Shah," writes historian April Summitt, "came out of the June riots stronger and more dictatorial than ever . . . unwittingly laying the foundation for the 1978 revolution."[36] His repressive response to the mullahs did little to dampen support from the Kennedy administration, which had abandoned its hope of real democratic reforms in favor of more pressing Cold War exigencies. The US-Iranian relationship would tighten considerably under Lyndon Johnson's presidency.

Johnson, who took over following Kennedy's November 1963 assassination, admired the shah's tough-guy tactics, regarding him as a defender of American Cold War interests in the Persian Gulf and beyond. As US involvement in Vietnam deepened, Iran would prove one of the only supporters of the American war to be found in the Third World. The shah could further be counted on to back US policies against Egypt and other Arab nationalists. Even as LBJ steered the United States toward a closer relationship with the shah, though, tensions persisted between the two countries throughout his administration. The fundamental point of contention was the shah's insatiable demand for military hardware. He lobbied the White House relentlessly for more military aid, growing increasingly frustrated by what he saw as ungrateful, disloyal treatment from Washington. Not only were Johnson administration officials limited in the amount of military aid they could provide Iran by US domestic political considerations and by Washington's increasing overextension in Vietnam; they were also concerned about the Iranian domestic political repercussions that could ensue from bloated arms deals. In March 1965, LBJ warned his newly appointed ambassador to Iran, Armin Meyer, that the shah "was tempted to spend far too much on fancy military hardware and not enough on meeting his own people's rising expectations."[37] A series of events in 1964 set the stage for such concerns about popular discontent within Iran and, once again, laid cobbles on the path to revolution in Iran more than a decade hence.

Iran, no stranger to tempestuous politics, saw yet another rash of protests erupt in response to the Status of Forces Agreement (SOFA) concluded between Washington and Tehran on October 13, 1964. The agreement, which extended sweeping diplomatic immunity to American personnel and their dependents, effectively exempting them from Iranian law, went significantly further than any such accord with American NATO allies. The Majlis, which could usually be counted on for a rubber stamp, approved the SOFA with a narrow vote of 74 in favor and 62 opposed.[38] Harkening memories of Iran's long history of subjugation by the British, the SOFA—which would come to be known in Iran as the Capitulations Agreement—"reinforced the shah's image as a Cold War client of the United States."[39] Twelve days after it was signed, parliament voted to authorize the Iranian government to accept a $200 million loan from private American banks for the purpose of buying US military equipment, sparking outrage from across the political spectrum at what appeared to be the shah's blatant sellout of Iranian sovereignty in exchange for a bigger and better arms stockpile.

Khomeini led the opposition, with a fiery speech that Bill has described as "one of the most important and moving political statements made in Iran" in the twentieth century. The Ayatollah lambasted the United States and its Iranian marionette, the shah, for their efforts to destroy the nation's dignity, integrity, and autonomy. "They have reduced the Iranian people to a level lower than that of an American dog," claimed Khomeini, referring to the terms of the SOFA. "If someone runs over a dog belonging to an American, he will be prosecuted. Even if the shah himself were to run over a dog belonging to an American, he would be prosecuted. But if an American cook runs over the shah, the head of state, no one will have the right to interfere with him."[40] Close government surveillance and intense political pressure had failed to muzzle Khomeini after his arrest in 1963, prompting Iranian security officers in early November 1964 to round him up and force him into exile in Turkey.

Throughout 1965, the shah struggled to fend off a rise in violent political extremism among secular and religious opponents. On January 21, 1965, prime minister Hassan Ali Mansur was assassinated by a radical Islamists, followed that April by a second attempt on the shah's life, this time by one of his own discontented imperial guardsmen. The shah's response was, unsurprisingly, a tighter crackdown on opposition. He sacked the current head of SAVAK, replacing him with Gen. Nimatullah Nassiri, who "began a period of secret police control that made him one of the most feared and detested officials in Iran."[41] By the mid-1960s, the shah's administration had largely succeeded in silencing political opposition within Iran, thereby forcing it underground and in exile, where it would germinate intense hatred of his regime and the Americans with which it was associated.

At the same time, the shah made overtures to the Soviet Union in pursuit of a more independent foreign policy for Iran. In June 1965, the shah made an official state visit to the Soviet Union. Then, in January 1966, Moscow and Tehran signed a major commercial agreement that bound the Soviets to build a steel mill, a gas pipeline, and a mechanical engineering plant in Iran. The agreement precipitated a "flurry of economic activity" between Iran and Eastern European countries and prompted the shah to announce his intention to purchase $110 million in military supplies from the Soviet Union. Several factors contributed to the shah's decision to pursue rapprochement with the Kremlin. Washington's refusal to fulfill his arms requests left him feeling vulnerable in the face of perennial threats from the Soviet Union and from Iran's Arab neighbors. He was frustrated at being charged "discriminatory fees" for American military equipment and having his security needs dictated to him by American advisors, venting to CIA official Kermit Roosevelt that he was "tired of being treated like a schoolboy."[42] Furthermore, he was offended by what he perceived as America's infidelity, claiming that it "treated its enemies better than its friends."[43] The shah felt that the United States took for granted his support reining in radical Arab nationalism, his unwavering defense of American policy in Vietnam, and his willingness to position Iran as the front line of defense against Soviet aggression in the Persian Gulf. Perhaps the best evidence for this was Washington's refusal to join Iran in supporting Pakistan in the 1965 Indo-Pakistan War over Kashmir, which seemed to demonstrate that CENTO membership promised no guarantee of American protection.[44] Adding to the shah's concern about the fickle nature of his American ally was the niggling fear that he could be "Diem'ed," meeting the same fate that befell South Vietnam's slaughtered president, should he outlive his usefulness.[45]

Even with all of these caveats, the US-Iranian relationship grew steadily closer and more dynamic under LBJ. The shah never intended for his rapprochement with the Soviet Union to undermine Iran's attachment to the United States, merely to demonstrate his government's autonomy and make clear that the Iranians would not be taken for granted. His gambit worked, especially as he began to second-guess the wisdom of closer relations with Moscow in the wake of the Seven-Day War. In late 1967, following the shah's state visit to the United States, the Johnson administration finally acquiesced to supply Iran with a good chunk of the military aid he requested. And on November 30, Washington officially ended direct economic assistance to

Iran "based on a formal determination that Iran was no longer a less developed country."[46] This move, made possible by a sharp rise in Iranian oil revenues, was symbolic of a more equal dynamic emerging between the two countries that would underpin the shift from a patron-client relationship to a partnership under President Richard Nixon.

The imperative for such a partnership emerged after Britain announced on January 16, 1968, that it would withdraw all of its military forces from the Persian Gulf by 1971. Britain's retreat, undertaken as part of a larger fiscal austerity project in the face of a severe economic crisis, threatened to leave a gaping power vacuum in the strategically vital, oil-rich region. LBJ, dismayed by the "British withdrawal from world affairs," bemoaned the burden it placed on the United States "to man the ramparts alone."[47] But with Johnson beset by crisis amid the Tet Offensive in Vietnam that would soon lead him to announce his decision not to run for reelection, this novel crisis in the Persian Gulf would be left to Nixon and his national security advisor, Henry Kissinger, to solve.

On July 25, 1969, during a press conference in Guam after witnessing the splashdown in the Pacific Ocean of the Apollo astronauts following their return from the first landing on the moon, Nixon laid the groundwork for a fundamental shift in US-Iranian relations. Outlining his intention to "Vietnamize" the Vietnam War, while articulating a broader policy that would prevent the United States from getting dragged into similar regional conflicts, the president made clear that America's Asian allies would henceforth be responsible for shouldering the burden of their own defense. Promising that the United States would honor its treaty commitments and provide military and economic aid to regional allies, he noted, "We should assist, but we should not dictate."[48] The Nixon Doctrine, as this policy would become known, quickly extended to the rest of the Third World, where Nixon and Kissinger sought reliable regional partners who could help them avoid costly distractions as they pursued their primary geostrategic goals of détente with the Soviet Union and rapprochement with China.

The shah wasted no time in lobbying Nixon to back Iran as the pro-Western power best suited to fill the vacuum that was set to emerge in the Persian Gulf following Britain's scheduled withdrawal. Seeing an opportunity, finally, to secure his long-sought arsenal, he deployed the language and logic of the Nixon Doctrine to argue that the United States should supply him with the weapons necessary for Iran to spearhead the defense of the

Persian Gulf, obviating the need for American military intervention. The move toward just such a partnership during Nixon's tenure was gradual. At first, unsure of the shah's ability to deliver on his bold regional defense promises, Nixon and Kissinger continued to follow their predecessor's policy of balancing Iran and Saudi Arabia as twin pillars of the Persian Gulf. But the new administration, worried about the long-term stability of the Saudi regime, began shifting toward "a policy of Iranian primacy in substance while paying lip service to Saudi-Iranian cooperation."[49]

Washington's increasing reliance on Iran was facilitated by a warm personal relationship between Nixon and the shah dating back to the former's first vice-presidential trip to Tehran in 1953, shortly after the coup against Mosaddeq. The two leaders' mutual admiration stemmed from a shared aversion to communism, a commitment to realpolitik, and a disdain for American intellectuals.[50] In the early 1970s, when the Iranian leader clamped down his system of domestic political repression and control, inaugurating what amounted to a reign of terror that would eventually spur the very extremism that brought down his regime, Nixon praised him as "decisive, confident, strong, kind, thoughtful," a modernizing monarch whose developmental success American officials heralded as a model for other states in the region.[51] In an Oval Office conversation in April 1971, mulling over whether the shah would in fact be capable of filling the power vacuum Britain left in its wake, Nixon mused to his advisors: "If he could do it, it'd be wonderful, because he's our friend. . . . He runs a damn tight shop [sic]. . . . I like him, I like him, and I like the country. And some of those other bastards out there I don't like."[52]

Iran's capacity to serve as the guarantor of American interests in the region was put to the test in November 1971, when India intervened in Pakistan's civil war on the side of Bangladesh. Nixon wanted to help Pakistan, an ally that had served as a critical intermediary between Beijing and Washington, but he faced a torrent of domestic political opposition to the Pakistani slaughter of Bengali civilians. He turned to the shah, who was equally interested in supporting Pakistan, a CENTO ally whose defeat, the Iranian leader feared, could facilitate the expansion of Chinese communist influence in the region as well as generate troublesome border crises that Iran desperately sought to avoid. Nixon and Kissinger, working around a US law prohibiting third-party arms transfers, secretly channeled weapons through Iran to Pakistan's Yahya Khan. The arrangement served as a test run for a full American commitment to the shah as its regional proxy under the rubric of the Nixon Doctrine.

That full commitment came in May 1972, during Nixon's brief stopover in Tehran on the way home from a summit in Moscow, when he famously beseeched the shah to "protect me."[53] This followed on the heels of a treaty of friendship concluded the previous month between the Soviet Union and Iraq, which was currently engaged in a series of violent border clashes with Iran. In exchange for the shah's protection, Nixon authorized the sale of large quantities of sophisticated American weapons to Iran, including coveted fighter jets and laser-guided bombs. With a mix of surprise and elation, the shah boasted, Nixon "gave me everything I asked for."[54] During Nixon's administration, annual US military sales to Iran mushroomed from $94.9 million in 1969 to $2.55 billion in 1977, by which point Iran's military and security establishments accounted for more than 40 percent of the national budget.[55] Nixon and Kissinger's decision to go all in with the shah was rooted in their belief that American and Iranian interests were aligned and that the shah had demonstrated the mettle necessary to protect them. As Kissinger put it, "On all major international issues, the policies of the United States and the policies of Iran have been parallel and therefore mutually reinforcing."[56]

As part of his embrace of the shah, Nixon also pledged support for Iran's secret war in Kurdistan, where the shah backed the Kurdish separatist Peshmerga army led by Mustafa Barzani. Neither Nixon nor the shah were particularly interested in Kurdish independence; rather, they sought to tie down Soviet-backed Iraqi forces in stalemated Kurdistan, thereby neutralizing Iraq as a military threat to Iran and weakening Soviet influence in the Gulf. Nixon and Kissinger insisted that US aid for the Kurds remain plausibly deniable, to avoid scuttling progress in the realm of Soviet-American détente. Between 1972 and 1975, the United States passed millions in aid and supplies through Iran to Barzani's forces only to leave Nixon's successor, Gerald Ford, holding the bag when the shah presented Washington with a cease-fire agreement negotiated with his Iraqi nemesis, Saddam Hussein. The United States had little choice but to acquiesce. The June 1975 Algiers Agreement followed a series of bloody clashes along the Iran-Iraq border, and an Iraqi offensive against the Kurds that would have required a major commitment of Iranian troops to put down. With the two countries perched dangerously on the precipice of a major war, Hussein and the shah agreed to demarcate and

carefully police their borders, giving Iran sovereignty over the hotly contested Shatt al-Arab waterway along the Iran-Iraq border. In turn, the shah
agreed to halt all support for the Kurds. The Peshmerga, which had not been
consulted about the negotiations, was summarily crushed after fifteen long
years of fighting the Iraqi army. Reactions were harsh across the Third World,
where onlookers condemned the United States and its venal proxy for the
blatant hypocrisy of sacrificing allied liberation fighters in pursuit of land
and oil.[57]

The American people, generally sympathetic to the Kurds, also lashed
out at Kissinger and the shah for the volte-face. In the domestic political context germinated by the Watergate scandal, Nixon's resignation, and the igno-
minious American retreat from Vietnam, public attitudes about the proper
role for the United States in the world were shifting seismically. Americans
who had long accepted at face value official justifications for Cold War foreign policies were now starting to reject the amoral practice of realpolitik and
the partnerships it spawned with anticommunist autocrats like the shah. A
rising chorus of voices called for a more moral approach to foreign policy, less
focused on crushing communism and more attentive to human rights.[58] In
1974, the heavily Democratic House and Senate passed a new Foreign Assistance Act aimed at curtailing arms sales to governments that violate the
human rights of their citizens. This shined a hazy light on the shah, whose
ascension to primacy in the Persian Gulf, increasing control over the Iranian
political sphere, and burgeoning national wealth due to increased oil revenues only heightened his inclination to crack down on opposition. Growing
concerns about Washington's ongoing commitment to the shah provided the
backdrop for negotiations initiated in 1974 for an agreement on nuclear
exports to Iran.

The talks, which began under Nixon in 1974, proceeded from the shah's
announcement of a Fifth Development Plan (1973–1977), designed to thrust
Iran into the ranks of the world's leading industrial economies through a
rapid expansion of the nation's energy program.[59] Following the 1973 Arab-
Israeli War, Iran's oil revenues increased nearly eightfold from $2.4 billion in
1972 to $18.5 billion in 1974.[60] With soaring oil prices filling the Iranian cof-
fers, the shah aimed to build dozens of nuclear power plants across the country. He was spurred on by European, American, and Japanese investors who
sought to leverage access to high technology as a way to strengthen ties with
Middle Eastern oil suppliers, in the hope of inoculating themselves against

future oil shocks.[61] Kissinger in particular saw a strategic opportunity "to tie up Middle East capital in a way that would make future oil embargos extremely painful for the suppliers." As historian Jacob Hamblin writes, "Reducing their capital cushion would ensure that, in a moment of crisis, the Middle East countries would be concerned about the bills they had to pay, and would not so easily reduce their oil production."[62] Iran seemed the perfect test case for such a strategy. Kissinger deemed the shah a more reliable long-term partner than his Saudi counterparts, and, perhaps more importantly, the Iranian economy—driven by developmentalism, with a high population relative to its oil supplies—made it more vulnerable to the US strategy.

In May 1974, however, before Kissinger and the shah could launch their negotiations, India's peaceful nuclear explosion, "Smiling Buddha," altered the politics of nuclear proliferation in ways that would ultimately scuttle the deal. Although Iran was a party to the 1968 Treaty on the Non-Proliferation of Nuclear Weapons (NPT), the shocking Indian test made Americans skittish about furthering the spread of nuclear technology in the Third World. Concern over Iran's nuclearization was particularly acute, in light of simmering public discomfort with the shah's apparent megalomania and the propensity for precipitous policy shifts signaled by his cavalier abandonment of the Kurds. It was of no help that the shah, just weeks after Smiling Buddha, made statements to the press indicating that Iran "certainly" intended to pursue nuclear weapons, "and sooner than one would think."[63] An immediate campaign by Iranian spokesmen to deny and reframe the shah's statement failed to assuage American concerns.

"The main obstacle to a nuclear deal," writes Alvandi, "was the unwillingness of the United States to allow Iran to reprocess spent nuclear fuel, a sensitive technology that would also allow Iran to stockpile plutonium for a nuclear weapons program."[64] Ford and Kissinger continued to negotiate under these constraints but failed to reach a deal by the time they left office. The pressures of proliferation politics intensified during the 1976 presidential campaign, contributing to Jimmy Carter's adoption of even stricter terms for the Iranians after he moved into the White House in January 1977. The Iranians, meanwhile, were incensed by the imposition of more stringent requirements on their nuclear program than what was enshrined in the NPT. Extra safeguards written into bilateral deals with the United States and other nuclear powers not only reeked of a double standard; they struck the shah as an infringement on Iran's national sovereignty. By 1978, though deeply dissatisfied with his inability to gain control of the entire nuclear fuel cycle, the shah had compromised to conclude a nuclear cooperation agreement with West Germany, signed on to build an Iranian enrichment facility in France, and informally initialed a deal with the US administration to purchase eight nuclear reactors. Before the Carter administration could formalize that agreement, however, massive riots broke out in Iran, auguring a revolution to which American officials remained largely oblivious.

Although the Iranian Revolution took the Americans by surprise, they might have seen the writing on the wall much earlier had they not maintained the Cold War tunnel vision that kept them married to the shah, even as he put Carter's human rights commitment to the test, and even as it became increasingly clear that his regime was crumbling in the face of massive popular resistance. In fact, the collapse of the shah's regime began as early as 1975, when the oil bubble that had been financing his modernization projects—including the nuclear program—burst, plunging Iran's budget into a deep deficit. As a sharp economic retraction gripped the country, popular discontent with the shah's corrupt, authoritarian rule rose to the surface. By mid-1976, he and his advisors recognized the urgent need to liberalize Iran's political system in an attempt to release mounting pressure and break the cycle of resistance and repression that was progressively weakening his grip on power. The shah hoped that by implementing a series of calculated reforms, he could co-opt revolutionary forces as he had done successfully with the White Revolution in 1963. By the time he initiated these reforms in early 1977, he was aware of the cancer that would soon end his life, and he sought to quell unrest in order to ensure the smooth succession of his sixteen-year-old son, the Crown Prince Reza.[65] The Iranian regime enacted a fiscal austerity program, the strategic release of political prisoners, the partial loosening of censorship laws, and the establishment of study groups and commissions to collect dissenters' complaints and grievances. Rather than diffuse pent-up political pressures as intended, though, the shah's superficial liberalization project unleashed revolutionary forces that could no longer be contained. "The regime's inept responses to the crisis only polarized the situation," writes Middle East scholar Mehran Kamrava, "by helping fan the flames of political discontent that had long been suppressed, making heroes and martyrs out of ordinary demonstrators, and further demonizing the shah and the whole Pahlavi establishment before the court of public opinion."[66] What had started as a series of scattered grassroots strikes and demonstrations across the country began to coalesce into a revolutionary movement, which a range of antishah political figures emerged in competition to lead.

Among those who rose to the revolutionary fore were long-suppressed political parties on the left like the Tudeh and the National Front; guerrilla organizations including the socialist Islamic mujahideen and the Maoist fedayeen that had been responsible for scattered antigovernment terrorist attacks; a host of independent intellectuals; and Islamic clerics. Of these, the clerics were by far the most significant force. They enjoyed relative protection from the excesses of SAVAK while benefiting from the imprimatur of religious authority. Critically, "the central role of mosques as popular social institutions and gathering places afforded clerics a ready and highly receptive audience with whom they could communicate in a language both easily understandable and emotionally compelling."[67] The size of that audience grew steadily after 1975, as the oil revenue bust led to high rates of unemployment and rural-to-urban migration that, in turn, sparked a religious revival as Iranian youth flocked to Shia Islam "as a force of liberation and refuge from the oppressive secular politics of Pahlavi rule."[68] Clerics maneuvered into prime position to mold the country's disparate riots and strikes into a concerted revolution. And the Ayatollah Khomeini, preaching pitch-perfect revolutionary rhetoric from the seat of his exile in Najaf, Iraq, emerged as the movement's symbolic leader.

Khomeini, who had made his bones in 1963 calling for the shah's removal, found the fraught Iranian public in the late 1970s much more receptive to his revolutionary rhetoric. Not only did he condemn the shah as a traitor, he blasted the United States as the "Great Satan" for its role in exploiting the nation's politics and corrupting Iran's traditional Islamic culture, and he exalted those rebelling against repressive Pahlavi rule. The Iranian regime's attempts to discredit Khomeini misfired spectacularly. In early January 1978, a Pahlavi functionary published a scathing attack on the Ayatollah in a leading Tehran newspaper. Clerics and students in the holy city of Qum responded the next day with massive demonstrations and protest movements to which the shah's police responded by firing into the crowds, killing two dozen people and wounding many more. This incident sparked a surge of antigovernment protests and violent clashes around the country. As Iranian security forces responded with violence, the demonstrations only grew larger and more united, forcing religious moderates and secular leaders to align with the extremists. "Careful research," claims James Bill, "indicates that an estimated 10,000 to 12,000 persons were killed and another 45,000 to 50,000 injured during the fourteen-month revolutionary upheaval."[69]

Throughout this period, Khomeini issued a steady drumbeat of revolutionary pronouncements. Couching his appeals to the everyday suffering and complaints of the Iranian masses in religious terms, he earned the sacred title of Imam (head of the Islamic community). He directed the movement from his perch in Najif until October 8, 1978, when the shah compelled Iraq to expel him, after which he continued to operate out of a small home in a Parisian suburb. There he enlisted the support of a number of Western-educated Iranians, many of whom had studied in the United States, as spokespersons and collaborators to lead "what had now become a revolution of historic proportions."[70] Claiming medical necessity, the shah fled the country on January 18, 1979. Before he left, in a last-ditch effort to salvage the monarchy, he appointed Shapour Baktiar, a former National Front figure, as the last in a revolving door of prime ministers. By then, the streets of Iran were flooded with millions of protestors demanding the shah's death, an end to the monarchy, and the return of Ayatollah Khomeini. On February 1, 1979, after nearly fifteen years in exile, Khomeini came back to Tehran. On February 11, following what would become known as the "Ten Days of Dawn," the Iranian military—already gutted by desertions and insubordination—surrendered to Khomeini's Islamic Revolutionary Council (IRC). The Pahlavi monarchy had reached an inglorious end.

Khomeini's political philosophy was rooted in the belief that "the true tenets of Islam had been corrupted by heretical Western influences through the instrument of secular, modernizing rulers such as the shah."[71] To restore Iranian society to the path of righteousness, he maintained, it was essential to create a truly Islamic form of government. On March 30 and 31, Khomeini presided over a national referendum in which the Iranian people were asked the simple question, "Should Iran be an Islamic republic?" With results that strain credulity, over 98 percent of the 20 million ballots cast confirmed that it should. Proclaiming April 1 "Islamic Republican Day," Khomeini announced that "the referendum is unprecedented in history—to establish a government of righteousness and to overthrow and bury the monarchy in the rubbish pile of history."[72] So began Iran's Islamic Republic, which would soon verge into a phase of radicalism and brutality. As Khomeini worked to consolidate his power, he leveraged the specter of external threats as a means of distracting attention from Iran's domestic problems, building nationalist support for his movement, and extinguishing internal opposition.

The leaders of the Islamic Republic, suspicious of hostility from both superpowers, enumerated several Soviet and American actions following the revolution as evidence of their intentions to destroy the new regime. When it came to the Soviet Union, Iranian leaders pointed to the invasion of Afghanistan in December 1979, the steady flow of Soviet arms to Iraq as it fought against Iran, and revelations of espionage by Tudeh Party members as indications of Soviet hostility. The United States was even more suspect on the grounds of its long, checkered history of subversive intelligence operations in Iran, a practice that continued during and after the revolution, implicating some of Khomeini's moderate rivals as collaborators. Moreover, on the US side, Islamic leaders saw enmity in congressional condemnations of the revolution and especially in the Carter administration's decision to allow the exiled shah to enter the United States for medical treatment. That decision precipitated the hostage crisis that, taken together with Washington's tilt toward Iran in the Iran-Iraq War, would further erode US-Iranian relations.

In both the Soviet and American cases, these actions stemmed largely from their mutual failure to apprehend how fully the Islamic Revolution in Iran circumvented the bipolar ideological structure of the Cold War.[73] Accustomed to slotting nationalist movements into communist/noncommunist binaries to determine which could be co-opted and which should be opposed, neither superpower was equipped to respond to "an ideology centered on the Third World itself, through which *both* [Soviet and American] projects of modernization could be condemned."[74] While Soviet officials were more proactive in their early overtures to Khomeini than were the Americans, their interactions with the new regime were colored by the assumption that it would ultimately end up in the Western camp due to a shared opposition to communism. The United States, meanwhile, was slow to accept the reality of the shah's overthrow. Until late 1978, Carter expressed optimism that the shah could stay in power for years to come. As the writing on the wall became clearer, Washington officials eschewed contact with Khomeini and his radical cohort, opting instead to build connections with moderate revolutionary figures whom they hoped might continue, in some form, Iran's long-standing promotion of American interests in the Persian Gulf. Carter's hard line against Khomeini—justified on standard Cold War grounds of the imperative to prevent disorder upon which Soviets could capitalize, while securing local allies to do Washington's bidding—was in part a function of bureaucratic infighting that elevated the voice of the administration's Cold War hawk, National Security Advisor Zbigniew Brzezinski, over the more dovish Secretary of State Cyrus Vance.

It was Brzezinski who spearheaded the most catastrophic miscalculation in Washington's postrevolutionary policy: its preoccupation with the moderates.[75] The overwhelming US focus on building relationships with moderates, including the Islamic Republic's first prime minister, Mehdi Bazargan, resulted in a failure to establish any meaningful ties with extremist leaders and cast suspicion on the moderates themselves. It also lent credibility to Khomeini's accusations that the United States was working to overturn the forces of Iranian nationalism, just as it had done in 1953 and continued to do ever since through its support for the shah. On October 22, 1979, against this backdrop of growing anti-Americanism and after months of temporizing, Carter made the fateful decision to allow the shah into the United States for cancer treatment. The move, which seemed to pile on evidence of an American plot to overthrow the Islamic Republic and restore the shah to his throne, was greeted immediately by throngs of protest on the streets of Iran.

On November 4, a group of nearly five hundred student protestors who would call themselves "Students Following the Imam's Path" scaled the walls of the US embassy in Tehran, taking hostage sixty-one American diplomats in retribution for American imperialism, and to neuter their counterrevolutionary potential.[76] Two days later Bazargan, frustrated not only with the Americans' imprisonment but with the increasingly radical direction of the revolution, resigned his post. He was replaced by another moderate figure, Abolhassan Banisadr, with whom US officials tried to negotiate, only to discover that the extremists—with Khomeini's encouragement—would consistently prevent him from delivering on his promises. Khomeini, for his part, initially expressed muted disapproval for the embassy raid but quickly became an ardent supporter of the student hostage takers when it became clear that their bold play had earned them overwhelming popular support. "Khomeini's handling of what evolved into the 'hostage crisis,'" writes Kamrava, "was representative of his modus operandi as a shrewd, populist political animal. Every time events of this nature happened—and in revolutionary Iran they happened a lot—he would initially sit back and gauge the popular response, then opt for the most 'revolutionary' (i.e. radical) option."[77]

On November 9, 1979, demonstrators burn an American flag atop the wall of the US embassy in Tehran, Iran, where students were holding American hostages. (AP Photo/Thierry Campion, File)

On April 7, 1980, after months of heartbreaking diplomatic failures, missteps, and betrayals in its attempts to free the hostages, the United States finally terminated diplomatic relations with the Islamic Republic. A few weeks later, Carter authorized Operation Eagle Claw, a military operation to free the hostages. On April 24, an elite commando unit comprising eight helicopters took off from an aircraft carrier in the Persian Gulf with orders to attack the embassy compound in Iran and rescue the hostages. Two of the helicopters were stricken with mechanical problems in the Iranian desert, leading the US to abort the mission. Foul weather on the retreat contributed to one of the helicopters colliding with a US transport plane on the ground, killing eight US servicemen. The botched mission was a tragic humiliation for the United States and a political catastrophe for Carter, who was encountering one foreign policy disaster after another in the midst of a reelection campaign.[78] For Khomeini and the extremists, the American invasion of Iran—bungling as it may have been—justified holding the hostages even longer and spurred a more violent purge of moderate rivals. The hostage crisis would drag out for another eight months, during which time Carter would be routed at the ballot box by his Republican challenger, Ronald Reagan. Finally, as Reagan was being sworn into office on January 20, 1981, the hostages were flown out of Iran on a pair of Algerian aircraft that inexplicably lingered on the tarmac for hours until the US transfer of power was complete. Gary Sick, a White House insider who has written extensively about the crisis, points to clandestine contacts between the Reagan campaign and the Iranian hostage takers that suggest the possibility that neither the benefit of the crisis to Reagan's campaign nor the timing of the hostages' release was any coincidence.[79]

The 444-day hostage crisis was as politically advantageous to Khomeini and the extremists as it was to Reagan. Coupled with the Iraqi invasion of Iran on September 22, 1980, it enabled them to rally the Iranian public behind a campaign of resistance to outside aggression and facilitated a "reign of terror" against their domestic political opponents.[80] In June 1981, a period of relative moderation in the Iranian Revolution ended following the removal of Prime Minister Banisadr, on suspicion of conspiring with the mujahideen against the republic. Thereafter, the term "moderate" became a pejorative, as anyone who disagreed with the "Imam's line" was condemned as a "counter-revolutionary," a "monarchist," a "hypocrite," or a lackey of "the Great Satan."[81] Just days after Banisadr's ouster, a massive terrorist attack on the headquarters of Khomeini's Islamic Republican Party (IRP) launched a full-scale civil war that provoked the Imam to approve a relentless campaign of repression. Vicious cycles of escalating violence ensued between the mujahideen and the IRP, resulting in the total annihilation of the former by mid-1982, after which the Islamic Republic made quick work of the intelligentsia and the Tudeh Party, which its leaders accused of conspiring with the Soviet Union.[82] By 1984, Khomeini and the Islamic Republic had cemented their control over Iranian politics.

Iraq's initial invasion of Iran in the fall of 1980, following a series of escalating border clashes, was designed to strike while the Iranian military was weak and distracted. Saddam Hussein, who had taken power in Iraq in 1979, was responding to Khomeini's pledges to export Islamic fundamentalism to Iraq and throughout the region. He believed Iran to be so weakened by revolutionary upheaval that it would collapse in the face of an overpowering assault from its neighbor. Hussein's narrow goal was to force Iran to revise the 1975 Shatt al-Arab agreement, but more broadly he hoped to destroy the revolutionary regime and assert Iraqi dominance in the Persian Gulf. Iraqi forces made early gains but, following a series of missteps, suffered an unexpectedly vigorous retaliation from Iran. Khomeini pledged to fight until Hussein was overthrown.

The Iran-Iraq War provided leaders of the Islamic Republic with a concrete enemy around which they could rally nationalist sentiment. "Despite the catastrophic invasion of its territory and the burdens of war," writes Ray Takeyh, "the Islamic Republic welcomed the conflict as a means of consolidating its power, displacing its rivals, and transforming Iran's political culture."[83] The regime's propaganda cast the war as "a gift to its Muslim constituents and an opportunity to confirm their faith through deed."[84] By framing military service not just as an act of patriotism but, more significantly, as a form of martyrdom, Khomeini and his cohort cemented the discursive connection between God and the Islamic Republican government. The upshot of this, however, was that the regime linked its legitimacy to victory in battle, foreclosing diplomatic solutions and fueling a drawn-out, bloody stalemate.

Iran's siege mentality was intensified by the fact that Iraq was supported, to varying degrees, by both the United States and the Soviet Union. France, Saudi Arabi, Jordan, Egypt, Morocco, and a host of smaller regional states also lined up against Iran, with only Syria, and to a lesser extent Libya and Algeria, backing the Islamic Republic. Soviet support for Iraq, constant throughout the war, became decisive after 1986, transforming "Iraq's static defense into an offensive juggernaut that began to score victories on the battlefield."[85] The United States remained officially neutral, but by 1983 it began to lean decidedly toward Iraq, which it regarded as the lesser of two evils. A few years later, though, American officials began to fear that an impending Iranian victory could coincide with the collapse of the Islamic Republic, making way for the Soviet Union to fill the void in the Persian Gulf unchallenged. Equally ominous was the prospect that the revolutionary government would emerge victorious and survive to spread its pernicious influence to neighboring conservative Gulf states.

These fears, combined with mounting concern over an ongoing hostage crisis in Lebanon, led the NSC and CIA, with Reagan's approval, to launch an illegal scheme to sell Iran arms in exchange for help securing the release of American hostages. Khomeini, facing his own declining health, international isolation, a deteriorating domestic situation, and the threat of the Soviet military presence in neighboring Afghanistan, was just as willing as the Americans to swallow his bile and resume relations in some form. Ultimately, though, public revelations of the Iran-Contra affair in 1987 proved humiliating to the Reagan administration, "undercutting administration objectives overseas and impairing U.S. standing in the world," and further damaging prospects for US-Iranian rapprochement.[86] Later that year, US forces found themselves engaged directly with Iran's navy in the Persian Gulf. Serious clashes in 1987 and 1988 culminated with the tragic downing of an Iranian civilian aircraft, killing all 290 people on board.

This sparked fears of a US entry into the Iran-Iraq War that, combined with an overwhelming new Iraqi offensive financed by the Soviet Union and Saddam Hussein's persistent use of chemical weapons, persuaded Iran to accept a UN-brokered cease-fire.[87] By the war's end in August 1988, more than a million people had been killed, and tens of thousands taken as prisoners of war. The economic cost of the war was equally staggering, totaling hundreds of billions of dollars. The war had no winners, as both sides were left exaggerating the other side's losses while downplaying their own problems.[88] Iranian leaders used the war successfully to consolidate their power but emerged from it scarred by the experience of international isolation and committed to a foreign policy of self-sufficiency and self-reliance.[89] That insularity and distrust of the international community would generate grave crises surrounding its highly secretive nuclear program, the program Kissinger had encouraged it to develop.

The Iran-Iraq War provided a glimpse of the post–Cold War future, pointing to "the likelihood of resurgent regional conflicts in the Global South as the U.S.-Soviet rivalry began to wind down."[90] Saddam Hussein, facing a crisis of legitimacy following the disastrous Iran-Iraq War, would quickly go on to pursue even riskier international provocations to consolidate his power. The first of these came on August 2, 1990, as Iraqi tanks rolled into Kuwait, inviting the first instance of post–Cold War cooperation between Moscow and

Washington, and inaugurating an era of direct confrontation with the West, especially the United States. The United States, after 1988, had pursued a brief policy of dangling the normalization of diplomatic relations with Iraq as a carrot to induce Hussein to moderate his use of chemical and biological weapons, to encourage Iraqi cooperation in brokering an Arab-Israeli deal, and to make inroads into the country's oil market. But it was quick to abandon this tack, reclassifying Hussein's Iraq as a "rogue state" of the sort national security strategists had just posited would emerge to threaten US interests in the wake of the Soviet collapse.[91] The Americans had, over the previous decade, responded to threatening developments in Iran and Afghanistan by building up a military presence in the Gulf with which it would oppose Hussein's adventurism and that would "repeatedly propel them into armed conflict."[92]

Much of that armed conflict came in response to Islamic terrorism, largely inspired by the Iranian Revolution, the assassination of Egyptian president Anwar Sadat, and the mujahideen's victory over the Soviets in Afghanistan, and fueled by popular media depictions of Western profligacy. A fundamentalist ideology emerged that justified political violence on religious grounds, and Iran took the lead in backing organizations like Hizballah in Lebanon. By the late 1990s, Islamic fundamentalist forces were largely suppressed in the Middle East, and the page seemed to be turning with Iran's 1997 election of the moderate Mohammad Khatami as prime minister. The focus of Islamic terrorism turned to Afghanistan, under the control of the Taliban, which gave sanctuary to al-Qaeda leader Osama bin Laden. He declared war on the United States, culminating in the dramatic attacks on the World Trade Center and the Pentagon on September 11, 2001, attacks that provoked George W. Bush's "War on Terror." That war included ill-conceived invasions and occupations of Iraq and Afghanistan, and the designation of Iran, along with North Korea and Syria, as the "Axis of Evil" for its state sponsorship of terrorism. In the years since the Iranian Revolution, relations between the United States and Iran have remained tense, despite periodic efforts at rapprochement. Iran's support for Islamic fundamentalists, its controversial nuclear program, and its blistering critiques of American culture and foreign relations prove remarkably enduring. So, too, have American conceptions of Iran as an enemy not only of American national security but of the American way of life.

Conclusion

A clear pattern emerges from the case studies in this book: the interconnect-edness of events in the decolonizing world. The outbreak of war in Korea directly affected Washington's strategic assessment of disparate events in India, Vietnam, and Iran, inspiring policies that shaped the long-term political development of each country. Nehru's vision for nonalignment influenced Nasser's conception of Arab nationalism and informed Kwame Nkrumah and Patrice Lumumba's embrace of Pan-Africanism. A nuclear test in India altered the prospects for Iran's nuclear program. The Vietnam War was shaped by the same Sino-Soviet rivalry that it would ultimately help transform, along with the very nature of the Cold War international system. And the US defeat in Vietnam, the Sino-Soviet split, and Cuba's revolutionary foreign policy spurred Soviet intervention in faraway Angola. These are but a few examples of such interconnectedness that stemmed from the fact that decolonization constituted a global process, a sweeping imperative to replace the existing international order with something new. As empires collapsed in the face of internal weakness and anticolonial challenges, vacuums of power emerged around the world, begging to be filled. The Cold War conflict between the Soviet Union and the United States was part and parcel of this global reconfiguration, a competition between the world's two mightiest powers to answer the question of what would replace the imploding imperial system.

Anticolonial nationalists came to understand themselves as participants in a shared anticolonial movement, seeking not only to overthrow colonial regimes but to replace them with power structures of their own design. They pursued not only the formal removal of colonial governments but also the nationalization of resources, the redress of long-standing grievances, the restoration of autonomy in domestic politics and foreign affairs, and the revision of cultures, borders, and economic structures in ways that sometimes pitted them violently against one another. Solidarity of action proved more difficult to attain than solidarity of spirit—especially as Third World leaders found themselves pinched between the agendas of rival superpowers—but the collective consciousness of the Global South, rooted in a shared history of oppression, exploitation, and racial discrimination, would prove enduring; all the more enduring because of the persistence of those abuses in the post-colonial era.

The Soviet Union and the United States emerged from the ashes of World War II as rival superpowers whose ideologies of communism and liberal democratic capitalism, respectively, underpinned their quests to fill power vacuums left in the wake of Europe's fast-receding empires. The interconnectedness of the Third World during the Cold War was, of course, amplified tremendously by the strategic outlooks of officials in Washington and Moscow who collapsed events in all corners of a heterodox decolonizing world into a simple Cold War framework. Although the Cold War started on a European continent divided in two by an "Iron Curtain," Soviet and American officials by the mid-1950s had largely shifted their focus to the Third World, on which they transposed this concept of binary division. Anticolonial nationalists, as they navigated unique paths to independence, found themselves ensnared in superpower politics for a host of ideological, strategic, and economic reasons. Some, like the shah of Iran, Ngo Dinh Diem of South Vietnam, Le Duan of North Vietnam, and each of the fronts in Angola's civil war, actively sought attachment to one Cold War camp or another. But almost all Third World leaders would find themselves, at some point, playing the superpowers off one another in pursuit of leverage in their quests for aid and security guarantees. As the Indian and Egyptian cases demonstrate, even the most stalwart efforts to remain nonaligned often proved impossible to sustain, as Soviet and American leaders dangled desperately needed economic and military aid to lure neutralists into their respective camps.

The revolutionary project of decolonization posed a grave threat to the United States, whose hegemonic global position was implicated in European colonialism. In the name of a bold effort to remake the world in its own liberal democratic capitalist image, American officials would largely replicate the power dynamics of the colonial system that they so fervently condemned. Washington's Cold War national security strategy was framed around the imperative of preventing Soviet expansion, but it regularly sought to contain any forces of nationalism that threatened to displace Western power in the Third World, communist or not. The United States pushed its allies to devolve political power to postcolonial elites but intervened extensively through overt manipulation and covert action to determine who those elites were, and how they would govern, in ways that prevented newly independent countries from navigating their own paths, however messy, from colonial subjectivity to national autonomy. A rhetorical commitment to liberalization and modernization—although often earnestly held—could not mask Washington's pattern of support for authoritarian dictators who would protect Western economic and security interests at the expense of democratic development. And following the logic of containment, Washington largely replaced European colonial power with American-centric neocolonial power bolstered by institutions like the IMF, the World Bank, and the United Nations.

The Soviet Union, for its part, saw both opportunity and peril in the global reconfigurations wrought by decolonization. Anticolonial movements not only dislodged the entrenched dominance of its western European and Japanese rivals in strategically vital and resource-rich parts of the globe; they also shared with Marxism-Leninism blistering critiques of colonialism—and often capitalism—that buoyed hopes that they would gravitate naturally to the Soviet camp. At the same time, the Kremlin trod carefully, seeking to avoid drawing the United States into direct conflict, even as it courted potential Third World allies. China, which rose to the fore as a rival communist power just as the Soviet-American gaze shifted to the Third World, cast itself as a radical anticolonial power. Beijing acted as an accelerant to Cold War conflict, provoking Moscow to pursue a greater degree of intervention than it desired and heightening Washington's perception of threat. The reconfiguration of this Cold War triad by the early 1970s altered the logic of intervention but retained the pattern of pigeonholing Third World crises into Cold War frameworks.

Superpower intervention in the decolonizing world took many forms. The Soviet Union and the United States, and to a lesser degree China and Cuba, pursued modernization and development projects consisting of economic aid, technical assistance, and tutelage in political and economic planning. Amid a deeply ideological Cold War contest, the goal was not only to win allies but to mold them in their own respective images in ways that would prove their civilizational superiority, thereby forestalling subversion and attracting additional converts. These projects were underpinned by robust covert operations generally designed, in the American case, to advance friendly regimes and thwart leftist rivals and, in the Soviet case, to strengthen challengers to US-backed clients. By the early 1960s, the focus on modernization and development largely gave way to an increasing pattern of supplying arms and military advice and, in cases like Vietnam and Afghanistan, direct military intervention. This militarization wrought havoc across the Third World, costing untold millions of lives, scarring landscapes, cultures, and political systems, and stoking enmities that would fuel future wars.

In 1991, the Soviet collapse sent a wave of triumphalism crashing over the United States. The end of the Cold War was greeted as a "sweeping defeat for totalitarianism" and a "sweeping victory for democracy."[1] History, it seemed, had climaxed with "the triumph of the West, of the Western *idea.*"[2] This assessment reflected the simple reality that the democratic West outlasted the Soviet bloc in the Manichean superpower struggle, but it elided the fact that Western ascendance was secured through economic and military support for antidemocratic forces like Joseph Mobutu, the shah of Iran, and Ngo Dinh Diem, among many others across the Third World. It ignored the reality that postcolonial processes of state-making—indeed of securing real independence—were not only incomplete and ongoing but irrevocably denatured by decades of superpower interventionism that had deepened a host of domestic and regional rivalries, spawned a series of brutal and protracted wars, armed Third World governments to the teeth (in some cases with nuclear weapons), encouraged authoritarianism, suppressed democratic movements, and chipped away at cultural autonomy, all while generating economic stagnation and dependence. Ignoring these facts not only contorted Americans' assessments of the past; it also warped their predictions of what was to come.

Hailing the end of the Cold War as the close of a historical epoch, American triumphalists failed to apprehend that the collapse of the Soviet Union was not so much the end of an era as a major disruptive episode within the ongoing process of decolonization. It was not an exclamation point but a semicolon in the treatise of modern world history. If the post–World War II world was defined by a global struggle to replace the collapsing imperial order with a new international system, a solution had not yet been achieved. Even the notion of a singular moment of Cold War triumph fails to account for the gradual changes to the international system that had, by the time of the Soviet collapse, rendered the Cold War of the 1950s unrecognizable. By the 1970s, the communist bloc fragmented and superpower alliances were radically reconfigured. Novel ideologies, most notably the revolutionary Islamism forged in Iran, had emerged to compete with socialism and liberal democracy for the souls of mankind. The supposed bipolarity of the Cold War's early years had, by the time the conflict ended, been replaced by a more overtly fragmentary geopolitical reality that would change but not disappear with the removal of the Soviet Union as a putative superpower.

The "clash of civilizations" that political scientist Samuel P. Huntington predicted would replace the Cold War as the next great conflict to grip the world was, in fact, nothing new; the clashes he anticipated amounted to a continuation of the decolonizing process stripped of Cold War constraints.[3] The United States would thereafter approach a world gripped by the struggles of postcoloniality, which it had led the way in militarizing and polarizing, in the absence of the Cold War framework that it had developed to decode— and oversimplify—a vast array of global conflicts. In the years immediately following the Soviet collapse, the United States occupied a position of uncontested hegemony but struggled to establish a clear set of rules to govern its international behavior. The interventionism of the Cold War years continued apace but in the absence of a coherent national security paradigm. The terrorist attacks on September 11, 2001, focused American officials on terrorism as a new global threat against which US foreign policy could be organized. In many ways, the ensuing War on Terror adopted many of the same characteristics as the Cold War, as Americans were mobilized—at home and abroad— against an existential threat that was as ideological as it was violent. Radical Islam became the new global contagion ostensibly aimed at extinguishing freedom in favor of tyranny. So began a new era of direct military interventions, to address problems with deep roots in the Cold War, that have ended in spectacular catastrophe. The eerily similar images of the fall of Saigon in 1975 and the collapse of the Afghan government in 2021 point to fundamental flaws, and a heavy dose of hubris, inherent in Washington's interventionist approach to Third World challenges.

Today's world is replete with evidence that the end of the Cold War was not, in fact, a great and final victory for liberal democracy, nor did it mark an end to the process of decolonization. Autocracies and kleptocracies rule much of the world, a world mired in stark wealth inequalities that overwhelmingly favor former colonial metropoles. Regional wars rooted in ethnic, religious, and national animosities rage, often fueled by weapons supplied by the United States, Russia, and China. Nuclear crises stemming from Cold War–era proliferation, and terrorist activities inspired by Cold War and post–Cold War interventions, periodically grace the headlines. Racism and xenophobia persist across Europe and the United States, which have recently witnessed the rise of right-wing populist governments. A world once thought to be unified behind the principles of liberal democracy has proven woefully incapable of responding to global challenges like the COVID-19 pandemic, climate change, and narcotics trafficking. To blame all of today's problems on the Cold War would be facile. Although some of these issues—especially militarized hot wars fueled by foreign arsenals—are direct descendants of the Cold War, many others are simply a function of the superpowers' disruptions, distortions, and derailment of the decolonizing process that began before the Cold War and was far from completed by its end. In 1961, the West Indian postcolonial philosopher Frantz Fanon warned: "The question which is looming on the horizon, is the need for a redistribution of wealth. Humanity must reply to this question, or be shaken to pieces by it."[4] Persistent global inequities not only of wealth but of power, culture, and autonomy—inequities with roots in colonialism and branches in the Cold War—are, indeed, causing mighty quakes.

Acknowledgments

Among many inspirations for this book, my undergraduate students at Williams College top the list. Students in my seminar on the Cold War and decolonization, while making their way through stacks of award-winning books and articles, often ask me to assign more compact, chronological case studies to help them unravel the dizzying complexities of Cold War international history. As excited as they are by what they are reading, they often find themselves confused about how things fit together and exhausted by the late nights spent reading massive tomes. Amid the plethora of scholarship on various aspects of the Cold War and decolonization published over the last two decades—some narrow, others sweeping, and many excellent—I have struggled to find the classroom-ready readings they request. Thanks to the tremendous legwork put in by so many scholars, however, I realized I had the tools at my disposal to write a book that would introduce students to the complex interconnections between the Cold War and decolonization in a broad yet digestible way. I can only hope this book gives my students—and many others—what they need to wrap their minds around how the Cold War's collision with decolonization played out in key parts of the world.

I owe a debt of gratitude to the scholars cited in this book, and to many others who have informed my thinking about twentieth-century international history. Jason Parker and William Roger Lewis, directors of the National History Center's International Seminar on Decolonization, as well as my 2011 seminar cohort, inspired me to think expansively about decolonization. Despite my temporal distance from graduate school, the imprint of my involvement with the UCSB Center for Cold War Studies (now the Center for Cold War Studies and International History)—especially the influence of Fredrik Logevall, Tsuyoshi Hasegawa, Salim Yaqub, and my cohort of graduate students—can be readily detected in this work. My colleagues in the Williams College history department have proven inspirational and remarkably supportive of my meandering scholarly interests. Support from the Mellon Foundation in the form of a New Directions Fellowship, and from the Williams College dean of the faculty, has been instrumental in facilitating the completion of this book. Of course, all mistakes are my own.

Kathryn Statler deserves special thanks for helping me think about this book as a way to continue producing useful scholarship while making time to spend with my family, especially during my daughter's precious baby and toddler years. Not only did this largely synthetic project keep me close to home while Mia learned to walk, talk, and—as it turns out—develop some sick ninja warrior skills, it proved perfectly suited to pandemic-era lockdown. At the University Press of Kentucky, I also thank Natalie O'Neal Clausen, Melissa Hammer, Allison Webster, and Andy Johns, as well as the two anonymous reviewers, for their thoughtful guidance throughout the process of putting this book between two covers.

Last, but far from least, I owe my deepest thanks to my family. My parents' early encouragement set me up to pursue a career that allows me to follow my curiosity, and I cannot imagine a better gift. My husband, Bill—my best friend—enables me to see myself and my work as something far more valuable than I would ever imagine without his support. My daughter, Mia, inspires me to do my very best work but never at the expense of soaking up her one-and-only childhood.

Notes

Introduction

1. Prasenjit Duara, "Introduction: The Decolonization of Asia and Africa in the Twentieth Century," in *Decolonization: Perspectives from Now and Then,* ed. Duara (New York: Routledge, 2004), 2; see also Raymond F. Betts, "'Decolonization': A Brief History of the Word," in *Beyond Empire and Nation: The Decolonization of African and Asian Societies,* ed. Els Bogaerts and Remco Raben, *1930s–1970s,* 23–37 (New York: Brill 2012).

2. Leslie James and Elizabeth Leake, eds., introduction to *Decolonization and the Cold War: Negotiating Independence* (New York: Bloomsbury Academic, 2015), 2.

3. Dietmar Rothermund, *The Routledge Companion to Decolonization* (New York: Routledge, 2006), 1–4.

4. Todd Shepard, *The Invention of Decolonization: The Algerian War and the Remaking of France* (Ithaca, NY: Cornell University Press, 2006), 6.

5. Odd Arne Westad, *The Global Cold War: Third World Interventions and the Making of Our Times* (New York: Cambridge University Press, 2007), 66–72.

6. Robert J. McMahon, ed., *The Cold War in the Third World* (New York: Oxford University Press, 2016), 3.

7. Westad, *The Global Cold War,* 3.

8. Matthew Connelly, *A Diplomatic Revolution: Algeria's Fight for Independence and the Origins of the Post–Cold War Era* (New York: Oxford University Press, 2002).

9. Lorenz M. Lüthi, *Cold Wars: Asia, the Middle East, and Europe* (Cambridge: Cambridge University Press, 2020), 261–306.

10. Westad, *The Global Cold War,* 396.

11. McMahon, *The Cold War in the Third World,* 7.

12. Westad, *The Global Cold War,* 2.

1. Decolonization and the Cold War

1. See Santanu Das, ed., *Race, Empire, and First World War Writing* (New York: Cambridge University Press, 2014).

2. George H. W. Bush, quoted in Melvyn P. Leffler, *For the Soul of Mankind: The United States, the Soviet Union, and the Cold War* (New York: Hill and Wang, 2007), 3.

3. Michael H. Hunt, *Ideology and U.S. Foreign Policy* (New Haven, CT: Yale University Press, 1987).

4. Erez Manela, *The Wilsonian Moment: Self-Determination and the International Origins of Anticolonial Nationalism* (New York: Oxford University Press, 2007), 31–34; Thomas J. Knock, *To End All Wars: Woodrow Wilson and the Quest for a New World Order* (Princeton, NJ: Princeton University Press, 1992), 6.

5. Manela, *The Wilsonian Moment*, 37.

6. Mario R. DiNunzio, ed., *Woodrow Wilson: Essential Writings and Speeches of the Scholar President* (New York: New York University Press, 2006).

7. Michael Weiner, "Comintern in East Asia, 1919–39," in *The Comintern: A History of International Communism from Lenin to Stalin*, ed. Kevin McDermott and Jeremy Agnew (New York: St. Martin's, 1997), 159–60.

8. Jonathan Haslam, *Russia's Cold War: From the October Revolution to the Fall of the Wall* (New Haven, CT: Yale University Press, 2011), 146.

9. Victoria de Grazia, *Irresistible Empire: America's Advance through 20th Century Europe* (Cambridge, MA: Belknap Press of Harvard University Press, 2005).

10. Haslam, *Russia's Cold War*, 2.

11. Melvyn P. Leffler, *The Specter of Communism: The United States and the Origins of the Cold War, 1917–1953* (New York: Hill and Wang, 1994), 9.

12. For an alternative view, see Frank Castigliola, *Roosevelt's Lost Alliances: How Personal Politics Helped Start the Cold War* (Princeton, NJ: Princeton University Press, 2012). Castigliola suggests that FDR might have been able to temper—or even to stave off—the Cold War rivalry through his personal politics that Truman lacked the experience and the temperament to continue.

13. George Orwell, "You and the Atom Bomb," *Tribune*, October 19, 1945.

14. Melvyn P. Leffler, *A Preponderance of Power: National Security, the Truman Administration, and the Cold War* (Stanford, CA: Stanford University Press, 1992).

15. "The Kennan 'Long Telegram,'" Moscow, February 22, 1946, in *Origins of the Cold War: The Novikov, Kennan, and Roberts 'Long Telegrams' of 1946*, rev. ed., ed. Kenneth M. Jensen, 17–31 (Washington, DC: United States Institute of Peace Press, 1993).

16. Arnold A. Offner, *Another Such Victory: President Truman and the Cold War, 1945–1953* (Stanford, CA: Stanford University Press, 2002), 128.

17. "Churchill's 'Iron Curtain' Speech, "Sinews of Peace," March 5, 1946, History and Public Policy Program Digital Archive, CWIHP archives, https://digitalarchive.wilsoncenter.org/document/116180.

18. Odd Arne Westad, *The Cold War: A World History* (New York: Basic, 2017), 55–56.

19. March 12, 1947, "Special Message to the Congress on Greece and Turkey: The Truman Doctrine," in *Public Papers of the Presidents of the United States: Harry S. Truman* (Washington, DC: US Government Printing Office, 1963), 176–80.

20. Caroline Kennedy-Pipe, *Russia and the World, 1919–1991* (New York: Oxford University Press, 1998), 81.

21. Odd Arne Westad, *The Global Cold War: Third World Interventions and the Making of Our Times* (New York: Cambridge University Press, 2007), 118.

22. "National Security Council Report, NSC 68, 'United States Objectives and Programs for National Security,'" April 14, 1950, History and Public Policy Program Digital Archive, US National Archives, http://digitalarchive.wilsoncenter.org/document/116191.

23. Robert J. McMahon, "How the Periphery Became the Center: The Cold War, the Third World, and the Transformation of U.S. Strategic Thinking," in *The Shifting Margins of US International Relations since World War II*, ed. Bevan Sewell et al. (Lexington: University Press of Kentucky, 2017), 19–35.

24. Andrew L. Johns, preface to Kathryn C. Statler and Andrew L. Johns, eds., *The Eisenhower Administration, the Third World, and the Globalization of the Cold War* (Lanham, MD: Rowman and Littlefield, 2006), vii.

25. See Ellen Schrecker, *Many Are the Crimes: McCarthyism in America* (New York: Little, Brown, 1998); M. J. Heale, *American Anticommunism: Combatting the Enemy Within, 1830–1970* (Baltimore, MD: Johns Hopkins University Press, 1990), 167–90.

26. John Lewis Gaddis, *Strategies of Containment: A Critical Appraisal of American National Security Strategy during the Cold War*, rev. and expanded ed. (New York: Oxford University Press, 2005), 134–35.

27. Quoted in Gaddis, *Strategies of Containment*, 139.

28. For a more detailed discussion of the effects of Stalin's death on the Cold War, see Klaus Larres and Kenneth Osgood, eds., *The Cold War after Stalin's Death: A Missed Opportunity for Peace?* (Lanham, MD: Rowman and Littlefield, 2006).

29. Vladislav M. Zubok, *A Failed Empire: The Soviet Union in the Cold War from Stalin to Gorbachev* (Chapel Hill: University of North Carolina Press, 2007), 104; Vladislav Zubok and Constantine Pleshakov, *Inside the Kremlin's Cold War* (Cambridge, MA: Harvard University Press, 1996), 184–85.

30. Zubok, *A Failed Empire*, 95.

31. Jeremy Friedman, *Shadow Cold War: The Sino-Soviet Competition for the Third World* (Chapel Hill: University of North Carolina Press, 2015), 27.

32. Friedman, *Shadow Cold War*, 2.

33. Friedman, *Shadow Cold War*, 4–5.

34. Friedman, *Shadow Cold War*, 14.

35. Kwame Nkrumah, *Neo-Colonialism: The Last Stage of Imperialism* (New York: International, 1966).

36. Alfred Sauvy, "Three Worlds, One Planet," August 14, 1952, in Todd Shepard, *Voices of Decolonization: A Brief History with Documents* (New York: Bedford/St. Martin's, 2015), 60–62; Vijay Prashad, *The Darker Nations: A People's History of the Third World* (New York: New Press, 2007), 10.

37. Prashad, *The Darker Nations*, xvii.

38. Quoted in Prashad, *The Darker Nations,* 34; for a full discussion of the Bandung Conference, see 31–50.

39. Salim Yaqub, *Containing Arab Nationalism: The Eisenhower Doctrine and the Middle East* (Chapel Hill: University of North Carolina Press, 2004), 34.

40. Roy Allison, *The Soviet Union and the Strategy of Non-Alignment in the Third World* (Cambridge: Cambridge University Press, 1988), 2–3.

41. Robert J. McMahon, *The Limits of Empire: The United States and Southeast Asia since World War II* (New York: Columbia University Press, 1999), 31–45.

42. Westad, *The Global Cold War,* 119–23.

43. Yaqub, *Containing Arab Nationalism,* 37–55; Haslam, *Russia's Cold War,* 151–56 and 173–74.

44. Westad, *The Global Cold War,* 126; Yaqub, *Containing Arab Nationalism,* 58.

45. Quoted in Zubok, *A Failed Empire,* 139.

46. Friedman, *Shadow Cold War,* 29–35.

47. Quoted in Haslam, *Russia's Cold War,* 150.

48. Dwight D. Eisenhower: "Annual Message to the Congress on the State of the Union," January 9, 1958, online by Gerhard Peters and John T. Woolley, The American Presidency Project, http://www.presidency.ucsb.edu/ws/?pid=11162.

49. Westad, *The Global Cold War,* 130.

50. Harold Macmillan, "Wind of Change" speech, February 3, 1960, in Todd Shepard, *Voices of Decolonization: A Brief History with Documents* (New York: Bedford/St. Martin's, 2015), 138–40.

51. Fredrick Cooper, *Africa since 1940: The Past of the Present* (New York: Cambridge University Press, 2002), 66–77.

52. Todd Shepard, *The Invention of Decolonization: The Algerian War and the Remaking of France* (Ithaca, NY: Cornell University Press, 2006), 2.

53. Matthew Connelly, *A Diplomatic Revolution: Algeria's Fight for Independence and the Origins of the Post–Cold War Era* (New York: Oxford University Press, 2002), 277; Connelly, "Taking off the Cold War Lens: Visions of North-South Conflict during the Algerian War for Independence," *American Historical Review* (June 2000): 739–69.

54. Friedman, *Shadow Cold War,* 56.

55. Robert B. Rakove, *Kennedy, Johnson, and the Nonaligned World* (New York: Cambridge University Press, 2013), xxi.

56. Walt W. W. Rostow, *The Stages of Economic Growth: A Non-Communist Manifesto* (Cambridge: Cambridge University Press, 1960).

57. Michael E. Latham, *The Right Kind of Revolution: Modernization, Development, and U.S. Foreign Policy from the Cold War to the Present* (Ithaca, NY: Cornell University Press, 2011), 52–58.

58. John F. Kennedy: "Special Message to the Congress on Foreign Aid," March 22, 1961, online by Gerhard Peters and John T. Woolley, The American Presidency Project, http://www.presidency.ucsb.edu/ws/?pid=8545.

59. Rakove, *Kennedy, Johnson, and the Nonaligned World*, xxi.

60. Westad, *The Global Cold War*, 146.

61. Piero Gleijeses, *Conflicting Missions: Havana, Washington, and Africa, 1959–1976* (Chapel Hill: University of North Carolina Press, 2002), 16.

62. Zubok, *A Failed Empire*, 144.

63. Quoted in Lorenz M. Lüthi, *The Sino-Soviet Split: The Cold War in the Communist World* (Princeton, NJ: Princeton University Press, 2008), 227.

64. Friedman, *Shadow Cold War*, 40; Haslam, *Russia's Cold War*, 193.

65. Lüthi, *The Sino-Soviet Split*, 244. As Lüthi makes clear, Mao's renewed insistence on ideological radicalism in foreign policy was due at least as much to his domestic concerns about the rise of revisionism and the resurgence of capitalism in China as it was a response to the conflicts with Khrushchev over Cuba and India discussed here.

66. Lüthi, *The Sino-Soviet Split*, 277.

67. Friedman, *Shadow Cold War*, 104.

68. Zubok, *A Failed Empire*, 199.

69. Westad, *The Global Cold War*, 168.

70. Lien-Hang T. Nguyen, "The Vietnam Decade: The Global Shock of the War," in *The Shock of the Global: The 1970s in Perspective*, ed. Niall Ferguson, Charles S. Maier, Erez Manela, and Daniel J. Sargent (Cambridge, MA: Harvard University Press, 2010), 159.

71. Jeremy Suri, *Power and Protest: Global Revolution and the Rise of Détente* (Cambridge, MA: Harvard University Press, 2003), 164.

72. Jeffrey Kimball, *Nixon's Vietnam War* (Lawrence: University Press of Kansas, 1998), 119.

73. Odd Arne Westad, "The Great Transformation: China in the Long 1970s," in *The Shock of the Global*, ed. Ferguson et al., 76

74. Vladimir O. Pechatnov, "Soviet-American Relations through the Cold War," in *The Oxford Handbook of the Cold War*, ed. Richard H. Immerman and Petra Goode (New York: Oxford University Press, 2013), 112; Haslam, *Russia's Cold War*, 271 and 312–13.

75. Quoted in Westad, *The Global Cold War*, 241.

76. This section draws heavily on Westad, *The Global Cold War*, 208–49.

77. Pechatnov, "Soviet-American Relations," 113.

78. David F. Schmitz and Vanessa Walker, "Jimmy Carter and the Foreign Policy of Human Rights: The Development of a Post-Cold War Foreign Policy," *Diplomatic History* 28, no. 1 (January 2004): 113.

79. See Barbara J. Keys, *Reclaiming American Virtue: The Human Rights Revolution of the 1970s* (Cambridge, MA: Harvard University Press, 2014).

80. January 29, 1981, "The President's News Conference," in *Public Papers of the Presidents of the United States. Ronald Reagan (1981)* (Washington, DC: US Government Printing Office, 1982), 57.

81. Haslam, *Russia's Cold War*, 338.

2. India

1. Nehru's speech can be found in Sarvepalli Gopal, ed., *Jawaharlal Nehru: An Anthology* (Delhi, India: Oxford University Press, 1980), 76–77.

2. Robert J. McMahon, *The Cold War on the Periphery: The United States, India, and Pakistan* (New York: Columbia University Press, 1994), 3.

3. Margaret W. Fisher, "India's Jawaharlal Nehru," *Asian Survey* 7, no. 6 (June 1967): 363–73.

4. For more on Nehru's conception of nonalignment, see Jawaharlal Nehru, "Indian Foreign Policy (Selected Statements)," *India Quarterly* 42, no. 1 (January-March, 1945): 74–75.

5. Quoted in Fisher, "India's Jawaharlal Nehru," 366.

6. Quoted in H. W. Brands, *India and the United States: The Cold Peace* (Boston: Twayne, 1990), 34.

7. Michael Latham, *The Right Kind of Revolution: Modernization, Development, and U.S. Foreign Policy from the Cold War to the Present* (Ithaca, NY: Cornell University Press, 2011), 66.

8. Latham, *The Right Kind of Revolution,* 68–69.

9. Sergey Radchenko, "India and the End of the Cold War," in *The End of the Cold War and the Third World: New Perspectives on Regional Conflict,* ed. Artemy Kalinovsky and Radchenko (New York: Taylor and Francis, 2011), 173.

10. McMahon, *The Cold War on the Periphery,* 38.

11. Vojtech Mastny, "The Soviet Union's Partnership with India," *Journal of Cold War Studies* 12, no. 3 (Summer 2010): 52.

12. McMahon, *The Cold War on the Periphery,* 46.

13. Brands, *India and the United States,* 28.

14. McMahon, *The Cold War on the Periphery,* 37–41.

15. McMahon, *The Cold War on the Periphery,* 68–72.

16. Brands, *India and the United States,* 38.

17. McMahon, *The Cold War on the Periphery,* 32–34.

18. Quoted in Brands, *India and the United States,* 49.

19. McMahon, *The Cold War on the Periphery,* 56 and 64.

20. Andrew J. Rotter, *Comrades at Odds: The United States and India, 1947–1964* (Ithaca, NY: Cornell University Press, 2000), 21.

21. McMahon, *The Cold War on the Periphery,* 60.

22. McMahon, *The Cold War on the Periphery,* 81.

23. Quoted in Brands, *India and the United States,* 53.

24. McMahon, *The Cold War on the Periphery,* 82–88.

25. Waheguru Pal Singh Sidhu, "The Accidental Global Peacekeeper," in *India and the Cold War,* ed. Manu Bhagavan (Chapel Hill: University of North Carolina Press, 2019), 85–86.

26. McMahon, *The Cold War on the Periphery,* 91–102.

27. Daniel Immerwahr, *Thinking Small: The United States and the Lure of Community Development* (Cambridge, MA: Harvard University Press, 2015), 4.

28. Immerwahr, *Thinking Small*, 72–100.

29. McMahon, *The Cold War on the Periphery*, 123–24.

30. Quoted in Robert B. Rakove, *Kennedy, Johnson, and the Nonaligned World* (New York: Cambridge University Press, 2013), 5

31. Quoted in Roby C. Barrett, *The Greater Middle East and the Cold War: U.S. Foreign Policy under Eisenhower and Kennedy* (New York: I. B. Taurus, 2007), 24.

32. McMahon, *The Cold War on the Periphery*, 179.

33. Quoted in Barrett, *The Greater Middle East*, 26.

34. Barrett, *The Greater Middle East*, 27.

35. Quoted in Rakove, *Kennedy, Johnson, and the Nonaligned World*, 5

36. McMahon, *The Cold War on the Periphery*, 190

37. Brands, *India and the United States*, 83–84.

38. Rakove, *Kennedy, Johnson, and the Nonaligned World*, 9.

39. Brands, *India and the United States*, 85.

40. Mastny, "The Soviet Union's Partnership with India," 53.

41. McMahon, *The Cold War on the Periphery*, 217.

42. Radchenko, "India and the End of the Cold War," 174.

43. Mastny, "The Soviet Union's Partnership with India," 52.

44. Brands, *India and the United States*, 86.

45. Mastny, "The Soviet Union's Partnership with India," 54–55.

46. McMahon, *The Cold War on the Periphery*, 220–23.

47. Quoted in McMahon, *The Cold War on the Periphery*, 218.

48. McMahon, *The Cold War on the Periphery*, 220–23.

49. *Foreign Relations of the United States, 1955–1957*, vol. 8: *South Asia,* ed. Robert J. McMahon and Stanley Shaloff (Washington, DC: US Government Printing Office, 1987), Document 5; McMahon, *The Cold War on the Periphery*, 230.

50. David C. Engerman, "Learning from the East: Soviet Experts and India in the Era of Competitive Coexistence," *Comparative Studies of South Asia, Africa, and the Middle East* 33, no. 2 (2013): 229; McMahon, *The Cold War on the Periphery*, 225–27.

51. David C. Engerman, "South Asia and the Cold War" in *The Cold War in the Third World,* ed. Robert J. McMahon (New York: Oxford University Press, 2013), 67.

52. Rakove, *Kennedy, Johnson, and the Nonaligned World*, 25–26; Engerman, "Learning from the East," 232.

53. Radchenko, "India and the End of the Cold War," 174.

54. Engerman, "Learning from the East," 229–32.

55. Quoted in McMahon, *The Cold War on the Periphery*, 212 and 233.

56. McMahon, *The Cold War on the Periphery*, 237–39.

57. Brands, *India and the United States*, 96.

58. Mastny, "The Soviet Union's Partnership with India," 56.

59. Jeremy Friedman, *Shadow Cold War: The Sino-Soviet Competition for the Third World* (Chapel Hill: University of North Carolina Press, 2015), 42.

60. Lorenz Lüthi, *The Sino-Soviet Split: The Cold War in the Communist World* (Princeton, NJ: Princeton University Press, 2008), 141–46.

61. Mastny, "The Soviet Union's Partnership with India," 57.

62. Quoted in McMahon, *The Cold War on the Periphery*, 272.

63. Rakove, *Kennedy, Johnson, and the Nonaligned World*, xxi and 62–63.

64. McMahon, *The Cold War on the Periphery*, 272–73.

65. Quoted in McMahon, *The Cold War on the Periphery*, 277.

66. McMahon, *The Cold War on the Periphery*, 240–69.

67. Rakove, *Kennedy, Johnson, and the Nonaligned World*, 105–11.

68. Quoted in Rakove, *Kennedy, Johnson, and the Nonaligned World*, 184.

69. Rakove, *Kennedy, Johnson, and the Nonaligned World*, 163.

70. Quoted in McMahon, *The Cold War on the Periphery*, 286.

71. Mastny, "The Soviet Union's Partnership with India," 58.

72. Brands, *India and the United States*, 103.

73. Mastny, "The Soviet Union's Partnership with India," 61–62.

74. McMahon, *The Cold War on the Periphery*, 292.

75. Mastny, "The Soviet Union's Partnership with India," 62–63.

76. Rakove, *Kennedy, Johnson, and the Nonaligned World*, 164.

77. Rakove, *Kennedy, Johnson, and the Nonaligned World*, 170–71.

78. Rakove, *Kennedy, Johnson, and the Nonaligned World*, 202–3.

79. McMahon, *The Cold War on the Periphery*, 324–25.

80. Brands, *India and the United States*, 115.

81. McMahon, *The Cold War on the Periphery*, 327–32.

82. Mastny, "The Soviet Union's Partnership with India," 64.

83. Papul Jayakar, *Indira Gandhi: An Intimate Biography* (New York: Pantheon, 1988), 28.

84. Brands, *India and the United States*, 119–20.

85. Quoted in Jayakar, *Indira Ghandi*, 138.

86. McMahon, *The Cold War on the Periphery*, 8 and 335.

87. Quoted in Jayakar, *Indira Gandhi*, 140.

88. Mastny, "The Soviet Union's Partnership with India," 64.

89. Brands, *India and the United States*, 130; Mastny, "The Soviet Union's Partnership with India," 66.

90. Quoted in Brands, *India and the United States*, 121.

91. Brands, *India and the United States*, 124–37.

92. Quoted in Brands, *India and the United States*, 131.

93. Mastny, "The Soviet Union's Partnership with India," 70. For more on Nixon and Kissinger's support for Pakistan, see Paul Thomas Chamberlin, *The Cold War's Killing Fields: Rethinking the Long Peace* (New York: HarperCollins, 2018), 254–70.

94. Richard M. Nixon, *RN: The Memoirs of Richard M. Nixon* (New York: Grosset and Dunlap, 1978), 527.

95. Lorenz M. Lüthi, "Non-Alignment, 1961–74," in *Neutrality and Neutralism in the Global Cold War*, ed. Sandra Bott, Jussi M. Hanhimaki, Janick Schaufelbuehl, and Marco Wyss (London: Routledge, 2015), 100; Radchenko, "India and the End of the Cold War," 175.

96. Roy Allison, *The Soviet Union and the Strategy of Non-Alignment in the Third World* (New York: Cambridge University Press, 1988), 218.

97. Radchenko, "India and the End of the Cold War," 175; Mastny, "The Soviet Union's Partnership with India," 71.

98. Mastny, "The Soviet Union's Partnership with India," 75.

99. Lüthi, "Non-Alignment, 1961–74," 100.

100. Mastny, "The Soviet Union's Partnership with India," 72; Lüthi, "Non-Alignment, 1961–74," 101.

101. Mastny, "The Soviet Union's Partnership with India," 73.

102. Mastny, "The Soviet Union's Partnership with India," 74–75.

103. Radchenko, "India and the End of the Cold War," 175.

104. Radchenko, "India and the End of the Cold War," 177.

105. Radchenko, "India and the End of the Cold War," 179.

106. Radchenko, "India and the End of the Cold War," 188.

107. Mastny, "The Soviet Union's partnership with India," 78–79.

108. Radchenko, "India and the End of the Cold War," 173–84.

109. Radchenko, "India and the End of the Cold War," 182–89; Mastny, "The Soviet Union's Partnership with India," 81–83.

110. Radchenko, "India and the End of the Cold War," 187–88; Mastny, "The Soviet Union's Partnership with India," 85.

3. Egypt

1. Erez Manela, *The Wilsonian Moment: Self-Determination and the International Origins of Anticolonial Nationalism* (New York: Oxford University Press, 2007), 66–67.

2. Manela, *The Wilsonian Moment*, 63.

3. Manela, *The Wilsonian Moment*, 65.

4. Manela, *The Wilsonian Moment*, 141.

5. Manela, *The Wilsonian Moment*, 145.

6. Manela, "'Peoples of Many Races': The World beyond Europe in the Wilsonian Imagination," in *Jefferson, Lincoln, and Wilson: The American Dilemma of Race and Democracy*. ed. John Milton Cooper and Thomas J. Knock (Charlottesville: University of Virginia Press, 2010), 198.

7. Douglas Little, *American Orientalism: The United States and the Middle East since 1945* (Chapel Hill: University of North Carolina Press, 2008), 160.

8. Quoted in Peter L. Hahn, *Crisis and Crossfire: The United States and the Middle East since 1945* (Washington, DC: Potomac, 2005), 1–2.

9. Melvyn P. Leffler, *A Preponderance of Power: National Security, the Truman Administration, and the Cold War* (Stanford, CA: Stanford University Press, 1992), 238.

10. Dean Acheson, *Present at the Creation: My Years in the State Department* (New York: Norton, 1967), 219.

11. March 12, 1947, "Special Message to the Congress on Greece and Turkey: The Truman Doctrine," in *Public Papers of the Presidents of the United States: Harry S. Truman* (Washington, DC: US Government Printing Office, 1963), 176–80.

12. Jonathan Haslam, *Russia's Cold War: From the October Revolution to the Fall of the Wall* (New Haven, CT: Yale University Press, 2011), 151–52.

13. Salim Yaqub, *Containing Arab Nationalism: The Eisenhower Doctrine and the Middle East* (Chapel Hill: University of North Carolina Press, 2004), 25.

14. Philip Zelikow, "The World of 1956," in *Suez Deconstructed: An Interactive Study in Crisis, War, and Peacemaking*, ed. Zelikow and Ernest May (Washington, DC: Brookings Institution Press, 2018), 25.

15. Quoted in Little, *American Orientalism*, 126.

16. Hahn, *Crisis and Crossfire*, 15.

17. Dietmar Rothermund, *The Routledge Companion to Decolonization* (New York: Routledge, 2006), 113–14.

18. Little, *American Orientalism*, 165; Yaqub, *Containing Arab Nationalism*, 27.

19. Tarek Osman, *Egypt on the Brink: From the Rise of Nasser to the Fall of Mubarak* (New Haven, CT: Yale University Press, 2010), 66.

20. Zelikow, "The World of 1956," 22.

21. Laurie Brand, *Official Stories: Politics and National Narratives in Egypt and Algeria* (Palo Alto, CA: Stanford University Press, 2014), 27.

22. Osman, *Egypt on the Brink*, 54–57.

23. Little, *American Orientalism*, 166.

24. Yaqub, *Containing Arab Nationalism*, 31–32.

25. Little, *American Orientalism*, 128; Zelikow, "The World of 1956," 15–17.

26. Quoted in Vladislav M. Zubok, *A Failed Empire: The Soviet Union in the Cold War from Stalin to Gorbachev* (Chapel Hill: University of North Carolina Press, 2007), 110.

27. Jonathan B. Alterman, "Cairo," in *Suez Deconstructed*, ed. Zelikow and May, 112.

28. Yaqub, *Containing Arab Nationalism*, 38–39.

29. Little, *American Orientalism*, 168; Hahn, *Crisis and Crossfire*, 28–30.

30. Haslam, *Russia's Cold War*, 154–55.

31. Little, *American Orientalism*, 130.

32. Zelikow, "The World of 1956," 27.

33. Robert St. John, *Boss: The Story of Gamal Abdel Nasser* (New York: McGraw-Hill, 1960), 210.

34. Quoted in Alterman, "Cairo," 109.

35. Hahn, *Crisis and Crossfire*, 41–42.

36. Alterman, "Cairo," 123.

37. Osman, *Egypt on the Brink,* 51.

38. Quoted in Alterman, "Cairo," 157.

39. Alterman, "Cairo," 243.

40. Quoted in Little, *American Orientalism,* 91.

41. Zelikow, "Final Observations: No End of Lessons," in *Suez Deconstructed,* ed. Zelikow and May, 312–17; Yaqub, *Containing Arab Nationalism,* 51–55.

42. Osman, *Egypt on the Brink,* 66

43. Yaqub, *Containing Arab Nationalism,* 68.

44. Quoted in Little, *American Orientalism,* 132.

45. January 5, 1957, "Special Message to the Congress on the Situation in the Middle East," in *Public Papers of the Presidents of the United States: Dwight D. Eisenhower (1957)* (Washington, DC: US Government Printing Office, n.d.), 6–16.

46. Yaqub, *Containing Arab Nationalism,* 98–99, 103, 114.

47. Yaqub, *Containing Arab Nationalism,* 164.

48. Yaqub, *Containing Arab Nationalism,* 177.

49. Little, *American Orientalism,* 182.

50. Yaqub, *Containing Arab Nationalism,* 201–2.

51. Quoted in Little, *American Orientalism,* 136.

52. Yaqub, *Containing Arab Nationalism,* 205.

53. Yaqub, *Containing Arab Nationalism,* 255.

54. Little, *American Orientalism,* 95–97 and 185; Hahn, *Crisis and Crossfire,* 45.

55. Carolyn Kennedy-Pipe, *Russia and the World, 1919–1991* (New York: Oxford University Press, 1998), 135–36; Galia Golan, *Soviet Policies in the Middle East: From World War II to Gorbachev* (New York: Cambridge University Press, 1990), 54–57.

56. Little, *American Orientalism,* 99–102; Hahn, *Crisis and Crossfire,* 50–55; Yaqub, *Imperfect Strangers: Americans, Arabs, and U.S.–Middle East Relations in the 1970s* (Ithaca, NY: Cornell University Press, 2016), 18–19.

57. Osman, *Egypt on the Brink,* 73.

58. Jason Brownlee, *Democracy Prevention: The Politics of the U.S.-Egyptian Alliance* (New York: Cambridge University Press, 2012), 15–18.

59. Kennedy-Pipe, *Russia and the World,* 135; Golan, *Soviet Policies in the Middle East,* 69–75.

60. Hahn, *Crisis and Crossfire,* 55–57; Yaqub, *Imperfect Strangers,* 25–29.

61. Yaqub, *Imperfect Strangers,* 25–39.

62. Quoted in Yaqub, *Imperfect Strangers,* 48.

63. Quoted in Brand, *Official Stories,* 73.

64. Golan, *Soviet Policies in the Middle East,* 77–78.

65. Brownlee, *Democracy Prevention,* 20.

66. Yaqub, *Imperfect Strangers,* 53.

67. Brand, *Official Stories,* 75.

68. Quoted in Yaqub, *Imperfect Strangers,* 141.

69. Hahn, *Crisis and Crossfire,* 57–61.

70. Yaqub, *Imperfect Strangers,* 141–43.

71. Brownlee, *Democracy Prevention,* 5.

72. Yaqub, *Imperfect Strangers,* 150.

73. Yaqub, *Imperfect Strangers,* 151. Participants included the United States, the Soviet Union, Israel, Egypt, and Jordan. Syria declined an invitation to attend, refusing to negotiate with Israel until it had withdrawn from Arab land.

74. Brand, *Official Stories,* 81.

75. Quoted in Yaqub, *Imperfect Strangers,* 168.

76. Little, *American Orientalism,* 108.

77. Yaqub, *Imperfect Strangers,* 13.

78. Brownlee, *Democracy Prevention,* 23.

79. Brownlee, *Democracy Prevention,* 25.

80. Quoted in Yaqub, *Imperfect Strangers,* 252.

81. Quoted in Brand, *Official Stories,* 83.

82. Brownlee, *Democracy Prevention,* 31–32.

83. Yaqub, *Imperfect Strangers,* 261–267; Hahn, *Crisis and Crossfire,* 63–64.

84. Quoted in Yaqub, *Imperfect Strangers,* 267.

85. Quoted in Brownlee, *Democracy Prevention,* 35.

86. Yaqub, *Imperfect Strangers,* 271.

87. January 23, 1989, "State of the Union Address—Delivered before a Joint Session of the Congress," in *Public Papers of the Presidents of the United States: Jimmy Carter (1980–1981, Book 1)* (Washington, DC: US Government Printing Office, 1981), 194–99.

88. Quoted in Yaqub, *Imperfect Strangers,* 333.

89. Brownlee, *Democracy Prevention,* 40.

90. Brand, *Official Stories,* 92.

91. Quoted in Brand, *Official Stories,* 94.

92. Hahn, *Crisis and Crossfire,* 78.

93. Brownlee, *Democracy Prevention,* 51.

94. Brownlee, *Democracy Prevention,* 57.

95. Lorena De Vita, "The Cold War in the Middle East," *Atlantisch Perspectief* 43, no. 6 (2019): 37.

4. The Congo

1. Elizabeth Schmidt, *Foreign Intervention in Africa: From the Cold War to the War on Terror* (New York: Cambridge University Press, 2013), 57.

2. Lise Namikas, *Battleground Africa: Cold War in the Congo, 1960–1965* (Washington, DC: Woodrow Wilson Center Press, 2013), 36.

3. Quoted in Ludo De Witte, *The Assassination of Lumumba,* trans. Ann Wright and Renée Fenby (New York: Verso, 2001), xxii

4. David Van Reybrouck, *Congo: The Epic History of a People* (New York: HarperCollins, 2014), 243.

5. On limited educational opportunities for Black Africans in the Belgian Congo, see Herbert Weiss, "The Congo's Independence Struggle Viewed Fifty Years Later," *African Studies Review* 55, no. 1 (April 2012): 110; and Weiss, *Political Protest in the Congo: The Parti Solidaire Africain during the Independence Struggle* (Princeton, NJ: Princeton University Press, 1967), 6–7.

6. Van Reybrouck, *Congo,* 230.

7. Quoted in Van Reybrouck, *Congo,* 233.

8. Quoted in Van Reybrouck, *Congo,* 238.

9. Quoted in Van Reybrouck, *Congo,* 250.

10. Odd Arne Westad, *The Global Cold War: Third World Interventions and the Making of Our Times* (New York: Cambridge University Press, 2007), 137.

11. Sergey Mazov, *A Distant Front in the Cold War: The USSR in West Africa and the Congo, 1956–1964* (Washington, DC. Woodrow Wilson Center Press, 2010), 2.

12. Namikas, *Battleground Africa,* 47.

13. Ryan M. Irwin, "Sovereignty in the Congo Crisis," in *Decolonization and the Cold War: Negotiating Independence,* ed. Leslie James and Elizabeth Leake (New York: Bloomsbury Academic, 2015), 208.

14. For insight into the monumental task newly decolonized states faced in establishing postcolonial governments, see Fred Inglis, "What Was the Third World Revolution?," in *Life among the Anthros and Other Essays* (Princeton, NJ: Princeton University Press, 2012), 240.

15. Weiss, "The Congo's Independence Struggle Viewed Fifty Years Later," 110.

16. Quoted in De Witte, *The Assassination of Lumumba,* 1; Emmanuel Gerard and Bruce Kuklick, *Death in the Congo: Murdering Patrice Lumumba* (Cambridge, MA: Harvard University Press, 2015), 22.

17. De Witte, *Assassination of Lumumba,* 2.

18. Patrice Lumumba, Speech at the Ceremony at the Proclamation of the Congo's Independence, June 30, 1960, in Lumumba, *The Truth about a Monstrous Crime of the Colonialists* (Moscow: Foreign Languages Publishing House, 1961), 44–47.

19. De Witte, *Assassination of Lumumba,* 3.

20. Irwin, "Sovereignty in the Congo Crisis," 203; De Witte, *Assassination of Lumumba* 6; Namikas, *Battleground Africa,* 64.

21. Weiss, "The Congo's Independence Struggle Viewed Fifty Years Later," 113–14.

22. Namikas, *Battleground Africa,* 64.

23. Quoted in Crawford Young, "Ralph Bunche and Patrice Lumumba: The Fatal Encounter," in *Trustee for the Human Community: Ralph J. Bunche, the United Nations, and the Decolonization of Africa,* ed. Robert A. Hill and Edmond J. Keller (Athens: Ohio University Press, 2010), 130.

24. Young, "Ralph Bunche and Patrice Lumumba," 137.

25. Van Reybrouck, *Congo,* 295.

26. Erik Kennes and Miles Larmer, *The Katangese Gendarmes and War in Central Africa: Fighting Their Way Home* (Bloomington: Indiana University Press: 2016), 41–60.

27. Irwin, "Sovereignty in the Congo Crisis," 205.

28. Irwin, "Sovereignty in the Congo Crisis," 206.

29. Quoted in Namikas, *Battleground Africa*, 67; see also Van Reybrouck, *Congo*, 297.

30. Quoted in Namikas, *Battleground Africa*, 68.

31. Quoted in Namikas, *Battleground Africa*, 68.

32. Madeline G. Kalb, *The Congo Cables: The Cold War in Africa from Eisenhower to Kennedy* (New York: Macmillan, 1982), 7.

33. Quoted in Namikas, *Battleground Africa*, 70.

34. Mazov, *A Distant Front in the Cold War*, 93; Mark Mazower, *No Enchanted Palace: The End of Empire and the Ideological Origins of the United Nations* (Princeton, NJ: Princeton University Press, 2009), 149.

35. Both quoted in Mazov, *A Distant Front in the Cold War*, 95.

36. Irwin, "Sovereignty in the Congo Crisis," 210.

37. Quoted in Namikas, *Battleground Africa*, 74.

38. Mazov, *A Distant Front in the Cold War*, 98.

39. Mazov, *A Distant Front in the Cold War*, 102.

40. Quoted in Van Reybrouck, *Congo*, 301.

41. *Foreign Relations of the United States, 1958–1960*, vol. 11: *Africa*, ed. Harriet Dashiell Schwar and Stanley Shaloff (Washington, DC: US Government Printing Office, 1992), Document 140, Memorandum of Discussion at the 452d Meeting of the National Security Council, July 21, 1960.

42. Thomas Borstelmann, *The Cold War and the Color Line: American Race Relation in the Global Arena* (Cambridge, MA: Harvard University Press, 2001), 129.

43. Quoted in Mazov, *A Distant Front in the Cold War*, 100.

44. Borstelmann, *The Cold War and the Color Line*, 130.

45. Namikas, *Battleground Africa*, 82.

46. Mazov, *A Distant Front in the Cold War*, 105.

47. *Foreign Relations of the United States, 1958–1960*, vol. 11: *Africa*, Document 179, Telegram from the Embassy in the Congo to the Department of State, August 17, 1960.

48. *Foreign Relations of the United States, 1958–1960*, vol. 11: *Africa*, Document 180, Memorandum of Discussion at the 456th Meeting of the National Security Council, August 18, 1960.

49. Namikas, *Battleground Africa*, 93; Mazov, *A Distant Front in the Cold War*, 110.

50. Lawrence Devlin, *Chief of Station, Congo: A Memoir of 1960–67* (New York: Public Affairs, 2007), 66.

51. *Foreign Relations of the United States, 1958–1960*, vol. 11: *Africa*, Document 189, Editorial Note.

52. Devlin, *Chief of Station,* 67.

53. Quoted in Mazov, *A Distant Front in the Cold War,* 113.

54. Quoted in Mazov, *A Distant Front in the Cold War,* 114.

55. Quoted in Mazov, *A Distant Front in the Cold War,* 116.

56. Van Reybrouck, *Congo,* 241 and 247.

57. Mazov, *A Distant Front in the Cold War,* 120.

58. Kalb, *The Congo Cables,* 105.

59. Quoted in Kalb, *The Congo Cables,* 111.

60. Quoted in Jason C. Parker, *Hearts, Minds, Voices: US Cold War Public Diplomacy and the Formation of the Third World* (New York: Oxford University Press, 2016), 114.

61. De Witte, *Assassination of Lumumba,* 59; Van Reybrouck, *Congo,* 307.

62. Namikas, *Battleground Africa,* 119.

63. Quoted in Namikas, *Battleground Africa,* 120

64. Mazov, *A Distant Front in the Cold War,* 162.

65. Quoted in De Witte, *Assassination of Lumumba,* 78.

66. De Witte, *Assassination of Lumumba,* xiii. Historian Georges Nzongola-Ntalaja similarly argues that it was "a culmination of two interrelated assassination plots by Belgian and American governments, which used Congolese accomplices and a Belgian execution squad to carry out the deed" (Georges Nzongola-Ntalaja, "Patrice Lumumba: The Most Important Assassination of the 20th Century," *The Guardian,* January 17, 2011).

67. Robert B. Rakove, *Kennedy, Johnson, and the Nonaligned World* (New York: Cambridge University Press, 2013), 98.

68. James Meriwether, *Proudly We Can be Africans: Black Americans and Africa, 1931–1965* (Chapel Hill: University of North Carolina Press, 2002), 233–40; Namikas, *Battleground Africa,* 134.

69. Namikas, *Battleground Africa,* 127–29.

70. Alessandro Iandolo, "Imbalance of Power: The Soviet Union and the Congo Crisis," *Journal of Cold War Studies* 16, no. 2 (Spring 2014): 33.

71. Namikas, *Battleground Africa,* 187.

72. Namikas, *Battleground Africa,* 182.

73. Matthew Hughes, "Fighting for White Rule in Africa: The Central African Federation, Katanga, and the Congo Crisis, 1958–1965," *International History Review* 5, no. 23 (September 2003).

74. Van Reybrouck, *Congo,* 326.

75. Namikas, *Battleground Africa,* 209.

76. See Piero Gleijeses, *Conflicting Missions: Havana, Washington, and Africa, 1959–1976* (Chapel Hill: University of North Carolina Press, 2002), 77–123.

77. Namikas, *Battleground Africa,* 219.

78. Irwin, "Sovereignty in the Congo Crisis," 214.

79. Rakove, *Kennedy, Johnson, and the Nonaligned World,* 134.

80. Namikas, *Battleground Africa,* 227–228.

81. Iandolo, "Imbalance of Power," 55.

82. Namikas, *Battleground Africa*, 231.

83. Quoted in Van Reybrouck, *Congo*, 376.

5. Vietnam

1. I am using "the Vietnam War" to describe the conflict between the United States and South Vietnam on one side and North Vietnam and the National Liberation Front on the other.

2. Mark Philip Bradley, *Imagining Vietnam & America: The Making of Postcolonial Vietnam, 1919–1950* (Chapel Hill: University of North Carolina Press, 2000), 10–25.

3. Sophie Quinn-Judge, "Ho Chi Minh: Nationalist Icon" in *Makers of Modern Asia*, ed. Ramachandra Guha (Cambridge, MA: Harvard University Press, 2014), 68–69.

4. Peter Zinoman, *The Colonial Bastille: A History of Imprisonment in Vietnam, 1962–1940* (Berkeley: University of California Press, 2001), 286.

5. David Marr, "Ho Chi Minh's Independence Declaration," in *Essays into Vietnamese Pasts*, ed. K. W. Taylor and John K. Whitmore (Ithaca, NY: Cornell University Press, 1995), 225.

6. Mark Atwood Lawrence, *Assuming the Burden: Europe and the American Commitment to War in Vietnam* (Berkeley: University of California Press, 2005), 20.

7. Mark Atwood Lawrence, *The Vietnam War: A Concise International History* (New York: Oxford University Press, 2008), 30.

8. Mark Philip Bradley, *Vietnam at War* (New York: Oxford University Press, 2009), 44.

9. Pierre Asselin, *Vietnam's American War: A History* (New York: Cambridge University Press, 2018), 51–53.

10. See Shawn McHale, "Understanding the Fanatic Mind? The Viet Minh and Race Hatred in the First Indochina War (1945–1954)," *Journal of Vietnamese Studies* (October 2009): 98–138; Christopher Goscha, "A Popular Side of the Vietnamese Army: General Nguyen Binh and War in the South," in *Naissance d'un État-Parti: Le Viêt Nam depuis 1945*, ed. Goscha and Benoit Tréglodé (Paris: Indes Savantes, 2004), 325–53.

11. Christopher E. Goscha, "Courting Diplomatic Disaster? The Difficult Integration of Vietnam into the Internationalist Communist Movement (1954–1950)," *Journal of Vietnamese Studies* 1, no. 1–2 (2006): 59–103.

12. Goscha, "Courting Diplomatic Disaster," 90.

13. Lawrence, *Assuming the Burden*, 282, 280.

14. Asselin, *Vietnam's American War*, 66–67.

15. See John Prados, *The Sky Would Fall: Operation Vulture: The U.S. Bombing Mission in Indochina* (New York: Dial, 1983).

16. Asselin, *Vietnam's American War,* 68–70.

17. Christopher J. Goscha, "'Hell in a Very Small Place': Cold War and Decolonization in the Assault on the Vietnamese Body at Dien Bien Phu," *European Journal of East Asian Studies* 9, no. 2 (2010): 219.

18. Asselin, *Vietnam's American War,* 77.

19. Jessica M. Chapman, *Cauldron of Resistance: Ngo Dinh Diem, the United States, and 1950s Southern Vietnam* (Ithaca, NY: Cornell University Press, 2013), 70–74.

20. For more on Diem and Nhu's efforts to maneuver the former into office, see Edward Miller, "Vision, Power, and Agency: The Ascent of Ngo Dinh Diem, 1945–1954," *Journal of Southeast Asian Studies* 35, no. 3 (October 2004): 433–58.

21. Edward Miller, *Misalliance: Ngo Dinh Diem, the United States, and the Fate of South Vietnam* (Cambridge, MA: Harvard University Press, 2013).

22. Seth Jacobs, *America's Miracle Man in Vietnam: Ngo Dinh Diem, Race, Religion, and U.S. Intervention in Southeast Asia* (Durham, NC: Duke University Press, 2005).

23. Edward Miller, "Religious Revival and the Politics of Nation Building: Reinterpreting the 1963 'Buddhist Crisis' in South Vietnam," *Modern Asian Studies* 49, no. 6 (2015): 1959.

24. Pierre Asselin, *Hanoi's Road to the Vietnam War, 1954–1965* (Berkeley: University of California Press, 2013), 15.

25. Jessica Elkind, "'The Virgin Mary Going South': Refugee Resettlement in South Vietnam, 1954–1956," *Diplomatic History* 38, no. 5 (November 2014): 987–1016.

26. Asselin, *Hanoi's Road to the Vietnam War,* 43.

27. Asselin, *Hanoi's Road to the Vietnam War,* 53, 64–65.

28. Quoted in Asselin, *Hanoi's Road to the Vietnam War,* 70.

29. Asselin, *Vietnam's American War,* 93.

30. Quoted in Asselin, *Hanoi's Road to War in Vietnam,* 81.

31. Robert K. Brigham, *Guerrilla Diplomacy: The NLF's Foreign Relations and the Vietnam War* (Ithaca, NY: Cornell University Press, 1999), 9–11; Asselin, *Hanoi's Road to the Vietnam War,* 89.

32. David Hunt, *Vietnam's Southern Revolution: From Peasant Insurrection to Total War* (Amherst: University of Massachusetts Press, 2008), 31.

33. Bradley, *Vietnam at War,* 90–91.

34. Quoted in Chapman, *Cauldron of Resistance,* 191.

35. Fredrik Logevall, *Embers of War: The Fall of an Empire and the Making of America's Vietnam* (New York: Random House, 2012), 703.

36. Quoted in Fredrick Logevall, *The Origins of the Vietnam War* (New York: Pearson Education Limited, 2001), 46.

37. Logevall, *The Origins of the Vietnam* War, 42.

38. Seth Jacobs, *The Universe Unraveling: American Foreign Policy in Cold War Laos* (Ithaca, NY: Cornell University Press, 2012), 3–4.

39. Quoted in Logevall, *The Origins of the Vietnam War*, 44.

40. Philip E. Catton, *Diem's Final Failure: Prelude to America's War in Vietnam* (Lawrence: University Press of Kansas, 2003).

41. Miller, "Religious Revival and the Politics of Nation Building."

42. Fredrik Logevall, *Choosing War: The Lost Chance for Peace and the Escalation of War in Vietnam* (Berkeley: University of California Press, 2001).

43. Asselin, *Vietnam's American War*, 107–9.

44. Martin Grossheim, "The Lao Dong Party, Culture and the Campaign against 'Modern Revisionism': The Democratic Republic of Vietnam Before the Second Indochina War," *Journal of Vietnamese Studies* 8, no. 1 (2013): 81–82.

45. Lien-Hang T. Nguyen, *Hanoi's War: An International History of the War for Peace in Vietnam* (Chapel Hill: University of North Carolina Press, 2012), 75.

46. Nick Turse, *Kill Anything That Moves: The Real American War in Vietnam* (New York: Metropolitan, 2013).

47. Asselin, *Vietnam's American War*, 121.

48. Nguyen, *Hanoi's War*, 109.

49. Chen Jian, "China, the Vietnam War, and Sino-American Rapprochement, 1968–1973," in *The Third Indochina War: Conflict between China, Vietnam, and Cambodia, 1972–1979*, ed. Odd Arne Westad and Sophie Quinn Judge (New York: Routledge, 2006), 33–64.

50. Bao Ninh, *The Sorrow of War* (New York: Riverhead, 1993).

51. Tuong Vu, *Vietnam's Communist Revolution: The Power and Limits of Ideology* (New York: Cambridge University Press, 2017), 238.

52. Balázs Szalontai, "From Battlefield into Marketplace: The End of the Cold War in Indochina, 1985–1989," in *The End of the Cold War and the Third World: New Perspectives on Regional Conflict*, ed. Artemy Kalinovsky and Sergey Radchenko (New York: Routledge, 2011), 156.

53. Odd Arne Westad, "From War to Peace," in *The Third Indochina War: Conflict between China, Vietnam and Cambodia, 1972–79*, ed. Westad and Sophie Quinn-Judge (New York: Routledge, 2009), 1.

6. Angola

1. Piero Gleijeses, *Visions of Freedom: Havana, Washington, Pretoria, and the Struggle for Southern Africa* (Chapel Hill: University of North Carolina Press, 2013), 13.

2. David Birmingham, *A Short History of Modern Angola* (New York: Oxford University Press, 2015), 102.

3. Birmingham, *A Short History of Modern Angola*, 71.

4. Elizabeth Schmidt, *Foreign Intervention in Africa: From the Cold War to the War on Terror* (New York: Cambridge University Press, 2013), 79.

5. Birmingham, *A Short History of Modern Angola*, 68–71.

6. Pierro Gelijeses, *Conflicting Missions: Havana, Washington, and Africa, 1959–1976* (Chapel Hill: University of North Carolina Press, 2002), 238.

7. Odd Arne Westad, *The Global Cold War: Third World Interventions and the Making of Our Times* (New York: Cambridge University Press, 2007), 210.

8. Arthur Jay Klinghoffer, *The Angolan War: A Study in Soviet Policy in the Third World* (Boulder, CO: Westview, 1980), 13.

9. Schmidt, *Foreign Intervention in Africa*, 81.

10. Steven F. Jackson, "China's Third World Foreign Policy: The Case of Angola and Mozambique, 1961–1993," *China Quarterly* 142 (June 1995): 391.

11. Caryle Murphy, "Rebel Poet-Doctor," *Washington Post,* September 12, 1979; Birmingham, *A Short History of Modern Angola,* 103.

12. Candace Sobers, "Interdependence, Intervention, and Internationalism: Angola and the International System, 1974–1975," *Journal of Cold War Studies* 21, no. 1 (Winter 2019): 104.

13. Birmingham, *A Short History of Modern Angola,* 76.

14. Jeremy Ball, "'At Least in Those Days We Had Enough to Eat': Colonialism, Independence, and the Cold War in Catumbela, Angola, 1974–1977," in *Local Consequences of the Global Cold War,* ed. Jeffrey A. Engel (Washington, DC: Woodrow Wilson Center Press, 2007), 281–82.

15. Luís Nuno Rodrigues, "The United States and Portuguese Decolonization," *Portuguese Studies* 29, no. 2 (2013): 165.

16. Rodrigues, "The United States and Portuguese Decolonization," 170–73.

17. Schmidt, *Foreign Intervention in Africa,* 82.

18. Rodrigues, "The United States and Portuguese Decolonization," 177.

19. Sobers, "Interdependence, Intervention, and Internationalism," 105.

20. Birmingham, *A Short History of Modern Angola,* 79.

21. Bruno C. Reis, "Decentering the Cold War in Africa: The Portuguese Policy of Decolonization and Détente in Angola and Mozambique (1974–1984)," *Journal of Cold War Studies* 21, no. 1 (Winter 2019): 13; Westad, *The Global Cold War,* 220.

22. Quoted in Ball, "At Least in Those Days We Had Enough to Eat," 277.

23. Quoted in Gleijeses, *Conflicting Missions,* 233.

24. Gleijeses, *Conflicting Missions,* 233.

25. Ball, "At Least in Those Days We Had Enough to Eat," 277.

26. "Mario de Andrade, 62, a Founder of Angola's Governing Movement," *New York Times,* August 27, 1990; Gleijeses, *Conflicting Missions,* 236–238; Westad, *The Global Cold War,* 217.

27. Rodrigues, "The United States and Portuguese Decolonization," 182.

28. Gleijeses, *Conflicting Missions,* 277.

29. Westad, *The Global Cold War,* 215–22.

30. Gleijeses, *Conflicting Missions,* 243.

31. Raymond L. Garthoff, *Détente and Confrontation: American-Soviet Relations from Nixon to Reagan,* rev. ed. (Washington, DC: Brookings Institution, 1994), 583.

32. Gleijeses, *Conflicting Missions,* 244.

33. "Text of the Alvor Agreement between Portugal and the Angolan Liberation Movements," in *Decolonization: A Publication of the UN Department of Political Affairs, Trusteeship and Decolonization* 2, no. 4 (March 1975), UN Library, March 27, 1975, UN/SA Collection, https://www.un.org/dppa/decolonization/sites/www.un.org.dppa.decolonization/files/decon_num_4–1.pdf.

34. Gelijeses, *Conflicting Missions,* 251.

35. Jackson, "China's Third World Foreign Policy," 401–2.

36. Tiago Moreira de Sá, "'The World Was Not Turning in Their Direction': The United States and the Decolonization of Angola," *Journal of Cold War Studies* 21, no. 1 (Winter 2019).

37. Gleijeses, *Conflicting Missions,* 242.

38. Quoted in Vladislav M. Zubok, *A Failed Empire: The Soviet Union in the Cold War from Stalin to Gorbachev* (Chapel Hill: University of North Carolina Press, 2003), 252.

39. Milorad Lazic, "Comrades in Arms: Yugoslav Military Aid to Liberation Movements of Angola and Mozambique, 1961–1976," in *Southern African Liberation Movements and the Global Cold War 'East': Transnational Activism, 1960–1990,* ed. Lena Dallywater, Chris Saunders, and Helder Adegar Fonseca (Boston: Walter de Gruyter, 2019), 170; Gelijeses, *Conflicting Missions,* 252.

40. Westad, *The Global Cold War,* 222.

41. Moreira de Sá, "The World Was Not Turning in Their Direction," 60.

42. James H. Meriwether, *Tears, Fire, and Blood: The United States and the Decolonization of Africa* (Chapel Hill: University of North Carolina Press, 2021), 184.

43. Gleijeses, *Conflicting Missions,* 356.

44. Moreira de Sá, "The World Was Not Turning in Their Direction," 61.

45. Gleijeses, *Conflicting Missions,* 273–75.

46. Tyrone L. Groh, *Proxy War: The Least Bad Option* (Stanford, CA: Stanford University Press, 2019), 158; Westad, *The Global Cold War,* 230.

47. Groh, *Proxy War,* 164; Gleijeses, *Conflicting Missions,* 276.

48. Gleijeses, *Conflicting Missions,* 301.

49. Westad, *The Global Cold War,* 177; Fidel Castro, December 1975, "African Blood Runs through Our Veins," in *Cuba and Angola: Fighting for Africa's Freedom and Our Own,* ed. Mary-Alice Waters (New York: Pathfinder, 2013), 31–33.

50. Gleijeses, *Conflicting Missions,* 7–8.

51. Gleijeses, *Conflicting Missions,* 269.

52. Gelijeses, *Conflicting Missions,* 305–8.

53. Gleijeses, *Conflicting Missions,* 307; Westad, *The Global Cold War,* 235.

54. Quoted in *Conflicting Missions,* 311.

55. Gleijeses, *Conflicting Missions,* 330; *Foreign Relations of the United States, 1969–1976,* vol. 28: *Southern Africa,* ed. Myra F. Burton (Washington, DC: US Government Printing Office, 2011), 83; Director of Central Intelligence Bush to the Chairman of the House Appropriations Subcommittee on Defense (Mahon), March 18, 1976.

56. Gleijeses, *Conflicting Missions,* 332.

57. Robert David Johnson, "The Unintended Consequences of Congressional Reform: The Clark and Tunney Amendments and U.S. Policy toward Angola," *Diplomatic History* 27, no. 2 (April 2003): 215.

58. Gleijeses, *Conflicting Missions,* 342.

59. Christopher Saunders, "The South Africa-Angola Talks, 1976–1984: A Little-Known Cold War Thread," *Kronos* 37 (November 2011), 105.

60. Quoted in Gelijeses, *Conflicting Missions,* 345.

61. Gleijeses, *Conflicting Missions,* 390–91.

62. Westad, *The Global Cold War,* 237.

63. Garthoff, *Détente and Confrontation,* 588.

64. Soviet Politburo member Andrei P. Kirilenko quoted in Garthoff, *Détente and Confrontation,* 588.

65. Westad, *The Global Cold War,* 232–243.

66. Gleijeses, *Conflicting Missions,* 8–9.

67. Garthoff, *Détente and Confrontation,* 591.

68. David Birmingham, *Empire in Africa: Angola and Its Neighbors* (Athens: Ohio University Press, 2006), 116; Gleijeses, *Visions of Freedom,* 73

69. Birmingham, *A Short History of Modern Angola,* 90.

70. Gleijeses, *Conflicting Missions,* 372.

71. Birmingham, *Empire in Africa,* 118; Birmingham, *A Short History of Modern Angola,* 73.

72. Gleijeses, *Visions of Freedom,* 118.

73. Gleijeses, *Visions of Freedom,* 213–16.

74. Gleijeses, *Visions of Freedom,* 163.

75. Gleijeses, "A Test of Wills: Jimmy Carter, South Africa, and the Independence of Namibia," *Diplomatic History* 34, no. 5 (November 2010): 889.

76. Westad, *The Global Cold War,* 331; Nancy Mitchell, *Jimmy Carter in Africa: Race and the Cold War* (Stanford, CA: Stanford University Press, 2016); Gleijeses, "A Test of Wills," 884–87.

77. Flavia Gasbarri, "The Reagan Administration and the Cold War Endgame in the Periphery: The Case of Southern Africa," in *The Reagan Moment: America and the World in the 1980s,* ed. Jonathan R. Hunt and Simon Miles (Ithaca, NY: Cornell University Press, 2021), 348.

78. Kathryn O'Neill and Barry Munslow, "Ending the Cold War in Southern Africa," *Third World Quarterly* 12, no. 3/4 (1990–1991): 91.

79. Gleijeses, *Visions of Freedom,* 199.

80. Gleijeses, *Visions of Freedom,* 249.

81. Gasbarri, "The Reagan Administration and the Cold War Endgame in the Periphery," 351.

82. Odd Arne Westad, *The Cold War: A World History* (New York: Basic, 2017), 532.

83. Gleijeses, *Visions of Freedom,* 296.

84. "Address to the 40th Session of the United Nations General Assembly in New York, New York, October 24, 1985," in *Public Papers of the Presidents of the United States: Ronald Reagan (1985, Book 2: June 29–December 31, 1985)* (Washington, DC: US Government Printing Office, 1988), 1286–90.

85. William Minter, "The U.S. and the War in Angola," *Review of African Political Economy* 50 (March 1991): 136–37.

86. Westad, *The Cold War: A World History,* 536.

87. Westad, *The Global Cold War,* 391.

88. Gleijeses, *Visions of Freedom,* 402–3.

89. Westad, *The Global Cold War,* 391.

90. Gleijeses, *Visions of Freedom,* 431

91. "Resolution 435" (1978), September 29, 1978, https://peacemaker.un.org /sites/peacemaker.un.org/files/NM_780929_SCR435%281978%29.pdf.

92. Gleijeses, *Visions of Freedom,* 450–81; O'Neill and Munslow, "Ending the Cold War in Southern Africa," 81–84; "Agreement among the People's Republic of Angola, the Republic of Cuba, and the Republic of South Africa" (Tripartite Agreement), December 22, 1988, https://peacemaker.un.org/angola-tripartite-agreement88.

93. Ian Van Der Waag, "Angola," in *Twentieth Century War and Conflict: A Concise Encyclopedia,* ed. Gordon Martel (New York: John Wiley and Sons, 2014), 9.

94. Lydia Polgreen, "Angolans Come Home to 'Negative Peace,'" *New York Times,* July 30, 2003.

7. Iran

1. Jalal Al-i Ahmad, "Diagnosing an Illness," in *Decolonization: Perspectives from Now and Then,* ed. Prasenjit Duara (New York: Routledge, 2004), 60.

2. James A. Bill, *The Eagle and the Lion: The Tragedy of American-Iranian Relations* (New Haven, CT: Yale University Press, 1988), 16; Roham Alvandi, *Nixon, Kissinger, and the Shah: The United States and Iran in the Cold War* (New York: Oxford University Press, 2014), 7; Valdislav M. Zubok, "Stalin, Soviet Intelligence, and the Struggle for Iran, 1945–1953," *Diplomatic History* 44, no. 1 (2020): 25.

3. Bill, *The Eagle and the Lion,* 18.

4. Alvandi, *Nixon, Kissinger, and the Shah,* 9.

5. Bill, *The Eagle and the Lion,* 30.

6. Galia Golan, *Soviet Policies in the Middle East: From World War II to Gorbachev* (New York: Cambridge University Press, 1990), 29.

7. Quoted in Zubok, "Stalin, Soviet Intelligence, and the Struggle for Iran," 28.

8. Mark J. Gasiorowski, "U.S. Perceptions of the Communist Threat in Iran during the Mossadegh Era," *Journal of Cold War Studies* 21, no. 3 (Summer 2019): 190.

9. Quoted in Malcolm Byrne, "Factors Influencing U.S. Policy toward Iran, 1945–1953," in *Mohammad Mosaddeq and the 1953 Coup in Iran*, ed. Mark J. Gasiorowski and Byrne (Syracuse, NY: Syracuse University Press, 2004), 211.

10. Byrne, "Factors Influencing U.S. Policy towards Iran," 204–5.

11. Quoted in Alvandi, *Nixon, Kissinger, and the Shah*, 11.

12. Quoted in Byrne, "Factors Influencing U.S. Policy towards Iran," 208.

13. Gasiorowski, "U.S. Perceptions of the Communist Threat, 191.

14. Alvandi, *Nixon, Kissinger, and the Shah*, 14.

15. Quoted in Gasiorowski, "U.S. Perceptions of the Communist Threat," 197.

16. Alvandi, *Nixon, Kissinger, and the Shah*, 15.

17. Gasiorowski, "U.S. Perceptions of the Communist Threat," 202–5.

18. Gasiorowski, "U.S. Perceptions of the Communist Threat," 210.

19. Gasiorowski, "U.S. Perceptions of the Communist Threat," 214–15; Gasiorowski, "The CIA's TPBEDAMN Operation and the 1953 Coup in Iran," *Journal of Cold War Studies* 15, no. 4 (Fall 2013): 18.

20. Zubok, "Stalin, Soviet Intelligence, and the Struggle for Iran," 32.

21. Zubok, "Stalin, Soviet Intelligence, and the Struggle for Iran," 24.

22. Gasiorowski, "U.S. Perceptions of the Communist Threat," 186.

23. Hugh Wilford, "'Essentially a Work of Fiction': Kermit 'Kim' Roosevelt, Imperial Romance, and the Iran Coup of 1953," *Diplomatic History* 40, no. 5 (2016): 923.

24. Alvandi, *Nixon, Kissinger, and the Shah*, 17–18.

25. Bill, *The Eagle and the Lion*, 94.

26. Bill, *The Eagle and the Lion*, 112.

27. Bill, *The Eagle and the Lion*, 99.

28. Bill, *The Eagle and the Lion*, 115.

29. Bill, *The Eagle and the Lion*, 119.

30. Zubok, "Stalin, Soviet Intelligence, and the Struggle for Iran," 21; Golan, *Soviet Policies in the Middle East*, 178.

31. April R. Summitt, "For a White Revolution: John F. Kennedy and the Shah of Iran," *Middle East Journal* 58, no. 4 (Autumn 2004): 142; David R. Collier, "To Prevent a Revolution: John F. Kennedy and the Promotion of Democracy in Iran," *Diplomacy and Statecraft* 24 (2013): 462.

32. Collier, "To Prevent a Revolution," 465.

33. Collier, "To Prevent a Revolution," 464.

34. Bill, *The Eagle and the Lion*, 150.

35. Golan, *Soviet Policies in the Middle East*, 178–79.

36. Summitt, "For a White Revolution," 571.

37. Quoted in Andrew L. Johns, "The Johnson Administration, the Shah of Iran, and the Changing Pattern of U.S.-Iranian Relations, 1965–1967," *Journal of Cold War Studies* 9, no. 2 (Spring 2007): 70.

38. Bill, *The Eagle and the Lion*, 157.

39. Alvandi, *Nixon, Kissinger, and the Shah*, 24.

40. Quoted in Bill, *The Eagle and the Lion,* 159.

41. Bill, *The Eagle and the Lion,* 163.

42. Quoted in Bill, *The Eagle and the Lion,* 170.

43. Johns, "The Johnson Administration, the Shah of Iran," 83.

44. Johns, "The Johnson Administration, the Shah of Iran," 72.

45. Johns, "The Johnson Administration, the Shah of Iran," 90–91.

46. Johns, "The Johnson Administration, the Shah of Iran," 88.

47. Quoted in Alvandi, *Nixon, Kissinger, and the Shah,* 33.

48. *Public Papers of the Presidents of the United States: Richard Nixon (1969)* (Washington, DC: US Government Printing Office, 1971), 544–56.

49. Alvandi, *Nixon, Kissinger, and the Shah,* 50.

50. Alvandi, *Nixon, Kissinger, and the Shah,* 39.

51. Alvandi, *Nixon, Kissinger, and the Shah,* 40 and 53; Bill, *The Eagle and the Lion,* 184–90.

52. *Foreign Relations of the United States, 1969–1976,* vol. E-4: *Documents on Iran and Iraq, 1969–1972,* ed. Monica Belmonte (Washington, DC: US Government Printing Office, 2006), Document 122; Alvandi, *Nixon, Kissinger, and the Shah,* 58.

53. *Foreign Relations of the United States, 1969–1976,* vol. E-4: *Documents on Iran and Iraq, 1969–1972,* ed. Belmonte, Document 201; Salim Yaqub, *Imperfect Strangers: Americans, Arabs, and U.S.-Middle East Relations in the 1970s* (Ithaca, NY: Cornell University Press, 2016), 53

54. Quoted in Alvandi, *Nixon, Kissinger, and the Shah,* 63.

55. Alvandi, *Nixon, Kissinger, and the Shah,* 64; Bill, *The Eagle and the Lion,* 202.

56. Quoted in Bill, *The Eagle and the Lion,* 203.

57. Bill, *The Eagle and the Lion,* 207.

58. See Barbara J. Keys, *Reclaiming American Virtue: The Human Rights Revolution of the 1970s* (Cambridge, MA: Harvard University Press, 2014).

59. Alvandi, *Nixon, Kissinger, and the Shah,* 130–32.

60. Mehran Kamrava, *The Modern Middle East: A Political History since the First World War,* 3rd ed. (Berkeley: University of California Press, 2013), 148.

61. The "Group of Six," including the United States, Britain, France, West Germany, Italy, and Japan, coordinated a strategy to tie up Middle East capital in bilateral technology and infrastructure deals.

62. Jacob Darwin Hamblin, "The Nuclearization of Iran in the Seventies," *Diplomatic History* 38, no. 5 (2014): 1118.

63. Quoted in William Burr, "A Brief History of U.S. Iranian Nuclear Negotiations," *Bulletin of Atomic Scientists* (January/February 2009): 22.

64. Alvandi, *Nixon, Kissinger, and the Shah,* 130.

65. Bill, *The Eagle and the Lion,* 220–22.

66. Kamrava, *The Modern Middle East,* 150.

67. Kamrava, *The Modern Middle East,* 150–53.

68. Bill, *The Eagle and the Lion*, 218.

69. Bill, *The Eagle and the Lion*, 236.

70. Kamrava, *The Modern Middle East*, 153. On the transnational nature of the Iranian revolution and the roles played by American-educated Iranians, see Matthew K. Shannon, *Losing Hearts and Minds: American-Iranian Relations and International Education during the Cold War* (Ithaca, NY: Cornell University Press, 2017).

71. Gary Sick, *All Fall Down: America's Tragic Encounter with Iran* (New York: Random House, 1986), xviii.

72. Quoted in R. K. Ramazani, "Iran's Revolution: Patterns, Problems, and Prospects," *Independence without Freedom: Iran's Foreign Policy* (Charlottesville: University of Virginia Press, 2020), 39.

73. Bill, *The Eagle and the Lion*, 275.

74. Odd Arne Westad, *The Global Cold War*, 295.

75. Bill, *The Eagle and the Lion*, 278.

76. Sixteen days into the crisis, thirteen Black and female hostages were released, thanks to diplomatic intervention by the Palestinian Liberation Organization (PLO), which acted in response to the vocal support it had received from African Americans. The PLO continued to work thereafter for the release of the remaining hostages, to no avail (see Yaqub, *Imperfect Strangers*, 303 and 322–23).

77. Kamrava, *The Modern Middle East*, 159.

78. On the US domestic political implications of the hostage crisis, see David Farber, *Taken Hostage: The Iran Hostage Crisis and America's First Encounter with Radical Islam* (Princeton, NJ: Princeton University Press, 2009).

79. Sick, *All Fall Down*, 294–328.

80. Kamrava, *The Modern Middle East*, 161.

81. Kamrava, *The Modern Middle East*, 156.

82. Bill, *The Eagle and the Lion*, 270–73.

83. Ray Takeyh, "The Iran-Iraq War: A Reassessment," *Middle East Journal* 64, no. 3 (Summer 2010): 367.

84. Takeyh, "The Iran-Iraq War," 366.

85. Bill, *The Eagle and the Lion*, 306.

86. Malcolm Byrne, *Iran-Contra: Reagan's Scandal and the Unchecked Abuse of Presidential Power* (Lawrence: University Press of Kansas, 2014), 4.

87. Takeyh, "The Iran-Iraq War," 381.

88. Kamrava, *The Modern Middle East*, 206.

89. Takeyh, "The Iran-Iraq War," 383.

90. Paul Thomas Chamberlin, "Rethinking the Middle East and North Africa in the Cold War," *International Journal of Middle East Studies* 43, no. 2 (May 2011): 318.

91. Peter L. Hahn, *Crisis and Crossfire: The United States and the Middle East since 1945* (Washington, DC: Potomac, 2005), 106.

92. Yaqub, *Imperfect Strangers*, 304.

Conclusion

1. John Lewis Gaddis, "Toward the Post-Cold War World," *Foreign Affairs* 70, no. 2 (Spring 1991): 103.

2. Francis Fukuyama, "The End of History?," *National Interest* 16 (Summer 1989): 3–18.

3. Samuel P. Huntington, "The Clash of Civilizations?," *Foreign Affairs* 22, no. 3 (Summer 1993): 22–49.

4. Frantz Fanon, *The Wretched of the Earth* (New York: Grove, 2005).

Bibliography

Published Primary Sources

"Agreement among the People's Republic of Angola, the Republic of Cuba, and the Republic of South Africa" (Tripartite Agreement). December 22, 1988. https://peacemaker.un.org/angola-tripartite-agreement88.

Al-i Ahmad, Jalal. "Diagnosing an Illness." In *Decolonization: Perspectives from Now and Then,* edited by Prasenjit Duara, 56–63. New York: Routledge, 2004.

"Churchill's 'Iron Curtain' Speech, "Sinews of Peace." March 5, 1946. History and Public Policy Program Digital Archive, CWIHP archives. https://digitalarchive.wilsoncenter.org/document/116180.

DiNunzio, Mario R., ed. *Woodrow Wilson: Essential Writings and Speeches of the Scholar President.* New York: New York University Press, 2006.

Eisenhower, Dwight D. "Annual Message to the Congress on the State of the Union." January 9, 1958. Online by Gerhard Peters and John T. Woolley, The American Presidency Project. http://www.presidency.ucsb.edu/ws/?pid=11162.

———. "Inaugural Address." January 20, 1953. Online by Gerhard Peters and John T. Woolley, The American Presidency Project. http://www.presidency.ucsb.edu/ws/?pid=9600.

Foreign Relations of the United States, 1955–1957. Vol. 8: *South Asia,* edited by Robert J. McMahon and Stanley Shaloff. Washington, DC: US Government Printing Office, 1987.

Foreign Relations of the United States, 1958–1960. Vol. 11: *Africa,* edited by Harriet Dashiell Schwar and Stanley Shaloff. Washington, DC: US Government Printing Office, 1992.

Foreign Relations of the United States, 1969–1976. Vol. E-4: *Documents on Iran and Iraq, 1969–1972,* edited by Monica Belmonte. Washington, DC: US Government Printing Office, 2006.

Foreign Relations of the United States, 1969–1976. Vol. 28: *Southern Africa,* edited by Myra F. Burton. Washington, DC: US Government Printing Office, 2011.

Gopal, Sarvapelli, ed. *Jawaharlal Nehru: An Anthology.* Delhi, India: Oxford University Press, 1980.

Jensen, Kenneth M., ed. *Origins of the Cold War: The Novikov, Kennan, and Roberts "Long Telegrams" of 1946.* Rev. ed. Washington, DC: United States Institute of Peace Press, 1993.

Kennedy, John F. "Special Message to the Congress on Foreign Aid." March 22, 1961. Online by Gerhard Peters and John T. Woolley, The American Presidency Project. http://www.presidency.ucsb.edu/ws/?pid=8545.

Lenin, Vladimir Il'ich. *Imperialism, the Highest Stage of Capitalism: A Popular Outline.* New York: International, 1939.

Lumumba, Patrice. *The Truth about a Monstrous Crime of the Colonialists.* Moscow: Foreign Languages Publishing House, 1961.

"National Security Council Report, NSC 68, 'United States Objectives and Programs for National Security.'" April 14, 1950, History and Public Policy Program Digital Archive, US National Archives. http://digitalarchive.wilsoncenter.org/document/116191.

Nehru, Jawaharlal. "Indian Foreign Policy (Selected Statements)." *India Quarterly* 42, no. 1 (January-March, 1945).

Nixon, Richard M. *RN: The Memoirs of Richard M. Nixon.* New York: Grosset and Dunlap, 1978.

Nkrumah, Kwame. *Neo-Colonialism: The Last Stage of Imperialism.* New York: International, 1966.

Orwell, George. "You and the Atom Bomb." *Tribune,* October 19, 1945.

Public Papers of the Presidents of the United States: Harry S. Truman. Washington, DC: US Government Printing Office, 1963.

Public Papers of the Presidents of the United States: Dwight D. Eisenhower (1957). Washington, DC: US Government Printing Office, n.d.

Public Papers of the Presidents of the United States: Richard Nixon (1969). Washington, DC: US Government Printing Office, 1971.

Public Papers of the Presidents of the United States: Jimmy Carter (1980–1981, Book 1). Washington, DC: US Government Printing Office, 1981.

Public Papers of the Presidents of the United States: Ronald Reagan (1981). Washington, DC: US Government Printing Office, 1982.

Public Papers of the Presidents of the United States: Ronald Reagan (1985, Book 2: June 29–December 31, 1985). Washington DC: US Government Printing Office, 1988.

"Resolution 435" (1978). September 29, 1978. https://peacemaker.un.org/sites/peacemaker.un.org/files/NM_780929_SCR435%281978%29.pdf.

Rostow, Walt W. W. *The Stages of Economic Growth: A Non-Communist Manifesto.* Cambridge: Cambridge University Press, 1960.

Shepard, Todd. *Voices of Decolonization: A Brief History with Documents.* New York: Bedford/St. Martin's, 2015.

"Text of the Alvor Agreement between Portugal and the Angolan Liberation Movements." In "Decolonization: A Publication of the UN Department of Political Affairs, Trusteeship and Decolonization." Vol. 2, no. 4 (March 1975),

UN Library, March 27, 1975, UN/SA Collection. https://www.un.org/dppa /decolonization/sites/www.un.org.dppa.decolonization/files/decon_num_4–1 .pdf.

Secondary Sources

Acheson, Dean. *Present at the Creation: My Years in the State Department*. New York: Norton, 1967.

Allison, Roy. *The Soviet Union and the Strategy of Non-Alignment in the Third World*. Cambridge: Cambridge University Press, 1988.

Alterman, Jon B. "Cairo." In *Suez Deconstructed: An Interactive Study in Crisis, War, and Peacemaking*, edited by Philip Zelikow and Ernest May, 107–23. Washington, DC: Brookings Institution Press, 2018.

Alvandi, Roham. *Nixon, Kissinger, and the Shah: The United States and Iran in the Cold War*. New York: Oxford University Press, 2014.

Asselin, Pierre. *Hanoi's Road to the Vietnam War, 1954–1965*. Berkeley: University of California Press, 2013.

———. *Vietnam's American War: A History*. New York: Cambridge University Press, 2018.

Ball, Jeremy. "'At Least in Those Days We Had Enough to Eat': Colonialism, Independence, and the Cold War in Catumbela, Angola, 1974–1977." In *Local Consequences of the Global Cold War*, edited by Jeffrey A. Engel, 275–96. Washington, DC: Woodrow Wilson Center Press, 2007.

Bao Ninh, *The Sorrow of War*. New York: Riverhead, 1993.

Barrett, Roby C. *The Greater Middle East and the Cold War: U.S. Foreign Policy under Eisenhower and Kennedy*. New York: I. B. Taurus, 2007.

Betts, Raymond F. "'Decolonization' A Brief History of the Word." In *Beyond Empire and Nation: The Decolonization of African and Asian Societies, 1930s–1970s*, edited by Els Bogaerts and Remco Raben, 23–38. New York: Brill, 2013.

Bill, James A. *The Eagle and the Lion: The Tragedy of American-Iranian Relations*. New Haven, CT: Yale University Press, 1988.

Birmingham, David. *Empire in Africa: Angola and Its Neighbors*. Athens: Ohio University Press, 2006.

———. *A Short History of Modern Angola*. New York: Oxford University Press, 2015.

Borstelmann, Thomas. *The Cold War and the Color Line: American Race Relation in the Global Arena*. Cambridge, MA: Harvard University Press, 2001.

Bradley, Mark Philip. *Imagining Vietnam and America: The Making of Postcolonial Vietnam, 1919–1950*. Chapel Hill: University of North Carolina Press, 2000.

———. *Vietnam at War*. New York: Oxford University Press, 2009.

Brand, Laurie. *Official Stories: Politics and National Narratives in Egypt and Algeria*. Palo Alto, CA: Stanford University Press, 2014.

Brands, H. W. *India and the United States: The Cold Peace*. Boston: Twayne, 1990.

Brigham, Robert K. *Guerrilla Diplomacy: The NLF's Foreign Relations and the Vietnam War.* Ithaca, NY: Cornell University Press, 1999.

Brownlee, Jason. *Democracy Prevention: The Politics of the U.S.-Egyptian Alliance.* New York: Cambridge University Press, 2012.

Burr, William. "A Brief History of U.S. Iranian Nuclear Negotiations." *Bulletin of Atomic Scientists* (January/February 2009): 21–34.

Byrne, Malcolm. "Factors Influencing U.S. Policy toward Iran, 1945–1953." In *Mohammad Mosaddeq and the 1953 Coup in Iran,* edited by Mark J. Gasiorowski and Byrne, 201–26. Syracuse, NY: Syracuse University Press, 2004.

———. *Iran-Contra: Reagan's Scandal and the Unchecked Abuse of Presidential Power.* Lawrence: University Press of Kansas, 2014.

Castigliola, Frank. *Roosevelt's Lost Alliances: How Personal Politics Helped Start the Cold War.* Princeton, NJ: Princeton University Press, 2012.

Catton, Philip E. *Diem's Final Failure: Prelude to America's War in Vietnam.* Lawrence: University Press of Kansas, 2003.

Chamberlin, Paul Thomas. *The Cold War Killing Fields: Rethinking the Long Peace.* New York: HarperCollins, 2018.

———. "Rethinking the Middle East and North Africa in the Cold War." *International Journal of Middle East Studies* 43, no. 2 (May 2011): 317–19.

Chapman, Jessica M. *Cauldron of Resistance: Ngo Dinh Diem, the United States, and 1950s Southern Vietnam.* Ithaca, NY: Cornell University Press, 2013.

Collier, David R. "To Prevent a Revolution: John F. Kennedy and the Promotion of Democracy in Iran." *Diplomacy and Statecraft* 24 (2013): 456–75.

Connelly, Matthew. *A Diplomatic Revolution: Algeria's Fight for Independence and the Origins of the Post-Cold War Era.* New York: Oxford University Press, 2002.

———. "Taking off the Cold War Lens: Visions of North-South Conflict during the Algerian War for Independence," *American Historical Review* (June 2000): 739–69.

Cooper, Fredrick. *Africa since 1940: The Past of the Present.* New York: Cambridge University Press, 2002.

Dallywater, Lena, Helder Adegar Fonseca, and Chris Saunders, eds. *Southern African Liberation Movements and the Global Cold War 'East': Transnational Activism, 1960–1990.* Boston: Walter de Gruyter, 2019.

Das, Santanu, ed. *Race, Empire, and First World War Writing.* New York: Cambridge University Press, 2014.

De Grazia, Victoria. *Irresistible Empire: America's Advance through 20th Century Europe.* Cambridge, MA: Belknap Press of Harvard University Press, 2005.

De Vita, Lorena. "The Cold War in the Middle East," *Atlantisch Perspectief* 43, no. 6 (2019): 34–37.

De Witte, Ludo. *The Assassination of Lumumba.* Translated by Ann Wright and Renée Fenby. New York: Verso, 2001.

Devlin, Lawrence. *Chief of Station, Congo: A Memoir of 1960–67.* New York: Public Affairs, 2007.

Duara, Prasenjit, ed. *Decolonization: Perspectives from Now and Then.* New York: Routledge, 2004.

Elkind, Jessica. "'The Virgin Mary Going South': Refugee Resettlement in South Vietnam, 1954–1956." *Diplomatic History* 38, no. 5 (November 2014): 987–1016.

Engel, Jeffrey A., ed. *Local Consequences of the Global Cold War.* Washington, DC: Woodrow Wilson Center Press, 2007.

Engerman, David C. "Learning from the East: Soviet Experts and India in the Era of Competitive Coexistence." *Comparative Studies of South Asia, Africa, and the Middle East* 33, no. 2 (2013): 227–38.

———. "South Asia and the Cold War." In *The Cold War in the Third World,* edited by Robert J. McMahon, 67–84. New York: Oxford University Press, 2013.

Fanon, Frantz. *The Wretched of the Earth.* New York: Grove, 2005.

Farber, David. *Taken Hostage: The Iran Hostage Crisis and America's First Encounter with Radical Islam.* Princeton, NJ: Princeton University Press, 2009.

Fisher, Margaret W. "India's Jawaharlal Nehru." *Asian Survey* 7, no. 6 (June 1967): 363–73.

Friedman, Jeremy. *Shadow Cold War: The Sino-Soviet Competition for the Third World.* Chapel Hill: University of North Carolina Press, 2015.

Fukuyama, Francis. "The End of History?" *National Interest* 16 (Summer 1989): 3–18.

Gaddis, John Lewis. *Strategies of Containment: A Critical Appraisal of American National Security Strategy during the Cold War.* Rev. and expanded ed. New York: Oxford University Press, 2005.

———. "Toward the Post-Cold War World." *Foreign Affairs* 70, no. 2 (Spring 1991): 102–22.

Garthoff, Raymond L. *Détente and Confrontation: American-Soviet Relations from Nixon to Reagan.* Rev. ed. Washington, DC: Brookings Institution, 1994.

Gasbarri, Flavia. "The Reagan Administration and the Cold War Endgame in the Periphery: The Case of Southern Africa." In *The Reagan Moment: America and the World in the 1980s,* edited by Jonathan R. Hunt and Simon Miles, 345–64. Ithaca, NY: Cornell University Press, 2021.

Gasiorowski, Mark J. "The CIA's TPBEDAMN Operation and the 1953 Coup in Iran." *Journal of Cold War Studies* 15, no. 4 (Fall 2013): 4–24.

———. "U.S. Perceptions of the Communist Threat in Iran during the Mossadegh Era." *Journal of Cold War Studies* 21, no. 3 (Summer 2019): 185–221.

Gerard, Emmanuel, and Bruce Kuklick. *Death in the Congo: Murdering Patrice Lumumba.* Cambridge, MA: Harvard University Press, 2015.

Gleijeses, Piero. *Conflicting Missions: Havana, Washington, and Africa, 1959–1976.* Chapel Hill: University of North Carolina Press, 2002.

———. "A Test of Wills: Jimmy Carter, South Africa, and the Independence of Namibia." *Diplomatic History* 34, no. 5 (November 2010): 853–91.

———. *Visions of Freedom: Havana, Washington, Pretoria, and the Struggle for Southern Africa.* Chapel Hill: University of North Carolina Press, 2013.

Golan, Galia. *Soviet Policies in the Middle East: From World War II to Gorbachev.* New York: Cambridge University Press, 1990.

Groh, Tyrone L. *Proxy War: The Least Bad Option.* Stanford, CA: Stanford University Press, 2019.

Goscha, Christopher. "Courting Diplomatic Disaster? The Difficult Integration of Vietnam into the Internationalist Communist Movement (1954–1950)." *Journal of Vietnamese Studies* 1, no. 1–2 (2006): 59–103.

———. "'Hell in a Very Small Place': Cold War and Decolonization in the Assault on the Vietnamese Body at Dien Bien Phu." *European Journal of East Asian Studies* 9, no. 2 (2010): 201–23.

———. "A Popular Side of the Vietnamese Army: General Nguyen Binh and War in the South." In *Naissance d'un État-Parti. Le Viêt Nam depuis 1945,* edited by Goscha and Benoit Tréglodé, 325–53. Paris: Indes Savantes, 2004.

Grossheim, Martin. "The Lao Dong Party, Culture and the Campaign against 'Modern Revisionism': The Democratic Republic of Vietnam Before the Second Indochina War." *Journal of Vietnamese Studies* 8, no. 1 (2013): 80–129.

Hahn, Peter L. *Crisis and Crossfire: The United States and the Middle East since 1945.* Washington, DC: Potomac, 2005.

Hamblin, Jacob Darwin. "The Nuclearization of Iran in the Seventies." *Diplomatic History* 38, no. 5 (2014): 1114–35.

Haslam, Jonathan. *Russia's Cold War: From the October Revolution to the Fall of the Wall.* New Haven, CT: Yale University Press, 2011.

Heale, M. J. *American Anticommunism: Combatting the Enemy Within, 1830–1970.* Baltimore, MD: Johns Hopkins University Press, 1990.

Hunt, David. *Vietnam's Southern Revolution: From Peasant Insurrection to Total War.* Amherst: University of Massachusetts Press, 2008.

Hunt, Jonathan R., and Simon Miles, eds. *The Reagan Moment: America and the World in the 1980s.* Ithaca, NY: Cornell University Press, 2021.

Hunt, Michael H. *Ideology and U.S. Foreign Policy.* New Haven, CT: Yale University Press, 1987.

Huntington, Samuel P. "The Clash of Civilizations?" *Foreign Affairs* 22, no. 3 (Summer 1993): 22–49.

Iandolo, Alessandro. "Imbalance of Power: The Soviet Union and the Congo Crisis." *Journal of Cold War Studies* 16, no. 2 (Spring 2014): 32–55.

Immerwahr, Daniel. *Thinking Small: The United States and the Lure of Community Development.* Cambridge, MA: Harvard University Press, 2015.

Inglis, Fred "What Was the Third World Revolution?" In *Life among the Anthros and Other Essays,* edited by Clifford Geertz and Inglis, 236–52. Princeton, NJ: Princeton University Press, 2012.

Irwin, Ryan M. "Sovereignty in the Congo Crisis." In *Decolonization and the Cold War: Negotiating Independence,* edited by Leslie James and Elizabeth Leake, 203–18. New York: Bloomsbury Academic, 2015.

Jackson, Steven F. "China's Third World Foreign Policy: The Case of Angola and Mozambique, 1961–1993." *China Quarterly* 142 (June 1995): 388–422.

Jacobs, Seth. *America's Miracle Man in Vietnam: Ngo Dinh Diem, Race, Religion, and U.S. Intervention in Southeast Asia.* Durham, NC: Duke University Press, 2005.

———. *The Universe Unraveling: American Foreign Policy in Cold War Laos.* Ithaca, NY: Cornell University Press, 2012.

James, Leslie, and Elizabeth Leake, eds. *Decolonization and the Cold War: Negotiating Independence.* New York: Bloomsbury Academic, 2015.

Jayakar, Papul. *Indira Gandhi: An Intimate Biography.* New York: Pantheon, 1988.

Jian, Chen. "China, the Vietnam War, and Sino-American Rapprochement, 1968–1973." In *The Third Indochina War: Conflict between China, Vietnam, and Cambodia, 1972–1979,* edited by Odd Arne Westad and Sophie Quinn Judge, 33–64. New York: Routledge, 2006.

Johns, Andrew L. "The Johnson Administration, the Shah of Iran, and the Changing Pattern of U.S.-Iranian Relations, 1965–1967." *Journal of Cold War Studies* 9, no. 2 (Spring 2007): 64–94.

Johnson, Robert David. "The Unintended Consequences of Congressional Reform: The Clark and Tunney Amendments and U.S. Policy toward Angola." *Diplomatic History* 27, no. 2 (April 2003): 215–43.

Kalb, Madeline G. *The Congo Cables: The Cold War in Africa from Eisenhower to Kennedy.* New York: Macmillan, 1982.

Kamrava, Mehran. *The Modern Middle East: A Political History since the First World War.* 3rd ed. Berkeley: University of California Press, 2013.

Kennedy-Pipe, Caroline. *Russia and the World, 1919–1991.* New York: Oxford University Press, 1998.

Kennes, Erik, and Miles Larmer, *The Katangese Gendarmes and War in Central Africa: Fighting Their Way Home.* Bloomington: Indiana University Press, 2016.

Keys, Barbara J. *Reclaiming American Virtue: The Human Rights Revolution of the 1970s.* Cambridge, MA: Harvard University Press, 2014.

Kimball, Jeffrey. *Nixon's Vietnam War.* Lawrence, KS: University Press of Kansas, 1998.

Klinghoffer, Arthur Jay. *The Angolan War: A Study in Soviet Policy in the Third World.* Boulder, CO: Westview, 1980.

Knock, Thomas J. *To End All Wars: Woodrow Wilson and the Quest for a New World Order.* Princeton. NJ: Princeton University Press, 1992.

Larres, Klaus, and Kenneth Osgood, eds. *The Cold War after Stalin's Death: A Missed Opportunity for Peace?* Lanham, MD: Rowman and Littlefield, 2006.

Latham, Michael E. *The Right Kind of Revolution: Modernization, Development, and U.S. Foreign Policy from the Cold War to the Present.* Ithaca, NY: Cornell University Press, 2011.

Lawrence, Mark Atwood. *Assuming the Burden: Europe and the American Commitment to War in Vietnam.* Berkeley: University of California Press, 2005.

————. *The Vietnam War: A Concise International History.* New York: Oxford University Press, 2008.

Leffler, Melvyn P. *For the Soul of Mankind: The United States, the Soviet Union, and the Cold War.* New York: Hill and Wang, 2007.

————. *A Preponderance of Power: National Security, the Truman Administration, and the Cold War.* Stanford, CA: Stanford University Press, 1992.

————. *The Specter of Communism: The United States and the Origins of the Cold War, 1917–1953.* New York: Hill and Wang, 1994.

Little, Douglas. *American Orientalism: The United States and the Middle East since 1945.* Chapel Hill: University of North Carolina Press, 2008.

Logevall, Fredrik. *Choosing War: The Lost Chance for Peace and the Escalation of War in Vietnam.* Berkeley: University of California Press, 2001.

————. *Embers of War: The Fall of an Empire and the Making of America's Vietnam.* New York: Random House, 2012.

————. *The Origins of the Vietnam War.* New York: Pearson Education, 2001.

Lüthi, Lorenz M. *Cold Wars: Asia, the Middle East, and Europe.* Cambridge: Cambridge University Press, 2020.

————. "Non-Alignment, 1961–74." In *Neutrality and Neutralism in the Global Cold War,* edited by Sandra Bott, Jussi M. Hanhimaki, Janick Schaufelbuehl, and Marco Wyss, 90–107. London: Routledge, 2015.

————. *The Sino-Soviet Split: The Cold War in the Communist World.* Princeton, NJ: Princeton University Press, 2008.

Manela, Erez. "'Peoples of Many Races': The World beyond Europe in the Wilsonian Imagination." In *Jefferson, Lincoln, and Wilson: The American Dilemma of Race and Democracy,* edited by John Milton Cooper and Thomas J. Knock, 184–208. Charlottesville: University of Virginia Press, 2010.

————. *The Wilsonian Moment: Self-Determination and the International Origins of Anticolonial Nationalism.* New York: Oxford University Press, 2007.

Marr, David. "Ho Chi Minh's Independence Declaration." In *Essays into Vietnamese Pasts,* edited by K. W. Taylor and John K. Whitmore, 221–31. Ithaca, NY: Cornell University Press, 1995.

Martel, Gordon, ed. *Twentieth Century War and Conflict: A Concise Encyclopedia.* New York: John Wiley and Sons, 2014.

Mastny, Vojtech. "The Soviet Union's Partnership with India." *Journal of Cold War Studies* 12, no. 3 (Summer 2010): 50–90.

Mazov, Sergey. *A Distant Front in the Cold War: The USSR in West Africa and the Congo, 1956–1964.* Washington, DC: Woodrow Wilson Center Press, 2010.

Mazower, Mark. *No Enchanted Palace: The End of Empire and the Ideological Origins of the United Nations.* Princeton, NJ: Princeton University Press, 2009.

McHale, Shawn. "Understanding the Fanatic Mind? The Viet Minh and Race Hatred in the First Indochina War (1945–1954)." *Journal of Vietnamese Studies* (October 2009): 98–138.

McMahon, Robert J., ed. *The Cold War in the Third World*. New York: Oxford University Press, 2016.

———. *The Cold War on the Periphery: The United States, India, and Pakistan*. New York: Columbia University Press, 1994.

———. "How the Periphery Became the Center: The Cold War, the Third World, and the Transformation of U.S. Strategic Thinking." In *Foreign Policy at the Periphery: The Shifting Margins of US International Relations since World War II*, edited by Bevan Sewell et al., 1935. Lexington: University Press of Kentucky, 2017.

———. *The Limits of Empire: The United States and Southeast Asia Since World War II*. New York: Columbia University Press, 1999.

Meriwether, James. *Proudly We Can Be Africans: Black Americans and Africa, 1931–1965*. Chapel Hill: University of North Carolina Press, 2002.

———. *Tears, Fire, and Blood: The United States and the Decolonization of Africa*. Chapel Hill: University of North Carolina Press, 2021.

Miller, Edward. *Misalliance: Ngo Dinh Diem, the United States, and the Fate of South Vietnam*. Cambridge, MA: Harvard University Press, 2013.

———. "Religious Revival and the Politics of Nation Building: Reinterpreting the 1963 'Buddhist Crisis' in South Vietnam." *Modern Asian Studies* 49, no. 6 (2015): 1903–62.

———. "Vision, Power, and Agency: The Ascent of Ngo Dinh Diem, 1945–1954." *Journal of Southeast Asian Studies* 35, no. 3 (October 2004): 433–58.

Minter, William. "The U.S. and the War in Angola." *Review of African Political Economy* 50 (March 1991): 135–44.

Mitchell, Nancy. *Jimmy Carter in Africa: Race and the Cold War*. Stanford, CA: Stanford University Press, 2016.

Moreira de Sá, Tiago. "'The World Was Not Turning in Their Direction': The United States and the Decolonization of Angola." *Journal of Cold War Studies* 21, no. 1 (Winter 2019): 52–65.

Murphy, Caryle. "Rebel Poet-Doctor." *Washington Post*, September 12, 1979.

Namikas, Lise. *Battleground Africa: Cold War in the Congo, 1960–1965*. Washington, DC: Woodrow Wilson Center Press, 2013.

Nguyen, Lien-Hang T. *Hanoi's War: An International History of the War for Peace in Vietnam*. Chapel Hill: University of North Carolina Press, 2012.

———. "The Vietnam Decade: The Global Shock of the War." In *The Shock of the Global: The 1970s in Perspective*, edited by Niall Ferguson, Charles S. Maier, Erez Manela, and Daniel J. Sargent, 159–72. Cambridge, MA: Harvard University Press, 2010.

Nzongola-Ntalaja, Georges. "Patrice Lumumba: The Most Important Assassination of the 20th Century." *The Guardian*, January 17, 2011.

Offner, Arnold. *Another Such Victory: President Truman and the Cold War, 1945–1953*. Stanford, CA: Stanford University Press, 2002.

O'Neill, Kathryn, and Barry Munslow. "Ending the Cold War in Southern Africa." *Third World Quarterly* 12, no. 3/4 (1990–1991): 81–96.

Osman, Tarek. *Egypt on the Brink: From the Rise of Nasser to the Fall of Mubarak.* New Haven, CT: Yale University Press, 2010.

Parker, Jason C. *Hearts, Minds, Voices: US Cold War Public Diplomacy and the Formation of the Third World.* New York: Oxford University Press, 2016.

Pechatnov, Vladimir O. "Soviet-American Relations through the Cold War." In *The Oxford Handbook of the Cold War,* edited by Richard H. Immerman and Petra Goode, 107–32. New York: Oxford University Press, 2013.

Pipes, Richard. *Russia under the Bolshevik Regime.* New York: Knopf, 1993.

Prados, John. *The Sky Would Fall: Operation Vulture: The U.S. Bombing Mission in Indochina.* New York: Dial, 1983.

Prashad, Vijay. *The Darker Nations: A People's History of the Third World.* New York: New Press, 2007.

Quinn-Judge, Sophie. "Ho Chi Minh: Nationalist Icon." In *Makers of Modern Asia,* edited by Ramachandra Guha, 6–92. Cambridge, MA: Harvard University Press, 2014.

Radchenko, Sergey. "India and the End of the Cold War." In *The End of the Cold War and the Third World: New Perspectives on Regional Conflict,* edited by Artemy Kalinovsky and Sergey Radchenko, 173–91. New York: Taylor and Francis, 2011.

Rakove, Robert B. *Kennedy, Johnson, and the Nonaligned World.* New York: Cambridge University Press, 2013.

Ramazani, R. K. *Independence without Freedom: Iran's Foreign Policy.* Charlottesville: University of Virginia Press, 2020.

Reis, Bruno C. "Decentering the Cold War in Africa: The Portuguese Policy of Decolonization and Détente in Angola and Mozambique (1974–1984)." *Journal of Cold War Studies* 21, no. 1 (Winter 2019): 3–51.

Rodrigues, Luís Nuno. "The United States and Portuguese Decolonization." *Portuguese Studies* 29, no. 2 (2013): 164–85.

Rothermund, Dietmar. *The Routledge Companion to Decolonization.* New York: Routledge, 2006.

Rotter, Andrew J. *Comrades at Odds: The United States and India, 1947–1964.* Ithaca, NY: Cornell University Press, 2000.

Saunders, Christopher. "The South Africa-Angola Talks, 1976–1984: A Little-Known Cold War Thread." *Kronos* 37 (November 2011): 104–19.

Schmidt, Elizabeth. *Foreign Intervention in Africa: From the Cold War to the War on Terror.* New York: Cambridge University Press, 2013.

Schmitz, David F., and Vanessa Walker. "Jimmy Carter and the Foreign Policy of Human Rights: The Development of a Post-Cold War Foreign Policy." *Diplomatic History* 28, no. 1 (January 2004): 113–43.

Schrecker, Ellen. *Many Are the Crimes: McCarthyism in America.* New York: Little, Brown, 1998.

Shannon, Matthew K. *Losing Hearts and Minds: American-Iranian Relations and International Education during the Cold War.* Ithaca, NY: Cornell University Press, 2017

Shepard, Todd. *The Invention of Decolonization: The Algerian War and the Remaking of France.* Ithaca, NY: Cornell University Press, 2006.

Sick, Gary. *All Fall Down: America's Tragic Encounter with Iran.* New York: Random House, 1986.

Sidhu, Waheguru Pal Singh. "The Accidental Global Peacekeeper." In *India and the Cold War,* edited by Manu Bhagavan, 79–99. Durham: University of North Carolina Press, 2019.

Sobers, Candace. "Interdependence, Intervention, and Internationalism: Angola and the International System, 1974–1975." *Journal of Cold War Studies* 21, no. 1 (Winter 2019): 97–124.

St. John, Robert. *Boss: The Story of Gamal Abdel Nasser.* New York: McGraw-Hill, 1960.

Statler, Kathryn C., and Andrew L. Johns, eds. *The Eisenhower Administration, the Third World, and the Globalization of the Cold War.* Lanham, MD: Rowman and Littlefield, 2006.

Summitt, April R. "For a White Revolution: John F. Kennedy and the Shah of Iran." *Middle East Journal* 58, no. 4 (Autumn 2004): 560–75.

Suri, Jeremy. *Power and Protest: Global Revolution and the Rise of Détente.* Cambridge, MA: Harvard University Press, 2003.

Szalontai, Balázs. "From Battlefield into Marketplace: The End of the Cold War in Indochina, 1985–1989." In *The End of the Cold War and the Third World: New Perspectives on Regional Conflict,* edited by Artemy Kalinovsky and Sergey Radchenko, 155–72. New York: Routledge, 2011.

Takeyh, Ray. "The Iran-Iraq War: A Reassessment." *Middle East Journal* 64, no. 3 (Summer 2010): 365–83.

Tuong Vu. *Vietnam's Communist Revolution: The Power and Limits of Ideology.* New York: Cambridge University Press, 2017.

Turse, Nick. *Kill Anything That Moves: The Real American War in Vietnam.* New York: Metropolitan, 2013.

Van Reybrouck, David, *Congo: The Epic History of a People.* New York: HarperCollins, 2014.

Waters, Mary-Alice, ed. *Cuba and Angola: Fighting for Africa's Freedom and Our Own.* New York: Pathfinder, 2013.

Weiner, Michael. "Comintern in East Asia, 1919–39." In *The Comintern: A History of International Communism from Lenin to Stalin,* edited by Kevin McDermott and Jeremy Agnew, 158–90. New York: St. Martin's, 1997.

Weiss, Herbert. "The Congo's Independence Struggle Viewed Fifty Years Later." *African Studies Review* 55, no. 1 (April 2012): 109–15.

———. *Political Protest in the Congo: The Parti Solidaire Africa in during the Independence Struggle.* Princeton, NJ: Princeton University Press, 1967.

Westad, Odd Arne. *The Cold War: A World History.* New York: Basic, 2017.

———. "From War to Peace." In *The Third Indochina War: Conflict between China, Vietnam and Cambodia, 1972–79,* edited by Westad and Sophie Quinn-Judge, 1–11. New York: Routledge, 2009.

———. *The Global Cold War: Third World Interventions and the Making of Our Times.* New York: Cambridge University Press, 2007.

———. "The Great Transformation: China in the Long 1970s." In *The Shock of the Global: The 1970s in Perspective,* edited by Niall Ferguson, Charles S. Maier, Erez Manela, and Daniel J. Sargent, 65–79. Cambridge, MA: Harvard University Press, 2010.

Wilford, Hugh. "'Essentially a Work of Fiction': Kermit 'Kim' Roosevelt, Imperial Romance, and the Iran Coup of 1953." *Diplomatic History* 40, no. 5 (2016): 922–47.

Yaqub, Salim. *Containing Arab Nationalism: The Eisenhower Doctrine and the Middle East.* Chapel Hill: University of North Carolina Press, 2004.

———. *Imperfect Strangers: Americans, Arabs, and U.S.–Middle East Relations in the 1970s.* Ithaca, NY: Cornell University Press, 2016.

Young, Crawford. "Ralph Bunche and Patrice Lumumba: The Fatal Encounter." In *Trustee for the Human Community: Ralph J. Bunche, the United Nations, and the Decolonization of Africa,* edited by Robert A. Hill and Edmond J. Keller, 148–206. Athens: Ohio University Press, 2010.

Zelikow, Philip. "The World of 1956" and "Final Observations: No End of Lessons." In *Suez Deconstructed: An Interactive Study in Crisis, War, and Peacemaking,* edited by Zelikow and Ernest May, 11–28. Washington, DC: Brookings Institution Press, 2018.

Zinoman, Peter. *The Colonial Bastille: A History of Imprisonment in Vietnam, 1962–1940.* Berkeley: University of California Press, 2001.

Zubok, Vladislav M. *A Failed Empire: The Soviet Union in the Cold War from Stalin to Gorbachev.* Chapel Hill: University of North Carolina Press, 2007.

———. "Stalin, Soviet Intelligence, and the Struggle for Iran, 1945–1953." *Diplomatic History* 44, no. 1 (2020): 22–46.

Zubok, Vladislav M., and Constantine Pleshakov. *Inside the Kremlin's Cold War.* Cambridge, MA: Harvard University Press, 1996.

Index

Studies in Conflict, Diplomacy, and Peace

Series Editors: George C. Herring, Andrew L. Johns, and Kathryn C. Statler

This series focuses on key moments of conflict, diplomacy, and peace from the eighteenth century to the present to explore their wider significance in the development of U.S. foreign relations. The series editors welcome new research in the form of original monographs, interpretive studies, biographies, and anthologies from historians, political scientists, journalists, and policymakers. A primary goal of the series is to examine the United States' engagement with the world, its evolving role in the international arena, and the ways in which the state, nonstate actors, individuals, and ideas have shaped and continue to influence history, both at home and abroad.

Advisory Board Members

Books in the Series

Truman, Congress, and Korea: The Politics of America's First Undeclared War
Larry Blomstedt

The Legacy of J. William Fulbright: Policy, Power, and Ideology
Edited by Alessandro Brogi, Giles Scott-Smith, and David J. Snyder

The Gulf: The Bush Presidencies and the Middle East
Michael F. Cairo

Remaking the World: Decolonization and the Cold War
Jessica M. Chapman

Reagan and the World: Leadership and National Security, 1981–1989
Edited by Bradley Lynn Coleman and Kyle Longley

A Diplomatic Meeting: Reagan, Thatcher, and the Art of Summitry
James Cooper

American Justice in Taiwan: The 1957 Riots and Cold War Foreign Policy
Stephen G. Craft

Soccer Diplomacy: International Relations and Football since 1914
Edited by Heather L. Dichter

Diplomatic Games: Sport, Statecraft, and International Relations since 1945
Edited by Heather L. Dichter and Andrew L. Johns

Nothing Less Than War: A New History of America's Entry into World War I
Justus D. Doenecke

Aid under Fire: Nation Building and the Vietnam War
Jessica Elkind

Enemies to Allies: Cold War Germany and American Memory
Brian C. Etheridge

Grounded: The Case for Abolishing the United States Air Force
Robert M. Farley

Foreign Friends: Syngman Rhee, American Exceptionalism, and the Division of Korea
David P. Fields

The Myth of Triumphalism: Rethinking President Reagan's Cold War Legacy
Beth A. Fischer

The American South and the Vietnam War: Belligerence, Protest, and Agony in Dixie
Joseph A. Fry

Lincoln, Seward, and US Foreign Relations in the Civil War Era
Joseph A. Fry

Made in United States
Troutdale, OR
07/31/2023

11705341R00192